KAFKA
and
Cultural Zionism

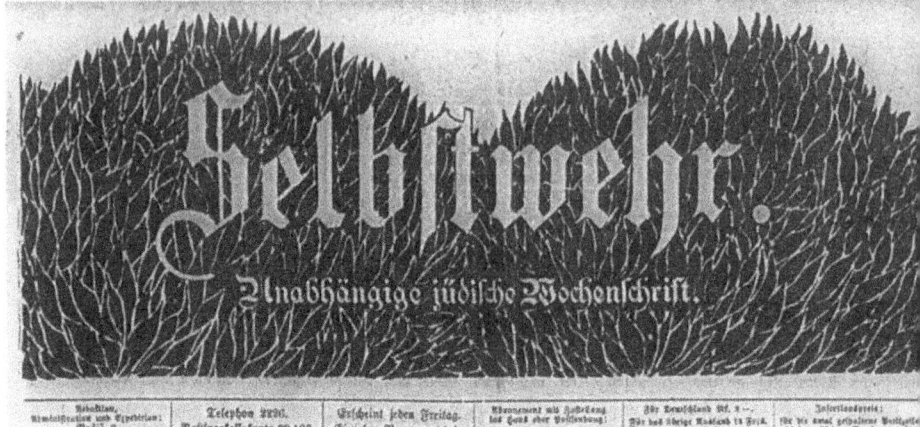

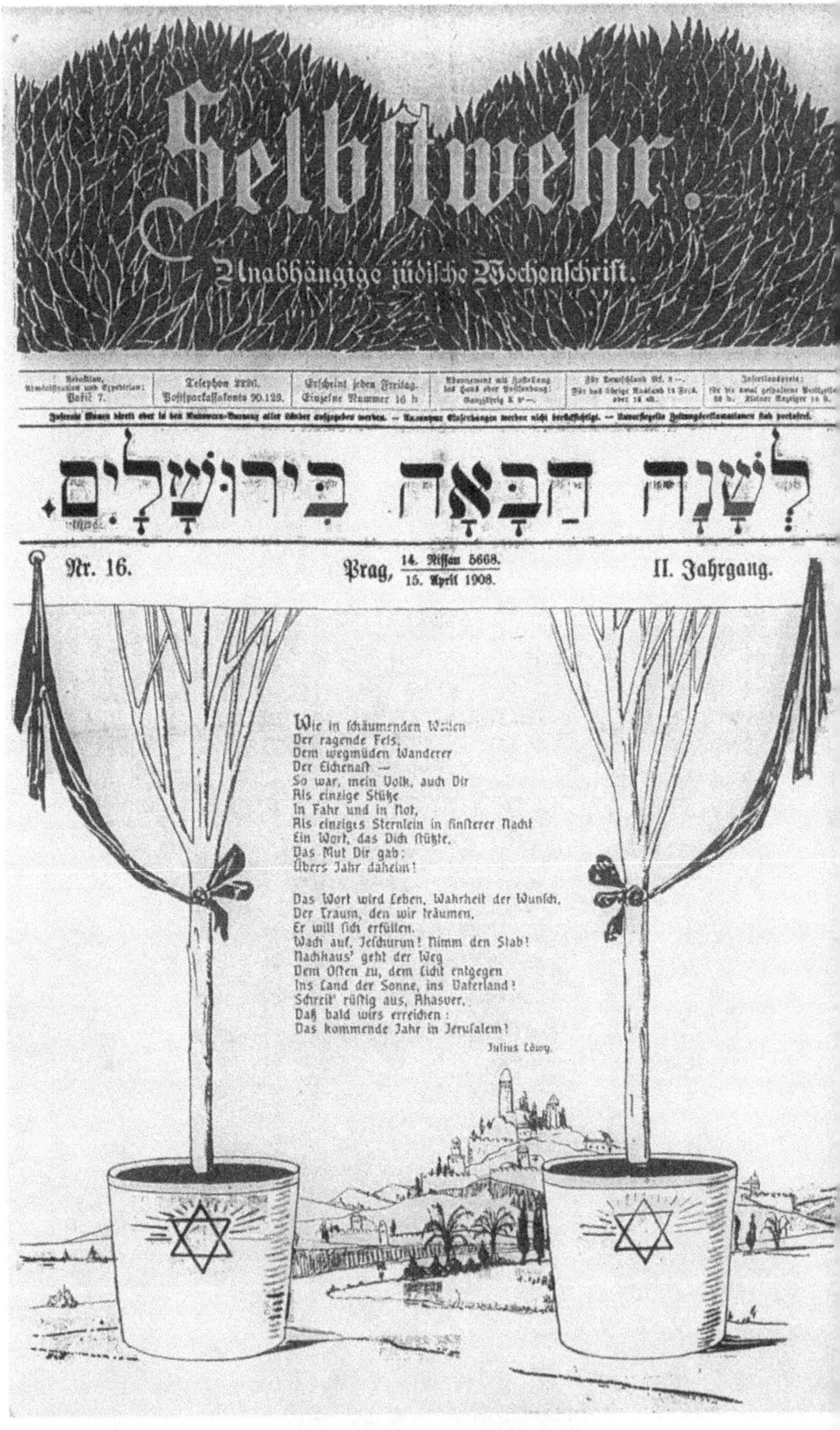

Selbstwehr.

Unabhängige jüdische Wochenschrift.

Telephon 2236. Postsparkassakonto 90.129. | Erscheint jeden Freitag. Einzelne Nummer 16 h

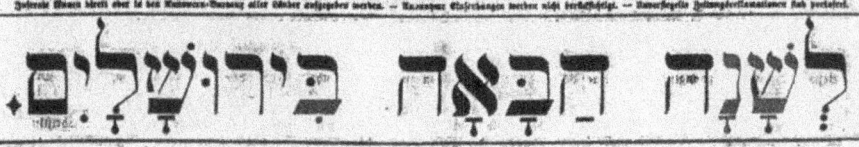

לשנה הבאה בירושלים.

Nr. 16. Prag, 14. Nissan 5668. / 15. April 1908. II. Jahrgang.

Wie in schäumenden Wellen
Der ragende Fels,
Dem wegmüden Wanderer
Der Eichenast —
So war, mein Volk, auch Dir
Als einzige Stütze
In Fahr und in Not,
Als einziges Sternlein in finsterer Nacht
Ein Wort, das Dich stützte,
Das Mut Dir gab:
Übers Jahr daheim!

Das Wort wird Leben, Wahrheit der Wunsch,
Der Traum, den wir träumen,
Er will sich erfüllen.
Wach auf, Jeschurun! Nimm den Stab!
Nachhaus' geht der Weg
Dem Osten zu, dem Licht entgegen
Ins Land der Sonne, ins Vaterland!
Schreit' rüstig aus, Ahasver,
Daß bald wirs erreichen:
Das kommende Jahr in Jerusalem!

Julius Löwy.

KAFKA
and
Cultural Zionism

Dates in Palestine

IRIS BRUCE

THE UNIVERSITY OF WISCONSIN PRESS

This book was published with generous support from the
Lucius N. Littauer Foundation.

The University of Wisconsin Press
1930 Monroe Street
Madison, Wisconsin 53711

www.wisc.edu/wisconsinpress/

3 Henrietta Street
London WC2E 8LU, England

Copyright © 2007
The Board of Regents of the University of Wisconsin System
All rights reserved

5 4 3 2 1

Library of Congress Cataloging-in-Publication Data
Bruce, Iris.
Kafka and cultural Zionism : dates in Palestine / Iris Bruce.
p. cm. — (Studies in German Jewish cultural history and literature)
Includes bibliographical references and index.
ISBN 0-299-22190-3 (hardcover : alk. paper)
1. Kafka, Franz, 1883–1924. 2. Kafka, Franz, 1883–1924—Themes, motives.
3. Jews—Identity. 4. Zionism in literature. I. Title.
PT2621.A26Z6453 2007
833′.914—dc22
2006031027

Frontispiece: Image from *Selbstwehr*

FOR

Kafka *and* Keeper

Date palms sway in the wind and ancient sycamores spread their shoots and give you shade.

—SHMUEL-YOSEF AGNON, *Only Yesterday* (1945)

My dear Fräulein Bauer,

In the likelihood that you no longer have even the remotest recollection of me, I am introducing myself once more: my name is Franz Kafka, and I am the person who greeted you for the first time that evening at Director Brod's in Prague . . . and who finally, with the very hand now striking the keys, held your hand, the one which confirmed a promise to accompany him next year to Palestine.

Now, if you still wish to undertake this journey—you said at the time you are not fickle, and I saw no signs of it in you—then it will be not only right but absolutely essential for us to start discussing this journey at once. For we shall have to make use of every minute of our holiday, which in any case is far too short, especially for a trip to Palestine.

—KAFKA, *Letters to Felice* (1912)

Climbing. *Snait*. It was a squirrel, it was a squirrel, a wild female nutcracker, a jumper, a climber, and her bushy tail was famous in all the forests. This squirrel, this squirrel was always travelling, always searching, it couldn't talk about this, not because it lacked the power of speech but because it had absolutely no time.

—KAFKA, *Wedding Preparations in the Country*
(date uncertain: 1919/1923)

Contents

List of Illustrations   xi

Acknowledgments   xiii

Abbreviations   xv

Introduction   3

1. Kafka's Jewish Prague (1883–1911)   12
2. The Yiddish Theater (1910–1913)   34
3. Anti-Semitism and Zionist Activities (1911–1915)   57
4. Forms of Cultural Renewal (1912–1917)   85
5. Kafka's Cultural Zionism (1914–1917)   113
6. Anti-Semitism and Self-Hatred (1916–1924)   138
7. The Dream of Palestine (1917–1924)   165

Conclusion   200

Notes   209

Works Cited   239

Index   253

Illustrations

1. Felix Salten's speech, "The Lapse from Judaism"   26
2. Advertisement for the Yiddish Theater   37
3. *Selbstwehr*'s response to anti-Semitic ritual murder smear campaign   64
4. Animal painting in Knesset Israel Synagogue in Toronto   164
5. Advertisement in *Selbstwehr* for the Jewish elementary school of Prague   176
6. *Selbstwehr* tribute to Kafka   207
7. Kafka's Talmud   238

Acknowledgments

Permission has been granted for the use of the following previously published material. Sections from "Of Devils and Demons and Absent Talmudists: Franz Kafka's Struggle with Philosophical Antisemitism in Hans Blüher's Secessio Judaica," in *Le Discours scientifique comme porteur de préjugés?/Scientific Discourse as Prejudice-Carrier?* ed. Alain Goldschläger and Clive Thomson (London, Ontario: Mestengo Press, 1998), 181–200, appear in chapter 6 in revised form. A few passages from "Elements of Jewish Folklore in Kafka's *Metamorphosis*," in Franz Kafka, *The Metamorphosis*, ed. Stanley Corngold (New York: Norton, 1996), 107–25, appear in slightly different form in chapter 4. Material from "Jewish Education: Borderline and Counterdiscourses in Kafka," in *Kafka, Zionism, and Beyond*, ed. Mark Gelber (Tübingen: Niemeyer Verlag, 2004), 107–45, has been revised and integrated into chapters 4 and 7. A few sections from "Seductive Myths and Midrashic Games in Franz Kafka's *Parables and Paradoxes*," *Carleton Germanic Papers* 25 (1997): 57–77, as well as from "Kafka and Jewish folklore," in *The Cambridge Companion to Franz Kafka*, ed. Julian Preece (Cambridge: Cambridge Univ. Press, 2002), 150–68, have been included in revised form in chapters 4, 6, and 7.

The groundwork for this study was laid by my Ph.D. dissertation, "A Life of Metamorphosis: Franz Kafka and the Jewish Tradition" (University of Toronto, 1991), which examined Kafka's interest in Judaism and Jewish folklore. I am thankful for a two-month DAAD (German Academic Exchange Service) Research Grant for Recent Ph.D.s in 1992, which enabled me to go to Germany to work with Kafka's personal library and the Zionist newspaper *Selbstwehr* at the Forschungsstelle für Prager

Deutsche Literatur (Research Center for Prague German Literature) in Wuppertal. I must also express my gratitude to the Social Sciences and Humanities Research Council of Canada for a three-year research grant (1992–95), which allowed me to pursue my research on Kafka and cultural Zionism in Germany at the Research Center in Wuppertal, the Stiftung "Neue Synagoge Berlin—Centrum Judaicum" in Berlin as well as in Prague at the Jewish Museum.

During my years of working on this book, I have had much support and would like to express my gratitude to the following individuals: Arno Pařik in the Jewish Museum of Prague for his invaluable assistance; Jürgen Born at the Research Center in Wuppertal for his friendship and helpfulness; the staff at the New Critical Edition of Kafka's works in Wuppertal; Tony Northey for his friendship and for generously sharing with me his vast knowledge of Kafka; the two anonymous readers for the University of Wisconsin Press for their careful reading of the manuscript and their helpful suggestions; my editors at the University of Wisconsin Press, Susanne Breckenridge and Sheila Moermond, and my copyeditor, Joanna Hildebrand Craig, for their careful preparation of the manuscript; Phil Goldman and Nasrin Rahimieh for their personal and professional support. I also wish to thank all of my students who have inspired me in so many ways. Special thanks go to Stanley Corngold and Sander Gilman for all I've learned from them, for their true support and encouragement over so many years. It is hard to put into words how much I owe to them.

Though a long distance away, my mother, Anneliese Pöhling, was always there for me. Don and Benjamin were remarkably patient and understanding, having to live with Kafka for an eternity, and never failed me in their support. It is truly amazing how Benjamin always found time in his incredibly busy life for my many translation questions! Michael faithfully read different versions of the manuscript and helped with Kafka's Hebrew book, Josephine's singing, and the English translations. I would also like to thank Arnd Bohm, Barbara Havercroft, and particularly Sylvia Söderlind for their friendship and moral support over many years. Finally there is the "zoo" to acknowledge, whose presence was felt at all stages of the conception of the book: Tic Tac, Latke, Saffie, and Keeper, who now takes me for walks by the "ocean."

Abbreviations

B   Benjamin, Walter. *Benjamin über Kafka: Texte, Briefzeugnisse, Aufzeichnungen.* Ed. Hermann Schweppenhäuser. Frankfurt: Suhrkamp, 1981.

BB   Kafka, Franz. *Beim Bau der chinesischen Mauer und andere Schriften aus dem Nachlaß in der Fassung der Handschrift.* Ed. Hans-Gerd Koch. Frankfurt: Fischer Taschenbuch Verlag, 1994.

BF   Kafka, Franz. *Briefe an Felice.* Ed. E. Heller and J. Born. Frankfurt: Fischer, 1976.

BK   Kafka, Franz. *Beschreibung eines Kampfes und andere Schriften aus dem Nachlaß in der Fassung der Handschrift.* Ed. Hans-Gerd Koch. Frankfurt: Fischer Taschenbuch Verlag, 1994.

BKB   *Max Brod, Franz Kafka: Eine Freundschaft.* Bd. 2, Briefwechsel. Ed. Malcolm Pasley. Frankfurt: Fischer, 1989.

BKR   *Max Brod, Franz Kafka: Eine Freundschaft.* Bd. 1, Reiseaufzeichnungen. Ed. Malcolm Pasley. Frankfurt: Fischer, 1987.

BM   Kafka, Franz. *Briefe an Milena.* Ed. Jürgen Born and Michael Müller. Frankfurt: Fischer Taschenbuch Verlag, 1986.

BO   Kafka, Franz. *Briefe an Ottla und die Familie.* Ed. H. Binder and K. Wagenbach. Frankfurt: Fischer, 1981.

Br   Kafka, Franz. *Briefe, 1902–1924.* Ed. Max Brod. Frankfurt: Fischer, 1975.

BV	Kafka, Franz. *Brief an den Vater*. Frankfurt: Fischer, 1979.
C	*Franz Kafka: Eine Chronik*. Ed. Roger Hermes, Waltraud John, Hans-Gerd Koch, and Anita Widera. Berlin: Verlag Klaus Wagenbach, 1999.
CJ	Kieval, Hillel. J. *The Making of Czech Jewry: National Conflict and Jewish Society in Bohemia, 1870–1918*. New York: Oxford Univ. Press, 1988.
CS	Kafka, Franz. *The Complete Stories*. Ed. Nahum N. Glatzer. New York: Schocken, 1971.
DF	Kafka, Franz. *Dearest Father: Stories and Other Writings*. Trans. Ernst Kaiser and Ethel Wilkins. New York: Schocken, 1954.
DI	Kafka, Franz. *The Diaries of Franz Kafka, 1910–1913*. Ed. Max Brod. Trans. Joseph Kresh. New York: Schocken, 1948.
DII	Kafka, Franz. *The Diaries of Franz Kafka, 1914–1923*. Ed. Max Brod. Trans. Martin Greenberg, with Hannah Arendt. New York: Schocken, 1949.
E	Kafka, Franz. *Erzählungen und andere ausgewählte Prosa*. Ed. Roger Hermes. Frankfurt: Fischer, 1996.
FK	Brod, Max. *Franz Kafka: A Biography*. Schocken: New York, 1960.
FK1	Brod, Max. *Über Franz Kafka*. Frankfurt: Fischer, 1977.
H	Kafka, Franz. *Hochzeitsvorbereitungen auf dem Lande und andere Prosa aus dem Nachlaß*. Ed. Max Brod. Frankfurt: Fischer, 1980.
K	Kafka, Franz. *Tagebücher in der Fassung der Handschrift: Kommentarband*. Eds. Hans-Gerd Koch, Michael Müller, and Malcolm Pasley. Frankfurt: Fischer, 1990.
KB	Born, Jürgen. *Kafkas Bibliothek: Ein beschreibendes Verzeichnis*. Frankfurt: Fischer, 1990.
KF	*Kafkas letzter Freund: Der Nachlaß Robert Klopstock, 1899–1972*. Ed. Hugo Wetscherek. Vienna: Inlibris, 2003.
KH	*Kafka Handbuch Bd. 1: Der Mensch und seine Zeit*. Ed. Hartmut Binder. Stuttgart: Alfred Kröner Verlag, 1979.
KK	Binder, Hartmut. *Kafka-Kommentar zu sämtlichen Erzählungen*. 1975. Munich: Winkler Verlag, 1986.

LF	Kafka, Franz. *Letters to Felice*. Ed. Erich Heller and Jürgen Born. Trans. James Stern and Elisabeth Duckworth. New York: Schocken, 1973.
LFF	Kafka, Franz. *Letters to Friends, Family, and Editors*. Trans. Richard and Clara Winston. New York: Schocken, 1977.
LM	Kafka, Franz. *Letters to Milena*. Trans. Philip Boehm. New York: Schocken, 1990.
LOF	Kafka, Franz. *Letters to Ottla and the Family*. New York: Schocken, 1882.
NII	Kafka, Franz. *Nachgelassene Schriften und Fragmente* II. Ed. Jost Schillemeit. Frankfurt: Fischer, 1992.
NIIA	Kafka, Franz. *Nachgelassene Schriften und Fragmente* II. Apparatband. Ed. Jost Schillemeit. Frankfurt: Fischer, 1992.
PK	Brod, Max. *Der Prager Kreis*. Frankfurt: Suhrkamp, 1979.
S	*Selbstwehr* [Independent Jewish weekly, Prague].
SL	Brod, Max. *Streitbares Leben, 1884–1968*. München: F. A. Herbig, 1969.
T	Kafka, Franz. *Tagebücher in der Fassung der Handschrift*. Eds. Hans-Gerd Koch, Michael Müller and Malcolm Pasley. Frankfurt: Fischer, 1990.
W	Kafka, Franz. *Wedding Preparations in the Country and Other Posthumous Prose Writings*. Trans. E. Kaiser and E. Wilkins. Notes by Max Brod. London: Secker & Warburg, 1954.
Z	Kafka, Franz. *Zur Frage der Gesetze und andere Schriften aus dem Nachlaß in der Fassung der Handschrift*. Ed. Jost Schillemeit. Frankfurt: Fischer Taschenbuch Verlag, 1994.

KAFKA
and
Cultural Zionism

Introduction

> And incidentally, won't you tell me what I really am: in the last *Neue Rundschau, Metamorphosis* is mentioned and rejected on sensible grounds, and then says the writer: "There is something fundamentally German about K's narrative art." In Max's article on the other hand: "K's stories are among the most typically Jewish documents of our time." A difficult case. Am I a circus rider on 2 horses? Alas, I am no rider, but lie prostrate on the ground.
> —*Letters to Felice* (1916)

Franz Kafka (1883–1924) considered it quite typical for many Jews of his time to be torn between identities. In February 1919 he characterized the twenty-eight-year-old Julie Wohryzek (1891–1944), later his fiancée, as "a common and yet astounding phenomenon. Not Jewish and yet not not-Jewish, not German and yet not not-German, crazy about the movies, about operettas and comedies, wears face powder and veils, possesses an inexhaustible and nonstop store of the brashest Yiddish expressions, in general very ignorant, more cheerful than sad—that is about what she is like" (LFF 213 [Br 252]). As a remedy, he asked his friend Max Brod (1884–1968) to send Julie a copy of "Die dritte Phase des Zionismus" (The Third Phase of Zionism)[1] and discussed Brod's study with her (LFF 213, 214 [Br 252, 253]). Kafka often expressed ambivalence about his own identity as well. In January 1914, for instance, he pointed out his great distance from Jews in general: "What have I in common with Jews? I have hardly anything in common with myself and should stand very quietly in a corner, content that I can breathe" (DII 11 [T 622]). For many critics these types of statements suggest Kafka's ambiguous feelings about his heritage. At the same time, though, they have to acknowledge that many other statements reveal precisely the opposite: how much Kafka identified with other Jews and Jewish culture. Especially after 1917 his interest was so great that he taught himself Hebrew and increasingly supported the Zionist movement. Changed attitudes toward a cultural heritage during different phases in a person's lifetime are far from unusual, but scholarship on Kafka and Judaism has continually tried to "pin him down." This state of affairs is aptly described by Marthe Robert:

> [Kafka] never quite corresponds to one's view of his interests and aims, especially not in the realm, so inadequately described, of his relations with Judaism and the Jews, where every writer tends to appropriate him, or at least to define him according to the writer's own requirements. Assimilated Jew, anti-Jewish Jew, anti-Zionist, Zionist, believer, atheist—Kafka was indeed all of these at different times in his development, sometimes all at once.[2]

It appears that Kafka has resisted many such attempts at classification or labeling, making room for more critical commentary.

The present study focuses on Kafka's individual type of cultural Zionism. Cultural Zionism is to be distinguished from Theodor Herzl's political Zionism, whose foremost goal was the foundation of a secular Jewish state. The philosophy of cultural or spiritual Zionism developed in opposition to political Zionism and placed the emphasis on reviving Jewish culture in the Diaspora. Kafka was familiar with the different philosophies of the cultural Zionists Ahad Ha'am (Asher Ginsberg 1856–1927), Martin Buber (1878–1965), Nathan Birnbaum (Mathias Acher 1864–1937), and Micha Josef Berdyczewski (1865–1921; later known as bin Gorion) and especially with the ideas and writings of his friends Hugo Bergmann (1883–1975), Felix Weltsch (1884–1964), and Max Brod. To be sure, of the approximately twenty thousand Jews living in Prague during Kafka's lifetime,[3] only a small number of intellectuals were Zionists. However, the growing Zionist movement was an important intellectual presence, and many of his friends were Zionists. The aim of my study, therefore, is to lay out the formative influences (family and personal history, historical events, readings, cultural interests, and activities) that led Kafka to become engaged in Zionist activities and to compare and contrast his practical, cultural Zionism with the beliefs and convictions of other contemporary Zionists.

The subtitle, *Dates in Palestine,* is intentionally ambivalent and speaks of many "dates"—real and imagined, realized or not. It refers to the historical dates and facts that led to Kafka's romantic preoccupation with Palestine as well as to cultural events involving Palestine and to Zionist

Introduction 5

engagements supporting and furthering the country's political, economic, and cultural growth. It alludes to his date or planned rendezvous with his fiancée Felice Bauer (1887–1960) in Palestine, to his further (eventually aborted) plans to visit friends there, and to his final wish to emigrate there with his last companion, Dora Diamant (1898–1952). It also refers to the travels to Palestine undertaken by friends and acquaintances. A final association is the actual fruit that grows abundantly in Palestine. In 1918 Kafka composed a sketch about his vision of life in an early kibbutz, entitled "The Workers without Possessions" (W 119–20 [NII 105–7]). Here bread, water, and dates constitute the sole nourishment. Given the personal and political nostalgia inherent in this sketch and Kafka's inability to realize any of his plans to go there, "Dates in Palestine," ultimately comes to stand for a dream unfulfilled.

SCHOLARLY BACKGROUND

After World War II and well into the 1990s, German scholars scarcely dealt with Kafka's Judaism, and most of the books and articles on this subject were written in English, French, and Italian—by scholars outside the German world. "The recognition of Kafka in respect to Judaism in general or to some of its main currents had been argued from the beginning by scholars like Max Brod, Gershom Scholem and Walter Benjamin; however, the German literary establishment initially addressed it only with great hesitation."[4] After the *Shoah*, German scholarship was reluctant to emphasize specifically Jewish characteristics, and textimmanent criticism was for a long time a convenient theoretical excuse, since it created the impression of unbiased, nonideological scholarship. As a result, debates and controversies ensued amongst scholars that were sometimes more ideologically and personally motivated than academically founded.[5] The post–World War II Jewish editors of Kafka's work were also responsible for the lack of research in this area because German editions did not include all relevant material. It is important to recognize the obvious suppression and omission of matters relating to Judaism in Kafka's diaries and personal correspondence. For instance, M. I. Pinès's Yiddish literary history *L'Histoire de la littérature judéo-allemande* (The History of German-Jewish Literature),[6] which Kafka read in 1912, has been largely ignored by scholars. Until the publication of the critical edition of Kafka's diaries (1990), several crucial pages of diary entries were missing in the German edition: all of Kafka's notes on Pinès. "By one of the anomalies of textual history, the notes that Kafka took from Pinès are available only in the English translation of his diaries, having been omitted by Brod from the German edition."⁷ Pinès's study is especially significant because it represents a greatly needed correction to the romanticized representation of Jewish *shtetl* life in the first half of the twentieth century, as well as after World War II. Furthermore, Claude Mauriac, in 1956, expressed regret at the cuts undertaken by Willy Haas in his 1952 edition of Kafka's letters to his lover Milena Jesenskà (1896–1944), the Czech journalist and translator of Kafka's stories who later died in the concentration camp Ravensbrück.⁸ Haas stressed that he did in fact keep most of Kafka's references to Judaism despite strongest misgivings. But as the recent edition of the letters shows, Haas cut many critical remarks that Kafka made, such as his highly suggestive and telling commentary on Milena's article "The Devil at the Hearth," in which he examines Jewish-Christian relationships (LM 229–31 [BM 309–13]). Over the last years, the new critical editions of Kafka's works have finally given scholars access to previously inaccessible material and have been invaluable in reexamining and reestablishing Kafka's relation to Judaism. Pinès's literary history as well as the omitted commentary by Kafka on Milena's "The Devil at the Hearth" article both have a central place in my study.

Considering how much historical and cultural documentation has been made available over the years, one should think that there would be more consensus when it comes to an evaluation of the "facts." Ironically, the opposite is true as scholars continue to argue for a mystic/nonmystic, Zionist/non-Zionist, enlightened/anti-Enlightenment Kafka. This suggests that there is yet a more fundamental problem facing critics engaged in reconstructing the pre-Holocaust period. Hillel Kieval sums it up in a simple phrase: "There are no archival collections that document the early history of Zionism in Prague; one is forced to rely on contemporary press accounts and reminiscences" (CJ 224n.5). What is true of the history of Zionism in Prague is true of much of Eastern European Jewish history before World War II. Kafka scholarship was exceptionally lucky when his personal library was discovered in 1982, by chance, in a second-hand bookstore in Munich (KB 7). The fact remains that many documents needed to reconstruct this period are forever lost. Consequently, the criteria and methods used to evaluate the available data are frequently determined by the individual scholar's own area of research or personal background and presuppositions. The contradictory interpretation of Kafka's speech on the Yiddish language (1912) by two historically oriented scholars is a case in point.

Giuliano Baioni regards Kafka's tone toward his "enlightened" audience as "hostile, ironic, aggressive and provocative."[9] For Régine Robin, however, Kafka's speech reveals quite the opposite: "Kafka could not, whatever he may have said, abandon the point of view of the Haskalah [Jewish Enlightenment] regarding Yiddish."[10] There is clearly a need for a more historically based approach to Kafka's knowledge and perception of Eastern European Jewish culture.

An important study in this regard is Sander Gilman's *Franz Kafka, the Jewish Patient* (1995),[11] which thoroughly documents the racial climate in Kafka's time. Gilman attempts to "reconstruct the contemporary discourses that Kafka consciously or unconsciously repressed by reinscribing them into a new literary tradition, the high modern" (3–4). He then reads Kafka's fiction, his personal correspondence, as well as his diaries through contemporary stereotypes and shows that while Kafka's personal writings discuss contemporary realities, they nonetheless also reveal that he largely internalized the racial discourses of his time. Both physically and mentally, Kafka becomes the "Jewish Patient" who represses the "stereotype of the Jew" (3), especially in his fiction, where he "removes any specifically 'Jewish' overtones" (26). Gilman is not alone in his belief that Kafka was unable to deal with contemporary reality. Many psycho-biographical-historical readers of Kafka before him (such as Marthe Robert, Anne Oppenheimer, Jean Jofen, or Ritchie Robertson) have been puzzled by the fact that the word "Jew" never appears in his fiction and have discussed Kafka's self-hatred, his supposed uneasiness with his Jewish heritage, and other such matters.[12] Pavel Petr is one of the few critics who quite rightly, to my mind, disagrees with such readings, "which acquire a central position in Kafka scholarship when the experience of the holocaust is projected onto Kafka."[13]

Furthermore, Gilman's position that Kafka "fled" into high modernism instead of addressing the ideological climate of his day is reminiscent of the Marxist rejection of Kafka in the 1930s: the Marxist critics also "reproached [Kafka] for resorting to 'modernism,' a mode condemned for ideological insufficiency, particularly to the extent that it failed to record or represent the historical circumstances from which alienation emerged."[14] Though no Marxist, Gilman, like Georg Lukács or Günter Anders, faults Kafka for not being more critical of contemporary ideologies. The connection between these scholars is the history of fascism and the Holocaust. Gilman acknowledges: "my reading of Kafka's imaginary world must be in light of my own fantasy of my world after the *Shoah*" (7). By stretching the time frame beyond Kafka's death and concluding with the Holocaust in his last chapter, "Kafka goes to Camp," Gilman emphasizes the continuity of racial discourses in Kafka's time that led to the "final solution." Gilman's shift in focus is crucial because readers and critics generally do not make the connection between Kafka and the Holocaust. Had he lived longer and stayed in Europe, he likely would not have survived—virtually his entire family died in concentration camps. This Vanished World was, after all, very much Kafka's world, too. However, Gilman's climactic ending also contains an ideological position, prepared for by the rhetorical construction of his overall argument, a "why did he not see and talk about this more" accusation. But it is too easy to adopt this stance in hindsight (from a postwar perspective that Kafka never had), easy in view of the overwhelming presence of racial discourses that Gilman has collected and condensed into one book and isolated from the many other contemporary discourses that are equally significant for Kafka's time. Walter Benjamin well understood that Kafka had "no far-sightedness or 'prophetic vision.' Kafka eavesdropped on tradition, and he who listens intently does not see."[15] Benjamin did not live to see the atrocities of the death camps, but he saw enough to distance Kafka from the impending catastrophe and to grant him the space for creative freedom that Kafka found in his art: "His gestures of terror are given scope by the marvelous *field for play (der herrliche Spielraum)* which the catastrophe will not entail" (G. Scholem, ed., *Correspondence*, 224 [B 86]).

Given the massive quantity of Kafka scholarship, what could this study contribute? My book tells a fascinating story that has not figured prominently in the secondary literature: Kafka's relation to cultural Zionism. The first books to address this topic were Giuliano Baioni's carefully researched *Kafka: Letteratura ed ebraismo* (Literature and Judaism; 1984), which has not been translated into English, and Ritchie Robertson's groundbreaking study *Kafka: Judaism, Politics and Literature* (1985). More recently, Scott Spector's *Prague Territories: National Conflict and Cultural Innovation in Franz Kafka's Fin de Siècle* (2000) has examined several writers from the Prague Circle from the perspective of cultural Zionism. And finally, a collection of essays, *Kafka, Zionism, and Beyond* (2004), addressed "Kafka's complicated Zionist connection, or better manifold connections, [which] are largely unappreciated in scholarship and mostly unknown, outside small pockets of specialized readerships."[16] I am greatly indebted to all of the scholars in this field.

Naturally, by placing Kafka and his writings into the framework of cultural Zionism, I do not wish to suggest that cultural Zionism dominated Kafka's life to the exclusion of everything else. Kafka obviously had much else in his life and indeed many other interests that had nothing to do with Judaism. Rather, it is my contention that Kafka did not repress half as much as critics have assumed and that his literature contains more contemporary social reality than is generally acknowledged. Kafka's writings are not devoid of contemporary discourses but include many more besides anti-Jewish stereotypes. The experience of fascism and the Holocaust has been the main problem faced by all commentators on Kafka's relation to Judaism. It is responsible for the peculiar silence in postwar German studies, for the many omissions in standard Kafka editions, for the romanticized treatment of prewar Jewish culture, and, last but not least, for the condemnation of Kafka, the writer, for lacking a sufficiently strong political stance.

Certainly, by placing Kafka in an entirely anti-Semitic environment, one immediately loses Kafka's humor, his playfulness, his puns. Very few critics have written about the lighthearted and intellectually challenging Kafka whom Max Brod and other contemporaries remember. Yet Kafka's last diary entry contradicts the common defeatist representation of his character: "Every word . . . becomes a spear turned against the speaker. Most especially a remark like this. And so ad infinitum. The only consolation would be: it happens whether you like or no. And what you like is of infinitesimally little help. More than consolation is: You too have weapons" (DII 232–33 [T 926]). Here Kafka appears neither as a victim nor as someone who is rendered passive and despairing owing to his existential predicament. On the contrary, his military metaphors strike a combative note when he describes the fundamental ambiguity of language, communication, and reception, and it is significant that he ends on an affirmative note. There remains a firm belief (which is "more than consolation") that everyone ("You too") has weapons.

Walter Benjamin in 1934 was the first to stress Kafka's rebelliousness, and his insight has lost none of its importance today: "[Kafka's writings] do not modestly lie at the feet of doctrine, as aggadah [legends, anecdotes] lies at the feet of halakha [Law]. When they have crouched down, they unexpectedly raise a mighty paw against it."[17] Benjamin's analogy between Kafka's fiction and a certain kind of Talmudic commentary establishes a similarly subversive intention for Kafka's literary commentaries, which he sees as continually challenging conventional modes of thinking. My reading of Kafka's literature runs along these lines: we need to go beyond the *Shoah* and reconstruct Kafka's social environment in order to make visible again his potential for humor and playfulness, his rebelliousness, and the challenge—the "weapons"—in his writing.

In order to prove this thesis, I have attempted to recreate Kafka's place within his historical "(con)text"[18] as well as establish his knowledge of Judaism and the extent of his involvement in Jewish affairs. Given the largely ideological nature of previous criticism, I have tried to keep my biographical-historical narrative as matter-of-fact as possible in order to avoid elaborate interpretation. Factual errors are frequently due to careless scholarship: a blatant example is when one biography claims that Kafka's last companion, Dora Diamant, "ended up in Palestine" and another speculates that Kafka's fiancée Julie Wohryzek "probably" died in a mental home in the 1920s, a few years after Kafka broke up with her.[19] Both statements are incorrect: Dora escaped to England and died there in 1952; Julie got married and died in Auschwitz in 1944.[20] I have corrected numerous errors in empirical records. Furthermore, the largely archival character of this study makes available to the reader as many original sources as possible, and many of these are translated here for the first time. Whenever possible I have used (or modified) standard translations throughout. Unless otherwise indicated, all translations are my own. In addition, this study is meant to serve as a bridge between German and English scholarship. For this reason, all quotations from Kafka's personal and literary writings are followed by page references to English translations as well as to the original German source in brackets.

My final goal was to embed Kafka's literature in the documentary, archival narrative. Kafka's literary texts (as well as texts by his contemporaries) are mentioned briefly or integrated more fully into the historical narrative if they contain elements from contemporary historical discourses. Longer textual analyses of his fragments and short stories appear in separate sections and mostly at the end of individual chapters. Rather than give an exhaustive reading of any one of the larger novels, I focus mainly on Kafka's shorter texts in order to demonstrate how contemporary discourses manifest themselves in his writings over the years. While it has not been my intention to suggest that these texts should always be interpreted within an all-Jewish framework, I wanted to create a solid base for future interpretive, interdiscursive analyses of Kafka's life and fiction. My own study contends that although we find a wealth of allusions to contemporary culture in Kafka's literature, his frequently ironic representation of

Jewish and non-Jewish racial discourses allows us to see his literature—not exclusively but at least a substantial part of it—as his own private counterdiscourse that attempts to "contest the period's dominant discursive structures."[21]

The book consists of seven chapters arranged in a roughly chronological order; they overlap and at times extend beyond the main time frame of a particular chapter. This overlap was not only unavoidable but in fact desirable in order to retain the multidimensional significance of many events in Kafka's life. The chapters develop particular aspects of Kafka's contact with Judaism without heeding strict chronological limits in order to show themes of continuity or discontinuity in Kafka's life. I chose to use a condensed treatment of issues that were important to Kafka over writing a Kafka biography with little bits and pieces of his relation to Judaism distributed loosely throughout the text.

I avoided Gustav Janouch's *Conversations with Kafka* as a source, since, as has been pointed out repeatedly, the material is largely anecdotal and thus unreliable.[22] I do, however, make ample use of contemporary documents, including texts Kafka either read or owned; literary and theoretical works of his friends Max Brod, Oskar Baum (1883–1941), Felix Weltsch, and Hugo Bergmann; articles from contemporary journalism, such as *Der Jude, Palästina,* and other relevant Zionist publications (especially Kafka's favorite Prague Zionist newspaper *Selbstwehr,* "the Zionist voice in Czechoslovakia" [PK 117]); works of Jewish fiction and history; recollections by contemporaries; Kafka's own letters and diaries; and, finally, Kafka scholarship that relates to the topic in question. At times I provide multiple quotations from various sources concerning a certain topic or event in order to build a rich sociohistorical context for the reader.

Having established the framework of this study, let us now turn our attention to Franz Kafka.

≫ I ≪

Kafka's Jewish Prague

(1883–1911)

THE FAMILY: HERMANN KAFKA'S SOCIAL MOBILITY

Franz Kafka's mother, Julie Löwy (1855–1934), came from a well-to-do family of scholars, doctors, and rabbinic authorities who held religion and German culture in high esteem. She was from Poděbrady, a small Czech town to the east of Prague, but her family moved to Prague around 1876–77.[1] Recording his family history in December 1911, Kafka depicts his mother's great-grandfather, Joseph Porias (KH 124), as a very learned and pious man, respected by Christians and Jews alike: "during a fire a miracle took place as a result of his piety, the flames jumped over and spared his house while the houses around it burned down" (DI 197 [T 319]). Furthermore, Kafka tells us that his Hebrew name, Amschel, derives from his "mother's maternal grandfather," Adam Porias (1794–1862). He was "a very pious and learned man with a long, white beard" who took ritual baths "in the river every day, even in winter, when he chopped a hole in the ice for his bath" (DI 197 [T 318]). However, two generations later, as Kafka reports with a touch of irony, the last direct ancestors of these impressive maternal relatives were crazy Uncle Nathan (1824–?), Kafka's great-uncle, and Esther (1830–1859), his grandmother (DI 198 [T 319]). Over the years, and with assimilation, little remained of the family's Judaism. Kafka's uncles, for instance, were given Germanic names: Alfred (1852–1923), Richard (1857–1938), Joseph (1858–1932), Siegfried (1867–1942), and Rudolf (1861–1921), who converted to Catholicism.[2]

Kafka's father, Hermann Kafka (1852–1931), came from a less privileged family. He was born in the village of Osek/Ossek/Wossek (near

Strakonice/Strakonitz in southern Bohemia [Nekula 46]), which had a predominantly Czech population. His father, Jakob Kafka (1814–1889), was a kosher butcher who supported six children,[3] of which Hermann was the fourth. He had no more than the compulsory six years of schooling in the local Jewish school, where the language of instruction was German.[4] The languages he grew up with were German, Yiddish, and Czech.[5] He spoke German at home but would have picked up Czech and Yiddish in the Czech countryside, particularly when, at the age of fourteen, he left home and became a peddler in order to earn a living. Hermann Kafka especially loved his time in the army (1872–75), "liked to talk about his soldiering even when he was an old man," and "used to sing soldiers' songs when he was in a good mood—which was not very often, admittedly" (FK 6). This is apparent in a dream Franz Kafka had in 1916 in which the father watches a military regiment marching down the street and exclaims, "That's something to look at as long as one can" (DII 146 [T 778]). After military service he resumed his earlier life of a peddler until around 1880, when he decided to move to Prague. Here he did not live in the Jewish ghetto but in the house of a cousin who was better off (Wagnerová 62). In 1882 he married Julie Löwy and opened his own store. In 1883 Franz Kafka was born.

Scholars have long believed that when he came to Prague, Hermann Kafka became "a member of the council of the synagogue in Jindrisska Street, the first Prague synagogue with Czech religious service."[6] However, no such synagogue turned up for this period (1890) in Marek Nekula's recent archival research. It is documented, however, that Hermann Kafka was a member of the Zigeunersynagoge (Gypsy Synagogue) in 1893 (a reform synagogue since 1883[7]) and that he favored the use of German (Nekula 23–26). Kafka's father then joined the Pinkassynagoge (Pinkas Synagogue), the second oldest synagogue in Prague which was (until today) situated right on the edge of the Old Jewish Cemetery. During Franz Kafka's childhood and adolescence, both of these synagogues were part of the old Jewish ghetto, which was eventually torn down (1895–1905). The Zigeunersynagoge was destroyed in 1906 (Rybar 45); the Pinkassynagoge was not. By 1911 we hear that the father had a seat in the oldest and most prestigious synagogue, the orthodox Altneusynagoge (Old New Synagogue) (DI 72 [T 47]), where the famous Rabbi Loew, who is known for the legend of the Golem, is said to have preached. Hermann Kafka's move from synagogue to synagogue parallels his successful social climb in the Prague Jewish community: considering his modest beginning, it did not take him long to elevate his social status, and by 1911 he was moving in the circles of the rich and prestigious who had a seat in the Altneusynagoge.

Kafka's parents ensured that their children would have the necessary linguistic advantages by sending them to German schools. The children also had German and Czech governesses, and later Franz Kafka took Czech language classes in his German high school (Nekula 25–26, 55–57, 139–51). Kafka's father successfully practiced an ambiguous cultural affiliation to protect his family from anti-Semitic riots, which occurred frequently with the rise of the Czech nationalist movement from 1897 on. Stölzl appropriately describes the father's method of protection as "double-tracked" (*Böhmen,* 51). He was equally practical in his business affairs when, after 1918, with the advent of the new Czech Republic, he changed the emblem of his store to make it look less Germanic: "Whereas earlier the jackdaw [Czech: *kavka*—the emblem of the store] still perches on a German oak twig, in the later years [of the Czech Republic] it perches again on less identifiable foliage" (Wagenbach, *Selbstzeugnisse,* 17).[8] Hermann Kafka was shrewd and tough and knew how to survive. None of these qualities made him endearing to his son.

Jewish Education at School, Home, or Synagogue

Franz Kafka learned little about Judaism in religion classes at school (KH 216–20). At the Altstädter Gymnasium, which he joined in 1893, the students were "mostly sons from rich Jewish families, sons of manufacturers and wholesalers."[9] Compulsory religion classes were taught by the Prague rabbi Nathan Grün.[10] But these classes made no lasting impression on Kafka, for he is silent on that matter. Max Brod's account must serve as an approximately accurate picture of the religious and cultural education a Jewish child received in Prague. The students had to learn by heart the basics of Hebrew and some passages from the Scriptures: "the names of the vowels, months, . . . the simplest forms of conjugation and . . . translations of a few biblical verses which we had learned by heart. This was the curriculum we had to master in a foreign idiom" (SL 222–23).

In the Kafka home, religious observance was reduced to a minimum. The family had a seder for Passover, but they limited themselves to one, instead of the traditional two days of observance. From the perspective of an adult in 1919, Kafka regarded this situation as "a farce, with fits of hysterical laughter" (DF 173 [Z 43]), and Binder even claims that he "ostensibly refused to eat unleavened bread [matzo] on Passover . . . and worked as on weekdays" (KH 219). However, their housekeeper, Anna Pouzarovà, remembers that the holidays in the Kafka household were a special occasion. Kafka was the only one who never ate matzo because he did not like it, though he loved *Mazze loks,* their special matzo pudding. The family may not have been very observant, and Kafka not very religious, but they did take out their special dishes for Passover and celebrated the holiday.[11]

Franz Kafka also did not receive much of a religious education in the synagogue. He went there with his father only four times a year (DF 172 [Z 42])—probably on the High Holy Days, Rosh Hashanah, Yom Kippur, and Passover, as well as on the emperor's birthday: "Around 1900 almost all Prague Jews—including the fathers of Kafka and Max Brod—could be called Four-Day-Jews, who went to the synagogue only on the three holiest holidays and on August 18 of each year, the birthday of Emperor Franz Josef I."[12] Kafka's father was not ignorant of the Scriptures, and Kafka, in fact, admired him for his courage when he was called up to the Torah (DF 173 [Z 43]) to recite the prayers in front of the congregation. Otherwise, though, he criticized him for regarding these functions as no more than a mere formality (DF 172 [Z 42]).

Going to the synagogue was primarily a social occasion, when one would go to see people and be seen in return. The presence of "'the sons of the millionaire Fuchs,' who were in the synagogue with their father at the high holidays" (DF 173 [Z 43]), seemed to be of greater importance than the religious ceremony. Though in those early years Kafka reproached himself "for not going to the synagogue enough, for not fasting, and so on" (DF 171 [Z 42]), in hindsight he mostly remembers his father's religious practices as "a mere scrap, a joke, not even a joke" (DF 172 [Z 42]), certainly not enough to be passed on (DF 174 [Z 44]). The lasting memory of the service was that he "yawned and dozed through the many hours (I don't think I was ever again so bored, except later at dancing lessons)" (DF 172 [Z 42–43]; see LF 502 [BF 700]). Kafka's bar mitzvah in the German Zigeunersynagoge in 1896 was announced in the local newspaper by the Christian term "confirmation," in keeping with his father's assimilationist thinking. Kafka plays down the traditional significance of the occasion, because it "meant no more than some ridiculous learning by heart" (DF 172–73 [Z 43]). He received a rudimentary training that enabled him to read the particular Hebrew passage he had to recite in front of the congregation, and afterward he made a little speech at home, which was also practiced beforehand (LM 153–54 [BM 207]).

Of the synagogues in Prague, Kafka preferred the larger family synagogue, the Pinkassynagoge, to the orthodox Altneusynagoge. In a long diary entry he caricatures the Kol Nidre evening service (ushering in Yom Kippur, the Day of Atonement) in the Altneusynagoge (1 October 1911): "The Altneu Synagogue yesterday. Kol Nidre. Suppressed murmur of the stock market. In the entry, boxes with the inscription: 'Merciful gifts secretly left assuage the wrath of the bereft' [*besänftigen den Unwillen*]" (DI 72 [T 47]). Grözinger takes Kafka's description as evidence of his religious sentiments (*Kabbala,* 28); however, the context puts Kafka's remarks into a highly ironic light: to have a seat in the Altneu Synagogue was a sign of prestige for Kafka's father, and Kafka was struck by the hypocrisy of all around him. His comments mock the prayers by likening them to the murmur of the stock market, and he also questions the pious behavior of three "apparently Eastern Jews. In socks. . . . Two are crying, moved only by the holy day?[13] One of them may only have sore eyes, perhaps" (DI 72 [T 47]).

Moreover, two days before the service Kafka had visited a well-known brothel, Salon Suha, and he now recognized "the family of [the] brothel owner" among the worshipers (DI 72–73 [T 48–49, K 25]; translation modified). The contrast between appearance and reality does not escape his irony. The traveling salesman's emphatic prayer (DI 72 [T 47–48]) appears hypocritical "in an environment where piety is measured by one's wealth, by the length of one's beard or orthodox attire, by the vigor with which one shook at prayer."[14] Kafka concludes that he "was stirred immeasurably more deeply by Judaism in the Pinkas Synagogue" (DI 72 [T 48]). This large family synagogue[15]—in contrast to the small, orthodox Altneu Synagogue–did not have the social pretense and money ("murmur of the stock market") behind it. Apart from such visits on the High Holy Days, Kafka's religious observance—in later years especially—was limited to social and family occasions.

SOCIALISM, ZIONISM, ANTI-SEMITISM

The Red Carnation

In 1893, when Kafka was ten years old and began to attend the Altstädter Gymnasium, the first Jewish nationalist organization was established in Prague under the name Maccabäa (CJ 93–95; KH 68). This was in response to the foundation of the anti-Semitic German nationalist student organization Germania in 1892 (KH 280), which had previously been the right-wing element of the liberal Lese- und Redehalle der deutschen Studenten in Prag (Reading and Lecture Group of German Students in Prague). Maccabäa's nationalist orientation soon lost momentum but was revived in 1899 when it became the Zionist Bar Kochba (1899),[16] named after Simon Bar Kochba, the leader of the Jewish revolt against Rome (132–35 CE). However, for the time being most Jewish students retained their membership in the liberal Lese- und Redehalle and continued to join (like Kafka, Bergmann, and Brod).

The year 1897 (Kafka was fourteen) marks the rise of the young Czech nationalist movement, which was frequently anti-Semitic. In April 1897 anti-Semitic speeches could be heard not far from Kafka's residence. A few months later Kafka experienced the so-called "December storm," the three days of anti-German as well as anti-Semitic rioting in Prague when German institutions and stores were attacked and "thousands of windows broken, including those of Max Brod's family" (Stölzl, *Böhmen*, 61, 63). This riot came in the wake of the resignation of the Austrian prime minister, Casimir Badeni, whose sympathy for Czech nationalism had made him introduce controversial language laws which "stipulated that all civil servants in Bohemia and Moravia had to offer evidence, no later than 1 July 1901, of written and oral command of both German and Czech or face dismissal" (CJ 72). Whereas most Czech civil servants knew German, many of their German counterparts were not so familiar with the Czech language. German government officials felt very threatened, the legislation became a political and racial issue, and soon riots broke out everywhere. In Prague the clashes between Czechs and Germans (which included the Jews) were especially virulent (CJ 73). Nothing seems to have happened to Kafka's father's shop: someone, supposedly, during an anti-Semitic riot had said, "Leave Kafka alone, he is a Czech" (Wagenbach, *Biographie*, 19).

In terms of political affiliation, the average Jewish response to the riots of 1897 was an increasing support for the Social Democratic Party. Many young Jews turned to Zionism (1897 also marks the meeting of the First Zionist Congress in Basel). Kafka himself became a socialist. His friend Hugo Bergmann, who attended the same elementary and high school, recalls that Kafka openly wore a red carnation to school to show his socialist sympathies: this is Kafka's first recorded political statement. Bergmann, however, whose family was very sympathetic to Zionism, identified more strongly with the Zionist movement: "Franz became a socialist, I became a Zionist in 1898. The synthesis of Zionism and Socialism did not yet exist. In 1899, when the Prague Zionists called their first public meeting, it was broken up by the socialists (who were all Jews) together with the Czech assimilationists."[17]

Anti-Semitic Trials: Tisza Eszlar, Dreyfus, Hilsner, Kishinev (1882 to 1903)

This period saw several major anti-Semitic trials: the Tisza Eszlar trial in Hungary (1882–83), the Dreyfus affair in France (1895), the Hilsner case in Bohemia (1899), and the Kishinev massacre in Russia (1903). With the exception of the Dreyfus affair, all trials and pogroms were linked with ritual murder or blood libel accusations—the anti-Semitic charge that Jews needed Christian blood for their Passover rituals and slaughtered Christian children to obtain it. Even the charges against Dreyfus can be seen as an extension of this medieval ritual murder myth, since he was accused of "stabbing" France in the back. Apart from the Hilsner trial, which continued until 1916, these events took place during Kafka's childhood.[18]

The Tisza Eszlar ritual murder trial in Hungary (1882–83) took place in the year of Kafka's birth. On 1 April 1882, during the Easter/Passover season, a fourteen-year-old girl disappeared, and even though it was thought that she had committed suicide in the river Tisza, a "local Catholic priest ... accused the Jews of ritual murder" (*Judaica* 15:1155).[19] This accusation was connected with the figure of the mythical Wandering Jew, who supposedly appeared in the form of a ritual slaughterer.[20] Several individuals were charged with the crime and tortured. Riots broke out, and a "protective association for Christians against the Jews" was founded (Wambach 115). Eventually a young boy, Móric Scharf, was charged with the murder and under duress made to testify against his family and fellow Jews. Scharf was pardoned after a long trial that began during the summer of 1883 and continued well into 1884. Kafka mentions this event in 1916 (LF 530 [BF 735]; see chapter 6).

The most well-known trial at the turn of the century was the Dreyfus affair in France: "In 1894 Alfred Dreyfus was charged with spying for the Germans. . . . Kafka was eleven at the time of the thirty-five year old Dreyfus's degradation in 1895; at the time of Dreyfus's second trial in 1899, he was sixteen; he was twenty-three when Dreyfus was finally acquitted and twenty-five when a final attempt was made to assassinate Dreyfus. All of these events haunted the front pages of the newspapers in Prague as elsewhere in the world" (Gilman, *Patient,* 69). Moreover, as Anthony Northey has discovered, Kafka had a personal connection to the case through his uncles Joseph and Alfred Löwy. Their mentors, the Bunau-Varillas, did a great deal to exonerate Dreyfus and, of course, drew the wrath of the anti-Dreyfusards. Kafka's uncles' lives were directly affected by these events when their French employers, the Bunau-Varillas brothers, "decided to find positions abroad for Alfred and Joseph" (Northey, *Relatives*, 13). The Dreyfus affair surfaces later in several of Kafka's literary texts, and it even appears in a fragment from 1917: "You know the Trocadéro in Paris?" (DF 53–54 [W 58, H 43–44]). Northey points out that because this fragment deals with a great trial, it "is perhaps no coincidence that Kafka chose the name Trocadéro, for at the time of his arrest Captain Dreyfus lived at number 6 avenue de Trocadéro, which was also the street in which the offices of [the employers of Kafka's uncle Joseph Loewy] were located" (*Relatives*, 41–42).

In addition, Kafka knew about the notorious Leopold Hilsner blood libel trial (1899–1916) in Polnà, Bohemia (LM 51 [BM 68]). Also during the Easter/Passover season (on 1 April 1899), the corpse of a murdered seamstress was found. Leopold Hilsner (1877–1927), an innocent "22 year-old Jewish vagabond of ill repute and low intelligence" (*Judaica* 8:496) and a shoemaker by profession, was accused of murdering the girl and sentenced to hang (CJ 74).

Again, the Prague newspapers reported on these events extensively, and Kafka must have also heard about this trial at home, because his father and the fathers of Max Brod, Franz Werfel, Felix Weltsch were all involved in the Central Association for the Preservation of Jewish Affairs, which "took a stand ... in 1899 during the Hilsner affair against the Jew-baiting of the Czechs and nationalistic German Christians" (KH 119; see Stölzl, *Böhmen*, 112). The Hilsner trial also brought with it "an unending trivial literature about ritual murder, a wave of picture postcards with Polna and Hilsner motifs swamped the land, the ritual murder became the attraction of many dioramas, pantoscopes and peep-show boxes in Bohemia" (Stölzl, *Böhmen*, 68). Like Dreyfus, Hilsner was not without support and "found his Émile Zola in the person of Tomàš G. Masaryk (1850–1937), professor of philosophy at the Czech University in Prague" (CJ 74). Masaryk was well-known for his political activities in the Czech national movement and in 1918 became the first president of the Czechoslovak Republic. He was instrumental in arranging a new trial in 1900 (CJ 74) but was not very successful in his defense of Hilsner because public opinion was against him. The case nonetheless made him famous. Court proceedings against Hilsner lasted until 1916, when Emperor Charles I succeeded to the Habsburg throne and, as one of his first acts, "set Hilsner free."[21]

Kafka was twenty years old when the notorious Kishinev massacre took place in Russia (6–7 April 1903); he mentions it in 1911 (DI 101–2 [T 89]; see chapter 2). This pogrom also originated with ritual murder accusations and then grew out of hand:

> when the body of a Christian child was found and a young Christian woman patient committed suicide in the Jewish hospital, the mob became violent. A blood libel . . . spread like wildfire. (It was proved that the child was murdered by his relatives and that the suicide of the woman was in no way connected with the Jews.) According to official statistics, 49 Jews lost their lives and more than 500 were injured, some of them seriously; 700 houses were looted and destroyed and 600 businesses and shops were looted . . . about 2,000 families were left homeless.[22]

Many critics have ignored or downplayed the effect of anti-Semitism on Kafka in his youth and adolescence simply because he did not talk about it a great deal. But the very fact that he remembered his father (in *Letter to His Father*) being so paranoid that he called his Czech employees "paid enemies" (DF 161 [Z 32]) indicates that Kafka was quite aware of his father's fear of the lower classes. The Dreyfus affair and the Hilsner blood libel trial in particular were constant reminders of the always-latent anti-Semitism in society that could quickly turn ugly.

University Years: Lese- und Redehalle, Bar Kochba, and the Foundation of Selbstwehr (1901–7)

In the fall of 1901, after his *Abitur* (high school graduation), Kafka attended university. Like most Jewish students, he and Hugo Bergmann joined the liberal student organization Lese- und Redehalle (KH 280), which "was by all odds the most dynamic and effective center of German culture in Prague, with a library second only to that of the university itself, regular weekly readings by prominent German literary figures, and organized concerts, art exhibits, and discussion groups on various cultural topics." It had a membership of "around 450 students in Kafka's day" (Pawel, *Nightmare,* 106), most of whom were Jewish. In 1892 already, when the German nationalists broke away and founded Germania in 1892, "they left the organization half-empty and ostentatiously Jewish" (CJ 93). Max Brod, who started university a year after Kafka, also joined the Lese- und Redehalle.

Here Brod and Kafka met for the first time in October 1902, when Brod gave a lecture on Arthur Schopenhauer. Both friends were actively involved in the Lese- und Redehalle until 1905 (KH 280–86), which reveals their closeness to German culture and thus their assimilationist leanings. But membership became less attractive over the next years since this liberal student organization lamely fought against the aggressive anti-Semitism of its offshoot, Germania. In 1908, Jewish students founded their own Lese- und Redehalle der jüdischen Hochschüler in Prag (Reading and Lecture Group of Jewish Students in Prague) (CJ 117). The Zionists taunted those Jews who stayed in the former Lese- und Redehalle and put up with humiliation as "Jews of the Hall" (die Hallejuden) or "Jewish Teutons" (jüdische Teutonen) (S 2 July 1909:2).[23]

Meanwhile, Hugo Bergmann had been moving increasingly toward Zionism. He wrote to Kafka in 1902–3:

> Do not believe that it was the feeling of compassion that changed me into a Zionist. My Zionism is replete with selfishness. I feel as though I want to fly, to create, but cannot; I have no more strength. For all this I feel that under other circumstances I could find the strength, that this uprootedness was not decreed to me from birth. And so Zionism is for me an expression of my yearnings for love. For I know that thousands are suffering exactly as I; I want to travel on their path, to work with them.... Perhaps one of these days we shall overcome [our] weakness. One of these days we shall stand firmly on our soil, and we shall no longer be lacking roots, detached and trembling as a reed. And perhaps, perhaps my strength will return again to me.[24]

Bergmann soon joined Bar Kochba[25] and became its chairman (1903–4). Under his influence "Bar Kochba's Zionism became decidedly non-Herzlian. It drew its main inspiration from the school of 'cultural Zionism' originating with Ahad Ha'am (Asher Ginsberg, 1856–1927) and transmitted to Bar Kochba through the mediation of Nathan Birnbaum (1864–1937), Berthold Feiwel (1875–1937), Martin Buber (1878–1965), and Bergmann himself" (CJ 101). In 1901, the Bergmann family (mother, father, and older brother) attended a lecture by Feiwel where he "introduced the program known as *Gegenwartsarbeit* [work in the present]–which stressed the amelioration of current cultural, economic, and political conditions among diaspora Jewry–as a necessary first stage in the Zionist revolution"

(CJ 102). Bergmann's "völkische Kleinarbeit" (practical community work), which later became so central in his own philosophy of Zionism, derived from Feiwel's *Gegenwartsarbeit*.

In addition, the Viennese Zionist Nathan Birnbaum had just published a book on Ahad Ha'am in German (1903) (CJ 101; 225–26n.35). Bergmann must have read this work and immediately understood the attraction of Ahad Ha'am's cultural Zionism for Jews who lived in the Diaspora for "at the first conference of Austrian Student Zionist Organizations in 1903, Hugo Bergmann declared that his colleagues did not intend to follow Herzl's policies with respect to the noninvolvement of Zionists in domestic affairs. Instead, he stressed the importance of Gegenwartsarbeit. This, in the context of Austria, was to entail struggling for the recognition of the Jewish nationality in secondary schools and at the university; educating Jewish youth in Zionism; attempting to bridge the 'gap' between Eastern and Western Jewry; and devoting oneself to the problems of the 'Jewish masses'" (CJ 102). In the summer of 1903, Bergmann and his wife, Else, traveled to Galicia "on a pilgrimage of authenticity, an eastward trek, which many who had read Buber and Ahad Ha'am had already taken in their imagination" (CJ 115).

Though Kafka was not involved in Zionist politics, he likely knew about the fighting within Bar Kochba around his friend Hugo Bergmann's political views. As Kieval points out, "not everyone within the organization approved of Bergmann's leadership or of Bar Kochba's exclusively cultural orientation" (CJ 116), and after he became chairman in 1903, those who were dissatisfied founded Barissia, the rival Zionist group to Bar Kochba, which endorsed Theodor Herzl's political Zionism. Barissia was a militant *schlagende Verbindung* (a fighting fraternity) whose members would challenge liberal Jews with "colours, songs, and fists" (CJ 117). In 1909 it lived up to its name as a dueling fraternity when it came to a "pistol duel" between Leo Herrmann of the Bar Kochba and the leader of Barissia (CJ 117–18). Barissia members also founded the Zionist newspaper *Selbstwehr*, the "Only Jewish Weekly in Bohemia, Moravia and Silesia,"[26] in March 1907, the same year Kafka graduated as Doctor of Law. *Selbstwehr*, which later acquired great importance in Kafka's life, came into being largely because of increasing anti-Semitism in Prague: one of its goals was to report on all anti-Semitic incidents, large and small, because there was no other paper that did so at the time.[27] This, then, is some of Kafka's background before 1909–10, the time when both he and Max Brod did come into closer contact with Zionism.

THE ZIONIST SCENE IN PRAGUE

Theodor Herzl or Ahad Ha'am

Kafka's first encounter with Zionism took place in 1909–10, when he and Max Brod became acquainted with the Zionist Bar-Kochba association (KH 375; PK 66). Ritchie Robertson claims that Bar-Kochba's "main ideological preceptor was not Theodor Herzl ... but Ahad Ha'am, the proponent of cultural Zionism," whose ideas were very popular "when Brod and Kafka first made contact with the Bar Kochba" (*Judaism*, 142). Though this is generally accurate,[28] Ahad Ha'am (his Hebrew pen name means "One of the People") and his theories are not mentioned a great deal—certainly not by Kafka in any of his writings and correspondence. And while he is referred to extensively in *Der Jude*, he does not figure prominently in the local *Selbstwehr*. By the time Kafka and Brod began to take note of Bar Kochba, Ahad Ha'am's philosophy had become increasingly infused with the Prague Zionists' own ideas.

According to Kieval, Bar Kochba went through three stages. The first stage lasted from 1901 to 1905 and was greatly influenced by the leadership of Hugo Bergmann and his version of cultural Zionism. The second stage was initiated when the rival Zionist group Barissia was founded in 1903 (KH 68; Goshen, "Students' Organizations," 174) and led to "Bar Kochba's 'political phase,'" during which a "counter-movement" to Bergmann was launched (CJ 99). The third neo-romantic stage—when Kafka and Brod had contact to the Bar Kochba—began with Martin Buber's visits to Prague (when he delivered his famous speeches on Judaism) and ended with World War I. The Zionists Hugo Herrmann (1887–1940) and his cousin Leo Herrmann (1888–1951) were instrumental during this third period. They came to study in Prague in 1906–7, joined Bar Kochba, and soon took on leadership (KH 372)—Leo from 1908 to 1909 and Hugo from 1909 to 1911. This last phase represented "the definite triumph of Bergmann's version of cultural Zionism, though perhaps in more romantic tones than before, and climaxed in the publication of Prague's Zionism's intellectual jewel, *Vom Judentum* (On Judaism), in 1914" (CJ 100). Max Brod was included in the volume, and Kafka owned the first edition—it was part of his personal library (KB 131).

In this third phase, Theodor Herzl, especially after his early death in 1904, was still the idol of many Zionists and was practically mythologized in *Selbstwehr*; the paper celebrated every Herzl anniversary enthusiastically and published many more articles on Herzl than on Ahad Ha'am. Hugo

Bergmann himself had a picture of Theodor Herzl on the wall in his home; in fact, this was where Max Brod, in 1910, first encountered Herzl (SL 49). Brod recalled that Bergmann on this visit introduced him to the writings of both Herzl and Ahad Ha'am.[29] And though Kafka never mentions Ahad Ha'am,[30] he was clearly familiar with the name and his philosophy of cultural Zionism through newspapers, lectures, and friends. He knew about Ahad Ha'am for certain in 1912 because he was discussed in the *Palästinaheft* (Journal of Palestine), which he owned and brought along to Max Brod's home the night he met Felice Bauer (see chapter 3).

Generally, Ahad Ha'am was perceived by many as a logical continuation of Herzl for advocating a more realistic type of Zionism, where every Jew in the Diaspora could be useful without having to move to Palestine immediately. But Ahad Ha'am was also a controversial figure whos ideas did not go unchallenged—in fact, one authority claims they were "rejected by the bulk of the Zionist movement."[31] Rather, it was Micha Josef Berdyczewski (1865–1821), Ahad Ha'am's intellectual opponent, who had a much greater impact on Kafka's Zionist friends. He was known as bin Gorion but is rarely mentioned by scholars today in relation to Prague Zionism. Berdyczewski's vision of cultural Zionism was very important for the Zionists around Bergmann.

Martin Buber and Felix Salten

Even though Zionism was becoming increasingly vocal, the number of fervent Zionists in Prague was still relatively small in 1909–10. Hugo Bergmann was an exception, while many others, like Brod and Kafka, were hesitant in their initial response to the movement. In 1909–10 Martin Buber came to Prague to present his famous *Three Speeches on Judaism*.[32] He had been invited as a guest speaker for Bar Kochba (along with the Viennese Zionist Felix Salten) on their very first *Festabend* (festive evening) organized by Leo Herrmann, who had by now become a prominent figure in Prague Zionist circles: first he was chairman of Bar Kochba (1908–9); then he took on the editorship of *Selbstwehr* (1910–13) (*Judaica* 8: 365). At the time Buber was known for his own philosophy of cultural Zionism, especially after his speech at the Third Zionist Congress in 1899, which "bore the influence... notably of Ahad Ha-Am, [and] emphasized the importance of education as opposed to a program of propaganda" (*Judaica* 4:1429). Buber fitted well into the cultural Zionist orientation of Bar Kochba with its mixture of Ahad Ha'am and Herzlian neo-romanticism.

Max Brod, who at this time belonged to Bar Kochba only "as guest and opponent" (SL 48), attended these speeches. Though organized by the Zionists, they were major events and attracted many Jews in Prague. Brod claims that Kafka was present at Buber's three lectures as well. Kafka must have attended at least one, since, in a letter to his later fiancée Felice Bauer in 1913, he refers to an earlier occasion when he saw Buber: "I have heard him before, I find him dreary; no matter what he says, something is missing" (LF 157 [BF 252]). Kafka was less than impressed with Buber. Hartmut Binder, though, recounts that Buber's first speech, "Judaism and the Jews" (20 January 1909; see *On Judaism*, 11–21), was a great success: "He spoke with such great fervor that the audience appeared to be nearly drunk afterwards" (KH 373–74).

However, it was Felix Salten—and not Buber—who spoke with such great enthusiasm and appealed to the large crowd. Salten's speech was also reprinted in full on the front and succeeding page of *Selbstwehr* (22 January 1910), whereas Buber was mentioned only briefly in a review of the evening on the third page. In fact, before the event Buber seems to have been a little apprehensive about having to speak together with Salten. He arrived a day early, to everyone's surprise, so that he would get to know the Zionist group (CJ 137); he wished "to know the precise content of Salten's talk so that he might tailor his own accordingly" (CJ 129), and before the lecture he "fretted privately to Herrmann that he did not feel that he could match the lively tone of Felix Salten's introductory speech" (CJ 137). Leo Herrmann advised Buber "to ignore the public, 'to speak only for us'" (CJ 137). And this is what he did. He talked about a mystical Jewish essence which every Jew could claim, the need for "new forms of a viable Jewish life. . . . . in a series of trancelike affirmations" (CJ 133). Though he had a "very select audience" (S 22 Jan. 1909:3), many of those present remained unconvinced. After the event another reviewer remarked that the audience responded more to Salten than to Buber and that there were "extremes in both speeches" that were nonetheless "pleasant": "Salten chatted about Jews and Judaism and thereby quickly gained his audience's attention; Buber, on the other hand, fought with Jews and emphasized not so much their suffering and their struggles with non-Jews, but rather their special inner world and their future.—Naturally, not everyone could follow these ideas, but those who did experienced a 'spiritual epiphany'" (S 22 Jan. 1909:3). The evening, then, was successful mostly because Felix Salten gave a brilliant performance.

Felix Salten (1869–1945), author of the children's tale *Bambi* (1923), lived in Vienna and was a journalist by profession and also a prolific writer of short stories, novels, and plays. Other than being known as an author of children's animal tales, little information is available on Salten today.³³ Virtually nothing is known about his Zionist sympathies. In his time, though, he was "the confident, young, national Jew Salten" (S 22 Jan. 1909:3), loved by many and hated by a few, notably by his Viennese contemporary, the famous journalist and satirist Karl Kraus (1874–1936), who berated him in his intellectual magazine *Die Fackel* (The Torch). According to Kraus, Salten could "be sensitive and out of love for Herrn Herzl take on the millennial pain of Judaism for a Zionist weekly. Herr Salten can do all sorts of things, but he is nothing."³⁴

In his speech for the Bar Kochba in 1909, "Der Abfall vom Judentum" (The Lapse from Judaism), Salten took conversion to Christianity as a point of departure, arguing against those who seem to think an "enlightened" Jew would not care about being Jewish. On the contrary, he insisted, an enlightened thinker would choose to be Jewish in full awareness of the Jewish contributions to Western culture. Salten singled out the Bible, in particular, as the foundation of Western culture and stressed that there was no need to feel thankful for being tolerated and accepted by "enlightened" gentiles. With great conviction he insisted further that it was wrong to see emancipation as a generous gesture or gift on the part of the gentiles: "Emancipation was no gift. It was the repayment of a right, and a repayment which was not entirely honest, because it had been withheld from the Jews for fifteen centuries." Ironically, by embracing emancipation

1. Felix Salten's speech, "The Lapse from Judaism"

and liberalism so full-heartedly and passing these ideas on to the next generation, the Jews made sure that their earlier oppressors would never more be reminded of their guilt: "They were so sensitive that they felt badly about reminding their former oppressors of the embarrassing past, that they had, in fact, once been oppressors" (S 22 Jan. 1909:1). This passive acceptance of earlier injustices, Salten argues, lies at the very heart of liberalism. But the bill is paid. Jews have survived for centuries, which is a sign of their strength, and the time has now come to launch a new future.

Salten was loved in Prague and invited again two years later as main speaker at a Bible evening for the third Bar Kochba Festabend (26 January 1911). The lecture room was packed: "A thundering applause is roaring through the hall as Felix Salten steps onto the podium. After only a few words everyone is mesmerized by his speech" (S 27 Jan. 1911:5). *Selbstwehr* again reprinted Salten's speech in its entirety. Buber, in turn, was guest speaker at the fifth Bar Kochba "festive evening" in January 1913. Kafka was present (BF 252–53)[35] and also heard Salten speak again in the following year.

Kafka and Buber

If Kafka did not attend Buber's first lecture in 1909, he may have heard his second or third speech. Buber's next talk, "Judaism and Mankind" (*On Judaism*, 22–33), in the Jewish City Hall (3 April 1910), was announced in *Selbstwehr*, and Buber himself was hailed as a new Theodor Herzl. Buber talked about the struggle for wholeness and the desire to overcome the experience of dualism (being torn between good and evil). A synthesis was achieved especially in the work of one man, Spinoza, and it also found an outlet when the inner flames of Jewish mysticism burst forth. But the time of redemption, according to Buber, is still to come—a time when the Jews will be freed for the good of mankind and another (yet unknown) synthesis is about to appear. Whatever form it may take, "it will, once again, demand unity" (*On Judaism*, 32). To realize this synthesis or wholeness—herein lies the function of the Jews for all mankind.

Friedrich Thieberger, Kafka's later Hebrew teacher, reviewed the lecture in *Selbstwehr* (S 8 Apr. 1910:4–5). He found the "method" of his reasoning questionable because Buber deduced conclusions from his perception of Jewish history, which he then formulated as natural laws that would equally determine Jewish history in the future (5). Furthermore, since Buber's lecture lacked a strong Herzlian message, Thieberger continued Buber's argument and added one himself: "However, in order to become full-blooded Jews [*Vollblutjuden*] again after centuries of living in exile, we can pick up the thread only where our forefathers left off: in the homeland of Palestine" (5). Though Buber did not end on this Zionist note, this is what the "inner Zionist circle" would have liked to hear. Many Zionists, even if they could not appreciate Buber's mysticism, sympathized with him because they believed he was advocating going to Palestine as the most logical solution. Another Zionist reviewer said that "here we can also follow the mystic Buber, who seeks the meaning of Judaism not in the past but in the future, in Jewish Palestine. Perhaps there the new Messiah will arise—for the whole world" (S 15 Apr. 1910:2). Thus, the evening ended on a very positive note: "Buber's speech made a profound impression. The hour was an intellectual experience" (S 8 Apr. 1910:5).

With the extensive advertising, many Jews in Prague were looking forward to Buber's third speech, "The Renewal of Judaism" (*On Judaism,* 34–55). The organizers expected such a great demand for tickets that individuals were asked to approach Bar-Kochba beforehand, with "admission only by personal invitation" (S 6 Dec. 1910:6). Buber's lecture took place in the Jewish City Hall. "This time everyone came who had attended the first two lectures; but in addition numerous others had arrived who stood in front of Buber in amazement. Virtually all those in Prague who were interested in Jewish culture were present: old and young, women and men. The Jewish Cultural Council had cancelled its meeting which had been planned for that hour" (S 23 Dec. 1910:3).

Buber discussed the future of Judaism, a messianic future as yet unknown to man. He distinguished the kind of renewal he had in mind from the one envisioned by Ahad Ha'am, who "anticipates a renewal with the establishment of a spiritual center in Palestine" (*On Judaism,* 38). For Buber a fundamental renewal could not originate in Palestine, where people would be trying to create a normal and settled life for themselves out of "the normal and confident existence of a settler in his own land." Rather, the Diaspora is the place of regeneration: a fundamental renewal can emerge only out of chaos, despair, struggle, strife, and yearning for order. What Buber called for was an "absolute," Nietzschean "change in all elements of life" (*On Judaism,* 39). *Selbstwehr* reported on the evening enthusiastically (S 23 Dec. 1910:3).

No matter which of these talks Kafka attended, his dismissive comments made clear that he was not impressed. Max Brod, however, found Buber absolutely fascinating; for him Buber's work bridged the gap between a lost Jewish past and the present assimilated condition (SL 228). Kafka did not share these sentiments; nonetheless, he participated in several cultural events put on by the Zionists. He was certainly not unknown to the Zionist circle in 1910: a month after Buber's second speech, Kafka's name is mentioned in *Selbstwehr* for the first time (13 May 1910) in honor of his promotion to *Anstaltskonzipist* (draftsman) (LF 84 [BF 153]), which gave him "full civil service tenure" (Pawel, *Nightmare* 188; C 57) in the Workmen's Accident Insurance Institute.

ZIONISM AND THE CRITIQUE OF ASSIMILATION

Assimilation as Disease

Zionism is generally seen as a reaction to anti-Semitism, but some, like the Zionist Adolf Böhm (1873–1941), make finer distinctions. Böhm argued that "it is quite wrong to believe that Zionism is a 'consequence' of anti-Semitism"; rather, anti-Semitism must be seen as "only the *incident* which made these people think about the relationship between Jews and non-Jews and investigate why this relationship today is an unhealthy one. For them anti-Semitism was a socio-pathological phenomenon; they were therefore looking for the source of the disease as well as for a cure. They found both—the malady as well as the remedy for the cure."[36] This disease was called "assimilation"—the noncritical acceptance of the norms and values of German middle class culture. Assimilation was a major concern for many young Jews, and this manifested itself in their rebellion against their assimilated fathers, "who had as yet been unable to see the error of their ways" (KH 371).

For the young generation of Zionists, condemning or fighting anti-Semitism was insufficient because no change could be expected from the outside environment; rather, one had to look within oneself and bring about a fundamental change of perception by reclaiming one's heritage. Freud had taught that acknowledging the "disease" was the first step toward a cure; what needed to be recognized was that Enlightenment goals had not led to equality, and that assimilation had caused a suppression of Jewish identity and psychological problems, such as self-hatred and Jewish anti-Semitism. The problematics of assimilation were frequent subjects of discussion among Kafka's friends.

Though Brod and Kafka initially rejected Zionism, their aloofness did not last long. They were made to acknowledge Zionism as a political force to be reckoned with when Max Brod was attacked in *Selbstwehr* for his noncritical representation of Jewish assimilation in his literary work and for his overall lack of a national consciousness. Initially, the Zionist Leo Herrmann had criticized Brod's novel *A Czech Servant Girl* in 1909 and then invited him to a discussion about Jewish nationalism (KH 375; SL 47, 221–22). This was Brod's initiation into the Zionist circle. It was also the first time he—and by extension Kafka—saw an issue of *Selbstwehr* (SL 221). They knew nothing about Zionism or about the Zionist newspaper before this time. In May 1911 Brod was attacked again, for his second novel, *Die Jüdinnen*[37] (Jewish Women)—this time by Leo Herrmann's cousin, Hugo Herrmann, the aforementioned Buber enthusiast (KH 373).

Zionist Dogmatism: *Die Jüdinnen*

Brod's *Die Jüdinnen* is set in a very assimilated Jewish environment. One of the main characters, Alfred, "belonged to those young Jews who are strongly attracted to all that is Arian and despise everything Jewish" (228). Alfred is a not-very-sophisticated caricature of a young assimilated Jew who identifies with German nationalism: "The consolidation of all Germans was his ideal," and he is a "lover of Wagner" (288, 231). Brod was widely criticized for this novel; many Zionists believed his ideological message was not strong enough, and for several years they hounded him with their criticism.

Herrmann's review is written in the form of a dialogue between two fictive characters, Raphael and Julius, who put the novel on trial: Raphael is the book's advocate, Julius is the prosecutor. The final "judgment" is negative. The prosecutor's argument is that this is not a "Jewish" novel; it is not even a novel but a "representation" of the most typical, the most common and ordinary, Jews around us. In particular the main character, Hugo Rosenthal, seems a very self-satisfied person, not someone who is a fighter for a cause (i.e., a Zionist). There are not many conflicts, and there is no tragic end; instead, the author simply wishes his character good luck at the end of the book, which is very poor construction. The worst, though, is that Brod never takes a stance vis-à-vis his characters. This is the greatest flaw, and that is why his work is definitely not a "Jewish novel":

> It would be the duty of this historical work to judge. However, the judgments of this insignificant, childlike Hugo Rosenthal alone are so disputable and doubtful that one can always defend a contrary judgment and certainly a different judgment. For we all know these people whom Hugo judges.... and this is why we have the right to pass any other judgment on them than Hugo, and this is what we will do. (S 19 May 1911:3)

This objectivism with its "annihilation of judgment" is apparently typical of Brod's work in general and justifies Herrmann's final "judgment" that Brod is simply "no writer" (3). It was then that Brod felt compelled to argue back. On 26 May the front page of *Selbstwehr* has Brod's rebuttal followed by Herrmann's final commentary.

As a result of this controversy, Kafka attempted several reviews of Brod's novel in his diary (DI 54–55, 59–60 [T 36, 159–61, 162]).[38] On the surface it appears as if Kafka is siding with the Zionist critique, criticizing Brod for blurring the Jewish element and giving him advice as to how it could be brought out more effectively. However, a closer look reveals that Kafka not only recreates the contemporary Zionist discourse but parodies it at the same time. In the end, the butt of the joke is not so much Max Brod's novel as the discourse of the Zionists who criticized Brod. The following analysis is based mainly on the second version, Kafka's longest review (DI 54–55 [T 159–61]).

First of all, Kafka scolds Brod—in a slightly humorous and ironic manner—for not presenting a solution to the Jewish question, which one has come to expect considering the recent trend in "contemporary Western European stories about Jews" (DI 59 [T 36]). Therefore, "offhand" (DI 55 [T 160]), the Zionists jump to conclusions. In both review versions Kafka uses the phrase "kurz entschlossen" (DI 55, 60 [T 36, 160]), which is rendered as "offhand" in English but really implies jumping to conclusions and thus ridicules the reviewer's impatient response and his lack of thought. In the first version, the formulation was more hesitant: "therefore it is possible that offhand the reader will recognize in this a fault of the *Jüdinnen*" (DI 60 [T 36]). Beginning the sentence with "kurz entschlossen" in the second version (T 160) emphasizes more strongly the hasty judgment or condemnation practiced in Zionist circles: "Offhand, we recognize this as a fault" (DI 55).

Not only does Kafka in this second version place greater emphasis on the hasty Zionist condemnation, he also tones down the "Jewishness" of these stories by replacing "zeitgenössische Judenerzählungen" (contemporary Jewish stories) with the more qualified statement: "In Western European stories, as soon as they want to include only a few groups of Jews" (DI 54 [T 159–60, 162]). The author of this review, unlike the Zionists, is not prone to hasty judgments. The judgmental tone is more than evident in Herrmann's play with the word *Urteil,* judgment, which, incidentally, occurs sixteen times in the word combinations *verurteilen, Urteil, urteilen* (judgment, to judge, to condemn).[39] Kafka's reformulation of the original syntax reveals his rhetorical intention, which is to parody Hugo Herrmann's dogmatic stance.

Kafka now tackles the reasons for the novel's flawed construction. The main flaw (of which the above-mentioned defect is a result) is that the gentile characters are missing, "who in other stories draw out the Jewishness" (DI 55 [T 160]). But this Zionist position is parodied immediately and twice. For one, the very next sentence is ironic: "That is just what we demand, no other principle for the organization of this Jewish material seems justified to us" (DI 55 [T 160]). The use of "we" indicates that Kafka is mimicking the dogmatic Zionist viewpoint.

Thus, Kafka makes fun of the claim that the novel is not particularly Jewish without the presence of gentiles through the following anecdote: "In the same way, too, the convulsive starting up of a lizard under our feet on a footpath in Italy delights us greatly, again and again we are moved to bow down, but if we see them at a dealer's by hundreds crawling over one another in confusion in the large bottles in which otherwise pickles are usually packed, then we don't know what to do" (DI 55 [T 161]). Kafka's unflattering analogy, which likens the Jews to lizards, is also a response to the reviewer's criticism that there was no ethnic specificity, not even one Jewish hero the reader could identify with, and that for this reason the Jews in Brod's novel are all equally nondescript. By lumping them all together, Kafka is parodying the reviewer's objection that we really do not know who or what we are dealing with unless there is a definite ethnic identity attached to individuals. Moreover, by countering Herrmann's eagerness to "type" with a metaphor from anti-Semitic discourse (the Jew as reptile or lizard was a common anti-Semitic stereotype [Gilman, *Patient*, 17]), Kafka adapts anti-Semitic rhetoric "for Jewish ends" (*Patient*, 106) in order to give a scathing critique of the reviewer's dogmatic position.[40]

Kafka further pursues the Zionist argument that the novel would be much more convincing if "ethnic difference" applied not to the Jews as a people but rather to individual Jews with whom the reader can identify. Thus Brod's two flaws (no solution to the Jewish question and no gentile characters) really come together in a third one, in that there is no individual leading character in Brod's novel who presents dramatic action, "who . . . attracts the best to himself and leads it nicely along a radius to the borders of the Jewish circle. It is just this that we will not accept, that the story can do without this youth, here we sense a fault rather than see it" (DI 55 [T 161]). This unsophisticated narrative device of employing a Jewish hero that the reader can identify with would presumably satisfy contemporary Zionist taste. Kafka's final remark—that though this error cannot be "seen," it can be "sensed" or "intuited"—places his entire commentary into an ironic light.

In his review, then, Kafka mocks the rules a contemporary Jewish story must conform to: Zionist taste "demands" first of all a gentile environment for contrast since otherwise the Jewish element cannot be seen. Beyond that one needs a strong Jewish character who can lead the reader to the very limit of the Jewish circle, where it clashes with the gentile world. This would point out "difference" most effectively. The ensuing awareness of difference would lead to an assertion of ethnic identity and thereby bring about the solution to the Jewish question that is missing in Brod. In short, Brod's novel is too universalist and individualistic to be acceptable in the Zionist climate. Brod himself countered the reviewer's attack (S 26 May 1911:1–2) by referring to Homer, Shakespeare, and Flaubert, none of whom created unambiguous one-dimensional characters, monological in the extreme.

Kafka and Brod both shared an initial dislike of the contemporary Zionist scene in Prague. Brod recalls that "in the beginning [he] used to go to the tiny, not very inviting Café Savoy on Ziegen square, where they gave the generally despised melodrama as a direct protest against Zionist academics" (FK 112). Kafka accompanied him several times (FK 110). Nonetheless, Brod's opposition to the Zionists was of short duration. The fact that the Zionists would not leave him alone with their criticism must have been a shock: in 1913 he still argued back (with Zionist hindsight or because he felt compelled to do so) that they had misunderstood his novel *Die Jüdinnen,* that he had all along intended "a vehement satire against the type of the 'educated' average Jewish woman" and that the problem of "mixed marriages" had been foremost on his mind (S 25–30 June 1913:4).

Brod never turned back and became a strong Zionist. Kafka, however, remained critical not only of the doctrinaire ideological stance of many of the Prague Zionists but also of the emotional effusiveness of a Martin Buber. Yet from now on a change in Kafka's attitude toward Judaism can be observed which took the form of an ever-increasing interest in Jewish culture. The catalyst for this change was the Yiddish theater group that Kafka became involved with in September 1911, a few months after he wrote the above review. It was because of his interest in Eastern European Judaism that Kafka eventually, if reluctantly, came to participate in Zionist activities as well.

2

The Yiddish Theater

(1910–1913)

Actors and Plays

"Authentic" Judaism and Assimilation

Kafka and Brod both enjoyed the Yiddish theater. Brod describes this experience as a "transformation," and his response sheds some light on Kafka's fascination as well: "What we saw was all false and miserable, but the truth shone through everything, the traditional, honorable, the delicate and the mighty, the boorish Shakespearean element, the New, which I cared about (and soon after Kafka as well). Initially, the miserable Café Savoy, where the greasy comedians performed their poor plays, was the opposite pole to the 'academic' Bar Kochba. . . . The theater had life, the club was dominated by theory" (SL 227). Kafka certainly attended one performance after the other and saw some of the plays several times. He loved the music, the actors' gestures, the sound of Yiddish and was enthralled by the singer Frau Klug ("I beamed when she sang, I laughed and looked at her all the time while she was on the stage, I sang the tunes with her, later the words" [DI 127 (T 217)]) and the actress Mania Tschissik (DI 127, 135 [T 228, 217]). He states that he "may have gone to 20 of their performances, and possibly not once to the German theater" (LF 26 [BF 73]).

After spending almost a month with the actors, Kafka articulated his first uneasiness with German culture:

> Yesterday it occurred to me that I did not always love my mother as she deserved and as I could, only because the German language prevented it.

The Jewish mother is no "Mutter," . . . [which] unconsciously contains, together with the Christian splendor Christian coldness also, the Jewish woman who is called "Mutter" therefore becomes not only comic but strange. Mama would be a better name if only one didn't imagine "Mutter" behind it. I believe that it is only the memories of the ghetto that still preserve the Jewish family, for the word "Vater" too is far from meaning the Jewish father. (DI 111 [T 102]; October 1911)

The coldness of the German word *Mutter* must be contrasted here with the warmer Yiddish expressions *Mame, Mamele,* or *Mamenyu*. As a lawyer, Kafka worked with "cold" legal German every day and was moved by the lively and creative colloquialisms of Yiddish. He was also jolted into an awareness of Zionist concerns through his encounter with the Yiddish actors. His critique of the German language as "foreign" was commonplace in contemporary Zionist discourse. In 1910, for instance, Hugo Herrmann admired Martin Buber for managing to pour his feelings into a "foreign language" (S 16 Dec. 1910:3). Walter Sokel rightly suggests that for Kafka, too, "the German linguistic medium is . . . a façade which has usurped the place of the original Jewish childhood self."[1]

Behind the façade, Kafka believed, there was not much Judaism to be recovered. This realization struck him during his nephew Felix's circumcision ceremony: "Today when I heard the *moule*'s assistant say the grace after meals and those present, aside from the two grandfathers, spent the time in dreams or boredom with a complete lack of understanding of the prayer, I saw Western European Judaism before me in a transition whose end is clearly unpredictable and about which those most closely affected are not concerned, but, like all people truly in transition, bear what is imposed upon them" (DI 190–91 [T 311–12]; Dec. 1911). The gap between modern reality and traditional religious practice was only too visible in Kafka's own family, where religious customs were performed mechanically but had otherwise lost their meaning. His relatives, whom he describes as "people truly in transition [who] bear what is imposed upon them," are not unlike the characters in Brod's novel *Die Jüdinnen*. Thus both Kafka and Brod shared the Zionists' concerns about assimilation, though neither of them believed in a political, Zionist solution at this time. Rather, they turned to the roots of the past, those "memories of the ghetto" that kept the Jewish family together and which were exemplified (to them) by Yiddish culture. Kafka's enthusiastic response to Brod's novel *Arnold Beer* testifies to this.

Arnold Beer: Das Schicksal eines Juden (The Fate of a Jew)[2] depicts the generational conflict between assimilated parents and their offspring. The son discovers a more "authentic" Jewish culture through his ninety-year-old grandmother, who is dying. The grandmother speaks a Silesian German mixed with so much Yiddish that the protagonist often cannot quite make out what she is saying. However, to him, she represents the old uncontaminated culture, since she is so different from his proper, acculturated mother. A prototypical Yiddish grandmother, she is not refined at all; she swears in Yiddish and says whatever happens to come to her mind without any consideration for the refined taste of her daughter. Brod's depiction of a more "authentic," nonassimilated Jewish life is very different from the idealized picture created by Martin Buber or the Yiddishist Nathan Birnbaum; in fact, Brod in his afterword expressly distances himself from the depictions of Jewish life by Buber and Birnbaum, among others (175–76). Upon reading the novel, Kafka sent Brod a card: "Your book has given me such pleasure. . . . I give you a hearty kiss."[3]

First Theater Group

The Yiddish theater is important because it represents the catalyst for Kafka's active interest in Judaism. Kafka had seen a few Yiddish plays by a Spiwakow Trupe[4] in 1910. Brod recalls that "Franz, after the first time I took him there, entered into the atmosphere completely" (FK 110) and enjoyed himself: "*Mensch muß man sein* [To Be a Human Being] was the title of an Eastern Jewish play that Kafka was especially fond of when he discovered it together with me in the small Prague 'Café Savoy.'"[5] When Kafka started keeping a diary regularly (from 1911 on), he mentions one of the actresses again, Frau Weinberg, comparing her with this year's Frau Klug (DI 86 [T 67]; K 30n.67). Both had beautiful voices: *Selbstwehr* applauded Frau Salcia Weinberg's musical talent (S 13 May 1910:4), and Frau Klug appears in Kafka's diary as the sprightly and enthusiastic twenty-six-year-old actress with her "always lively singing" (DI 184 [T 303]) who encourages the audience to sing along, including Kafka (DI 126, 127 [T 216, 217]).

Lemberg Theater Group (24 September 1911 to 21 January 1912)

The second Yiddish theater group called itself the German-Jewish Company from Lemberg (L'viv, Poland, now Ukraine). The actors were Flora (ca. 1885–?) and Süsskind Klug (1874–?), Mania (1881–1976) and Emanuel Tschissik (1867–1940?), Itzhak Löwy (1887–1942), Schamai (Sami)

Urich, Mano and R. Pipes, "with occasional performances by another husband-wife team," Zalmen (ca. 1874–1942) and Bashia Liebgold (ca. 1890–1942).[6] They had already performed all over Western Europe before they came to Prague.[7] Of the eleven or twelve plays they put on, two were musical melodramas (*Shulamith* and *Bar Kochba* by Abraham Goldfaden), and three were operettas (*Kol-Nidre* by Abraham Sharkansky, *Der Vitsekenig* by Sigmund Feinmann, as well as *Blimele, di perle fun Varshe* by Joseph Lateiner). Six other plays were dramatic comedies with ample room for musical interludes: *Der Meshumed* by Sharkansky, *Di Seydernacht* (almost an operetta itself) and *Dovids Fidele* by Lateiner, *Moyshe Kahyet* and *Reb Herzele Miyuches* by Moses Richter, and *Der vilder mensh* by Jakob Gordin (Massino, *Fuoco*, 32). Kafka saw all of these plays and also knew three more from which the actor Löwy read to him: *Got, mensh un tayvel*, *Di Shkhite*, and *Elisha ben Abuyah*, all by Jakob Gordin.[8]

The actors were in Prague from 24 September 1911 to 21 January 1912. Their performance started out in a very respectable location, the Hotel Zentral, but their time there was short.[9] A reviewer describes an evening that began with Yiddish folksongs and with the "male impersonator Frau Klug," "whose art, though she obviously amused the audience, resembled

2. Advertisement for the Yiddish Theater, *Selbstwehr*, 5 January 1912.

a not entirely tasteful cabaret style." This was followed by Abraham Sharkansky's operetta *Kol Nidre* (because of the approaching Yom Kippur holiday). Though the quality of the acting was said to be poor, the crowd was nonetheless enthusiastic (S 29 Sept. 1911:9). Kafka did not attend this performance.

The actors soon moved on to the cramped Café Savoy on Ziegenplatz (Goat Square), where all their future performances took place. The Café Savoy was a small and unattractive location (FK 112), decidedly low class. Kafka remarks that the doorman, "who used to work in a brothel and is now a pimp, shouted little Tschissik down" (DI 121 [T 208]). It was also hard for the actors to perform properly in such cramped quarters: "a narrow podium, behind it a green curtain, this was the stage.... The whole effect therefore depended almost entirely on the spoken word. This is where the actors excelled" (S 13 May 1910:4; DI 116 [T 201]). It was here, on 4 October 1911,[10] that Kafka saw his first play, *Der Meshumed* (The Apostate), by Sharkansky (DI 79–86 [T 57–68]), a satire about a converted Jew who denies his Jewish heritage. *Der Meshumed* preoccupied Kafka for days. He loved the music and was especially touched by Flora Klug's singing, which made him identify with being Jewish (DI 80–82 [T 59, 61]). He was also fascinated by the "talmudic melody of minute questions, adjurations or explanations" out of which he developed the imaginative metaphor of a screw twisting and turning, proud and yet humble, moving toward those who are questioned, "a great screw, proud in its entirety, humble in its turns" (DI 81 [T 60]). Kafka takes pride in his Jewishness, and we can see that he identifies with the play's "contempt ... for the Christian" (DI 85 [T 65]) when all of a sudden the one "important" Christian in the audience, a "representative of the government," appears to be no more than "a wretched person, afflicted with a facial tic" (DI 81 [T 59]). Yet, despite his enthusiastic response to the play, Kafka was critical about the quality of the performance: "Would like to see a large Yiddish theater as the production may after all suffer because of the small cast and inadequate rehearsal" (DI 87 [T 68]).

A few days later, Kafka went to see *Die Seydernacht* by Joseph Lateiner (DI 91 [T 74]).[11] The plot centers around a love story and includes a ritual murder threat around Passover, when a bottle of blood is hidden in the altar of the synagogue and discovered by the Jews just in time. Kafka found the action very gripping (DI 91 [T 74]) and again loved the music (DI 217 [T 352]).[12] These two plays were not very demanding intellectually; however, they represented a more assertive phase in Yiddish theater

The Yiddish Theater (1910–1913)   39

in which "conflicts between Jews and non-Jews were thematized in such a way that the hierarchy of values typical of a theater tradition formed by the Shylock cliché was decidedly turned upside down: now the villain is a Christian (as in Lateiner's *Seydernacht,* which picks up on the ritual murder lie) or a converted Jew, denying his heritage like the protagonist in Sharkansky's *Meschumed*" (Sprengel 13).

A postcard to Max Brod dated 12 October shows Kafka's eagerness to see the next play, this time by Abraham Goldfaden, the founder of the Yiddish theater: "Dear Max, we are ever so lucky. *Shulamith* by Goldfaden will be performed!" (BKB 96). In a more sophisticated fashion than Sharkansky or Lateiner, Goldfaden applied "the form of the opéra-comique to subjects taken from Jewish legend and history" (Sprengel 13). After seeing the performance the next day (DI 95–97 [T 79–83]), with Frau Tschissik in the title role, Kafka remarks that the play is really an "opera" and criticizes the fact that every sung play is called an "operetta" (DI 95 [T 79]). One of the songs in *Shulamith* is the famous Yiddish lullaby "Roshinkes mit Mandlen" (Raisins and Almonds). Kafka gives a detailed plot summary in his diary. But the evening was spoiled when, at the end of the performance, Kafka's later friend, the actor Itzhak Löwy (1887–1942), was beaten up by another actor right on the stage and subjected to further humiliation by the "headwaiter, R.," who tossed him out (DI 97 [T 81–83]). The scene was highly embarrassing and left the organizers disconcerted, because more plays had already been planned around upcoming events. In fact, the actors were warned that their performances would be canceled if they did not behave properly.

Kafka eagerly attended these plays and soon made the actors' personal acquaintance. He became especially fond of Löwy and saw him almost on a daily basis. Löwy was a vibrant character, filled with energy, "a man of continuous enthusiasm, known in Eastern Europe as a 'hot Jew'" (LF 29 [BF 77]). Some critics have speculated that there might have been a homoerotic interest on Kafka's part. If there was, it could not have lasted too long. For when Kafka invited him to the Czech National Theater on 16 October (DI 104–5 [T 93–94]), Löwy confided in Kafka that he had contracted syphilis, and Kafka also feared that Löwy might have lice (T 93).[13] But he continued his friendship with Löwy despite the dreaded lice and venereal disease. Löwy also gave solo performances, one of which Kafka attended the very next day (17 October). This recital was possibly part of the weekly readings in the Jewish Toynbee Hall, where charity performances took place (DI 101–2 [T 87, 88–89]; K 34n.88). The audience consisted largely of poor people; entry was free, and tea and cake were distributed (K 149n.610). Löwy recited stories by Sholom Aleichem, I. L. Peretz, and Morris Rosenfeld, and Chaim Nachman Bialik's famous poem "In Shkhite-Stot" (In the City of Slaughter) was read, about the 1903 Kishinev pogrom in Russia. Kafka mentions the pogrom in connection with "Schhite-Stot" (DI 102 [T 89]).

On 21 October Kafka went to see *Kol-Nidre* by Sharkansky, his fourth play (DI 107 [T 96]). He was not very impressed; though, as before, he did enjoy the humor. A note of higher quality supposedly existed in the works of Jakob Gordin, whose play *Der vilder mensh* (The Wild Man) Kafka saw on 24 October. Though Kafka criticizes that "the wild man delivers speeches humanly unintelligible but dramatically so clumsy that one would prefer to close one's eyes" (DI 112 [T 195–96]), Gordin was considered a major playwright in Kafka's time. He was also a favorite of Löwy's, who read to Kafka from his *Got, mensh un tayvel* (God, Human, and the Devil)—the Yiddish *Faust*—all afternoon the next day (DI 111 [T 195]). Gordin also wrote the Yiddish *King Lear*. A day later, in the Kaffee City coffeehouse, Löwy read from Gordin again, this time from *Elisha ben Abuyah* (DI 121 [T 208]).[14]

Both Abraham Goldfaden (1840–1908) and Jakob Gordin (1853–1909) were regarded as luminaries of the Yiddish theater, and memories of them were still vivid because the artists had only recently passed away. When Gordin died, *Selbstwehr* ran a long article on his life and work, praising him together with Goldfaden (S 2 July 1909:1). The younger generation considered Gordin's plays among the best that had been produced since Goldfaden, who to their taste was a little too sentimental. No mystic and no romantic, Gordin was "strong in the depiction of everyday life, he rises to the occasion when he paints common faces with his cool, rationalistic pen" (S 2 July 1909:3). Kafka heard a similar appraisal from the Yiddish actors (DI 112 [T 195]).[15] The first four plays that Kafka attended thus gave him an overview of the history of the Yiddish theater: "On top of the melodramatic stage production of legends (Goldfaden) and the clichéd purpose-plays (Lateiner), we now see a social-critical engagement with inner-Jewish problems [i.e., especially in Gordin]" (Sprengel 22).

Increasingly, though, it did not matter what Yiddish plays the actors put on: the quality of the acting deteriorated (DI 117 [T 202]). They planned a short break from 30 October to 15 November (K 59). But the Klugs were the only ones to leave because they wanted to be reunited with their three children. The other actors had not been able to make up their minds and decided on the spur of the moment to stay on longer (DI 130 [T 221]) and stage yet a few more performances of Goldfaden's operetta *Bar Kochba* (on 3, 4, 5 November). Kafka and Brod, as well as the Zionists around Hugo Bergmann, saw the play on 4 November (DI 134–37 [T 227–31]). But the performance turned out to be a disappointment all round.

Everyone seemed to have come with different expectations, none of which was fulfilled (DI 134–35 [T 227–29]). Brod's laudatory article in the *Prager Tagblatt* praised the quality of the acting and compared the performances with Greek theater, "where religious ceremonies appear on the stage with the same naiveté as here."[16] For the members of the Bar-Kochba,[17] the play did not reflect favorably on their club because the hero, Bar Kochba, kills his bride Dina's innocent father, Rabbi Eliazar, and soon after kills himself out of shame (Sprengel 123, 268). Interestingly enough, this performance was not mentioned in *Selbstwehr,* which usually announced and reviewed every significant Jewish event. However, as with the earlier plays, Kafka enjoyed the humor and found himself still laughing the day after when he thought back to some of the comical scenes (DI 136 [T 230]).

The theater group finally left on 6 November 1911 (DI 137 [T 231]), but after much quarrelling and confusion. Löwy slept in until four o'clock in the afternoon and made them miss their train. Then they still had not decided whether to go to Brünn or Nürnberg. During their quarrel Kafka suggested a stopover (DI 138, 141–42 [T 231–33, 237–38]) and Teblitz was mentioned, which sounded promising, for Kafka had a relative there who could help them. Not only did Teplitz have a large Jewish community, but "around 1907 a considerable numbers [sic] of Eastern Jews settled there." They still could not agree, so they drew lots. It was only when Teplitz came up three times that they finally made up their minds, and Kafka quickly wrote a letter of introduction to his relative, Dr. Josef Polacek (1874–1943), a step-son of his uncle Filip Polacek, who lived in Teplitz (DI 142 [T 238]). Of all his uncle's children, Josef was the only one "who remained a practicing Jew all his life," and Kafka "was obviously well aware of his relative's readiness to aid Jews. A member of the Teplitz Lodge of B'nai Brith and later a member of the executive of the Jewish Community Council as well as director of the Jewish hospital, Dr. Polacek was in a good position to make the actors' stay in Teplitz agreeable" (Northey, *Relatives,* 75–76).

After their short break, the Yiddish theater group returned to Prague on 16 November and resumed their performances. Kafka continued his friendship with the actors and again remained particularly close to Löwy. He wrote in his diary that on 24 November Löwy read to him from *Di Shkhite* ("one who is learning the slaughterer's art") by Gordin, and Kafka recorded Talmudic sayings from this play (DI 161–62 [T 265]). At the end of November there are further citations from the Talmud, which he heard from Löwy, as well as many anecdotes, and Kafka wrote down Löwy's autobiography in early December 1912 (DI 217–20 [T 352–56]), which left him under no illusions about Jewish life in Eastern Europe: "The night in the Yeshivah was unbearable.... the stench and the heat would not leave the rooms.... Everything was full of fleas" (DI 220 [T 356]; translation modified).

Kafka saw a few more plays, such as *Der Schneider als Gemeinderat* (Moishe Khayit als Gemaynderat; The Tailor as City Counseller) by Moses Richter on 11 December 1911. This time the Tschissiks had left because of another quarrel with the rest of the troupe and were replaced by the Liebgolds (DI 183–84 [T 301–2]). Kafka disliked the new actors (especially the replacement for Frau Tschissik) and, consequently, the whole play (DI 176 [T 290–91]). On 19 December the Tschissiks were back, and Kafka saw them in *Dawids Geige* (David's Violin) by Lateiner (DI 183–84 [T 301–2]). Furthermore, on 25 December he saw Lateiner's *Blümale oder die Perle von Warschau* (Blümale, or The Pearl of Warsaw [DI 198; T 319–20]) with Frau Tschissik in the leading role (K 83 no. 319).

The return of Frau Tschissik brought with it a flood of creativity. On 25, 26, and 27 December, Kafka wrote his famous essay on "minor literature" ("Literatur der kleinen Nationen" [Literature of Small Nations]), in which he examines the political nature of small literatures based on what he knew from Löwy about the present Jewish literature in Warsaw (DI 191–95 [T 312–15, 321–22, 326]). The expression "small nations" was a common contemporary political slogan, referring to the poorer and smaller countries of the Austro Hungarian Empire, especially Galicia. In 1909 a member of Parliament wrote that the government should be a "protector of small nations" (Hort der kleinen Nationen) (S 25 June 1909:1). The expression was also adopted by the Zionists. A headline on the front page of *Selbstwehr* ran "The Small Nations," a slogan that was described as "the catchword of the day" (S 19 Oct. 1917:1). The article discussed similarities between Jewish nationalism and that of other smaller nations.

Just as Kafka praised the "minor" literature of the Eastern European Jews, there were Jews, also Zionists, who praised the "minor" Czech performances. Hugo Herrmann, for instance, wrote about Lothar Suchý's

David in "glowing terms and added that it was a stark contrast to the sterile, mediocre offerings at the German theater" (CJ 113). Perhaps Kafka, too, took Löwy to the Czech National Theater (DI 104 [T 93]) as a way of showing that smaller nations could also have a national theater. In any event, the contact with the Yiddish actors made Kafka increasingly aware of the burning questions of his day: minority issues and the importance of having a cultural identity. In December 1911 he came to take an interest in his own background, as evidenced by his "Jewish autobiography" (DI 197–98 [T 318–19]), and his critical comments about his nephew Felix's circumcision appear in a different light when we consider that they were provoked by the presence of Löwy, who had accompanied Kafka to the ceremony.[18] The comparison with the circumcision rituals in Russia must have come from Löwy (DI 195–96 [T 316–17]).

In 1912 Kafka's interest in the Yiddish plays decreased markedly. On 5 January his friend Felix Weltsch accompanied him to the "big charity concert by the popular soubrette Mrs. Flora Klug" (DI 215 [T 348; K 87n.348]) and the play *Vicekönig* (Viceroy) by Sigmund Feinmann. Kafka remarked: "My receptivity to the Jewishness in these plays deserts me because they are too monotonous and degenerate into a wailing. . . . The people remain, of course, and I hold fast to them" (DI 215 [T 349]). Things were not going well for the actors (DI 217 [T 352]) when Frau Tschissik invited him to attend one more performance of *Seydernacht*. Their time in Prague was running out, but in these last weeks (they left 21 January 1912), Kafka was still quite preoccupied with them: "finally I spent a lot of time with the Jewish actors, wrote letters for them, prevailed on the Zionist society to inquire of the Zionist societies of Bohemia whether they would like to have guest appearances of the troupe; I wrote the circular that was required and had it reproduced; saw *Shulamith* once more and Richter's *Herzele Mejiches* for the first time, was at the folksong evening of the Bar Kokhba Society" (DI 223 [T 360]). The phrase "prevailed on the Zionist society to inquire" is quite telling. Considering the Zionists' negative response to the actors, there would have been no "circular" had it not been for Kafka's initiative, and it was printed in *Selbstwehr* ("Jewish Theater," S 26 Jan. 1912:6). Moreover on 18 January Kafka attended the "Evening of Jewish Folk Songs" (DI 223–24 [T 360–61]) in the Hotel Zentral at which the Yiddishist Nathan Birnbaum (1864–1937) spoke. Yiddish folk songs were sung this evening by the famous Berlin cantor Leo Gollanin, and well-known actress Margarethe Neff read Yiddish stories in German translation (K 91n.360). The Yiddish actors used this opportunity to put on a final performance of Moses Richter's *Reb Herzele Mejiches* the next day in honor of Nathan Birnbaum (K 91). This was the last play Kafka saw, because thereafter the actors left Prague.

KAFKA AND LÖWY

"An Introductory Talk on the Yiddish Language"

Although the Yiddish actors were gone, Kafka remained in contact with Löwy, who had not left with the rest of the group and performed on his own in the area around Prague. At the beginning of February, Kafka wrote him a letter of recommendation for an evening of recitals in another town, Trautenau (DI 228 [T 368]).[19] Kafka, however, increasingly felt "coolness toward Löwy" (DI 228 [T 369]); perhaps he wished Löwy had left with the others. Nonetheless, Kafka put much effort and energy into arranging a guest performance for him through the Bar Kochba (DI 232–35 [T 376–79; KH 393]),[20] at which time Kafka made his famous speech on the Yiddish language. Originally Oskar Baum had agreed to present the introductory lecture, but he suddenly withdrew and could not be persuaded by Kafka to reconsider (DI 232, 233 [T 374–75, 377]). Five days before the event, Kafka knew he had to give the speech himself. There was not much time to advertise the Yiddish evening, and he even went to a lecture by Rabbi Dr. Chanoch Heinrich Ehrentreu on "Jeremiah and His Time" to publicize the Löwy performance afterwards (DI 234 [T 377]; K 104).

The Yiddish evening took place on 18 February 1912. *Selbstwehr* announced that "Poetry by Rosenfeld, Frischmann, Reisen, Nomberg, Dranow, Bialik, Frug, Scholem Aleichem, hasidic songs" would be on the agenda (S 16 Feb. 1912:4). Kafka's "Introductory Talk on the Yiddish Language" (DF 381–86 [BK 149–53]) was clearly written for an "enlightened" audience, so much so that Régine Robin believes it not only shows Kafka's own "enlightened" attitude toward Yiddish—"Kafka maintains notions typical of the Haskalah"—but also that Kafka was never able to overcome these views (52). However, Kafka was painfully aware of the "enlightened" attitude of his audience and of the stigma that was attached to Yiddish in most circles. He did not have to look far: Hermann Kafka made it very clear that he considered Löwy a "useless relationship" and said about him, "'Whoever lies down with dogs gets up with fleas [*sic:* bedbugs]'" (DI 125, 131 [T 214, 223]).

A good example of the German Jews' uneasiness with Yiddish is the audience's response to the sweatshop poet Morris Rosenfeld (1862–1923) in 1908. After Rosenfeld's enthusiastic reception in Karlsbad, *Selbstwehr* was confident that "many a prejudice about Jewish language and culture would certainly have been destroyed" (S 7 Aug. 1908:5). A more typical reaction, though, presented itself in Prague a month later. Here Rosenfeld was introduced by Friedrich Adler, an enlightened Germanophile, who spoke "about the heroism of the Jews who had steadfastly held onto German culture and preserved their German language in a dialect which was called jargon or Yiddish. The Jews of Prague . . . as Germans were introduced by a German to the poetry of the 'German dialect poet' Morris Rosenfeld!" (S 25 Sept. 1908:2). Even with someone as popular as Rosenfeld, most Prague Jews could not overcome their prejudice about Eastern European culture. Kafka was therefore not very optimistic: "Although the regular guests and employees of the coffeehouse are fond of the actors, they cannot remain respectful amid the depressing impressions, and despise the actors as starvelings, tramps, fellow Jews, exactly as in the past" (DI 120–21 [T 207–8]). Kafka's skill in composing the introductory lecture on the Yiddish language lay in finding precisely the right tone for an "enlightened" audience.

Kafka's "Introductory Talk" is cleverly constructed. From the beginning he makes clear that he is not afraid of this evening's success. He will not even mention those "who take an arrogant attitude to Yiddish," yet at the same time he intends to clear the air immediately, knowing that no successful evening will be possible "so long as many of you are so frightened of Yiddish that one can almost see it in your faces" (DF 382 [BK 149]). Baioni regards the tone of Kafka's speech here as "hostile, ironic, aggressive and provocative" (*Letteratura,* 53). But why did he need to be aggressive with an audience that had, after all, chosen to come—unlike Kafka's own parents, who were not present (DI 235 [T 379]). And Kafka even admits that the audience's "fear" of jargon was very understandable. *Selbstwehr* reported after the event that Dr. Kafka's speech was "elegant and charming" (S 23 Feb. 1912: 3). If anything, his rhetoric of persuasion would have encouraged even opponents to give Yiddish a chance because no one would readily admit "fear" of jargon. Sharing with the audience the problematic at hand was an attempt to build a bridge for those who felt a little awkward but would not admit it. The very first sentence revealed this as well, when he reassured his audience that they would discover "how much more Yiddish [they] understand than [they] think" (DF 381 [BK 149]), which suggests that he intended to unmask "the Jewishness of the spectator masked behind assimilated cultivation" (Spector 88).

Kafka then presented a brief history of the Yiddish language (known to him through his reading of M. I. Pinès's Yiddish literary history, *L'Histoire de la littérature judéo-allemande* (DI 223 [T 360]), and proceeded with a German summary of the Yiddish poems that Löwy was to recite in the original immediately thereafter: "Die Grine" (The Greenhorn) by Morris Rosenfeld (1862–1923), "Sand und Sterne" (Sand and Stars) by Simon Samuel Frug (1860–1916), and "Die Nacht ist still" (The Night Is Silent) by David Frischmann (1859–1922) (BK 151). All three were well-known contemporary writers. In a long chapter on the socialist poet Rosenfield, Pinès described him as "the Heine of the ghetto" and "the one whose name is best known by the educated public outside of the ghetto" (*Histoire,* 268, 329–30). He also devoted a whole chapter to Frug, whose poem "Sand und Sterne" Kafka described as "a bitter commentary on a promise in the Bible that we shall be as the sand which is upon the seashore and as the stars of the heaven. Well, we are trodden down like the sand. When will it come true that we are as the stars?" (DF 384 [BK 151]) Frug was influenced by the poets Heine and Börne, and the poem's subject matter shows Frug's socialist Zionist orientation. As for David Frischmann, Pinès described him as "a talented poet and literary critic, whose work was dedicated foremost to Hebrew literature but who also wrote excellent pieces in Yiddish" (389). Frischmann traveled to Palestine in 1911 and 1912, and many of his stories and impressions of these travels were printed in *Selbstwehr* and other Zionist publications.

Kafka quickly dismissed the German summaries and translations, which was in keeping with his criticism of the German language as "cold," with its "Christian coldness" (DI 111 [T 102]): "Now you see, such explanations are quite useless" (DF 384 [BK 151]). In a clever tactical move, he stressed that every native speaker of German is in a most fortunate position, since the two languages are so closely related: "Fortunately, however, everyone who speaks the German language is also capable of understanding Yiddish. For . . . the superficial comprehensibility of Yiddish is a product of the German language; this is an advantage it has over all the other languages in the world" (DF 384 [BK 152]). Here Kafka undermined the commonly held view of the superiority of the German language, which was generally used to denigrate Yiddish, and turned it upside down in order to "upgrade" Yiddish. Switching the original German-Yiddish linguistic power relationship around, Kafka asserted the autonomy of Yiddish; the very closeness of the two languages means that Yiddish dies when it is translated into German: "The links between Yiddish and German are too delicate and significant not to be torn to shreds the instant Yiddish is transformed back into German, that is to say, it is no longer Yiddish that is transformed, but something that has utterly lost its essential character. If it is translated into French, for instance, Yiddish can be conveyed to the French, but if it is translated into German it is destroyed. *Toit,* for instance, is not the same thing as *tot* (dead), and *blüt* is far from being *[B]lut* (blood)" (DF 384–85 [BK 152]).

Despite his provocative conclusion, Kafka did allow the audience to come a step closer. Even if modern German seems far removed from Yiddish, he continued, the latter still surfaces in the language of trade with German Jews, where "many nuances remain to this day" (DF 385 [BK 152]), and especially in "thieves' cant [*Gaunersprache*]" (DF 382 [BK 150]), which likes to borrow from it.[21] Ultimately, the aim of Kafka's rhetoric was to open up the audience to an intuitive understanding of the Yiddish language. He believed that there still were, in every one of them, emotional bonds, "forces," that enabled them "to understand Yiddish intuitively" (DF 385 [BK 152]). At the end of his speech he conjured up a climactic vision of self-regeneration through Yiddish and ended on a humorous note:

> But once Yiddish has taken hold of you and moved you—and Yiddish is everything, the words, the Chasidic melody, and the essential character of this East European Jewish actor himself—you will have forgotten your former reserve. Then you will come to feel the true unity of Yiddish, and so strongly that it will frighten you, yet it will no longer be fear of Yiddish but of yourselves. You would not be capable of bearing this fear on its own, but Yiddish instantly gives you, besides, a self-confidence that can stand up to this fear and is even stronger than it is. Enjoy this self-confidence as much as you can! But then, when it fades out, tomorrow and later—for how could it last, fed only on the memory of a single evening's recitations!—then my wish for you is that you may also have forgotten the fear. For we did not set out to punish you. (DF 385–86 [BK 153])

Kafka's introduction was psychologically tailored to his "enlightened" audience and tactically astute. The reviewer in *Selbstwehr* later stated: "The audience, at first a little taken aback by the unfamiliar language, finally got in the right mood . . . and awarded Mr. Löwy with plenty of applause" (S 23 Feb. 1912: 3). The whole evening was a success, and Löwy had a little more money in his pockets.

Löwy: Last Contacts

Löwy left Prague at the end of February 1912 and for a while performed again with the old troupe in Berlin. Kafka had a lively correspondence with Löwy, who sent him pictures, posters, and newspaper reviews of their performances. Later that year, Kafka's interests shifted to his future fiancée, Felice Bauer, whom he met at Max Brod's home (DI 268–69 [T 431–32]; 13 Aug. 1912), where they also talked about the Yiddish actors (LF 25 [BF 72]). The Yiddish theater and the ensuing correspondence with Felice (20 Sept. 1912) together mark the beginning of Kafka's literary creativity: on the night of 22–23 September, he wrote "The Judgment" (DI 275–76 [T 460]), and in that period he began the *Amerika* novel (*The Man Who Disappeared*) and composed *The Metamorphosis* (September–December 1912). But the Yiddish theater was never far from his mind. On 3 November Kafka informed Felice that Löwy was presently in Berlin giving performances, encouraged her to see him (LF 26 [BF 72–73]), and mentioned one of their funny posters to her where Tschissik was described as a "primadonna" and Löwy even called himself "a dramatist" (LF 25–26 [BF 72]).[22] In February 1913 Kafka asked Felice to send him a review of the Löwy troupe's performance in Leipzig written by the expressionist writer and journalist Kurt Pinthus (1886–1975) (LF 179 [BF 281]).[23] In his article of 17 January 1913, Pinthus states that Löwy's group has been playing "back and forth in Berlin and Leipzig for the last few weeks" (Sprengel 305). They performed the same plays that Kafka saw, *Bar Kochba*, *Shulamith,* and *Seydernacht:* "The mighty hero and liberator Bar Kochba takes leave of his love in a renaissance room, with a half touching, half comical aria. A Persian army of three men is stomping over the stage to Jerusalem, singing a marching song. Oppressed pious Jews are sitting at the Passover meal and are accused of ritual murder." Löwy also gave a performance of Gordin's *Got, mensh un tayvel* (Sprengel 306), the Jewish *Faust*, from which he had read to Kafka in October 1911.

In March 1913 Löwy abandoned the old troupe, but he was still leading the same lifestyle. When Kafka saw him in Leipzig in March 1913,[24] he recounts that Löwy had formed a new company with whom "he was perpetually traveling back and forth . . . between Leipzig and Berlin, getting hardly any sleep" (LF 239 [BF 360]; see Massino, *Fuoco,* 58). It was a financial disaster for Löwy, and in April 1913 he returned to Prague sick and destitute and had to be hospitalized: "and thus he was left, ill, entirely without funds, heavily in debt, and without any prospects after such complete failure.... Perhaps he will now follow my advice and go to Palestine" (LF 239 [BF 360]). Kafka arranged yet one more evening for Löwy through the Bar Kochba organization (LF 264 [BF 392]).[25]

Löwy's recital took place in the Hotel Bristol on 2 June 1913. As Kafka told Felice, it was no success, "but at least Löwy has a little money now" (LF 267 [BF 396]). Löwy left Prague again, and in his letters from now on he repeatedly accused Kafka of not having supported him enough. In 1916 Kafka remarked that Löwy "is now having great success in Budapest, and is making wild (and by no means justified) accusations against me, saying I hadn't done enough for him here, had merely trifled with him" (LF 539 [BF 748]). Some of the actors from the old troupe (Klugs, Emanuel Tschissik) returned to Prague in 1916 with a new theater group to perform at the Jewish-Polish Orfeum, but Löwy was not among them. They likely came to entertain the Jewish refugees from the East who had come to Prague during WWI.[26] Kafka met Löwy for the last time in 1917 in Budapest, where he traveled with Felice Bauer to visit Felice's sister. After this visit he told Max Brod that Löwy had to remain in a sanatorium for three months (LFF 148 [Br 173; KH 490]). Kafka approached Martin Buber on Löwy's behalf, and Löwy sent Kafka an essay on the Yiddish theater for Buber's *Der Jude* (BB 137–42), which Kafka was willing to edit for him (LFF 148 [Br 173], H 113–17). Buber did show interest and asked to see the piece, but Kafka forewarned him that Löwy might never deliver.[27] There is no indication that any of them followed up on this project (KH 490).

Ritchie Robertson argues that "Löwy kept his admiration for Kafka all his life, if we can trust the evidence of the story 'A Friend of Kafka' by Isaac Bashevis Singer" (*Judaism*, 27–28). But an article on Brod and Kafka written by Löwy in 1934 suggests that Löwy was too busy surviving to remain grateful to Kafka. The occasion seems to have been Max Brod's fiftieth birthday, and since Kafka was long dead, Löwy gave all the praise to the more famous Brod instead: "Max Brod was the first to encourage me to appear in public with excerpts, songs, and scenes from Yiddish literature. Max Brod opened the 'evening,' to which the elite of Prague came" (Evelyn Beck 222). Löwy never mentions Kafka. He had a hard life, was in increasingly poor health,[28] and desperate: changing a few facts did not matter much if he could present himself in a better light through his association with Brod. In Singer's story "A Friend of Kafka,"[29] Löwy, in the early 1930s, is an older man and living on the edge, boasting of glorious times and connections with important personalities of his day. He has turned to writing newspaper articles[30] lately since he is no longer wanted as an actor, "but the editors were unanimous in rejecting his manuscripts" (277). In the story he lives in an unheated attic, cannot pay the rent, and has no money for food. He has turned into a *shnorrer*, borrowing money from everyone around him, but one who still "had the air of an important European celebrity" (277).

Life for Löwy and the actors became far more cruel: except for Frau Tschissik, they all seem to have perished in the Holocaust. The last we hear of Löwy is that he was deported to Treblinka in 1942; the Liebgolds died there as well, and the fate of the others remains unknown (Massino, *Fuoco*, 73–74).

Readings: Grätz, Fromer, and Pinès

Just before the actors left for their first break in early November 1911, Kafka began reading "den 'kleinen Grätz'" (the little Grätz) , or the *Popular History of the Jews*.[31] According to Max Brod, it was Löwy who introduced Kafka to his first scholarly books on Jewish history and Yiddish literature.[32] Kafka could have also come across them in his reading of *Selbstwehr,* where these books were advertised. The reviewer acknowledged that Graetz today was "dated and superceded in part" but concluded that "the smaller edition for the general public of 'Grätz' in three volumes is becoming increasingly popular, and the time will come when it will be shameful for a Jewish home to at the very least not own the 'little Grätz.'"[33] In his comments on the book (1 November 1911), Kafka was deeply touched by "the imperfection of the first settlements in the newly conquered Canaan and the faithful handing down of the imperfections of the popular heroes (Joshua, the Judges, Elijah)" (DI 125 [T 215]).

Also, before the actors' final departure (ca. January 21), Kafka was so busy with readings that between 6 and 24 January 1912 he had no time for diary entries: "For the following reasons have not written for so long: . . . read, and indeed greedily, Pinès's *L'Histoire de la littérature judéo-allemande,* 500 pages, with such thoroughness, haste and joy as I have never yet shown in the case of similar books; now I am reading Fromer, *Organismus des Judentums;* finally I spent a lot of time with the Jewish actors" (DI 223 [T 360]). Jakob Fromer's "Organismus des Judentums" (The Organism of Judaism) includes much historical information as well as descriptions of the lives and works of famous rabbis. It outlines the development of Talmudic literature and rabbinic interpretation and gives an overview of the life and work of key Talmudic interpreters from Hillel, Akiba, and Maimonides to Joseph Karo, who compiled the *Schulkhan Aruch,* the standard legal code of Judaism. He analyzes the content of the Mishnah, the nature of the Talmud, and the various forms of rabbinic interpretation in addition to providing many excerpts from the Talmud, complete with Rashi commentary and free translation. Fromer's work is scholarly and serious, and later on Kafka also read his edition of *Salomon Maimons Lebensgeschichte* (Salomon Maimon's Life History), in which Fromer, among other things, also explains rabbinic terminology and practice (LFF 173 [Br 203]).[34]

The third book Kafka read, Meyer Isser Pinès's *L'Histoire de la littérature judéo-allemande* (The History of German-Jewish Literature) is of considerable importance for an understanding of Kafka's knowledge of Jewish culture, especially since Kafka's notes, excerpts, and plot summaries from Pinès were not included in the German edition of Kafka's diaries until the recent publication of the critical edition. Pinès's study, a nearly 600-page-long doctoral dissertation, is a Yiddish literary history that was meant as an introduction to Yiddish literature and culture. It was aimed at a European audience unfamiliar with Yiddish culture and without access to many of its literary productions, since these texts were written in Hebrew characters. For this reason Pinès strove to give the reader as complete an overview as possible, providing the necessary cultural background as well as numerous excerpts and summaries from representative works of major Yiddish writers: "This is why we have added numerous excerpts, which we have translated, to our analysis and interpretation of these works." And he defends himself should this be considered excessive: "If we have sinned out of excess, one should be so kind as to overlook this fault which was virtually unavoidable in an attempt at a popularization which is the first of its kind in Europe" (6).

Régine Robin is critical of the book's ideological bias and believes its main effect on Kafka was to reinforce him in his romanticization: "The reading of Pinès comforts him in his anti-Haskalah vision of Yiddish literature, it strengthens his chagallian, nostalgic, popularist and backward-looking tendencies" (50). Robertson, in turn, claims that Pinès's study is of inferior quality: "[It] was the only account of the subject available to Kafka. Unfortunately it is full of errors, and aroused outrage when translated into Yiddish in the 1920's."[35] This judgment is surprising because Pinès is very scholarly indeed. In addition, he was translated into Yiddish already in 1911 and into German in 1913. As to the "outrage" his study created, Robertson does not give any sources, but the *Encyclopaedia Judaica* mentions that some scholars regarded the work as dilettantish.[36] However, "dilettantish" does not imply that it is "full of errors" but rather that it was not for the specialist—and Pinès's study was never meant for specialists. It would be doing the work an injustice, however, to call it merely a "popularization." Even if more rigorous criteria are applied to it, Pinès's study is, at the same time, a *scholarly* literary history as well. There are sixty-three pages of bibliography, a table of contents, and an index—scholarly apparatus unusual for French critical works at that time. A more recent evaluation of Pinès's work thus rightly calls it one of the two "earliest notable academic accounts of Yiddish literature."[37]

In *L'Histoire de la littérature judéo-allemande* the development of Yiddish literature is discussed up to the year 1890. The Yiddish writers who are examined in individual chapters are Mendele, Linetski, Frug, Dick, Schomer, Peretz, Rosenfeld, Spektor, Dienesohn, and Sholom Aleichem as well as the well-known dramatists of the Yiddish theater, Goldfaden, Gordin, and Lateiner. Pinès chose the year 1890 because the writers up to then all strove to make Yiddish an acceptable literary language. Pinès did not share the low regard the Jewish Enlightenment, the Haskalah movement, had for Yiddish (27). Kafka commented on the irony that in order to reach the masses, Haskalah writers had to resort to Yiddish, as much as this went against their principles, and thereby they inadvertently created the basis for the development of Yiddish literature (DI 224 [T 363]).

In his *Histoire*, Pinès is very critical of some Haskalah literature. The works presented are predominantly didactic; the excerpts Pinès gives are tedious, and Kafka took note of this (DI 225 [T 363]). Pinès's overall argument is that in Haskalah literature it is only with Mendele that the ideas of the Jewish Enlightenment find the first literary voice of quality in Yiddish literature. After Mendele, he maintains, it is Peretz, whose work returns to folk and Hasidic sources, elevating them above the works of the Jewish Enlightenment. Pinès devoted seventy pages to Mendele alone, twenty to a discussion of his novel *Di Kliatsche* (1876) (The Mare). He summarizes, quotes, and discusses Peretz's poetry (in a separate chapter) as well as twenty of his short stories, plus his *Travel Pictures* and his articles on social questions and the status of Yiddish. Among the stories are "In the Basement Dwelling," "A Musician Dies," "Mendel Braines," "The Rabbi's Pipe," "The Mad Talmudist," "Cabalists," "Between Two Peaks," "The Golem," and "The Dead Town," while "Bontsha Schweig" sets the tone for the whole study, having been discussed at length in the introduction.

Kafka was not impressed by Peretz's "bad Heine lyrics and social poems" (DI 226 [T 365]), but he notes down some of Pinès's commentary, most importantly his explanation of the death scene in Peretz's story "Cabalists": "death by a kiss: reserved only for the most pious" (DI 226 [T 366]; *Histoire*, 463n.1). The motif of the kiss later resurfaces at the end of Kafka's "A Hunger Artist."[38] In his chapter on Sholom Aleichem (S. Rabinovitsh, 1859–1916), whom he calls "the Mark Twain of the ghetto" (*Histoire*, 411), Pinès discusses the adventures of Menahem Mendel and Tevye the Dairyman, among others.

Kafka's notes are not just informative; he also records whatever strikes him as odd or interesting, such as, "Talmud: He who interrupts his study to say, 'How beautiful is this tree,' deserves death" (DI 225 [T 364]; *Histoire*, 284), and he rewrites the content of S. Frug's poem "La fille du Schamesch" (The Daughter of the Shames [synagogue caretaker]) in a Kafkaesque fashion, stripping a good story of its melodrama. Many of Kafka's notes reveal his interest in storytelling, but what is perhaps just as interesting is his translation of "il entend la voix de son fils qui étudie la Loi et qui pouvait devenir un grand en Israël" (he heard the voice of her son studying Torah and preparing to become one of the great scholars in Israel) as "die Stimme des Sohnes, der die Tora *lernt*" (Pinès, *Histoire*, 298; DI 223–24 [T 365]; my emphasis). Kafka knew to translate *la Loi* (the Law, das Gesetz) as *Tora* and *étudie* not as *studieren* (to study) but chose the correct term for reciting or reading from the Torah: *lernen* (*lejnen* in Yiddish).

Pinès also gives an overview of the Yiddish theater from the early Purim plays to the repertories of Goldfaden and Gordin (494–508). His evaluation of the literary value of Gordin, Lateiner, and Goldfaden would have confirmed Kafka in his earlier critical judgment. Pinès says of Goldfaden that "the number of his works is fairly extensive, but they have no literary value." At the same time he stresses their enormous popularity, especially through "the melodies which accompanied them [and] made the tour of the entire ghetto" (496, 497). He does not mention Sharkansky, but Lateiner for him falls into the same category: he considers his plays no more than "melodramas without psychological depth, without truthful characters." Gordin represents a new voice in the theater, one that allows the plays to emerge from "their lowliness and platitude." And even though Gordin is no "creative spirit," since he mostly adapts plays by Shakespeare, Goethe, or Lessing for the Yiddish stage, nonetheless (despite Gordin's didactic, "enlightened" orientation) Pinès has the highest praise for his achievement (499–501). He mentions his family dramas, in particular *Di Shkhite,* and discusses in great detail *Got, mensh un tayvel* and even *Elisha ben Abuyah* (502–5), all texts Kafka was familiar with.

Both Kafka and Pinès admired the fighting spirit of many of the literary works and the struggle for a Jewish identity. In 1911, before reading Pinès, Kafka commented that "Yiddish literature . . . is obviously characterized by an uninterrupted tradition of national struggle that determines every work" (DI 87 [T 68]). Pinès, too, characterized Yiddish literature as "a literature of combat" (*Histoire,* 6). Moreover, Kafka wrote the following lines in his diary: "Soldiers' song: They cut off our beards and earlocks. And they forbid us to keep the Sabbath and holy days" (DI 224 [T 362]). Pinès also discussed soldiers' songs in which the soldiers deplore their fate as conscripts and ends the chapter with a song whose refrain affirms Jewish identity: "the same refrain which seems inspired by the profound feelings of a people who, despite the attacks continually directed against them, have not lost consciousness of their dignity and who have loudly proclaimed the nobility of their destiny" (*Histoire,* 72). Kafka copied the refrain in his diary: "What we are, we are, / But Jews we are" (DI 224 [T 362]). At one point Pinès refers to Max Nordau at the Fifth Zionist Congress in Basel in 1901 (*Histoire,* 419). Coincidentally, without knowing each other, Kafka and Pinès both attended the 1913 Eleventh Zionist Congress in Vienna. Unlike Kafka, who simply went out of interest, Pinès appeared in the official listing of participants. Given his Zionist sympathies, it is not surprising that Pinès is critical of the Haskalah, the Jewish Enlightenment. What was at stake for Pinès and Kafka and other Haskalah writers (such as Mendele or Peretz) was the desire not to abandon a cultural heritage for the rather dubious and insecure belief in assimilation.

Ernst Pawel makes it sound as if the book was written from a Hasidic perspective when he describes it as "a massive work of decidedly anti-Enlightenment, pro-Hasidic slant" (*Nightmare,* 245). But Pinès, for one, rightly remarked that the "writers of the Enlightenment period . . . , other than two or three exceptions, amongst whom we find Linetski, only saw the ridiculous and crude elements in the hasidic movement" (*Histoire,* 473). Kafka made note of Isaac Joel Linetski's satire of Hasidic life, his autobiographical novel *Dos polnische juengel* (The Polish Lad) (T 364),[39] to which Pinès devoted a whole chapter. Despite his sympathetic commentary on Linetski, Pinès is very critical of the Hasidic movement: "Unfortunately,

Hasidism, which—let us not forget—was a movement of the ignorant masses, was unable to retain the nobility of its original role. From the very beginning it carried within itself the seeds of its ultimate degeneration" (*Histoire*, 472). Linetski's *The Polish Lad* (1875) contained one of the most virulent attacks on Hasidism of the period and was intended as a warning to young people. For Pinès, the satire was in fact the novel's most outstanding feature:

> But what constitutes the principal attraction of *The Polish Lad* is the satiric spirit which permeates it from one end to the other. The account of all the abuses, of the ignorance and infantile superstition of the hasidim, is placed in the mouth of a man who is himself a hasid and a faithful follower of the rabbi. And in this account the author succeeded in explaining in the smallest detail not only the manner of thinking but also the way the hasidim talk with all their technical expressions, for the most part borrowed from Hebrew, all the terms used by the hasidim when they talk of the rabbi, of his miracles or other spiritual matters related to their beliefs and their prejudices. (*Histoire*, 250)

This compassionate treatment of Linetski's *The Polish Lad* (1875) demonstrates that his book is not written from a "pro-Hasidic slant." Pinès had intimate knowledge of Jewish life and culture and was very careful to situate individual writers and their works within their particular historical, cultural, and personal circumstances. His literary history is analytic rather than judgmental and important for several reasons. First of all, he describes Yiddish culture from the perspective of an insider (which Kafka did not have) and from a point of view that is critical of the ideology of the Enlightenment (a view that Kafka shared). In addition, the world of Eastern European Yiddish culture depicted by Pinès with critical distance and from many angles (religious, historical, cultural, political) is much more realistic than the sentimental shtetl world that is re-evoked after World War II.

Pinès includes writers and stories that are often not included in the canon now and therefore represents a much-needed correction to many postwar anthologies. Due to the earlier-mentioned trend to romanticize Yiddish culture after World War II, satiric writers like Linetski or Moishe Nadir or even Mendele are not well represented in modern collections of Yiddish stories. As Milton Hindus puts it in his introduction to Linetski, "with the wide-spread tendency nowadays to idealize and even sentimentalize the Hasidic form of life which has largely disappeared, we are loath to look squarely at his little vignettes of Hasidic life at its worst. Caught in Linetski's pitiless lens, there is little of the quality that attracted Martin Buber to it" (20). The often scathing criticism of Jewish life in Eastern Europe that Mendele and Linetski offer may not fit into the postwar picture of shtetl life. Yet Kafka was familiar with these writers, and his own satires are at times not very different from theirs.

3

Anti-Semitism and Zionist Activities

(1911–1915)

The Specter of Ritual Murder

The Beilis Affair (1911–1913)

In 1911, when Kafka was twenty-eight years old, the famous Mendel Beilis trial began in Kiev, Russia. Kafka never explicitly mentions the Beilis affair, but the ritual murder trial left imprints on "The Judgment," *The Trial,* and "In the Penal Colony" (Band 179–81). The trial was the talk of the day and was covered extensively in the Prague newspapers. The Jewish population in Eastern Europe was especially vulnerable during Christian holidays, and pogroms around Easter as a result of ritual murder charges were almost predictable. The Beilis affair began at Eastertime, 20 March 1911, when the body of a twelve-year-old boy, Andrei Yushchinsky, was found in a cave on the outskirts of Kiev. Ritual murder accusations were immediately in the air. After several months of looking for a suspect, Menahem Mendel Beilis (1874–1924), a worker in a quarry near where the body was found, was charged with the murder. Beilis was the superintendent of a brick kiln, which was owned by another Jew on whose premises, supposedly, the boy had last been seen alive. As was revealed later, the police knew all along that Beilis was innocent because they had already traced the murder to a group of thieves. Yet ritual murder charges were laid anyway (*Judaica* 4:399–400).

In May 1911, on the same page where Kafka read Hugo Herrmann's critique of Brod's *Die Jüdinnen, Selbstwehr* published the contents of a flyer that was distributed at the murder victim's funeral:

Righteous Christians! Jews have slaughtered the young boy Andrej Justschinsky. Every year before their Easter celebrations they make it a practice to torture a dozen Christian boys to death, so that they can then pour their blood into matzo [unleavened bread]. . . . The examining doctors have found (?) that Justschinsky was chained by his torturers, his clothes were removed, and then he was stabbed while he was naked. They pierced his main arteries so that they would be able to draw as much blood as possible. In this fashion the Jews stabbed Justschinsky fifty times. Russian men! If you love your children, then beat up the Jews! Beat them until there is not a single Jew left in Russia! Show mercy for your children! Revenge the unfortunate martyrs. It is time, it is time! (S 19 May 1911:3)

Beilis was arrested in July, and the arrangements for his trial began in September. Not long after, the Yiddish theater group arrived in Prague. In October Löwy recited Bialik's famous poem, "In the City of Slaughter" (1904), written in response to the 1903 Kishinev pogrom, which had been incited by ritual murder accusations during the Easter period as well. The poem is a powerful condemnation of the massacre, the indifference of the people, and the absence of justice. Kafka remarked that this was "the one instance where the poet stooped from Hebrew to Yiddish, himself translating his original Hebrew poem into Yiddish, in order to popularize this poem which, by making capital [*ausbeuten*] out of the Kishinev pogrom, sought to further the Jewish cause [*für die jüdische Zukunft*]" (DI 101–2 [T 89]). Here Kafka is echoing a common Zionist slogan. The "Zionist national poet"[1] had close ties to Ahad Ha'am, and his poem was distributed widely and translated into Russian by the revisionist military Zionist leader Vladimir Jabotinsky (1880–1940). For Bialik, who had chosen Hebrew over Yiddish in the contemporary Yiddish-Hebrew language debate, this uncharacteristic descent into jargon, Yiddish, revealed his call for political action.

During the fall of 1911, when Kafka was enjoying the Yiddish plays, the atmosphere in Prague was becoming increasingly infected by a revival of the old ritual murder legend. The trial against Beilis was deliberately set to begin the following Easter so that it would arouse anti-Semitic sentiments. At the time of the trial, *Selbstwehr* reported how the repercussions were felt immediately in and around Prague: "Yet again the spectre of ritual murder is traversing the lands, spreading rumors and whispering into the ears of the people: the Jews are draining our blood. With giant steps the bloody fairy tale crosses borders, speaks all languages and knows all the hidden paths" (S 22 Mar. 1912:1). In Prague, a Czech anti-Semitic newspaper used the Beilis trial to rekindle the old ritual murder myth. In its Sunday entertainment section, it carried a large picture of the murdered boy in Kiev, showing the wounds inflicted on his head together with a detailed description of the alleged ritual murder. *Selbstwehr* reproduced this picture on the front page as well as the whole article in German translation (S 26 Apr. 1912:5). Feelings of anger and indignation ran high because the content of the Czech paper had passed the censorship office. The Central Association for the Preservation of Jewish Affairs (in which the fathers of Kafka, Brod, Weltsch, and Werfel were active) was now taking "the lead of the organized resistance against the journalistic smear campaign" (S 3 May 1912:1).

In the meantime, the trial of Beilis, after being repeatedly postponed, was finally announced for 15–19 October (S 17 May 1912:3). An incredible cover-up on the side of the authorities came to light. In December 1911 already, a journalist had provided the evidence of Beilis's innocence, but to no avail: Beilis was charged with the murder. The journalist then continued his research under assumed identities, amidst threats to his life. He submitted his evidence yet again, in January 1912 as well as in May, when the tide started turning.[2] It was now revealed that a policeman formerly in charge of the case had also been relieved of his duties because his investigations had not been "biased enough in the desired depiction of the 'ritual murder'" (S 21 June 1912:3). This policeman and the journalist had from then on pursued their investigations in private.

Kafka's "The Judgment," written in September 1912, contains a clear allusion to ritual murder when the friend from St. Petersburg, who encounters a riot on a business trip to Kiev, observes "a priest on a balcony who cut a broad cross in blood on the palm of his hand and held the hand up and appealed to the mob."[3] Clergymen often started ritual murder accusations and roused the masses. At the 1882–83 Tisza Eszlar trial in Hungary, a local priest had pushed for ritual murder charges even though the "murder" looked like a suicide. At the Beilis trial, too, a "Catholic priest with a criminal record" had "supplied 'scientific' evidence for the blood libel" and was "refuted by the Rabbi of Moscow" at the trial (*Judaica* 4:400). In November the vermin metaphor appears in Kafka's *The Metamorphosis*, the most obvious allusion to an anti-Semitic stereotype in his work. The protagonist, Gregor Samsa, literally becomes an ugly, smelly parasite, and when he is reduced to this reading by his environment, he is emptied of all other signification and dies. In both of these early texts, elements from present-day discourses become part of a larger framework of signification.

In December 1912 there were ritual murder accusations in Prague. At Christmas a religion teacher at the German Josephstädter school distributed ritual murder literature. *Selbstwehr* ran the story on the front page: "As everyone knows, the catechist there distributed booklets to the Christian students at Christmas time. They contained the story 'The Jewish Stone,' which describes in the most gruesome fashion how some Jews with their rabbi slaughter a little Christian child, cut up the body, drain its blood, and hang the body from a tree" (S 17 Jan. 1913:1). On the same page much is made of a new novel by Sholom Aleichem, *The Bloody Hoax*, which was inspired by the Beilis trial. Here Jew and Christian change roles and the Christian is accused of ritual murder: "The ritual murder lie is exposed not through a Jew, but it is through a Christian and Christian society that it is led towards its absurd conclusion" (1). The reviewer proposed a German translation, but no Jewish publisher should be approached so that a larger (Christian) market could be reached. He suggested "the combination of translator-publisher Max Brod=Axel Junker" (S 17 Jan. 1913:3). In this last year of the Beilis trial, Beilis and other ritual murder charges were still covered extensively in *Selbstwehr*. Despite the fact that the murder had been solved, the trial was dragged out until 28 October 1913. In the end, though, "the jury, composed of simple Russian peasants, after several hours of deliberation, unanimously declared Beilis 'not guilty'" (*Judaica* 4:399–400).

Evil Innocence: A Jewish Small-Town Novel

In January 1914 Kafka read Oskar Baum's novel, *Die böse Unschuld* (Evil Innocence)[4] (1913). Here a pogromlike scene describes "the riots of the radical Czechs, which are characteristically organized by a Jew and end with the smashing of windows and the demolition of Jewish stores" (S 20 Mar. 1914:1–2). The irony is that the anti-Semitic riots were arranged by a young Jewish socialist who identified with the Czech national movement. When the anti-Semitic Czech crowd calls for punishing the Jews, he takes the lead of the storming mob, charging toward the homes of his fellow Jews where they smash windows and destroy everything in their path. In the novel, as in real life, many Czechs disliked the Jews because they identified them with the dominant German power structure. When he was seven years old, Baum himself lost his eyesight in an attack provoked by anti-German sentiment (LF 74 [BF 139])—ironically, because the Czechs regarded him as German.

The overall theme of Baum's novel is the arbitrary psychology of scapegoating, suggested by the oxymoronic title *Evil Innocence*. Julius Budweiser, the protagonist, eventually understands that no one becomes a scapegoat because he or she is guilty. Paradoxically, the innocence of the accused is said to incite the crowd to violence. Thus, the social environment is regarded as guiltier than the "criminals" who are condemned. Even the mob is aware of this: what angers them most is that they know about the scapegoat's innocence (everyone supposedly feels this, even if only unconsciously). Baum's psychological reading of the victim-perpetrator dynamic also sheds light on the twisted psychology behind the mob's obsession with ritual murder. Thus, the evidence of the extensive cover-up which came to light during the Beilis trial may well suggest that it was precisely the victim's "wicked," "spiteful innocence" that incited the mob's anger even more.

The Beilis Trial: Kafka's *The Trial* and "In the Penal Colony"

Sander Gilman links the form of Joseph K.'s arrest in *The Trial* (1914) to the conviction of Dreyfus and points out that the ending "alludes to contemporary associations of ritual murder with ritual practice" (*Patient*, 102–3, 154). Yet Gilman never mentions the Beilis affair, though Kafka can be said to have blended particular details into his narrative. For instance, Joseph K.'s execution takes place in a "stone quarry" (the murder victim in real life was found in a cave outside of Kiev, and Beilis was charged because he worked in the nearby brick quarry). Moreover, K.'s futile attempts to exonerate himself echo an ironic passage in *Selbstwehr* two years earlier: "Well, [Beilis] still has not been convicted. The trial is still going on, the judgement has still not been revealed, and events could still occur which might prevent the worst" (S 12 Apr. 1912:1).[5] The similarity of syntax, vocabulary, and subject matter that this article shares with stylistic features of Kafka's writing suggests that what we now consider to be Kafkaesque, or absurd, could be found in the common rhetoric of everyday newspaper reports.

Likewise, there are echoes from contemporary events in "The Penal Colony," which Kafka wrote during his composition of *The Trial* (15–18 Oct. 1914). Among the many sources that have been identified is Octave Mirbeau's *The Garden of Torturers* (1898–99; 1902 in German), which was written "under the influence of the images of the Dreyfus Affair" (Gilman, *Patient*, 81).[6] Gilman also links the traveler's argument with the officer about the killing machine to the current debate on the cruelty of ritual animal slaughter (*Patient,* 150). The same connection between ritual murder and animal slaughter was made in the anti-Semitic press in relation to the Beilis trial: the stab wounds on the victim were said to have been "cold-bloodedly carried out *with a firm and calm hand,* which did not know the tremble of fear, . . . perhaps with a hand that is used to slaughter animals" (S 5 July 1912:3–4). A more overt allusion to the Beilis case can be seen in the description of the accused lying rigid while needles are puncturing their bodies. This is reminiscent of the picture of Beilis's supposed victim, which was reproduced in *Selbstwehr* in April 1912. The graphic description of the "ritual murder" accompanying the picture—which, incidentally, takes up over half the page (it was said to be reduced in size to the one that originally appeared in the Czech anti-Semitic newspaper!)—suggests further parallels:

> Before the torture the boy's clothes were removed except for his shirt. . . . His hands were tied firmly against his back, his mouth was completely gagged, his lips were pressed tightly against his teeth. . . . The *blood was drained* out of the boy while he was still alive, so that the dead body is entirely *without blood.* The numerous wounds, their particular type, and the way they were spread out on the body indicate that these were inflicted for the *purpose of torture. The torment was terrible.* The boy is pierced all over. Liver, lung, heart are all pierced through. . . . During the *draining of the blood* [*Blutabzapfung*] the boy was pierced further to *torture him more.* . . . When he had lost two thirds of his blood, his heart was pierced with the last (47th) cut. The cut was so strong and deep that imprints of the weapon could be seen around the heart on the victim's skin. During the whole torture, the boy was held in an upright position, the body slightly tilted to the side. (S 26 Apr. 1912:1)

The editors of *Selbstwehr* highlighted the nouns and phrases in italics through larger print, perhaps to draw attention to the current anti-Semitic rhetoric. In Kafka's "Penal Colony," as in the ritual murder description above, the accused have to remove their clothes, and the twelve-hour-long torture is literally a form of *Blutabzapfung,* draining of the blood: while the victims are still alive, their blood is drained into grooves that empty into a pit; after the torture, they themselves are thrown into the pit. At the end of the story, the officer takes off his clothes and subjects himself to the blood-letting procedure, but the machine breaks down when the representative of justice submits himself to "Justice": he is pierced not through his heart, as was done to those before him, but through his head (the picture of the boy in *Selbstwehr* shows his head pierced by multiple stab wounds). As in the newspaper article, the officer, too, remains upright during the whole procedure (of which Kafka's text says, "this was no exquisite torture . . . , this was plain murder" (CS 165 [E 195]), and the machine turns him sideways before the end. At this point, without releasing him into the pit, it keeps the officer suspended in the air, similar again to the description in the newspaper article, where the victim is "held in an upright position, the body slightly tilted to the side." The officer's lips in "Penal Colony" are also "firmly pressed together," and his body, too, is literally "pierced through" like the body of the dead boy in the newspaper: "through the forehead went the point of the great iron spike" (CS 166 [E 196]).

In "The Penal Colony," as in *The Trial*, the accused do not know the nature of their crime. The officer speaks only French to them (CS 142 [E 167])—the language of colonialism, an allusion to Dreyfus's "penal colony"—and they do not understand him. However, the guilt that is never disclosed in *The Trial* is identified here, since the religious commandments inscribed on the bodies of the accused reveal their transgressions. These commandments, though, are written in a script that hardly anyone can read, a script surrounded by many "flourishes" and "embellishments" (CS 149 [E 175]), which critics have said resemble Hebrew letters.[7] In the story they are transformed into an imaginary script that opens up to many readings. After all, the officer remarks that naturally it cannot be a "simple" script, because "it's not supposed to kill a man straight off, but only after an interval of . . . twelve hours" (CS 149 [E 175]). During this period, the victim would eventually learn to decipher his guilt "with his wounds" (CS 150 [E 176]), and at that climactic moment everyone would supposedly know that "Justice is being done" (CS 154 [E 181]). Yet when the Officer of the Law places himself under the torture machine, the whole exquisite justice system self-destructs, and he is denied the "promised redemption; what the others had found in the machine he had not found" (CS 166 [E 196]). Ironically, the fate of this last representative of "Justice" exposes his faith in the rituals of the past as barbarous and misguided.

"In the Penal Colony" merges echoes of Dreyfus and the Beilis trial with allusions to biblical exegesis and contemporary debates on slaughter, assimilation, and colonialism. But the instrument of torture is also a "writing machine." The officer's fanatical devotion to the written word, as well as the desired merging of script and body as a form of punishment that

3. *Selbstwehr*'s response to anti-Semitic ritual murder smear campaign

will make the ignorant "feel" the law, is certainly also reminiscent of the physicality of the writing process expressed in Kafka's famous statement: "I am made of literature, I am nothing else, and cannot be anything else" (LF 304 [BF 444]) The printing process of the torture machine is a relentless act of inscription that deconstructs the elaborate machinery of outdated beliefs.

ZIONIST ACTIVITIES

Bar Kochba Events

Kafka never engaged in an activist, political-theoretical type of Zionism; instead, he preferred community-oriented events put on by Bar Kochba. From 1912 on, he frequently participated in Zionist cultural activities, such as the aforementioned "Evening of Jewish Folk Songs" with Nathan Birnbaum, which took place on 18 January 1912. On this fourth festive evening of the Bar Kochba, Birnbaum's opening speech, "The Music of the Eastern Jews," was an appeal to the Western audience to appreciate Eastern Jewish culture. Like Max Nordau (1849–1923) and Martin Buber, he was another "enlightened" Western Jew who had undergone many "conversions." Birnbaum was originally from Vienna and had been an early admirer of Theodor Herzl. He published a pamphlet opposing assimilation in 1882 and helped establish Kadimah, the first Jewish nationalist-oriented student fraternity a year later. In 1885 he "founded and edited the first Jewish nationalist journal in German, *Selbst-Emanzipation* [Self-Emancipation], where he coined the term 'Zionism'" (*Judaica* 4:1040). Birnbaum was an important personality at the First Zionist Congress in 1897, where he spoke in favor of Ahad Ha'am's "vision of a modern Jewish cultural rebirth as the ultimate solution to the Jewish question" (CJ 101). In 1898 he broke with Herzl, left the Zionist movement, and became a champion of Diaspora nationalism: for him the Yiddish language was the national language of Jewish culture. In 1908 he moved east to Czernowitz (Chernivtsi) in the Bukowina (now Ukraine), at which time he is said to have had a religious experience. He stayed in Czernowitz until 1911 and published Yiddish newspapers (*Dos Folk* and *Vokhen-Blat*). Then he moved to Berlin and began spreading the word about Yiddish culture from Germany. By the time Kafka met him, Birnbaum had long abandoned his secular views and embraced religion.

As with Buber before, Kafka did not share Birnbaum's romanticized notions about Eastern European Judaism. He was unimpressed with his talk and made fun of him in his diary because his speech seemed artificial with the Yiddish flavor that he tried to give it whenever there was an awkward pause: "But from what I know of Löwy I think that these recurrent expressions, such as "Weh ist mir!" or "S' ist nischt" or "S'ist viel zu reden," are not intended to cover up embarrassment but are rather intended, like ever-fresh springs, to stir up the sluggish stream of speech that is never fluent enough for the Jewish temperament. But not in Birnbaum's case" (DI 223 [T 360–61]; the last sentence is missing in the English translation).

According to the reviewer in *Selbstwehr,* Birnbaum talked "at first with bitter accusations, then with fierce demands" about the prejudice that existed toward the Eastern Jews on the part of the Western Jews. The Eastern Jews are not Jews who are constantly whining, he said. On the contrary, "The Eastern Jews are people who are whole, vigorous, and full of the love of life. They have a strong, primitive humor which is more precious than the western Jewish joke." In Buberlike fashion he addressed the unity between "religion and culture," which is best expressed in the music of the synagogue, and briefly touched on "the significance of the hasidic world feeling for the Jewish psyche, which represents an internalized joyous life with God and with the world." Unlike Kafka, the reporter in *Selbstwehr* was thoroughly enthusiastic (S 26 Jan. 1912:5, 4). The highlight seems to have been the Yiddish songs sung by cantor Gollanin, whom Kafka had heard before. This was followed by recitals of Yiddish poems in German translation. Kafka was as unimpressed by the poems as he was with Birnbaum's speech (DI 224 [T 361]). From Kafka's speech on the Yiddish language, it is clear that he disliked it when Yiddish was translated into German.

On 28 January Kafka attended Dr. Felix Theilhaber's lecture "on the decline of the German Jews" (DI 229 [T 370]), based on his book by the same name. Theilhaber cited statistics which showed that the high rates of baptism, assimilation, and intermarriage would have severe consequences for the continuation of the Jewish "race." A lively discussion ensued, with Theilhaber vehemently opposing those who argued for intermarriage. Gilman reads Kafka's short summary of the main points of the lecture as a sign of his own "anxiety" (*Patient,* 124); however, Kafka seems rather entertained by the comic side of the discussion period: "Amusing scene when Prof. Ehrenfels, who grows more and more handsome and who—with his . . . full voice, which he modulates like a musical instrument, and a confident smile at the meeting—declares himself in favour of mixed races" (DI 229 [T 370–71]). It was well known that Christian Freiherr von

Ehrenfels (1859–1932) was himself a product of a mixed marriage (Gilman, *Patient*, 199) and that he—who so trustingly came out on the side of intermarriage in this debate—had indeed often in the past argued for the advantages of mixed parentage.

Ehrenfels was professor of philosophy at the Prague Karls University. Kafka knew him well; he had been his student during his university years, and he also attended further philosophy lectures by him in October 1913 (DI 304 [T 587]). This particular evening, *Selbstwehr* reported, ended in a dialogue between Theilhaber and Ehrenfels, with Theilhaber repeatedly countering Ehrenfels's argument for *Mischehen*, mixed marriages:

> Again Professor Ehrenfels entered the debate and declared after initial hesitation, that he for his own part regarded the mixing of the Jewish and Aryan race as desirable, however only when a selection had preceded it, which was not possible under the present social conditions. Dr. Theihaber spoke up vehemently against the mixing theory. The mixing of races generally leads to poor results. . . . The Jewish offspring have by far been the greatest Jew-haters. (S 2 Feb. 1912:4)

In his argument for a selective racial mixing, Ehrenfels has been influenced by the biological-racial medical theories of his time. Like Max Nordau and Cesare Lombroso, he believed in the superiority and inferiority of certain races and types. Given his own mixed ethnic background, Ehrenfels was caught in a double-bind of racial dialectics, needing to justify and legitimate his own successful and "superior" existence, which went counter to the medical theories of his day. Thus he saw "mixing" as desirable if a selection process had preceded it to ensure that the offspring would be "a new race, comprised of the best qualities of the constitutive races" (Gilman, *Patient*, 199).

Kafka's next evening with the Bar Kochba was his own Yiddish evening with Löwy (18 February 1912). Soon after he made note of a "Zionist meeting" in his diary with "Blumenfeld. Secretary of the World Zionist Organization" (DI 235 [T 379]; K 105). Kurt Blumenfeld (1884–1963), who had joined the Zionist movement in 1905 at the age of twenty-one, started out as a student leader and then moved up the ranks. In 1909 he became secretary of the German Zionist Organization and in 1911 general secretary for the World Zionist Organization (when the headquarters were moved from Cologne to Berlin). He was a great inspiration to many young people and was in charge of Zionist propaganda, education, and recruitment.[8] Blumenfeld became known for "his specific 'post-assimilation' Zionism" (*Judaica* 4:1140), an ideology that appealed to acculturated Jews

> who had discarded Judaism qua religion with its traditions but continued to sense a lack in their personal lives and a need for Jewish expression.... As a man who was at home in German classic literature, Blumenfeld concluded that there could be no true synthesis between *Deutschtum* and *Judentum* since *Deutschtum* as a cultural milieu was alien to the essence of *Judentum*. The individual Jew was rootless in Germany; his intellectual, cultural and emotional destiny could be expressed only in Zionism and Judaism.... The only way to ameliorate this situation was to immigrate to Palestine.... Blumenfeld's first concern was to uproot German Zionists from German culture and only secondarily to help them attain their own Jewish culture. He and other leading Zionists did not acquire a working knowledge of Hebrew until after their emigration to Palestine.[9]

Blumenfeld was one of the few leading (political) Zionists whom the Prague students could identify with because he "shared their views concerning the cultural component of the Jewish national rebirth" (CJ 102). His Zionism was a combination of cultural and practical Zionism; he was not very interested in theorizing but was known to seek out the public and is remembered "for his ability of winning people over, for the fascination he exerted especially on demanding intellectuals" (Ginat, 7, 19). One of these was Albert Einstein, his good friend. On the occasion of his visit to Prague, Blumenfeld spoke about "The Jews in Academic Life" (K 105). At some point Blumenfeld and Kafka also met and came to know each other.[10]

On 16 May 1912, Kafka went to hear Davis Trietsch (1870–1935), an expert on Palestine and the Orient, whose speech, "Palestine as Land of Colonialization," was organized by the Zionist District Committee for Bohemia (K 119). Kafka was enthusiastic: "A few days ago an excellent lecture by Davis Trietsch on colonization in Palestine" (DI 263 [T 423]; K 119). He was deeply interested in this kind of practical Zionism, and his library contains several journals that deal with agriculture, including reports about the "cultural flora of Palestine," "the significance of introducing the Karakul sheep into the agriculture of Palestine," "cotton harvest in Palestine in 1911," orange and wine production in the young colonies, etc. There were also reports about the planting of eucalyptus trees to drain the swamps so that the population would not die from malaria and discussions about the kinds of grains, fruit, and trees that could be cultivated, including "date palms."[11] It is, of course, impossible to date precisely the moment when Kafka acquired or read these texts, but we know that he was a subscriber to the Zionist monthly *Palästina* in 1912 (LF 61 [BF 121–22]).

A Date in Palestine: Felice Bauer

The first time Kafka met his later fiancée, Felice Bauer, at Max Brod's home on 13 August 1912 (DI 268–69 [T 431–32]), he happened to have the most recent issue of *Palästina* with him (KB 163–64). In his very first letter to Felice, on 20 September 1912, Kafka used her promise "to accompany him next year to Palestine" (LF 5 [BF 43] as a means of establishing contact. He considered himself fortunate to have brought the *Palästina* publication along because it immediately engaged everyone in a discussion of Palestine (LF 16 [BF 58]). Felice had observed in passing that she had learned Hebrew, and Kafka was very impressed: "Now it also transpired that you are a Zionist, and this suited me very well" (LF 15 [BF 58; translation modified]). Yet, when they actually tried to read some Hebrew, it turned out that she could not even translate the name "Tel awiw" (LF 15 [BF 58]).

Today's Tel Aviv-Yafo was established in 1909 as Ahuzat Bayit outside of the existing Arab neighborhoods of Yaffa. It was renamed Tel Aviv (Hill of Spring) in 1910 in honor of Theodor Herzl: *Tel Aviv* was the Hebrew title of Herzl's novel *Alt-Neuland* (Old-New Land, 1902), translated by none other than the well-known Zionist politician Nahum Sokolov. The name symbolizes the destruction of the ancient land and the hope for restoration or renewal, *tel* meaning "hill of ruins" and *aviv* "season of spring."

The *Palästina* issue that Kafka brought listed trips "To Palestine (Jaffa)" on the front page. One could choose between the cheaper mail boat and the more expensive express steamer. The trips were arranged by a travel agency in Vienna. The magazine also contained a long essay by Ahad Ha'am (translated from the Hebrew) that criticized Zionist theorists and political activists for losing sight of the most pressing current issues. He reiterated his firm belief that colonization could not be rushed, that first of all small colonies should be built and supported, and only this would slowly lead to the creation of a cultural center. All the while the continual growth of Jewish culture in Palestine would be an inspiration to Jews all over the world (*Palästina*, 169–84). His article encountered a great deal of opposition from different factions of the political-theoretical Zionist spectrum. It was followed by a long commentary from Adolf Böhm, a major commentator on Zionist affairs, editor of *Palästina,* and author of *The Zionist Movement* (1920). Böhm attempted to reconcile the different factions (i.e., the political and cultural Zionists) and pointed out the significance of Ahad Ha'am's critique for contemporary political Zionism.

More Dates in Palestine

On 12 September 1912 Kafka spent an evening at his home with Dr. Hugo Löw, Dr. Kellner, and Hugo Bergmann talking about Palestine. The occasion was Kellner's visit to Prague (from Palestine) and Löw's imminent departure for Palestine. Kafka put the evening into an ironic light:

> Another traveler to Palestine [*Palästinafahrer*]. Is taking his bar examination a year before the end of his clerkship and is leaving (in two weeks) for Palestine with 1, 200 K. Will try to get a position with the Palestine Office. All these travelers to Palestine [Dr. B(ergmann), Dr. K(ellner)] have downcast eyes, feel blinded by their listeners, fumble around on the table with the tips of their extended fingers, their voices quiver, they smile weakly and prop up these smiles with a little irony (DI 272 [T 437]; translation modified).

The English translation "emigrants to Palestine" loses the humor in Kafka's word coinage *Palästinafahrer,* which creates the impression of a vivid traffic of people coming and going to Palestine.

Kafka's friends went to Palestine during the Second Aliya, or wave of immigration, 1903–14, when approximately forty thousand Jews emigrated there. Hugo Löw, the editor of the *Prager Tagblatt,* was himself in the process of emigrating.[12] He was planning to work in the Palestine Office in Jaffa, which the Zionist Arthur Ruppin had opened in 1908. Bergmann, Kellner, and Löw were looking at the map and exchanging information and advice. Bergmann had visited Palestine in 1910, while Viktor Kellner (1887–1970), a leading member of Bar Kochba, had emigrated a year later and was now teaching at the first Hebrew High School in Jaffa (K 124), which later became the Herzlia Gymnasium.

The high school had been founded by Dr. Leo Metmann in 1905 with very few students; in May 1910 there were nineteen students and three teachers (S 13 May 1910:6). As a result of a substantial donation by a British donor—peace judge Jacob Moser, lord manor of Bradford—a new building was erected (the biggest building in Palestine at the time) and more teachers were hired, of whom Kellner was one. Moser donated the money on condition that the school be renamed after Herzl, and this is how it became the well-known Herzlia Gymnasium. A year later, in his article in *Selbstwehr,* Viktor Kellner recounts that the high school already had 254 students from all over the world (Russia, Rumania, Portugal, Australia, South Africa, and Canada), and about sixty new students were coming for the next year. The new building could hold a maximum of 500 students (S 22 Sept. 1911:2). During the course of the evening with Bergmann and Löw, Kellner "told [the group] that his students are chauvinists, have the Maccabees forever in their mouths and want to take after them" (DI 272 [T 437]).

After his emigration, Hugo Löw, too, would write regular literary and political columns in *Selbstwehr* from Palestine. At the time he still belonged to Bar Kochba's rival Zionist group, Barissia. He had been one of its founders and was a strong supporter of Herzl's political Zionism (CJ 116). But the division between the two Zionist factions played no role this evening, when sentiment and reverence toward Palestine outweighed political differences. Kafka frowned on this Buberlike neo-romanticism. Karl Kraus, whose anti-Zionist sympathies are well known, disliked it even more. In "Eine Krone für Zion" (A Crown for Zion), his polemic against Theodor Herzl, Kraus ridicules a Zionist delegate's emotional response to the Jewish national flag with the Mogen David blowing in the wind at the First Zionist Congress in Basel in 1897:

"There, what's that? My vision is suddenly blurred. The excitement of the last days, the journey, . . .—everything together—and then all of a sudden this sight! From the balcony of the Congress building, two mighty flags are fluttering in the pleasant evening wind. On a white field there are two wide blue stripes and above the field floats the Star of David! For the first time in my life I had seen a Jewish flag, a flag, *which everyone would recognize immediately as a Jewish one.* The voice of my dearest friends had not moved me as much as these new flags. I almost became sad." The excitement of the travels and the joy over the final arrival are expressed with such ecstatic rapture that one does not think one is reading a travel report from Basel but rather about the successful arrival of Jews in Palestine. The conversations during the journey are touching. . . . It is probably the noisiest train that has travelled this route. . . . Again and again one heard the words: "homeland, Zion, the Congress, Basel. If only we were there already."[13]

Kafka, too, felt uneasy when Zionism became a substitute religion. However, the Zionism of many of his friends and acquaintances was also very practical: they were committed cultural Zionists, and several were willing to make sacrifices and move to Palestine. In his letters to Felice, Kafka still sounds very enthusiastic about the possibility of having a rendezvous with her there. However, he soon learned that Felice's family did not approve of her traveling to Palestine (LF 8 [BF 47]), and she herself must have used the expense that such a journey entailed as an excuse: "And the enormous sum you mentioned as necessary for Palestine!" (LF 273 [BF 404]).[14]

THE RELUCTANT ZIONIST

Martin Buber in Prague

In 1913 Kafka's interest in Zionism cooled off considerably. Not having been impressed with Martin Buber's lectures in 1909–10, he was quite unenthusiastic about hearing Buber speak "on the Jewish Myth; .... But after Buber Eysoldt will be reading, and it is entirely on her account that I am going.... I am completely under the spell of her personality and her voice" (LF 157–58 [BF 252–53]). The event was the fifth yearly festive evening of the Bar Kochba, and many Prague Zionists were enthusiastic about Buber's arrival. A week before the talk, *Selbstwehr* printed a long article on Buber (S 10 Jan. 1913:2–4).[15] The advertisements highlighted especially the participation of "the greatest actress and elocutionist, Gertrud Eysoldt," from the Max Reinhardt ensemble of the Deutsches Theater in Berlin, who will "read Jewish myths and Martin Buber will present the introduction" (S 10 Jan. 1913:5). Like Kafka, many came especially to see the actress. Two weeks in advance already, *Selbstwehr* announced the texts she would recite:

> A.: 1. From the Bible: The Witch of Endor, The Wisdom of Solomon. 2. Primeval legends: Mercy and the Truth; The Bird Milham; The Earth Trembles under Cain's Feet; The First Idol; Lilith, the First Wife of Adam.—B.: Hasidic Legends (from 'The Legend of the Baal-Schem': From Army to Army; The Call. (S 3 Jan 1913:6)

After the performance a reviewer pointed out that the biblical legends in the first part of the evening were taken from Micha Josef Berdyczewski's (published under the name bin Gorion) volume "From Prehistoric Times," which was about to appear in print (S 24 Jan. 1913:3).[16] The second half consisted of recitations of some of Buber's Hasidic tales. That evening

Kafka could not have escaped from Martin Buber's "tepid things" (*lauwarme Sachen*) (LF 161 [BF 257]), as he called his legends. However, after the lecture he met Buber personally and thought he was "lively and simple and remarkable" (LF 161 [BF 257]). Kafka and Felice also visited Buber at his home in Berlin in May 1914, and Kafka thoroughly enjoyed the visit (LFF 107, 115; Buber, *Letters,* 156). From then on Buber and Kafka had professional contact as well.[17]

In the following months Kafka became increasingly irritated with the Zionists' persistent attempts to recruit new members: "Then I met an acquaintance, a Zionist student.... He stops me, invites me to an especially important evening meeting (how many similar invitations has he not wasted on me in the course of the years!); at that moment my indifference to him as a person, or to any form of Zionism, was immense and inexpressible" (LF 207–8 [BF 318]). During this period, his relationship to Felice was foremost on his mind: he had decided to propose to her, and in June they became engaged. On this occasion they likely received Richard Lichtheim's *Das Programm des Zionismus* (The Zionist Agenda, 1911),[18] as a present from Max Brod. This anti-Enlightenment study that holds emancipation and assimilation responsible for the present situation is dedicated to "my dear Franz Kafka and bride" (KB 117).

The Eleventh Zionist Congress in Vienna

A few months later, Kafka was interested enough to attend the Eleventh Zionist Congress in Vienna,[19] together with the expressionist poet Albert Ehrenstein (1886–1950), the poet-critic Otto Pick (1887–1940), and Lise Weltsch (1889–1974), cousin of Kafka's friend Felix Weltsch. A photograph taken in the Prater of Vienna on 7 September bears witness to their meeting.[20] Lise Weltsch was from a political Prague family; her brother was the well-known writer and Zionist Robert Weltsch, and her father, a lawyer by profession, was a strong Zionist. On this occasion, she was accompanying her father to the congress (KH 450 [T 1063]). Soon after, Lise took a position in the Zionist bureau in Berlin.

Also present at the congress were Kafka's friend Hugo Bergmann's wife, Else, who was accompanied by her brother, Klara Thein (1884–?), from the "Zionist district committee Prague" (K 161), and members of the Prague Bar Kochba (Stach, *Entscheidungen,* 405). Furthermore, the following names that were known to Kafka appear in the list of participants in the minutes of the congress: M. I. Pinès, listed as a delegate from Russia; Viktor Kellner, from Jaffa (where he was teaching at the Hebrew school);

and Davis Trietsch from Berlin, whose lecture on Palestine Kafka had attended in May 1912.[21]

This Zionist Congress was different from previous ones where the ideology of political Zionism had overshadowed all other Zionist concerns. After Herzl's death in 1904, David Wolffsohn (1856–1914) continued Herzl's political Zionism. But the rift between political and practical Zionists was becoming progressively wider. At the 1911 Zionist Congress the practical Zionists opposed the reelection of Wolffsohn, and the third president of the World Zionist Organization, Dr. Otto Warburg (1859–1938), who replaced Wolffsohn in 1912, was a practical Zionist, a botanist from Berlin. He remained president until 1920 and was replaced by Chaim Weizmann at the Twelfth Zionist Congress in 1921.

At the Eleventh Zionist Congress in 1913, the shift to cultural Zionism had just taken place. The main theme was "Palästinaarbeit," work for and in Palestine. In his opening speech, Warburg announced that "agriculture and gardening deserve primary consideration and the broadest scope" (*Stenographishes Protokoll*, 11). Much time at the congress was devoted to the settlements in Palestine, to the Jewish National Fund's fundraising campaigns, and to the work of the Palestine office in Jaffa. Another important matter was the foundation of a university in Jerusalem.

We know for certain that Kafka attended the morning sessions on 8 September 1913 because he wrote to Felice, "I went to the Zionist Congress this morning. I have no real contact. I feel it in certain respects, also for the entire concept, but not for the essential part" (LF 317 [BF 462]). Critics have assumed that he probably went to a lecture on "Jewish Cultural Work in Palestine" (C 107), but this lecture was moved.[22] As for the sessions he did attend, his notes reveal that Kafka, as well as his friends, found them very boring:

> Zionist Congress. Types with small round heads, firm cheeks. The workers' delegate from Palestine, permanent uproar [*ewiges Geschrei*]. Herzl's daughter. The former director of the Gymnasium in Jaffa. On the stairs, erect, scruffy beard, coat. Fruitless German speeches, much Hebrew, most work done in small committees. Lise W. is merely dragged along by the whole thing without participating, tosses paper balls into the hall, hopeless. Frau Thein. (LF 319 [BF 465], [T 1063–64])

Kafka's remark about the useless German speeches and the constant shouting refers to the morning session. The speeches were by the Zionist leaders Nahum Sokolov (1859–1936), Menahem Ussischkin (1863–1941) and Arthur Ruppin (1867–1943) (*Stenographishes Protokoll*, 240–254). Sokolov was the general secretary of the World Zionist Organization; he later became an important negotiator with the British for issuing the Balfour Declaration (1917). Ussischkin was a practical Zionist who was involved in establishing agricultural settlements and Jewish schools in Palestine, and he promoted the creation of a Hebrew University. Ruppin had moved to Palestine in 1908 to be the director of the Zionist Organization's Eretz Yisrael (Palestine) Office in Jaffa. He was responsible for buying land and building colonies and settlements.

Kafka's remark about "types with small round heads" is likely an ironic comment on Nahum Sokolov's introductory speech, which distinguished between three different types of delegates: the Jewish researcher, the Jewish banker, and the American statesman type, represented by Louis Brandeis, who had just sent a telegram in support of the congress (Bokhove, "Zionism," 36n.72; *Stenographishes Protokoll*, 241). While the first two speeches were brief, Ruppin's talk was very long and fixated on Zionist infighting concerning the activities of his office in Jaffa. He was especially obsessed with countering a particular Herr (Jacobus Henricus) Kann (1872–1944), a wealthy Jewish banker from the Hague and an old friend of Theodor Herzl and a Zionist not yet living in Palestine like himself. Moreover, the "workers' delegate" from Palestine, the delegate S. Tolkowski—an agricultural engineer and animal breeder—was a disillusioned *chaluz* (pioneer) who criticized the reality of life in Palestine: the settlers' lack of knowledge about agriculture, that orange trees were planted in entirely unsuitable ground, the lack of water for plants and of good drinking water for humans, the fact that malaria and typhoid fever were rampant. He also talked about the neglect of the Herzl house, which Bokhove believes "may explain Kafka's mentioning Herzl's daughter" ("Zionism," 36n.72; *Stenographishes Protokoll*, 255–56). Tolkowski was continually disrupted by shouts of disapproval from the audience, and a riotous, tense situation ensued which became hard for the conference chairman to control (in the afternoon session Arthur Ruppin took issue with the "workers' delegate" and put him in his place).

Kafka's negative description—"permanent shouting" (ewiges Geschrei), ineffective German speeches, much Hebrew—aptly characterizes this morning session. Some delegates forcefully demanded the use of Hebrew; others spoke in Yiddish, German, Polish, Russian. It was a linguistic experience. Kafka's comments would have been welcomed by Karl Kraus, who, with mean-spirited sarcasm, stressed "the linguistic confusion alone" at the First Zionist Congress in Basel (1897):

> In Basel, the manual gesturing, which all speakers had in common, has proven itself to be an insufficient means of communication. But at a gathering of 300 mixed Jews, who speak all languages, one could after all think of substituting them with interpreters, who can interfere in time when an excited Zionist, understandable only to his own compatriots, wishes to make a statement likewise with his own hands. What common bond should, after all, hold the interests together of German, English, French, Slavic and Turkish Jews so that they can make up a whole State? ("Krone für Zion," 307–8)

Moreover, Kafka mentions that the real work at the congress was done in the smaller sessions. Because of the large number of visitors, they had prepared many smaller sessions which had a more practical goal and a cultural orientation (S Aug. 29, 1913:1). In fact, it was suggested to the "workers' delegate" Tolkowski that he save his comments for one of those meetings, which he did. It is doubtful whether Kafka attended any of the afternoon sessions, especially after the fiasco of the morning session.[23] However, he may have returned to the Zionist Congress in the evening, for some of his previous remarks about the congress may refer to the last session, where one of the speakers was the former school director of the Jaffa Hebrew school (whom Kafka mentions and whom he must have known about through his friends Bergmann and Kellner).

The last session of the Zionist Congress began at nine o'clock with a lecture in Hebrew. If he did attend this big evening session, then Kafka heard the two speeches by Ussischkin and Weizmann, which had previously been advertised in *Selbstwehr* as highlights of the congress (and which had been moved from the morning to the evening session). Ussischkin seems to have spoken in Hebrew, Weizmann in German. Both lectures were solid political-historical analyses about the rise of anti-Semitism in Eastern Europe and the need for cultural Zionism and Jewish education. Together, Weizmann and Ussischkin presented convincing arguments for the establishment of a university in Palestine. The former school director of the Jaffa Gymnasium, Dr. Ben Zion Mossinsohn, was the last speaker that evening; he spoke (in Hebrew) in favor of founding a university. One of the resolutions to come out of this congress was to found the Hebrew University of Jerusalem. The session ended at one o'clock in the morning.

The audience was enthusiastic about these last speeches. Kafka, however, remained negative about his time in Vienna. In fact, he told Max Brod that he considered his visit there a waste of time: "It was all a useless business. It is hard to imagine anything more useless than such a congress. I sat in on the Zionist Congress as if it were an event totally alien to me, though, to be sure, I felt myself cramped and distracted by many other things" (LFF 100 [Br 120]; translation modified).

The Jewish Civil Servants' Club

Max Brod recalled that in December 1913 his own increasing participation in Zionist activities had caused a brief estrangement between Kafka and himself (FK 112). Kafka's moderate position was known in the Zionist community, for on 12 or 13 December he was asked to direct a discussion group in the "Jewish Civil Servants' Club,"[24] which was very divided because of the strong Zionist orientation of some members (DI 322 [T 613]; Binder, "*Selbstwehr*," 292). In the end, the more radical Zionists won this internal battle because only a few months later we hear that the "general assembly has come to the following conclusion: the organization is exclusively Zionist, has to address all Zionist questions and must work for the Zionist cause. . . . Its members are urged to learn Hebrew" (S 10 Apr. 1914:7). The experience of Zionist dogmatism, that one had to toe the line, must have contributed to the "estrangement" Brod refers to. Hugo Bergmann's talk "Moses and the Present" on 17 December 1913 left Kafka equally cold (DI 323–24 [T 616–17]). Yet he concludes that he actually likes the different streams in Judaism because they allow him to create a space for himself ("Man bekommt Platz") and to see his own position more clearly (DI 324 [T 617]). Brod recalls that the period of distance was over by 24 December (FK 113).

Felix Salten: "Jewish Modernity"

Kafka certainly enjoyed the sixth festive evening of the Bar Kochba, on 21 January 1914, at which Felix Salten gave a lecture on "Jewish Modernity." Kafka was accompanied by his sister Ottla (1892–1943) and other friends (DII 13 [T 626]). According to *Selbstwehr*, the Hotel Zentral was completely booked, and approximately three hundred people were unable to obtain seats. Salten took issue with the *Sprachkampf* (language battle) then raging in Palestine and favored Hebrew as the future language, joking, "Considering that so far one hasn't understood the Jews in the European languages, perhaps one will understand them in Hebrew" (S 6 Feb.

1914:1). He also spoke about modern Jewish art and the problematic of defining the "Jewish" artist. After Salten, the actor Rudolf Schildkraut recited texts from modern Jewish literature with great fervor: excerpts from *Der Graf von Charolais* (The Count of Carolais) by Richard Beer-Hofmann and Herzl's *Jewish State,* poems by Max Brod and Morris Rosenfeld, as well as the short story "The Sick Boy" by I. L. Peretz (S 6 Feb. 1914:2). Kafka recalled Ottla and her women friends' "enjoyment of the Salten-Schildkraut lecture" (DII 13 [T 626]). He also referred to "Ottla's Zionism" in his diary. Ottla was active in the Zionist Club of Jewish Women and Girls (DII 21 [T 638]), founded in 1912 and first chaired by Bergmann's wife, Else, then by Lise Weltsch, and then by Nelly Thieberger, sister of Kafka's later Hebrew teacher (KH 432; K 157 no. 626 [5]). Brod's wife, Elsa, was a member as well (KH 432). Kafka remarked how the activities of the last days, of which this evening was one, had given him "some resolution and hope" (DII 13 [T 626]).

LITERATURE AND SOCIAL REALITIES

"The Judgment" and *Arnold Beer*

Between 1898 and 1912 the demand for a "Jewish novel" was the topic of discussion in the leading Jewish journals and papers. Kafka's first major literary work, "The Judgment" (September 1912), written at a time when a great deal of ideological pressure was placed on Jewish authors to write "Jewish" literature, is clearly not a Zionist text. Already discussed was the reception in Zionist circles of Brod's first novel *Die Jüdinnen* (1911) as well as Kafka's parody of the Zionist Hugo Herrmann's dogmatic rejection of Brod's novel. Herrmann's "(ver)Urteil(en)" was a typical stance in contemporary Jewish journalism. Brod, therefore, was only too aware that his second novel, *Arnold Beer,* would be subjected to the same scrutiny. Thus, the very first sentence in his four-page afterword boldly announced that he saw his novel as the continuation of what he began in *Die Jüdinnen.* In order to prevent similar charges being leveled against *Arnold Beer* (that the characters are not likeable or heroic enough, that the book is not Jewish enough) Brod stressed that though he personally did not recognize a clearly identifiable Jewish type (male or female), he nonetheless had tried to create a type that is characteristic of smaller groups of Jews. In future works, Brod promised, he intended to create more and even contradictory character types for still other groups of Jews. It remains to be seen, he continued, if a higher Jewish type might perhaps eventually emerge from this variety or whether this notion would have to be discarded forever. In any event, he believed that his representation of Jewry was already more complex than what was presently available in the existing critical climate (*Arnold Beer,* 172, 173, 175–76).

Arnold Beer is the coming-of-age story of the protagonist, Arnold, a very assimilated young man with artistic inclinations who finds a purpose in life only after he identifies with his Yiddish-speaking grandmother and, through her, with the history of his people. He is not a Zionist yet, but his nationalist feelings are kindled, and at the end of the novel he moves his life in a different direction where he can dedicate himself to a cause. On the train to Berlin to become a journalist, he understands that what he always wanted is "to speak, to write, to be passionate, to be always on the run" (170). In a climactic ending, Arnold identifies with the whole Jewish nation and their struggle against adversity.

We know that Kafka loved Brod's novel. He also acknowledged the influence of *Arnold Beer* on "The Judgment" (DI 276 [T 461]). But unlike Brod, Kafka in his own work never even attempts to conform to current Zionist concerns. Karlheinz Fingerhut has therefore called "The Judgment" an "anti-*Beer*" text, for despite structural and thematic similarities, the endings are entirely opposed to one another: "Instead of throwing himself into the stream of life, like Beer, [Kafka's Georg Bendemann] throws himself into the river and drowns."[25] Fingerhut rightly concludes that in 1912 Kafka was not ready yet to follow Brod and Bergmann in their move toward Zionism (282). He was not willing to compromise his artistic integrity to a contemporary ideology.

To many critics, though, it seems as if Kafka, at least from 1914 on, identified increasingly with Zionism. For instance, he attended editorial meetings for *Selbstwehr* on a regular basis with Max Brod during World War I (Binder, "*Selbstwehr*," 284). But one has to consider here that most of the young Zionists had been drafted.[26] There was no one else left to keep the paper going. *Selbstwehr* also received no financial support during this period. Albrecht Hellmann (later Sigmund Kaznelson [1893–1959], the editor of *Selbstwehr* 1913–18 and husband of Lise Weltsch) recalled many discussions with Max Brod about financing between 1915 and 1917, at which Kafka was frequently present. One of their ideas to obtain more funding was to publish the volume *Das jüdische Prag* (Jewish Prague).[27] Kafka's involvement with *Selbstwehr* during this period is therefore no indication of an increasing commitment to Zionism. His continuing critical distance is revealed in the following two literary texts.

Hans Bloch's "Legende von Theodor Herzl"

Amongst friends and acquaintances, Kafka was known to be sympathetic to the Zionist movement. Thus, Felice's close friend Grete Bloch sent him one of her brother's stories to ask him for his opinion. Kafka was interested because Hans Bloch (1891–1943) was a medical doctor, well known as a Zionist in Berlin, and Max Brod knew him and respected his political engagement (LF 332 [BF 480]).[28] But Kafka was not impressed with his work and criticized it for its Buberlike pathos and expressionistic style (LF 419–20 [BF 594]). Bloch's "Die Legende von Theodor Herzl" (The Legend of Theodor Herzl),[29] which Kafka read in June 1914, represents different periods of Jewish history in allegorical fashion and critically exposes the consequences of the Enlightenment. Bloch depicts the period of Assimilation as the final stage where Jewish culture is almost forgotten. Then suddenly Theodor Herzl appears, who is called by his Hebrew name, Benjamin, and there is renewed hope. Though Herzl, like Moses, is unable to enter the Promised Land, there is hope for the next generation. Bloch's ecstatic, polemical discourse with a distinct Zionist solution was characteristic of many "reports" of life in Palestine, which were printed frequently in *Selbstwehr*.

Kafka disliked this racial discourse in Zionist literature and politics. He associated it with "Geschrei," shouting. He had used the phrase "ewiges Geschrei," permanent shouting, to refer to the speakers at the Zionist Congress (LF 319 [BF 465]). With Bloch, he criticized in particular the "Geschrei" (the "scream") of his expressionistic style, his "effusiveness with mere words": "('life in me began to rebel and let out a piercing cry like that of a mortally wounded beast,' etc.—no, that's no good, or rather it's childish and might mean anything). Undoubtedly he will write better things, or has already" (LF 420 [BF 594]).

What makes Bloch's legend interesting is his use of animal imagery. The Jews are initially represented as pre-Enlightenment Novalis-like cavemen. When they are released from the cave, they rush out like "ravenous beasts with glaring eyes and foaming jowls" (57). Kafka was familiar with the ferocious animal imagery that was frequently employed in Zionist texts to represent life in the Diaspora. Max Brod's Jews in *Arnold Beer* also inherited "that biblical anger with which a people, ravenous beasts from the desert, are pouring themselves over the Jordan" (170), a phrase that impressed some Zionists since it was quoted in *Selbstwehr* (S 3 May 1912:2). Later, we will see how Kafka uses similar animal imagery in "Jackals and

Arabs" (1917) and "A Report to an Academy" (1917) in order to represent Diaspora and acculturated Jews.

Kafka modified his earlier criticism of Bloch's legend on 6 August 1914: "What little there is about the Jewish villagers, for example, gives an impression of truth, but it is a universal Zionist yearning [*allgemeine zionistische Sehnsucht*], and in this first slight attempt within reach of all who have joined the ranks. Nevertheless, I do appreciate what there is" (LF 421 [BF 595–96]). Though he distances himself from those "who have joined the ranks," he also admits that he, too, understands the "universal Zionist yearning." This statement well sums up the ambivalent feeling Kafka had for Zionism at this time. Only a few days later, he described himself again as someone who is "excluded from every great soul-sustaining community on account of his non-Zionist (I admire Zionism and am nauseated by it), nonpracticing Judaism" (LF 423 [BF 598]).

In September 1915 Kafka's own legend, "Before the Law," was published in the Rosh Hashana issue of *Selbstwehr* (S 7 Sept. 1915:2–3). This legend not only avoids literary expressionism but also the "dryness of [Bloch's] entire allegory, which is nothing but an allegory, which says all there is to say without ever delving deeper or drawing one deeper into it" (LF 421 [BF 596]). Kafka clearly felt that Bloch was "limited by the allegory" (LF 421 [BF 596]).

Blumfeld's Blue-White Nightmare

"Before the Law" was Kafka's first literary piece in the Zionist newspaper *Selbstwehr*, and it did not take long before his name appeared more frequently in Zionist publications. However, Kafka was still skeptical of Zionism. Earlier in the year he had caricatured Zionist tenacity in the bachelor story "Blumfeld, an Elderly Bachelor" (February–March/April 1915). The most immediate association with the name "Blumfeld" would be the Zionist leader Kurt Blumenfeld, whom Kafka knew personally. The reference to Zionism is explicit in Blumfeld's companions, the "two small white celluloid balls with blue stripes" (CS 185 [E 221]). Critics have never identified the significance of the blue-white balls,[30] but blue-white, the colors of the Jewish flag, were specifically Zionist colors, and Blau-Weiss was also the name of the first Zionist youth movement in Germany (1912–29), whose principal leaders were Kurt Blumenfeld and Felix Rosenblüth.

Kafka himself said of the "Blumfeld" story that "in spite of all its truth it is wicked, pedantic, mechanical" (DII 114–15 [T 726]). Though the real

Blumenfeld was only thirty-one years old in 1915, Blumfeld in the story is a self-important, German[31] man who is getting on in years. He works in a linen factory, has nothing meaningful in his life, and desires company. Getting a dog might be a solution, but he thinks this is too much trouble and decides he wants an animal that shows the same kind of loyalty to its owner as a dog but does not need so much care, "an animal . . . which nevertheless, when Blumfeld feels like it, is promptly at his disposal with its barking, jumping, and licking of hands" (CS 184 [E 221]). When the blue-white balls become his companions instead, is the "barking, jumping, and licking of hands" an ironic description of the relationship between the nervous and immature Zionist youth groups and their leader? One evening when Blumfeld returns home from work, the blue-white balls are suddenly there, and they really do not give him one free minute: they are always on call, hounding him, ready to serve him whenever he makes the slightest move.

In June 1914 Kafka had characterized Bloch's "Legend of Theodor Herzl" as "a childish piece of work" (LF 420 [BF 594]), and almost two years earlier (September 1912) he had described the Palestine travelers who gathered at his home as a little immature in their romanticism (DI 272 [T 437]). Moreover, the way these tenacious blue-white balls bother Blumfeld wherever he goes is reminiscent of the obstinate Zionist student in February 1913 ("how many similar invitations has he not wasted on me in the course of the years!"). Within this context, Clayton Koelb's insightful point about the homonym "Bellen-Bällen" (balls-barking)[32] (which is the associative link in German between the dogs and the balls) suggests that Kafka is satirizing the excited political "barking" of the blue-white young balls (read: Zionist youth). By transforming the dog metaphor into the bouncy hyper blue-white balls, Kafka quickly makes Blumfeld's life hell and drives him to distraction.

In fact, Blumfeld's exasperation with the blue-white balls is almost prophetic. After *Selbstwehr* published Kafka's "Before the Law" (7 Sept. 1915), only a few months later the newspaper hailed his literary achievements when he received the Fontane Prize with blatant Zionist rhetoric: "Our contributor and political supporter [*Gesinnungsgenosse*] Dr. Franz Kafka, Prague, received the Fontane Prize from Carl Sternheim, on whom it had originally been bestowed" (S 10 Dec. 1915:7). Kafka's name also appeared in *Der Jude* "in an advertizement that 'Selbstwehr' had placed there, which names him as one of the staff members for 1916" (Binder, "*Selbstwehr*," 288–89). While this indicates that his name had become increasingly known in Zionist circles in Prague and beyond, it is doubtful that Kafka saw himself as a "political supporter," given his ironic distance.

To be sure, he was much more positive about Zionism than Karl Kraus; but there is a great deal of truth in Kraus's ironic statement: "The power of the Zionist promise is so compelling, that even he, who would like to distance himself, can shortly see his name in a printed list of party members" ("Krone," 299–300). After donating one schekel for Palestine, Kraus was exasperated "because the campaign officer constantly addresses me with 'my honorable, venerable political comrade [Gesinnungsgenosse],' afterwards waves to me with a friendly Zion greeting and only leaves out the usual postscript of 'Next Year in Jerusalem.' I had barely begun to see myself as a political supporter [Gesinnungsgenosse], when I ... recognized my name on the list of delegates for the Zionist congress, who had been recommended amongst numerous stockmarket visitors and other martyrs to the cause. What could possibly be next?" ("Krone," 300).

One could argue that Kafka's estrangement from Brod, which supposedly ended in December 1913, found literary expression in "Blumfeld" as well, because Blumfeld eventually overcomes his nightmare and takes control. His elaborately planned escape routes are depicted with irony, but he finally succeeds in imprisoning the balls in the wardrobe and escapes from them into fresh air. Moreover, after he arranges to pass the inherited balls on to some children in his building, the balls are never mentioned again but reappear in very different form as the story continues. In the second part of the story, Blumfeld seems to have transferred his nightmarish anxiety onto his assistants at work. Significantly, the word "childish," which is repeated over and over again, is now applied to Blumfeld's two assistants in his office who, like the balls before them, complicate his life and are said to have been a constant source of frustration and obsession for him. In hindsight it seems as if these assistants were the source of his frustration all along and Blumfeld's previous obsession with the blue-white balls only symptomatic of his frustration at work.

After the Zionist Congress Kafka softened his previous critical remarks by adding that his negative impression was partially due to the fact that he had also felt "cramped and distracted by many other things" (LFF 100 [Br 120]; translation modified). In this story, too, the narrator modifies his judgment. At first Blumfeld wants to "destroy the balls, and that in the near future, but not just yet, probably not until tomorrow" (CS 188 [E 225]). However, in the very next sentence this condemnatory verdict is already transformed into its opposite, revealing Blumfeld's ambiguous response to them: "If one looks at the whole thing with an unprejudiced eye, the balls behave modestly enough" (CS 188 [E 225]). The transformation of the two balls into the annoying assistants at Blumfeld's work is a transference, a sidestepping of the real issue, for once again Blumfeld (as with the balls before) needs to find a vent for his frustration and destroy his assistants; yet, again he cannot do it, since "they were after all only children, and Blumfeld could not very well knock children down" (CS 201 [E 241]). We can conclude that if the problem is not the distraction at work or the balls themselves, then the caricature of the tenacious, self-confident blue-white balls and their pedantic, self-centered, and humorless master, Blumfeld, reveals that the problem is Kafka himself, as well as Zionism and the empowerment that the ideology gives its members.

4

Forms of Cultural Renewal

(1912–1917)

Jiři Langer and Religious Revival

Kafka's and Brod's friend Jiři (Georg) Langer (1894–1943), brother of the playwright František Langer, came from a Czech Jewish family. His brother remembers him being drawn to mysticism and "poring over borrowed Hebrew folios" at the age of fifteen.[1] Jiři became so obsessed with reading the old books that he dropped out of school to devote himself entirely to Jewish Scripture, which his brother, a medical doctor, diagnosed as a case of "belated adolescent psychopathy" (*Nine Gates*, xiv). In 1913, Jiři went to Galicia to live with the Hasidim. After a few months with the Belzer Rebbe, he returned to Prague because he could "endure it no longer. This life of isolation from the rest of the world is intolerable. I feel disgusted with this puritanism, this ignorance, this backwardness and dirt. I escape. I travel back to my parents in Prague" (*Nine Gates*, 12).

Langer's stay at home created much turmoil; he returned "wearing ear-locks and a kaftan, to his family's horror, and carried his obedience to Hasidic customs so far that he refused to look any woman, even his mother, in the face" (Robertson, *Judaism*, 176).[2] He saw only a select circle of friends, was reading cabalistic literature, and otherwise kept aloof from the world. When he had a vision of the rabbi of Belz in the kitchen, beckoning him to return to Belz, he packed his bags again (*Nine Gates*, xviii).

Jiři lived with his rabbi for another few months until WWI broke out and they had to flee to Hungary. When he was informed he had to join the army, he returned to Prague and got drafted. But he did not last long in the military: in 1915 he was jailed in an army prison "for refusing to handle a rifle or work on the Sabbath" (Oppenheimer 297). Through the intervention of his brother, now a doctor with the army, he was diagnosed a "mental case" and released from his duties. Jiří never gave his brother any credit for his help but "was convinced that the rabbi of Belz had performed a miracle and delivered him from military service" (*Nine Gates*, xix, 21).

Kafka and Langer may have met for the first time at Max Brod's lecture, "Religion and Nation," in March 1915 (DII 119 [T 733]), put on by the Zionist Jüdischer Volksverein (Jewish People's Club).³ Brod had befriended Langer already (PK 182–83) and accompanied him several times to a wonder rabbi, the rabbi of Grodek, who had fled from Galicia and was now living in a suburb of Prague (FK 153). On another such occasion, in September 1915, Kafka came along (FK 153; DII 128–29 [T 751–52]), and in the following month he recorded "Langer's stories" (anecdotes about the Baal Shem Tov) in his diary (DII 138–40 [T 766–68]).

Jiří Langer was an excellent source of information about Hasidic life and folklore. Perhaps Kafka even heard from him about two central books for the Hasidim, which Langer said he carried with him everywhere. One of these was *Reshit Chochmah* (The Beginning of Wisdom), which was recommended to Langer by the rabbi of Belz himself, "a cabbalistic book of exercises for the ascetic. It inculcates humility and self-denial and . . . is the work of a famous cabbalist named Elija de Vidas who lived in Palestine at the end of the seventeenth century" (*Nine Gates*, 16–17). The other book was recommended by his fellow Hasidim, "'The Joys of Elimelech' (Noam Elimelech) by the 'Rebe Reb' Melech of Lizensk (Elimelech)" (*Nine Gates*, 17). Langer's own work, *Nine Gates to the Chassidic Mysteries*, was published much later (1937). This lively, funny, and provocative book is filled with Jewish lore. Langer tells one anecdote after another. Kafka may very well have been familiar with some of the stories recounted in it.

Langer was witty and outrageous in many respects. In late December 1916, Kafka recorded the following anecdote in his diary:

> With Langer: He will only be able to read Max's book thirteen days from now. He could have read it Christmas Day—according to an old custom you are not allowed to read Torah on Christmas (one rabbi made a practice of cutting up his year's supply of toilet paper on that evening), but this year Christmas fell on Saturday. In thirteen days, however, the Russian Christmas will be here, he'll read it then [*da wird er lesen*]. According to

a medieval tradition you may take an interest in belles lettres and other worldly knowledge only after your seventieth year, according to a more liberal view only after your fortieth year. Medicine was the only science in which you were allowed to take an interest. Today not even in that, since it is now too closely joined with the other sciences.—You are not allowed to think of the Torah on the toilet, and for this reason you may read worldly books there. A very pious man in Prague, a certain Kornfeld, knew a great deal of the worldly sciences, he had studied them all on the toilet. (DII 145 [T 776–77]; translation modified)

There is no way of knowing how Langer told these stories. The phrase "da wird er lesen" is Yiddish syntax and suggests that Langer may have recounted this anecdote in a mix of German and Yiddish.

At some point, Langer went to live with the Belzer rabbi again. In July 1916, Kafka visited him in the company of the rabbi in Marienbad and went on at least two evening walks with them (LF 475 [BF 666]; LFF 123 [Br 146]). He was especially fascinated by the openly displayed homosexuality of two Jews who "walk along like a pair of lovers, looking affectionately at one another and smiling, one with his hand thrust into his low-slung back pocket, the other looking more citified. Firmly locked arm in arm" (LFF 121 [Br 143]). What Jiří's brother never mentions is that Jiří himself was gay (Oppenheimer 300).

Langer was back in Prague in November 1917 looking for employment. Brod suggested that Kafka might perhaps support him for a position in his insurance company and assured him that Langer was desperate and would even shave off his beard (BKB 193). Still, Kafka said he could not put in a word for Langer: "The Institute is closed to Jews. . . . There is no explaining how two Jews, with the help of the third Jew, got in, and it won't happen again" (LFF 165 [Br 194]). Kafka knew full well that Langer would ask to be dispensed from work on Saturdays. However, he mischievously considered imposing Langer on his father and wanted to propose at home that he be given a job in his father's store. Not having found employment, Langer likely returned to his rabbi and lived in the East until the war was over. Some time after his return to Prague, he underwent a complete transformation. He shaved off his beard and from then on never looked like a Hasid again, nor did he ever go back East (*Nine Gates*, xx). Jiří Langer now turned to studying the writings of Sigmund Freud and applying them to Jewish ritual and Kabbala mysticism.

Kafka and Religious Revival

Unlike Buber or Langer, Kafka showed little interest in religious revivalism. However, he did become interested in Jewish religion through his contact with the Yiddish actors. In November 1911, Kafka recounted the following "Orthodox practice" of the *eruv*: "As a result of bribery the telephone and telegraph wires around Warsaw were put up in a complete [*vollkommenen*] circle, which in the sense of the Talmud makes the city a bounded area, a courtyard, as it were, so that on Saturday it is possible even for the most pious person to move about, carry trifles (like handkerchiefs) on his person, within this circle" (DI 166 [T 276]). Robertson takes this passage quite seriously and sees it as testifying to Kafka's knowledge of Orthodox Judaism (*Judaism*, 174). Yet, as much as this account conforms with religious practice, for an acculturated person it might sound rather incredible that all of Warsaw can be reduced to a medieval *Hof*, courtyard, and that it is dishonest "bribery" that enables the formation of this "perfect circle"—Kafka's juxtapositions and his choice of vocabulary suggest irony. According to religious law, the pious could indeed not even carry a handkerchief outside of the circle.

The anecdote originated with the actor Löwy, who had firsthand knowledge of Orthodox practice, since he came from a "well-off hasidic family in Warsaw" and grew up in a large hasidic community (Massino, *Fuoco*, 52–53). Unlike Langer, who was fascinated by Hasidic revivalism and wanted to be a Hasid, Löwy wanted to escape from this fate. In his autobiography (as Kafka copied it down), he recounts that he ran away at around the age of fourteen "when the constraint of life at home became unbearable for him" and traveled to a famous Yeshivah in Ostro, a "small place eight hours by train from Warsaw." Löwy turns it into a funny, dramatic story (DI 218–19 [T 354]). The irony in the end is that he did not even last longer than ten days in the yeshiva, and he never stayed there either but at an inn, because the conditions were intolerable. He quickly became so homesick that he returned to his family, to the orderly life he knew (DI 220 [T 356]). Coming from Löwy, is it likely that the previous anecdote about the "Orthodox practice" could have been meant seriously, or was he trying to impress Kafka and included the handkerchiefs to make him incredulous? Kafka himself liked that Löwy was "a man of continuous enthusiasm . . . a 'hot Jew'" (LF 29 [BF 77]) and a born storyteller: when he talks "his fire is infectious" (LF 267 [BF 396]).

Equally tongue-in-cheek is the anecdote about the "eighteen-minute matzos," which Löwy recounted to Kafka: "Pesach festival. An association of rich Jews rents a bakery, its members take over for the heads of the families all the tasks of producing the so-called eighteen-minute matzos: the fetching of water, the koshering, the kneading, the cutting, the piercing" (DI 132 [T 225]). The way this story is told (Kafka retelling Löwy) makes it sound as if these were the first "fast food," assembly line matzos, and creates a visual image reminiscent of a scene in a Chaplin film. Traditional kosher Passover matzos are indeed prepared in this timed fashion, with everyone rushing to get the dough ready before the eighteen minutes are over, because after that the dough becomes leavened. Moreover, in a Hasidic community the number eighteen has special significance: it stands for *chai*, life.

Another story that originated with Löwy is the following: "On Friday evening two angels accompany each pious man from the synagogue to his home; the master of the house stands while he greets them in the dining room; they stay only a short time" (DI 166 [T 276]). Here Kafka combines the greeting of the Sabbath angels at the beginning of the Sabbath with the folklore belief that each pious man receives an additional soul on the Sabbath and thus returns home with "two angels." Kafka cared little about religious practices, but he loved these anecdotes and all such creative storytelling.

Kafka would also attend religious services with friends, as in May 1915 when he went to a prayer service with Jewish refugees (DII 128 [T 745]). Yet, unlike Brod, who became fascinated by the religious revival around him ("Unusual circumstances of life had brought me near to a kind of religious fanaticism" [FK 153]), Kafka remained distanced. His response to the wonder rabbi of Grodek (DII 128-29 [T 751-52]) reveals only too clearly that the surrounding religiosity left him cold. After participating in a "'Third Meal' at the close of the Sabbath," Kafka commented, "If you look at it properly, it was just as if we had been among a tribe of African savages. Sheerest superstition" (FK 153). A year later, too, his response to Langer and the Hasidim in Marienbad is typically ironic (LFF 119-23 [Br 141-46]). Scholars have interpreted Kafka's humorous description in a serious fashion[4]; however, Kafka states his lack of belief: "Langer tries to find or thinks he finds a deeper meaning in all this; I think that the deeper meaning is that there is none and in my opinion this is quite enough" (LFF 122 [Br 145]). He also firmly acknowledges that the authority of the rabbi of Belzer is "absolutely a case of divine right, without the absurdity [*Lächerlichkeit*] that an inadequate basis would give to it" (LFF 122 [Br 145]); it is "a case of divine right" for those who believe, while those who lack the "inadequate basis"—like himself—might easily find the rabbi funny or absurd, *lächerlich*.

Yet Kafka enjoyed this visit with the Hasidim. We can see this in the humorously ironic description of the rabbi's intense interest in pipes for the steam bath—"[he] cannot take his eyes off the pipes, concerning which various opinions and counteropinions are exchanged" (LFF 123 [Br 145]) or in Kafka's account of the rabbi's admiration for eaves-troughs (LFF 123 [Br 146]). For someone from a big city, the rabbi's intense interest in these eaves-troughs may be funny; however, for someone from a small town in Eastern Europe, this was a novelty. In a letter to Felix Weltsch, Kafka was enthusiastic about the rabbi: "He alone would justify the trip from Karlsbad to Marienbad" (LFF 123–24 [Br 146]), and he had respect for this man who was "no doubt at present the chief representative of Hasidism" (LF 475 [BF 666]).

In contrast to Kafka, Langer was filled with reverence: "Although he is seriously ill, he talks cheerfully to everybody. We are conscious that his are no ordinary words even when he is talking about things which appear to be everyday matters. All his words, however small, are to be understood metaphorically. The whole time his thoughts are concentrated exclusively on supernatural matters" (*Nine Gates,* 20). Though not making light of Langer's devotion, or of the rabbi himself, Kafka's description nonetheless shows his amusement. In the Hasidic tales by Chajim Bloch, which Kafka greatly enjoyed, there are several anecdotes in which East meets West. One in particular illustrates a similarly humorous response to a rabbi:

"Bom, bom" [Candy]

Deeply absorbed in pious thoughts, he used to mutter to himself the words "bom, bom." A worldly child (Weltkind), who had come for advice in a private matter, could not help laughing when he heard the odd words "bom, bom" from the mouth of the rabbi. Then the Ruzhiner asked him: "Why are you laughing?" The visitor replied without any embarrassment: "Because the rabbi is saying 'bom, bom.'" The Ruzhiner addressed him again: "But do we not say and do we not repeat every day in the Shma prayer: 'Wedibartu bom?'" When the worldly child returned to the rabbi some time later, he was muttering "bom, bom." The rabbi turned to the visitor and asked what this meant and the worldly child replied: "Did the rabbi not tell me a while ago that this was written in the Holy Scripture?" The

Ruzhiner answered: "Yes, yes, but there are two 'bom.' For it is written, 'Zadikim jelchu bom' (the just are walking along these paths) 'posschim jikoschlie bom' (the transgressors are stumbling on these paths). And for that reason," the rabbi ended, "you too may say 'bom.'"[5]

A rabbi who says "bom, bom" is funny because the homonym in German, as in English, is "Bonbon," a candy. For an acculturated Jew like Kafka or the *Weltkind*, this would be the most immediate association. Kafka said of these tales that they were "the only Jewish literature in which I immediately and always feel at home" (LFF 147 [Br 172–73]). A playful attitude toward the religious tradition was typical of many Western Jews. Max Brod, for instance, remembers that the children in his family burst out laughing during the Passover seder whenever the word *bimhero* (soon) came up, because it sounded like "bim," the sound of a bell. The "syllable 'bim' was uttered as sharply as possible to imitate the sound of a bell. And whoever could produce the best effect was praised. After all, the word came up all too many times, it seemed to us as if it challenged us to caricature it" (SL 223).

A few months later, in October 1916, neither Kafka nor his family had sent a card to Felice Bauer's family for Rosh Hashanah. Kafka's mother was embarrassed when she received a card from Felice and replied, "We observed the Jewish holidays like good Jews. Over the New Year our business was closed for the 2 days, and yesterday, the Day of Atonement, we fasted and prayed a great deal" (LF 518 [BF 721]). Grözinger takes her remarks literally without contextualizing them and highlights Kafka's family's observance of religious holidays and their significance for him.[6] However, given her son's aloofness in religious matters, is it not likely that she was trying to reassure Felice that the family was indeed observing the holidays? As a matter of fact, Kafka knew Felice's mother had expected a card, but he had not sent one and insists, "I still would not have sent her New Year greetings.—Dearest, accept me as I am" (LF 520 [BF 723]). Generally, for Kafka as well as for many of his contemporaries, being Jewish was more "an ideological or racial category—not necessarily a religious one."[7]

Rewriting Myths and Legends

Talmudic Discourse and Midrash for Storytelling

Kafka found Talmudic discourse fascinating. In 1911 he remembered arguing "the existence of God with [Hugo] Bergmann in a talmudic style either my own or imitated from him" (DI 205 [T 333]). And in 1922 he proposed to Brod, "Call in a talmudist to give us a commentary on that!" (LFF 344 [Br 397]). This interest also shows in the books Kafka acquired and/or read,[8] and many readers have commented on this interest as well. The Canadian poet and novelist A. M. Klein perceptively referred to Kafka as "a sort of latter-day Maimonides" whose "entire opus is the *Song of Perplexity* itself."[9] And Jean Starobinski has described Kafka's "talent for argumentation and refined casuistry" especially well: "an idea ingeniously turned on all sides, a hypothesis open to all possibilities, the ever-vigilant objections, which you find in the disputations of the rabbis. In addition, the parable-like nature of Kafka's narratives recalls that concrete instantiation dear to the talmudists."[10] Significantly, in 1914, when Kafka was writing *The Trial*, he explicitly referred to his commentaries in "Before the Law" as "exegesis of the 'Legend'" (DII 101 [T 707]). Kafka's interest in rabbinic commentaries is also suggested by his attendance at the lecture noted in his diary in November 1915: "In the Altneu Synagogue at the Mischnah lecture. Home with Dr. Jeiteles. Greatly interested in certain controversial issues" (DII 143–44 [T 774]). The person he accompanied home was, in fact, the speaker.

Kafka was also well aware of the striking Midrashic narrative feature of continual narrative transformation. He may have found Buber's "drastic adaptation[s]" of the Hasidic tales "intolerable" (LF 164 [BF 260]), but Buber's "method" was no different from that of other writers engaged in retelling these stories. Chajim Bloch worried even less than Buber about authorship and authenticity. Bloch published tales about the Prague Golem (the man made of clay by Prague's Rabbi Loew in the sixteenth century), which were unacknowledged appropriations of Rabbi Yudl Rosenberg's tales.[11] As for Rabbi Rosenberg (the grandfather of Canadian novelist Mordecai Richler), his so-called original was fabricated, too, though he claims it was a precious, rare document written by Rabbi Loew's son-in-law. In the long run it matters little whether "Rosenberg was a literary forger and Bloch a plagiarist. . . . Both men gave shape, form, and continuity to legends that had a long oral tradition in Eastern Europe and had just begun to appear in print in the last half of the nineteenth century."[12] What is more important here is Bloch's conscious choice of translating into a very different style from Buber: he aimed at reproducing "the simple and often childishly awkward diction of the unknown author" (*Golem*, 14). Kafka certainly loved Bloch's tales: "The hasidic stories in *Jüdische Echo* may not be of the best, but for some reason I don't understand, all these stories are the only Jewish literature in which I immediately and always feel at home, quite apart from my own state of mind" (LFF 147 [Br 172–73]).[13] Little did he know that they were consciously composed in this very simple, naïve, and almost childlike language to market them. The Yiddish-sounding style, which Bloch tried to reproduce, was the opposite of Buber's mystical rhetoric.

Alexander Eliasberg's *Sagen polnischer Juden* (Tales of Polish Jews), which Kafka owned, was equally simple in style. His legends are taken from "yiddish books of devotion," especially from the "tremendously popular collection "K'hal Chassidim," as well as from monographs written about some of the Zaddikim and Zaddikim dynasties. Eliasberg makes a point of stressing that "virtually the entire translation is literally accurate."[14] Even Buber's style underwent a change years later. While in the early versions Buber "often uproots the narrative from the realm of the literal and down-to-earth and transplants it into a mystical realm,"[15] in 1916 already Max Brod commends Buber on the change in his more recent versions, "which seem to me much better, as a matter of fact more Jewish than the earlier stories, shorter, less pathetic, more talmudic as it were."[16] Incidentally, the same tales Kafka read in *Das Jüdische Echo* were later retold by Buber in his 1922 collection *Der grosse Maggid und seine Nachfolge* (The Great Maggid and His Successors).[17] Buber's versions here are less effusive and inventive than in his earlier renderings, and Kafka enjoyed them and took notes (DII 229, 230 [T 919, 922]). When Buber's rhetoric changed, Kafka's appreciation of his work changed accordingly.

The most important work for folklore, Talmudic style, and narrative transformations that Kafka owned was the 1913 edition of Micha Josef bin Gorion's (M. J. Berdyczewski) *Die Sagen der Juden* (The Legends of the Jews). Kafka had heard excerpts from it at the Buber-Eysoldt evening in January 1913. The legends in this volume are taken from Midrashic-Talmudic commentaries on the first nine books of *Genesis,* and bin Gorion describes his collection as "a new type of legendary midrash" (*Sagen,* xiii). The rabbinic term for "legends" is aggadah, and Midrash refers to the function these tales have within the rabbinic framework, the explication of Scripture, "to fill in the holes in Scripture through fantasy and legend, explication [*Auslegung*] and interpretation [*Deutung*]."[18]

Bin Gorion's collection vividly illustrates the creative, anecdotal side of rabbinic interpretation: "the motifs repeat themselves innumerable times and are varied; of each individual item we have the most dissimilar versions. Some differences are of a significant nature—the stories are virtually rewritten—, some differences are only minor, yet one version explains the next, and one complements the other" (xiii). Kafka also owned the first volume of bin Gorion's *Der Born Judas: Legenden, Märchen, Erzählungen* (1916) (The Well of Juda: Legends, Fairy Tales, Stories), which begins with the post-Talmudic period and ends with Hasidism. The original sources are again the Talmud and Midrash, and "the legends are kept in their short talmudic style."[19] This volume also contains texts that reveal the influence of the host culture: Greek Alexander legends as well as Indian wisdom literature. Here non-Jewish material is Judaized and placed, in a formal way, within a Jewish narrative context. Many versions are arranged according to motifs, under the heading of specific biblical and folk themes (*Sagen,* xiv).

Bin Gorion's work, then, introduced Kafka to the basic Midrashic narrative principle, which is one of continual narrative transformation: a constant metamorphosis of traditional motifs or historical and biblical content, including the appropriation of non-Jewish material within a distinctly Jewish discursive framework. Kafka's fondness for rewriting legends is evident in a comment to Max Brod of 1917: "and I would tell the Talmud story differently [Tractate Sukkah 52a]" (LFF 175 , 459n.131 [Br 206]), upon which he immediately proceeds to give his own short version. Scholars have discussed myths and legends in his *Country Doctor* collection (1917–19), his Midrashic retelling of the "Abraham" story (1921) (LFF 285–86 [Br 333–34]), as well as his transformation of the kabbalistic "divine kiss" in "A Hunger Artist" (1922).[20] Kafka frequently appropriated and rewrote motifs from the Jewish narrative tradition.

FOLKLORE AND MIDRASH IN KAFKA: TALES OF VERMIN AND DOORKEEPERS, OF GOLEMS AND SILENT SIRENS

Folklore and Folksong in *The Metamorphosis*

Kafka knew the metamorphosis motif from modern Yiddish fiction, which tends to treat metamorphoses humorously. In Kafka studies, however, the question of humor tends to be avoided.[21] After World War II, it is understandable that scholars would not readily regard the transformation of a human being into vermin as funny. George Steiner therefore argues that Kafka "saw, to the point of exact detail, the horror gathering.... Gregor Samsa's metamorphosis... was to be the literal fate of millions of human beings. The very word for vermin, *Ungeziefer,* is a stroke of tragic clairvoyance; so the Nazis were to designate the gassed."[22] By implication, however, a great deal of the humor in Yiddish literature would be lost if seen from only a post-Holocaust perspective.

In a nineteenth-century Yiddish story by A. B. Gotlober (1811–99), in which a man undergoes transformations from horse to fish, donkey, leech, dog, and pig, the protagonist is at one point transformed into a Hasidic singer who, at the moment of highest religious ecstasy, is so saturated with alcohol that he provokes a spontaneous combustion. Asked by the Angel of the Dead about his name, he replies, "Dead drunk, burnt to a crisp—how was I supposed to remember? ... He even wanted to get to work and whip me a bit, which is what he normally does to a corpse that can't tell him its name. But what can you whip if everything's burnt up? How could he whip a heap of cinders? The hell with it! He didn't fool around with me for long, he promptly told me my judgment ... and—*poof!* I was a horse!!"[23] After the Holocaust, readers may not find this funny, and Gregor's metamorphosis admittedly creates a similar problem. Yet, while stressing that "it is unlikely that many of Kafka's readers since the war have been able to detect the playful element in any of his death scenes," Stanley Corngold, for one, detects an "element of play" in the recurring motifs of "deaths and survivals" in Kafka's work.[24] Certainly, death and humor can be interrelated if the link is seen as an attempt to face the unimaginable and not succumb to despair or be driven into madness.

In *The Metamorphosis,* the mood at the outset is not one of terror; nor does Gregor view himself as a horrible monster. Having accepted the "reality" of his metamorphosis, he tries to picture an encounter between himself and his family and cannot "suppress a smile at the very idea of it" (CS 94 [E 103]). The humor in part derives from Gregor's split personality, which is in play when Gregor the human being, who has kept his reason, observes but is unable to control Gregor the vermin, who reacts instinctively. Gregor's attempt to hold back the chief clerk starts up a chain of comic reactions that begins to suggest a Chaplinesque tragicomedy[25]: it is both comic and tragic that he feels so sorry for his mother, and yet he cannot control his instinctive reactions. The sight of Gregor makes the mother first jump up into the air and then sit on the table and knock over the coffee. This in turn leads Gregor to "snap his jaws together several times" (CS 103 [E 114]; translation modified), which makes his mother faint. The climax is reached when the chief clerk jumps down the stairs. The importance of gesture and sound in this comic situation has a strong theatrical effect and quite possibly goes back to Kafka's experience of the Yiddish theater, since Chaplin's films came to Europe only in 1920.

In fact, one could argue that there is even a specific echo of the Yiddish theater, of Goldfaden's operetta *Shulamith*,[26] which featured the famous folk song "Roshinkes mit Mandlen" (Raisins and Almonds, 1880). After his metamorphosis, Gregor is offered raisins and almonds but rejects them along with other food (CS 108 [E 120]). He seems to be declining the "comfort food" of the Yiddish theater, yet the operetta itself was not very nostalgic and the folk song not placed in a romantic setting. The story of the original folk song goes as follows. "Roshinkes mit Mandlen" was a lullaby, which tells of a little white goat that goes to the market trading in raisins and almonds, and the prophesy that this will be the profession of a little baby in a cradle as well (*"Dos zigele is geforn handlen, dos vet sein dein baruf"* [The little goat has gone off to trade, this will be your profession]). The white goat is "the embodiment of Israel" and "kin to the kid in the final seder song, 'Had Gadya.'"[27] In the lullaby, "Mandeln" rhymes with "Handeln," a simple and obvious association—"Mandel" is also a common Jewish name, "Handel" a common Jewish trade—and Gregor Samsa just happens to be a *"Handelsreisender,"* a traveling salesman.

However, when we compare this original lullaby with the context in which the song appears in *Shulamith*, we see that Goldfaden introduced significant changes. In the operetta there is no mother who sings the lullaby. It was sung by a Jewish warrior-hero, Abisalom, in a militant setting in the desert when the hero longingly remembers his childhood.[28] Goldfaden was "an ardent Zionist" (Caplan 196) and had modified not only the context but also the lyrics of the original lullaby to raise national consciousness. With each subsequent stanza, the Jews are prophesied more wealth and power. This *yingele* will not just trade in raisins and almonds (and become a great Torah scholar), but he will get rich and see the world and become a wealthy banker at the stock market. In fact, the Russian government had shut down the Yiddish theater in 1883 because of operettas like *Shulamith* and *Bar Kochba,* for it feared the strong nationalism in these plays would cause unrest in the Jewish population (Caplan 198); Kafka knew this from Pinès (DI 227 [T 366]).

Though it will never be known if the entire song was sung by the actors in 1911, in today's available version, the phrase about getting very rich through trading is present, while the banker and stock market part are left out. To be sure, for Goldfaden, within his immediate historical circumstances (the extreme poverty and political powerlessness of Russian Jews, their lack of education and lack of a trade), the message was meant to be uplifting: his song prophesied a great future for the poor Jews of Russia.

Perhaps "it was his intention . . . to connect Israel with the promise of the Haskalah" (Caplan 198). Yet Kafka may have found this "future promise"—the way it comes across in the operetta—not very inspiring.

Before his metamorphosis, Gregor Samsa was already a dissatisfied and exhausted traveling salesman. The militant and capitalist context of "Roshinkes mit Mandlen" in *Shulamith* alone is a good reason for him to reject the "raisins and almonds." Gregor is a victim of capitalism and can barely pay off his parents' debts. Moreover, as Marvin Caplan remarks, "it is hard to imagine a song whose words are more likely to offend contemporary Jewish sensibilities than that beloved and quintessential Yiddish lullaby, 'Rozhinkes mit Mandlen,'" and he states that Goldfaden "chose to rework the lullaby into a prediction of great material success for his 'Yidele (little Jew)'; so much so, that his song comes uncomfortably close to suggesting the classic anti-Semitic notion of a world in the grip of powerful Jewish financiers" (193, 195). Perhaps it came across as equally disturbing to some contemporaries in Kafka's time. If the raisins and almonds in *The Metamorphosis* indeed allude to the operetta and the song, it is important to realize Kafka's irony here when he makes Gregor reject the "promising future" that was predicted by the song.

One could postulate that *The Metamorphosis* is an anti-*Shulamith* story similar to "The Judgment," which is arguably an anti-*Arnold Beer* story (reversing the optimistic, Zionist conclusion that could be drawn from Brod's novel). Thus, instead of turning into a warrior-hero in shining armor, Gregor becomes a vermin in armor ("his hard, as it were armor-plated, back" [CS 89; E 96]) who rocks himself like a baby in the cradle, returning him to the original lullaby. Ironically, Gregor once "used to be" a military officer; there is a picture of him "as a lieutenant, hand on sword, a carefree smile on his face, inviting one to respect his uniform and military bearing" (CS 101 [E 111]). But those days are over when he becomes a less impressive little *Handelsreisender*, trying to support his family, with no life of his own. The next and last stage in his life shows him transformed into vermin. In fact, both "The Judgment" and *The Metamorphosis* reverse the sequence of events: whereas *Shulamith* promises a metamorphosis from poor to rich and a heroic future, *The Metamorphosis* depicts the opposite as Gregor metamorphoses into one of the lowest forms of existence and an anti-Semitic stereotype.

Rejecting Goldfaden's Zionist message, Kafka turned to the stories in Pinès for inspiration. In Jewish folklore, metamorphosis expresses "the reality of Exile."[29] In Mendele's novel *The Mare* (discussed by Pinès especially in its relation to the experience of exile), a Wandering Mare states that she has been in this peculiar shape "as long as the Jewish Exile!"[30] The result of the specific historical exile is a more general, personal, "inner" exile, and thus transformations are also "a symbol for the exile of the soul" (Scholem, *Major Trends*, 281). There are different degrees of "inner" exile, because "banishment into the prison of strange forms of existence, into wild beasts, into plants and stones, is regarded as a particularly dreadful form of exile" (*Major Trends*, 282). This description allows us to see many of the animals in Kafka's stories—ranging from vermin to apes, jackals, the marten-like creature in the synagogue, dogs and mice, even the peculiar Odradek—as signifying different degrees of exile. In Jewish mysticism any transformation is also regarded as "part of the process of restoration, of *Tikkun*" (*Major Trends*, 283). In fact, the sole purpose of metamorphosis is "the purification of the soul and the opportunity, in a new trial, to improve its deeds" (*Encyclopaedia Judaica*, 7:575). The use of the word "trial" is significant here, in that it characterizes the process of striving for redemption that is initiated by the metamorphosis. ("Process" is also one of the meanings of the title of Kafka's novel *Der Proceß* [*The Trial*]!). The concept of ever-renewed trials for penitents constitutes a topos in Hasidic folklore.

Another recurring motif is the mystic longing for redemption. Atonement can be reached only by going through the ritual stages of punishment, including exile—according to the principle, "descent for the sake of ascent."[31] The concept of "turning" is crucial for redemption. Walter Benjamin comments on its importance for Kafka, whose "messianic category is that of the 'turning' [*Umkehr*] or the 'studying.'"[32] In Part 1 we see Gregor dancing around the lock in order to "turn" the key (CS 100 [E 110]). After he accomplishes this and reveals himself, his steps toward his family are rewarded with a kick from the father, which is ironically described as "a deliverance" (CS 105 [E 116]), and he is quickly sent back to his room. Later on, the music of the violin that Gregor and his family are drawn to is a key tragic motif associated with the longing for redemption. At this point, the whole family has reached the height of impurity, humiliation, and displacement, and thus they can respond to the music while the roomers cannot (CS 130 [E 149]). When Gregor hears his sister playing the violin, he feels "as if the way were opening before him to the unknown nourishment" (CS 130–31 [E 149]). Hearing the "divine" music, Gregor is ready one more time for the crucial process of "turning," but when "he had completed the turn around, he began at once to crawl straight back" (CS 135

[E 154]). What we have here resembles the continual longing for redemption and the many examples of "false" turning in Buber's Hasidic tales, where the very concept of "true" and "false" turning is a topos.

Gregor fails to reach redemption. Kurt Weinberg rightly points to "Kafka's rather dark irony,"[33] which emerges from the contrast between Gregor's death and the dawn of a beautiful spring day that brings about feelings of hope and liberation for the family. In fact, this seemingly positive ending contains yet another ironic twist, because the parents' final rise to power manifests itself in their sudden realization "that it would soon be time, too, to find [Grete] a good husband" (CS 139 [E 161]). This resolution makes the ending appear highly ironic, since the parents are planning to reestablish the traditional patriarchal power relationship. There is no contradiction in acknowledging the secular nature of Kafka's texts and arguing at the same time that he, nonetheless, makes use of motifs and narrative devices drawn from the folk and mystic Jewish tradition: the utilization of traditional, particularly religious, sources in secular writing is true of virtually all modern literatures. Gershom Scholem therefore regards Kafka's work as "a secular statement of the Kabbalistic world-feeling in a modern spirit."[34]

Josef K.: *Am ha aretz* before the Law

The numerous trials of penitents in Hasidic tales—mostly of ordinary humans who are tried for moral and religious shortcomings but have committed no serious crimes—suggest a connection between Gregor Samsa's "trial" and that of Josef K. in *The Trial*. This association is taken for granted in a Yiddish translation of *The Trial*, when the Hebrew word *gilgulim* (transformations) is used to describe the "trials" that merchant Block has suffered.[35] The translator, Yiddish poet Melech Ravitsh, also renders the title of Kafka's *Metamorphosis* as *Der gilgul* (afterword to *Prozes*, 237). From a different but equally secular perspective, *The Trial* represents another modern variation on the struggle for redemption.

Though this novel was never published during Kafka's lifetime, the legend "Before the Law" was his first literary piece in *Selbstwehr*, where it appeared without the long commentary that follows in the novel (S 7 Sept. 1915:2–3). Here, the man from the country passively lives out his life "before the law," intimidated by the lowest doorkeeper and afraid to enter the door that—as he is told when he is dying—was all along meant only for him. He is the opposite of what a Zionist hero should be. The protagonist Joseph K., however, rebels against his predicament, and if there is anything Zionist about him it would be his relentless struggle for vindication. Though no character in the text ever "succeeds" in vindicating himself—which defeats any political Zionist message—Kafka's interest in cultural rather than political Zionism manifests itself in his creation of a fictional world where the protagonist's existential battles are played out in language. Significantly, there is no closure after the death of the man from the country; as Michael Greenstein has pointed out: "No sooner is the door shut than the hermeneutic dialogue between K. and the priest begins, parodying the aporia between doorkeeper and visitor as well as talmudic commentaries on the Law."[36] The battle is about to begin as Kafka is mobilizing narrative discourses from the ancient Jewish past and confronting his modern protagonist with them.

That Josef K. is caught in an inescapable dilemma is not new or surprising. Caught in a web of various relations with authority figures who pronounce judgment, with women as mediators, or with dependents that act in accordance with orders from above, he becomes increasingly entangled and in the end dies a violent death. For the most part, therefore, *The Trial* has been understood as a "serious" text, though Max Brod pointed out the humorous dimension specifically for this novel: "When Kafka read from his work, this humor became especially obvious. Thus, for example, we friends of his could not stop laughing when he read out the first chapter of *The Trial*. He himself laughed so much that there were moments when he couldn't read any further. Astonishing enough, when you think of the fearful earnestness of this chapter. But that is how it was" (FK 178; translation modified). An illustration of this humor is a passage in the first chapter that parodies Josef K.'s loss of authority immediately after his arrest. K. is entangling himself in a linguistic trap set by the inspector, who makes him qualify individual utterances until they are transformed, distorted, or turned into their opposite.

> "You're no doubt greatly surprised by this morning's events?" asked the inspector, arranging with both hands the few objects lying on the nightstand. . . . "Of course," said K., . . . "of course, I'm surprised, but by no means greatly surprised." "Not greatly surprised?" asked the inspector. . . ." Perhaps you misunderstand me," K. hastened to add. "I mean—" . . . "I mean—" . . . "I'm of course greatly surprised, but when you've been in this world for thirty years and had to make your way on your own, as has been my lot, you get hardened to surprises and don't take them too seriously. Particularly not today's." "Why particularly not today's?"[37]

The narrative is marked by continual reversals, antithesis following antithesis, all of which creates ambiguity. Suddenly we start questioning the meaning of "surprised" and "by no means greatly surprised" and other clichéd expressions. These discursive features resemble Midrashic technique, which is "largely concerned with the smaller units of Scripture—verses, phrases, single words," and the situational comedy suggests that we are dealing with a kind of mock-Midrash here.[38]

In 1911 Kafka expressed his "repugnance for antitheses": "They are unexpected, but do not surprise, for they have always been there. . . . They make for thoroughness, fullness, completeness, but only like a figure on the 'wheel of life'; we have chased our little idea around the circle" (DI 157 [T 106]).[39] This foreshadows Josef K.'s dilemma, for "like a figure on the 'wheel of life,'" he will indeed chase his little ideas "around the circle." With its twisting and turning of meaning, the previous passage exposes the trial from the outset as a "farce" (the original German has "comedy")—this is at least how K. himself is inclined to see his arrest (*Trial*, 7 [*Proceß*, 13]).

What really comes "unexpectedly" and acts as an antithesis to common expectations is the arrest of a very ordinary person, Josef K. The German word for "trial," *Proceß*, means both trial in the legal sense and also a "'process' of whatever sort."[40] Thus, the title can be read literally as legal proceedings against K. and, figuratively, as K.'s way of "interpreting" these legal proceedings, which is a trial in itself. In Judaism there is a whole body of legal literature, halakha, which is "primarily concerned with law and codes of behavior."[41] The problem here, as in *The Trial*, is that "the Bible often states matters of law without clarification or detail" (Holtz, "Midrash," 181). Joseph K.'s "arrest" is anything but clear. No cause is indicated and no explanation given outside of the famous first sentence of the novel: "Someone must have slandered Joseph K., for one morning, without having done anything truly wrong, he was arrested" (*Trial*, 3 [*Proceß*, 9]). Corngold makes the important observation that "the narrative begins not with the first event of the plot but with a first interpretation of the event" (*Necessity of Form*, 223). From the very beginning, therefore, Josef K. has been placed into an arbitrary narrative situation and left to fend for himself.

The entire novel is about K.'s attempts to get to the truth of the matter. In the Talmud (as in *The Trial*) "clarity must be won; it is the goal, not the starting point."[42] Clarification, the search for meaning, is the function of Midrash, the process of interpreting, which "fill[s] in the gaps" (Holtz, "Midrash," 180). But Kafka is caricaturing Josef K., who does not know this method and cannot make sense of his situation, as the *am ha aretz*, who is ignorant of Scripture and becomes lost in the commentaries on the priest's "exegesis of the legend" (DII 101 [T 707]). In November 1911 Kafka mentioned an *am ha aretz* in his diary (DI 166 [T 276]), and a few weeks later he read in Fromer's *Organismus des Judentums* that according to rabbinic law an *am ha aretz* deserves the hardest punishment: "'An Am ha aretz,' says a rabbi a little drastically, 'should be torn apart like a fish, even if this happened on Yom Kippur, which falls on a Sabbath', i.e. on a day when work such as tearing something or someone apart is doubly prohibited" (65). When Kafka was a child, his father used to threaten him with the words "I'll tear you apart like a fish" (DF 152 [Z 23]), and through the *Letter to His Father*, this phrase has become part of the folklore of the Kafka household. In a diary entry, though, Kafka depicts the *am ha aretz* as a comic Sancho Panza figure accompanying the bookish Don Quixote (DI 166 [T 276]). Josef K. is another quixotic *am ha aretz* figure, whose quest for justice is a similar comical enterprise that is bound to fail.[43]

Like the man from the country in the legend "Before the Law," the central part of *The Trial*, Josef K. is ignorant of Scripture and the Law contained within it. Talmudic discourse is easily recognizable in the following explication: "he's well aware of the importance of his office, *for he says* 'I'm powerful'; he respects his superiors, *for he says:* 'I'm only the lowest doorkeeper'; when it comes to fulfilling his duty he can neither be moved nor prevailed upon, *for it says* of the man 'he wearies the doorkeeper with his entreaties'; . . . he can't be bribed, *for he says* of a gift" (*Trial*, 218; *Proceß*, 228–29; my emphasis). In rabbinic fashion, every interpretation is followed by the citing of a prooftext (the biblical point of departure for the interpretation) from the original legend, always introduced by phrases such as *for he says*.[44] But the logic of the "halakhic and talmudic reflection, which figures so prominently in 'Before the Law,'" is foreign to Josef K. and leads him "into unaccustomed areas of thought" (*Trial*, 223 [*Proceß*, 233–34]). Kafka expresses none of the confidence in religious texts that is revealed in the famous saying by Ben Bag Bag (a fictitious rabbi): "Turn it and turn it for all is in it and look in it and grow grey and old in it, and turn not away from it, for there is no better rule for thee than it."[45] For Josef K., all his challenging, questioning, "turning" brings only frustration and in the end contains "Nothing" that could save his life. K. never finds out what is happening to him or why; when his executioners come to get him, he still thinks this is part of the comedy and takes them to be "supporting actors" and asks what theater they are from (*Trial*, 226 [*Proceß*, 236]).

Kafka's ironic use of motifs from Jewish mysticism further underscores the satire. In Kabbala symbolism (which so permeates the Hasidic legends) there are palaces and chambers, the heavenly courtroom, scales of justice, penitents' trials, divine radiance, as well as metamorphoses. Scholem furthermore highlights the obstacles that have to be surmounted, such as "closed entrance gates" with "'gate-keepers' posted to the right and left of the entrance to the heavenly hall through which the soul must pass in its ascent." As in *The Trial*, there are also "discussions between the traveller and the gate-keepers" (*Major Trends*, 50, 53). Many scholars have pointed out these metaphors and foregrounded the mystic and religious dimensions, often seeing Kafka's writing in terms of a "negative theology."[46] After all, the doorkeepers are intimidating, the courtrooms sordid, and, though the man from the country sees emanations of light behind the doorkeeper, Josef K.'s mystic ascent seems unimaginable.

In fact, K.'s situation is utterly hopeless, for even if he managed to gain an "ostensible acquittal," nothing would be achieved, for he would be no closer to freedom than before. Kafka's wheel, once set in motion, keeps turning (like the machine in the "Penal Colony") only to lend support to the bureaucratic structure that upholds the Law: "The trial can't come to a standstill.... [It] must be kept constantly spinning within the tight circle to which it's artificially restricted" (*Trial*, 161 [*Proceß*, 169]; translation modified). Midrash often tries to make sense of hopeless narrative situations in a playful manner and escapes from the law through aggadah, the "method of 'creative exegesis.'"[47] In *The Trial*, too, relief from despair comes in the form of humorous legends and scenes interspersed throughout the narrative. For instance, Josef K.'s lawyer Huld recounts an anecdote that represents the absurdity of the court with its "petty lawyers" in a humorous fashion. He describes how "an elderly official, a decent, quiet gentleman, had studied a difficult case, rendered particularly complex due to the lawyer's petitions." Out of frustration, trying to prevent the lawyers from coming into court, "he went to the outer door, waited in ambush, and threw every lawyer who tried to enter down the steps." As they desperately needed admittance to the court, "because each day missed at court is a day lost," the lawyers decided that their best course of action would be to tire him out. By taking it in turns, they rushed up the stairs, "one lawyer at a time," so that the elderly official could throw every single one down to the bottom again "where he would then be caught by his colleagues. That lasted for about an hour; then the old gentleman ... grew truly exhausted and went back into his office" (*Trial*, 118–19 [*Proceß*, 125–26]). The lawyers'

Sisyphus-like activity reads like a Jewish joke from Chelm, the town of fools from Jewish folklore. The anecdote about the "petty lawyers," who willingly let themselves be thrown down the stairs in order to reach their goal, caricatures their insatiability and reduces the serious court proceedings to farce.

In the Yiddish translation of the novel, the artist Yossl Bergner has illustrated such humorous scenes. We see the lawyers tumbling down the stairs (*Prozes,* 160), or the big hole in the floor of the law offices over which the lawyers trip, while the accused beneath them, sitting on benches, are looking up to the ceiling at a leg sticking out (*Prozes,* 118). Another illustration shows the painter Titorelli twirling a hunchback around his head, a gesture reminiscent of the *kapora* ritual on Yom Kippur where a sacrificial chicken is circled around someone's head before it is slaughtered in atonement for everyone's sins (*Prozes,* 181; *Trial,* 142; *Proceß,* 150). An originally religious ceremony thus becomes a folkloristic motif in *The Trial.* More than that, Josef K. is sacrificed in a similarly brutal and senseless fashion. His ritualistic death in the quarry evokes the age-old anti-Semitic accusation of ritual murder, most recently revived in the Beilis trial; at the same time, it is also reminiscent of ritual slaughter. Like the innocent Mendel Beilis, Josef K. has been circling from one authority to another, feeding on "belief sustaining fictions"[48] but never making any progress in his case. As an *am ha aretz,* he is abandoned by the Law as well as by society.

Kafka criticized Bloch's "Legend of Theodor Herzl" for "the dryness of the entire allegory, which is nothing but an allegory, which says all there is to say without ever delving deeper or drawing one deeper into it" (LF 421 [BF 596]). Kafka's own legend is embedded in a much richer narrative that generates multiple layers of interpretation and continual deferrals of meaning. Considering, too, Kafka's ironic transformation of Jewish narrative forms and motifs (*am ha aretz,* doorkeeper motif, etc.), "Before the Law" could appropriately be described as an "unlimited allegory" or a counter-allegory. In *The Trial,* then, Kafka creates a modern Midrash where the commentary becomes its own aim. The predominance of form over content is its characteristic feature, in the sense that certain types of discursive structures, as well as the process of interpreting, are more important than the theme being interpreted. Indeed, the "process" of interpreting can be said to be the theme. "'Turn it and turn it over,' the sage Ben Bag Bag counseled the student of Torah. 'For everything is in it' (M. Avot 5.25)—provided you know how to read Torah: that is, to study midrashically" (Stern, *Parables,* 18). For the acculturated Josef K., "Nothing" is in it; he turns it and turns it only to get trapped in what Kafka calls elsewhere *stehender Sturmlauf*, immobile assaults (DI 157 [T 259–60]).

The Missing Golem and the Status of Kafka's Fragments

Kafka wrote a great many fragments, which have generally been ignored by critics and underrepresented in editions of his work. One of these, the Golem fragment of 1916, was never included in any edition of his literary texts and has now even been eliminated from the latest, "critical" edition of Kafka's diaries on the grounds that he had apparently crossed it out. Considering how hard it is for Kafka's fragmentary texts to gain literary status, I will give this text a title and reproduce it in its entirety.

"The Creation of the Golem" (1916)

It soon became known, of course, that the rabbi was working on a clay figure. Every door of every room in his house stood open night and day, it contained nothing whose presence was not immediately known to everybody. There were always a few disciples, or neighbors, or strangers wandering up and down the stairs of the house, looking into all the rooms and—unless they happened to encounter the rabbi himself—going anywhere they pleased. And once, in a washtub, they found a large lump of reddish clay.

The liberty the rabbi allowed everyone in his house had spoiled people to such a degree that they did not hesitate to touch the clay. It was hard, even when one pressed it one's fingers were hardly stained by it, its taste—the curious even had to touch their tongue to it—was bitter. Why the rabbi kept it in the washtub they could not understand.

Bitter, bitter, that is the most important word. How do I intend to solder fragments together into a story that will sweep one along?

A faint grayish-white smoke was lightly and continuously wafted from the chimney.

The rabbi, his sleeves rolled up like a washerwoman, stood in front of the tub kneading the clay which already bore the crude outline of a human form. The rabbi kept constantly before him the shape of the whole even while he worked on the smallest detail, the joint of a finger, perhaps. Though the figure obviously seemed to be acquiring a human likeness, the rabbi behaved like a madman—time and again he thrust out his lower jaw, unnecessarily passed one lip over the other, and when he wet his hands in the bucket of water behind him, thrust them in so violently that the water splashed to the ceiling of the bare vault. (DII 152–53)[49]

The Golem myth originates with sixteenth-century Rabbi Loew in Prague, who created this creature of clay to help the Jews in times of persecution. Over the centuries there have been many versions. Some artists have highlighted the potential for magic, mysticism, or horror inherent in these tales; others have used this prominent motif from Jewish folklore for political commentary, to recreate for *their* time a superhuman folk hero who can help fight injustice.

There are two Golem fragments in the old edition of Kafka's diary, one following the other; the text above is the longer and more developed version. The elimination of these crucial fragments is unfortunate, because they reveal Kafka's fondness for storytelling and how he, too, is engaged in rewriting myths and legends. In Jewish folklore the creation of the golem is generally clouded in mystery and secrecy, but in Kafka's reworking of the legend everything is open for everyone to see. Usually the golem's body is depicted as a monstrosity and associated with fear, but here there is no fear; everything is allowed in the rabbi's house, even the tasting of the clay becomes part of the ceremony. The clay tastes bitter and Kafka at this point opens up the possibility for a narrative digression, a whole new narrative seems to hinge on the word "bitter." But he abandons this idea and immediately proceeds with rewriting the creation story in Genesis. There is no snake, no deceit in the rabbi's house; this is the optimal space, the rabbi the perfect creator, throwing his mind and body fully into the act of creation.

The Golem fragment would have fit nicely into Nahum Glatzer's bilingual (German-English) volume, Franz Kafka, *Parables and Paradoxes* (1961),[50] the only edition which collects texts that originally appeared within a variety of contexts and genres (such as novel, short story, aphorisms, autobiographical writings, and personal correspondence) and organizes them in groups under specific themes. Regarding the selection criteria, the epilogue states: "In the pieces collected in this volume, Frank Kafka reexamined and boldly rewrote some basic mythological tales of Ancient Israel, Hellas, the Far East, and the West, adding to them creations of his own imagination." Of course there are parables and paradoxes in German and English editions of Kafka's short prose, but many of the pieces in Glatzer's edition were never included or disappeared within other texts because they were not arranged together.

In fact, the selection criteria of the first editors, Brod and Karl-Heinz Schoeps, were quite arbitrary, because some fragments seemed to them more "complete" while others, even if they had been deleted by the author, "turned out to be indispensable for the whole context, or at least of such relevance that we decided to include them." In general they "let themselves be guided by intuition as to which version was the better or more in keeping with the author's intention."[51] Considering that an arbitrary criterion of "completeness" determined the inclusion or exclusion of many texts, an equally arbitrary "canon" of Kafka texts was involuntarily created. Over the years, many editors have therefore added individual pieces. Unfortunately, the Golem fragment was never included.

Glatzer's collection of parables and paradoxes is important because it grants many fragments individual status as "literary texts." By integrating these fragments into a narrative sequence, it makes visible—more than any other edition—a very prominent feature of Kafka's narrative discourse. Like bin Gorion in *The Legends of the Jews,* Glatzer has included the various versions and arranged them according to motifs. Many of the texts are highly intertextual on the thematic, or aggadic, level, while their Midrashic narrative structure is one of continual narrative transformation. At times we can see Kafka's intertextual composition in a single sentence, as in one of the Abraham fragments: "He is afraid that after starting out as Abraham with his son he would change on the way into Don Quixote" (P 43).

Moreover, Glatzer groups "An Imperial Message" together with three fragments that have the same "oriental" subject matter and thus deliberately reinforces the "oriental" context. The "China" theme may not seem particularly Jewish, but it is again interdiscursive: the translator Clement Greenberg sees China as "Kafka's figure of speech for Diaspora Jewry."[52] The Oriental theme was also part of contemporary anti-Semitic discourses, which commonly depicted the Jew as Oriental (Gilman, *Patient,* 16–17, 68, 107–8, 198). In addition, "Chinese" motifs appear in many Jewish literary texts: themes of messengers, kings, the Chinese emperor can be found in folk and Hasidic tales with which Kafka was familiar, especially those by Peretz. It is also interesting that Kafka himself removed "An Imperial Message" from its original "Chinese" context for publication in an entirely Jewish framework, the Zionist newspaper *Selbstwehr* (S 24 Sept. 1919:4).

Glatzer's *Parables and Paradoxes* is unique in that it brought to life many fragments within the framework of a particular parabolic genre. Through translation and generic canonization, it brings into focus an essential dimension of Kafka's hermeneutic discourse (which has its origins in the earliest parabolic discourse, i.e. as found in biblical/rabbinic interpretation) and is at the same time an example of how a bilingual collection of texts within a target culture can contribute more to an understanding of an author's discourse than the editions in the source culture on which translations are generally based.

Midrashic Weapons in "The Silence of the Sirens"

"The Silence of the Sirens" (1917) appropriates Homeric myth through continual narrative transformations. Stéphane Mosès points out that its overall structure consists of "a maxim, a quotation from an ancient text, and the exegesis of that quotation . . . [which] brings to mind the composition of texts that are part of ancient Jewish literature, the *homiletic Midrashim*."[53] The maxim, which states that the following text will illustrate how innocent means can lead to rescue/salvation (the German "*Rettung*" implies both meanings), is drawn from an ancient text, Homer's *Odyssey*. But the "quotation" from this text is a transformation of the original already: in order to save himself from the Sirens, Odysseus puts wax into his ears so as not to hear their song. As a matter of fact, it was not Odysseus who put the wax into his ears but his sailors into theirs. It was the whole point of Homer's story that Odysseus would be able to hear the sirens and yet remain unharmed as he was tied to the mast. A second and more radical transformation is explicit in the title already: in Kafka's text the sirens do not sing; rather, their silence is said to be an even more powerful weapon than their song. Here we have a complete reversal of the original narrative situation. A further change is that the sirens actually appear as characters in Kafka's text. They are seen and not heard, whereas in Homer they are heard and not seen.[54] Finally, while Odysseus is crafty in Homer's version, in Kafka's text he is initially naive and innocent—but only to be metamorphosed again at the very end into someone so crafty that it surpasses human understanding.

Kafka's narrative is reminiscent of the hermeneutic method of Midrashic discourse, which strives "to fill in the holes in Scripture through fantasy and legend, explication [*Auslegung*] and interpretation [*Deutung*]" (bin Gorion, *Sagen,* 10). Filling in the narrative gaps means making the "void," any conceivable empty center, meaningful, and Kafka can be said to fill in the gaps in a meaningful manner: even though we do not hear the narrator ask questions, the whole narrative consists of answers to possible questions in the text. For instance, the fact that Odysseus puts wax into his ears in order to escape the power of the sirens' song seems to be a pretty straightforward statement (P 88). However, since we are also told that he is one among many "traveler[s]" (CS 431 [P 88]) that have gone on this quest, the question presents itself, "If it is as easy as all that, why did the others not hit upon this idea?" Why indeed, then, did no one else try what Odysseus did? The narrator remarks that "all the world knew" this could not possibly help (CS 431 [P 88]). But, one may well ask, if the whole world knew, then Odysseus surely must have heard about it, too. He may very well, the narrator says, but he just did not think of it. He had absolute faith, "trusted absolutely" *(er vertraute vollständig)* but not in God, only in himself and in his "little stratagem" (CS 431 [P 88]). This way Odysseus survives even the worst that could happen, the encounter with the sirens' silence: since he could not hear, he did not know of the sirens' silence, thus he could not but believe that they must be singing.

There are several questions that present themselves at this point. The shift in the narrative from Odysseus to the sirens suggests that we ask about the sirens first. How about the sirens then? They were so used to being unchallenged in their seductiveness; how were they able to stand this rejection? Not very well, we hear; their situation was utterly sad and hopeless: "But they—lovelier than ever—stretched their necks and turned, let their awesome hair flutter free in the wind, and freely stretched their claws on the rocks. They no longer had any desire to allure; all that they wanted was to hold as long as they could the radiance that fell from Ulysses' great eyes" (CS 431 [P 90]). Not interested in seducing anyone any more, the sirens are just about annihilated by this experience. Homer's text, on the other hand, told us nothing about the fate of the sirens at this crucial moment. The sirens' despair exposes Odysseus's survival as so dubious that Maurice Blanchot remarks: "He took no risks but admired the Sirens with the cowardly, unemotional, calculated satisfaction characteristic of the decadent Greek he was who should never have figured among the heroes of the *Iliad*."[55] The shift in the narrative focus from Odysseus to the sirens brings about a shift in the readers' sympathy: is Odysseus really so innocent? What was announced as "innocent elation over his little stratagem" (CS 431 [P 88]) seems anything but innocent as the roles of victim and hero are suddenly reversed: while originally it was Odysseus who was attracted to the sirens and likely to become their victim, now it is the sirens who are attracted to Odysseus and become his victims.

The last paragraph shifts back to Odysseus, and the next set of questions concerns him. Since Odysseus survived because he did not know that the sirens were silent, it seems logical to conclude that had Odysseus known, surely he would have died? But no . . . we cannot win.. There is another commentary, "A codicil to the foregoing" which "has also been handed down" (CS 432 [P 90]): it states that Odysseus, in fact, knew all along, was as clever as a fox, only pretended to be innocent and naive and played a little game not only with the sirens and the gods but also with the reader, we might add. In the end we are faced not only with the impending loss of "textual" but of "moral authority" as well, since moral values such as absolute innocence and shrewd deviousness appear to be equally effective and interchangeable.

Now if this is to be the proof the narrator has promised us to illustrate that childish means can lead to rescue, it has none of the positive, reassuring value it seemed to contain at the outset—rather, we have entered a Midrashic web and are groping for answers. We have increasingly moved away from any narrative assurance: any "authority" is shaken, be it Homer's original, textual, or moral authority, or even the reader's "authority" as interpreter of the text. Stanley Corngold has aptly characterized Kafka's narrative technique through the DNA metaphor of the "double helix." By this he means, metaphorically, "a certain turning, with many hesitations and returns, farther and farther away from a virtual origin."[56] This metaphor vividly illustrates the spiral progression of Midrashic reasoning and also raises the question of the loss of "authority." Walter Benjamin stressed that Kafka's writings "do not modestly lie at the feet of doctrine, as aggadah [legends, anecdotes] lies at the feet of halakha [Law]. When they have crouched down, they unexpectedly raise a mighty paw against it" (Scholem, *Correspondence,* 225 [B 87]). For many critics Kafka's aggadah indeed "devours" halakha. Gershom Scholem, however, argues that the rebellious nature is typical of aggadah generally and never constitutes a real threat to the Law.[57]

How indeed can one lose the authority of a text (by Homer) that in any event constitutes only a "virtual origin," since the source is transformed already before the Midrashic game begins? The fragment "Leopards in the Temple" demonstrates well how Kafka's "modern" challenge to traditional authority becomes part of the interpretive ceremony. Since the leopards' assault on traditional practice repeats itself again and again, it soon becomes predictable (P 92); thus, it is not surprising any longer but rather to be expected. The emphasis therefore shifts away from the "challenge" to authority and focuses instead on the interpretive skills that make this Midrashic exercise different from previous ones.

If this hermeneutic goal characterizes Kafka's narratives as well, then they certainly do not end in sheer negativity. Corngold, for one, regards Kafka's chiastic reversals and his constant deferral of meaning as affirmative: the original definitions are "enlarged, not cancelled. They are enlarged in a direction productive of meanings for the reader who is determined to pursue them" ("Double Helix," 124). In "The Silence of the Sirens" we saw the spiral movement of the narrative that always makes room for further narrative expansion. The narrator for his part seems to find the final logical conclusion quite convincing: "Perhaps he had really noticed, although here the human understanding is beyond its depths, that the Sirens were silent, and held up to them and to the gods the aforementioned pretense merely as a sort of shield" (CS 432 [E 352; P 90]). This is where Kafka's commentary ends, but again I think we are ready with another question. Granted, Odysseus played a clever little game, but why is his action said to surpass human understanding?

Kafka's writing, here and elsewhere, defers rather than destroys narrative authority. In Derrida the arbitrary relation between signifier and signified leads, by means of deferral, to an ultimate indeterminacy of meaning. But Derrida, in an interview, also distances himself from a type of deconstruction that is used "to dismantle systems. Personally, I don't subscribe to this model of deconstruction. . . . what has been called the deconstructive gesture . . . is accompanied, or can be accompanied . . . by an affirmation. It is not negative, it is not destructive. That is why the word 'deconstruction' has always bothered me."[58] Kafka's "deconstruction" is of this affirmative kind. Even if language as such is indeterminate, "meaning" can always be created anew through continual recontextualization, and, here, ensures Odysseus's survival. We were told explicitly by the narrator that the "song" of the sirens was deadly and that their "silence" would certainly kill: "In every logically conceivable case, [Odysseus] is necessarily condemned to failure" (Mosès, "Silence," 71). However, it is precisely because causal reasoning for Odysseus would so clearly mean "death" that Kafka makes him believe in his "little stratagem" that, in turn, gives him the determination he needs in order to survive: "the sirens literally vanished before his resolution" (CS 431 [E 352; P 90]). In fact, the logic of Midrashic reasoning often lies in the interpreter's "fertile imagination" (Holtz, "Midrash," 203), and it is artistic creativity, fiction, that fills in the narrative "gaps." Thus, it is quite fitting that it is Odysseus's unconscious or conscious creation of fiction that makes him survive.

Odysseus's voyage in "The Silence of the Sirens" is a textual odyssey. Only a skillful artist can survive this textual tempest and create meaning out of a language that is characterized by arbitrariness and that can be made to literally turn against itself as when, in our story, the thrust of the final commentary is aimed at the first. "Every word," says Kafka in his last diary entry, "becomes a spear turned against the speaker. Most especially a remark like this. And so ad infinitum. The only consolation would be: it happens whether you like or no. And what you like is of infinitesimally little help. More than consolation is: You too have weapons" (DII 232–33 [T 926]). Kafka's Midrashic narrative is a discourse of survival. It is obviously not Odysseus's innocent means that are responsible for his rescue, nor is it his moral integrity. In both commentaries, it is the artist's manipulation of language that makes Odysseus survive. Inviting objections to his narration and countering them at the same time, the narrator is exercising his linguistic weapons in the combat zone of the text.

※ 5 ※

Kafka's Cultural Zionism

(1914–1917)

Hugo Bergmann's "Practical Community Work"

The cultural Zionism Kafka was interested in came to him in mediated form through his friends Hugo Bergmann and Max Brod, who had infused the philosophy of Ahad Ha'am with their own ideas. Ahad Ha'am advocated the creation of a "spiritual centre"—a cultural elite—in Palestine from which "the spirit of Judaism will radiate ... to all the communities of the Diaspora, to inspire them with new life and to preserve the over-all unity of our people."[1] The New Jews in this spiritual center would be a product of their own land, immersed as they were in Jewish life in Palestine, and well prepared to establish the Jewish state of the future. Hugo Bergmann, however, believed it was detrimental to separate the "spiritual centre" from the rest of the Jewish people. He did not want the Diaspora Jews to merely support a goal (Palestine) that most people would never reach. The type of spiritual community Ahad Ha'am envisioned for Palestine must be possible for Jews in the Diaspora as well. Zionism should be more than formal lip service or fashionable political activism, which brought about no change in personal lifestyles. Bergmann wanted a cultural Zionism that effected a fundamental change in Diaspora existence, a Nietzschean "transevaluation of all values" (*Jawne*, 35), so that there would be no split between the body (in the Diaspora) and the "spirit" (in Palestine). He envisioned a "larger Zionism" that went beyond party politics, one that combined body and spirit through community involvement (*Jawne*, 7).

In his essay "Jawne and Jerusalem (The Zionist Problem according to M. J. Berdyczewski)" (1914), Bergmann therefore acknowledges the significance of Ahad Ha'am but aligns himself with Micha Josef Berdyczewski's theoretical writings, which emphasize more consistently than Ahad Ha'am's that the national foundation of Zionism exists independent of any ideology (*Jawne*, 38). Like Ahad Ha'am, Berdyczewski wrote in Hebrew around the turn of the century, but while the former was slowly being heard in the West, the latter was only known as bin Gorion, the editor of *Sagen der Juden* (Legends of the Jews), and his writings on cultural Zionism remained largely unacknowledged.[2] However, it was Berdyczewski, "the great antipode" to Ahad Ha'am (*Jawne*, 34), who had the most powerful impact on Bergmann's understanding of cultural Zionism. Bergmann's essay outlines Berdyczewski's reservations about Ahad Ha'am's focus on a spiritual center in Palestine. It is precisely this division between the spiritual center and the Jews in the rest of the world that is the problem. Berdyczewski bridges this hierarchy by identifying all Judaism with humanity: "We are Jews only because we are human beings that are part of the Jewish people and our humanity is our Judaism" (*Jawne*, 38).

"Jawne and Jerusalem" draws on an analogy from biblical history to illustrate the contemporary problem. After all, there once was a spiritual center in Jewish history, a long time ago, after the destruction of Jerusalem in 70 BCE, when the city Jawne became the new spiritual center that replaced Jerusalem. For Berdyczewski and Bergmann this point in history represents the beginning of the *Galuth,* exile, Diaspora, "its great error [*sein großer Irrtum*]: the separation of the body from the soul" (*Jawne*, 35). They believed that contemporary Zionism offered a chance to correct this "error." Moreover, the reasons for the Jews never having created a national home had always been seen as lying outside, in the prejudiced gentile environment. The major insight of present-day Zionism was the awareness of an "inner Jewish problem" (*Jawne*, 20): "But who are we? People of the Galuth. And this Galuth is an inner one, not an external one" (*Jawne*, 36). It will not do, Bergmann argued (interpreting Berdyczewski), to blame history or the Romans or other people among whom the Jews lived for this state of affairs, because there were historical moments when action could have been taken. The fact is that from the beginning, when Jerusalem was destroyed, the Jews did not want to make the sacrifice of fighting for their national existence, and they chose to leave even before they were expelled: the history of events could have been changed had there been one strong will and a spark of life (*Jawne*, 36). Berdyczewski therefore draws the conclusion that "the Jews *want* the Galuth" (*Jawne*, 37).

Contemporary Jews in the Diaspora are descendants of those Jews who left the threatened Jerusalem in order to lay the new foundation for a spiritual Judaism in Jawne. At this much later stage in history, they possibly "*want* the Galuth" even more than their forefathers did. Bergmann therefore places great emphasis on an" inner" regeneration of the Jewish people, which is just as significant as all the work for Palestine. Zionism should therefore "give those of us, who are not able to go to Palestine yet, the opportunity to offer our children as much Jewish education here as we possibly can" (*Jawne*, 15). Bergmann was very active himself: in 1913 he taught Hebrew classes to the Zionist Club of Jewish Women and Girls in Prague, and he was also involved in other community plans, such as the "founding of a Hebrew kindergarten."[3] These cultural activities, for Bergmann, were more important than political and theoretical Zionism: "We will move forward not only through the creation of committees and commissions but only and above everything through *völkische Kleinarbeit* [practical community work], which every one of us can participate in" (*Jawne*, 15; my emphasis). Kafka shared these views about the ineffectiveness of political Zionism to revitalize Jewish culture and took Hugo Bergmann's practical, cultural Zionism very seriously. The phrase "*völkische Kleinarbeit*" well describes his own Zionist activities, which included not only attending "Jewish parent evenings" but also his interest in the *Notschule* (emergency school) for Jewish refugees during World War I, his active support for the Berlin Jewish People's Home in 1916, and finally his involvement with the first Jewish elementary school in Prague.

JEWISH EDUCATION IN PRAGUE

In Kafka scholarship little is known about Kafka's interest in Jewish education, and Max Brod later reproached himself for not having stressed this enough: "Far too briefly did I discuss Kafka's support for the establishment of a modern Jewish school in Prague" (FK1, 271). The foundation of this small Jewish elementary school (1920–42) that Kafka, Brod and others worked for has a long history and was the subject of controversy in the Prague Jewish community, especially because growing Czech nationalism kept interfering with these endeavors and by 1913 had, in fact, led to the closing of nearly all private German-Jewish schools in Czech-speaking areas (Stölzl, *Böhmen,* 52).[4] Brod claimed that the assimilated Czech Jews "saw it as the main purpose of their lives to destroy Jewish schools. . . . Too much German was spoken in them, in towns with an entire Czech population. . . . Of the many schools which existed in Bohemia, not a single one survived."[5] The first documentary evidence of Kafka's interest in Jewish education is a year later, after the situation improved and the Jewish School Association succeeded "in introducing extracurricular courses in Jewish history and the Hebrew language for the students of Bohemian secondary schools" (CJ 119).

On 14 February 1914 Kafka went to his first Jewish parents' meeting in the Hotel Bristol, organized by the Zionist Cultural Commission for Bohemia. He attended a lecture on "Principles of a Jewish Education" by Professor Hugo Stein, who argued that "old history" should be made "young again by celebrating Chanukah and Purim" with the family, Jewish art should not be banned from the home, and Jewish literature and philosophy should be added to the bookshelves.[6] Stein also stressed that the Jewish woman was of primary importance and her status needed to be raised. Furthermore, he strongly felt that education should not lead to the typical Jewish "civil servant career" but rather "only to professions for which we feel love and strength," such as "in trade and craft, where there is always a lack of skilled workers" (S 6 Mar. 1914:3). Kafka's sister Ottla attended another meeting the following day (DII 21 [T 637]); otherwise there are no further personal comments by Kafka on these events. However, a few months later, on 2 August 1914, World War I broke out, and Prague suddenly found itself flooded with Jewish refugees from the East, and with them came many children who were in need of an education. An important stage of practical community work was about to begin.

The Jewish Refugees and the Refugee School

World War I forced thousands of Jews in Galicia and Bukowina to leave their homes and move west. They settled mostly in or around big cities such as Prague, Vienna, and Berlin. In Prague a "relief committee" was established to help these refugees. At the end of September 1914, there were only about 200 refugees in Prague, half of them Jewish (Kudela 125). The Jews who came at this time were mostly richer Jews from the cities of Galicia; however, from November on mostly poorer refugees arrived. In early November the relief committee was informed that they could expect 20,000 to 60,000 refugees and that most of them were Jews (Kudela 124, 123). All of a sudden, on one day alone "more than 2,000 Jews arrived at the train station Smichov, and there was another train coming the same day, filled with refugees" (Kudela 126). At the beginning of 1915 there were 10,000 refugees in Prague, and in April there were already 13,000 (more than 30,000 if we include the areas outside of Prague [Kudela 124–25, 128]). When the war was over and the refugees had moved on or been relocated back to Galicia, there were nonetheless still more than 5,000 refugees who had decided to stay in Prague (Kudela 133).

Many people helped out when the flood of refugees arrived. Marsha Rozenblit points out that "Zionist youth groups like Blau-Weiss in Prague did railroad station duty, providing food and information to the thousands of refugees who arrived daily, and adult Zionist groups worked with the IKG (Israelitische Kultusgemeinde [Jewish Cultural Community]) to provide shelter and work for the refugees. Members of Blau-Weiss also collected clothing for distribution in Prague" (70; S 30 Oct. 1914:1). But generally the ordinary Jews in the relief committee (not partial to any political orientation) helped most (Kudela 127). Kafka, like many others, became involved when the masses of poor refugees arrived in November 1914. He as well as Brod and Brod's mother (DII 97–98 [T 698–99]; K 169) were among the many who distributed clothing and food. With them was Chaim Nagler, whom Kafka mentions in his diary as Chaim Nagel (DII 97 [T 698]), the leader of the Prague Zionist youth groups who helped the relief committee.[7] In these refugee circles, Kafka also at some point met the Polish Zionist Abraham Grünberg, who arrived from Krakow in November. Kafka and Brod got to know him well and greatly respected him.[8]

The assimilated Jews of Prague did not exactly welcome this sudden invasion of destitute Eastern Jews. Max Brod relates an embarrassing scene, when "a Polish Jewess, while the clothes were being distributed, threw her clothes back at a Prague lady who had insulted her, with the words: 'The *mitzveh* [good deed] should really be worth more than your Schmattes'; in German: you should find it more important to help me than I should value your rags."[9] Kafka was present at this scene in the Tuchmachergasse (DII 97–98 [T 698]). Not only does Kafka record the Polish Jewess's name (Frau Lustig) and her response in his diary (DII 98 [T 699]), he also identifies the Prague lady who was so impolite: the lady in question, who actually screamed at the Polish Jewess for being so choosy, was, in fact, Max Brod's own mother! Kafka also mentions another Jewish woman, Frau Kannengießer from Tarnow (DII 97 [T 698–99]),[10] who is given old and dirty clothes because the clean clothes are kept for the richer Jews. He dryly comments that there is a whole separate room with better clothes for a higher clientele of refugees (DII 97 [T 699]).[11] While many Prague citizens helped in person, others, like Kafka's father, donated money through the Central Association for the Preservation of

Jewish Affairs, which "supported the Galician refugees during WWI who were streaming to Prague, as well as hungry fellow Jews in Palestine."[12]

At the beginning of 1915, with about 30,000 refugees in and around Prague (Kudela 125), schools had to be organized for more than 2,500 children. Kafka was very supportive of these schools, which were quickly established (S 30 Oct. 1914:1–2). In January 1915 a "head office of the Jewish School Board" was created in Prague (S 7 Jan. 1916:7). Thus, sooner than anyone had expected, the Zionists suddenly had a Jewish school in Prague, and they even had the Jews to go with it. As Brod remarks, "One of our postulates has fulfilled itself virtually unnoticed, so to speak: the National Jewish School" ("Erfahrungen," 33). In May 1915, Professor Dr. Alfred Engel, an important figure in Prague Zionist activities, writes that "an elementary school for girls and boys was launched a short while ago, 16 classes and divisions.... Today there are 51 male and female teachers at the school, among them many high school teachers" (S 21 May 1915:3). One source reports that Engel's school had 900 students in fifteen classes (Kudela 124n.9), and another mentions "1200 students in its regular classes and many others in its vocational classes" (Rozenblit 71; S 30 July 1915:1). With the increasing number of refugees, the school undoubtedly kept growing. The curriculum "inculcated Jewish nationalism and provided Hebrew language instruction along with a modern secular education," and the goal of the educational project was "to improve and remake [the refugees] in the image of western Jewry," or, as Engel put it, to "lay the foundation for a reinvigorated, modernized Jewry in Galizia" when these Jews would be sent home again (Rozenblit 71). In the following months many other little schools were designed that served less intellectual than practical purposes.[13]

During the years 1915–18, Max Brod taught classes on world literature at the refugee school, first only out of "a feeling of duty." Soon, however, he came to idealize the students as "true Jewesses in their innermost being, brought up in a Jewish environment, according to old customs and morals, infused with Jewish knowledge" ("Erfahrungen," 34). Kafka attended several of these classes (LFF 242, 471n.55 [Br 279, 512n.16]) and got to know Brod's students, such as "the girl from Lemberg," Fanny Reiß (DII 107 [T 715]; K 175). Fanny was also at Brod's lecture on "Religion and Nation" in March 1915, when Kafka met Jiří Langer for the first time (DII 119 [T 733]). A month later, Kafka mentions a visit to Brod's "Homer class for the Galician girls" (DII 119 [T 734]; K 181), and in May he spent a whole day with the refugees and even went to a prayer service with them: "Service in the Teingasse today, then Tuchmachergasse, then the soup kitchen" (DII 128 [T 745] translation modified; K 184).[14]

During this period he also accompanied Brod and Langer to the Hasidic rabbi of Grodek (DII 128 [T 751]) and a few days later reproached himself for not going to the Kol Nidre service when he saw a "little boy with prayer shawls ... running along at his father's side" (DII 130 [T 753]). In October and November he still had contact with Fanny Reiß and her sisters (DII 140–41, 143 [T 768–70, 774]), and he knew other refugee children as well (LF 533 [BF 740]). Finally, in December he took his nephew Felix to a Chanukah play performed by the children from Eastern Europe (LF 533 [BF 740]). We can see that Kafka frequently participated in activities with the refugees. In the following year, he stresses Brod's energy and dedication and mentions his own involvement as well: "[Max] held a course of 11 lectures this winter, as well as lecturing at the refugee school for 2 hours a week to more than 50 girls, whom I joined on an outing the other day, and for 1 hour in a Zionist girls' club" (LF 470 [BF 660]). Kafka certainly did not write much literature in 1915, and in 1916, too, his literary production was slow. It picked up only at the end of November, and especially in the first months of 1917. But back in 1916 he became entirely absorbed by a new educational matter, the foundation of the Jewish People's Home in Berlin.

THE JEWISH PEOPLE'S HOME IN BERLIN

The Jewish People's Home opened on 18 May 1916. From the beginning, Kafka took great interest in this home and, according to Brod, visited whenever he was in Berlin (PK 116). It was located in the Jewish slum of Berlin, the *Scheunenviertel* (Barn Quarter), where most of the refugees from Eastern Europe had settled during World War I. The People's Home was founded by Berlin medical student and Zionist Siegfried Lehmann (1892–1958) with the help of other "students, young merchants and women."[15] The first yearly report is dedicated to Max Brod, Martin Buber, Gustav Landauer, Siegbert Stern, and Rabbi Warschauer for their help and support. It was typed by Kafka's fiancée Felice Bauer (LF 509, 517 [BF 708, 719]), and when she sent it to him, he exclaimed: "Oh, the personal significance these pages have for me!" (LF 521 [BF 725]). The report mentions that the socialist revolutionary Gustav Landauer (1870–1919) gave the opening speech on Judaism and socialism.[16] Lehmann himself wrote the afterword on Jewish education and concludes with a quotation from Hugo Bergmann, endorsing his "larger Zionism" by encouraging the national Jew today to know the literature of the world (as well as Jewish literature) and interpreting the "demand for Jewish nationalism" the way Bergmann had defined it, in the sense that "more Judaism" means "more humanism [*mehr Menschentum*]" ("Bericht," 18). Here we have another echo of Berdyczewski's vision of cultural Zionism.

The report gives detailed information about the organization of the People's Home and the available educational facilities. There were kindergartens, youth clubs, dance and music lessons, and Hebrew classes. Even though both boys and girls received Hebrew lessons, the genders were generally kept separate. While the girls were sewing or learning about "duties towards the family, the Jewish woman" (11), the boys had classes on bookbinding and instruction in a joiner's workshop, and a "gardening group" was planned (10). The emphasis in the home lay clearly on practical education, "especially in the domain of trade and agriculture" (19). The Zionist model realized here is similar to what was presented in theory at the first parents' evening that Kafka attended in 1914.

Moreover, the report stated that the helpers were encouraged to live right in the People's Home, or at least very close by to ensure that they had as much contact as possible with the little community. "Lehmann was attempting to apply the innovative concept of English social reformers, the Settlement House, where the permanent workers and those whom they served live together as a collective."[17] These settlement houses were nineteenth-century community-oriented educational facilities, intended to educate the working classes. The report mentions that they were looking to England as well as to the United States ("Bericht," 5). In fact, there were "some 56 [settlement houses] in Britain by 1926 (41 of them in London) and approaching 400 being established in the United States by 1910."[18] For classes with older boys, the People's Home applied the democratic American model of self-administration so that the children would learn to choose their own representatives ("Bericht," 7). This innovative idea of the settlement house was important for Kafka because such close contact gave Western Jews like him the opportunity to learn from these Eastern refugees. For the moment only three of the helpers had been able to move in, and Kafka was hoping the situation would improve after the war (LF 522 [BF 725]).

Felice's involvement with the People's Home came about through Kafka. While on holiday with her in Marienbad (3–13 July 1916), he had mentioned the Jewish People's Home and Felice had expressed interest.[19] Already on 19 July, Kafka informed her that an invitation was on its way

(LF 476 [BF 667]). From this time on he kept reminding her in his letters to follow up on her promise: when she felt unsure, he urged her on, and at the end of August he even offered to pay all her expenditures.[20] Finally, in September, Felice went and Kafka responded enthusiastically: "That you have at last got together, you and the Home, is certainly the most important thing; everything else ... will solve itself" (LF 498 [BF 693]). By way of preparation, he recommended *Memoiren einer Sozialistin* (Memoirs of a Female Socialist), an autobiographical novel by the German feminist Lily Braun (LF 498 [BF 694]).[21]

On Felice's first visit to the People's Home, she witnessed a heated debate between the scholar Gershom Scholem (1897–1982), who was nineteen at the time, and Siegfried Lehmann, who presented a talk on "The Problem of a Jewish-Religious Education," which Kafka thought addressed "the fundamental question which in my opinion can never lie dormant, but will continue to flare up time and again, to disturb the very foundations of Zionism" (LF 498 [BF 694]). The problem, as Kafka saw it, was that many Zionists considered a traditional religious education much less important than a revival of national consciousness. He was very skeptical about the kind of education the refugee children would receive:

> Since people are sewn into their skins for life and cannot alter any of the seams ... one will try to imbue the children ... with the spirit and more indirectly the mode of life of their helpers. In other words one will try to raise them to the standard of the contemporary, educated, West European Jew, Berlin version, which admittedly may be the best type of its kind. With that, not much would be achieved. If, for instance, I had to choose between the Berlin Home and another where the pupils were the Berlin helpers ... and the helpers simple East European Jews from Kolomyja or Stanislawow, I would give unconditional preference to the latter Home—with a great sigh of relief and without a moment's hesitation. (LF 500 [BF 697])

Kafka always stressed that it was important not to forget who was being helped. For him the Western Jews needed the Eastern Jews, and not the other way round ("Zionism and sweeping enthusiasm are not enough" [LF 522, BF 725]). Scholem's views on the People's Home lend support to Kafka's apprehensive remarks. Scholem had been present at several previous meetings and described "an atmosphere of aesthetic ecstasy" where poems by Franz Werfel were read out aloud.[22] As a matter of fact, he had attended Lehmann's talk because he expected it to challenge and provoke him, for he "sensed in it the lack of seriousness which expressed itself in the group's interpretations of Buber's interpretations of Hasidism without their knowing anything about historical Judaism" (*Jerusalem*, 78). Not surprisingly, a serious controversy ensued between Scholem and Lehmann, with Scholem demanding "that people learn Hebrew and go to the sources instead of occupying themselves with such literary twaddle" (*Jerusalem*, 79).

Kafka was familiar with this problem because a similar situation existed in Prague: "The discussion you describe is typical; theoretically I am always inclined to favor proposals such as those made by Herr Scholem, which demand the utmost, and by so doing achieve nothing. So one simply mustn't appraise such proposals and their value by the actual result laid before one. . . . Actually, Scholem's proposals in themselves are not impracticable" (LF 505 [BF 703–4]). In a political sense, Scholem's position would not have an immediate impact on a revival of national consciousness. At the same time, mastering the "sources" was a tremendously ambitious project but not unrealizable. In contrast to many Western Zionists "who throng to the synagogue simply because they are Zionists," Kafka thought this was hypocritical; but he stressed the importance of a formal religious education, though he himself could not pretend to be part of it: "The synagogue is not a place one can sneak up to. . . . I should have to tell the children . . . that owing to my origin, my education, disposition, and environment I have nothing tangible in common with their faith (*keeping the Commandments is not an outward thing; on the contrary, it is the very essence of the Jewish faith*)" (LF 502–3 [BF 700]; my emphasis). A year after these comments, Kafka himself decided to go "back to the sources" by studying Hebrew, which he pursued until the end of his life.

When Kafka's letters to Felice Bauer appeared fifty years later, Scholem was pleased to discover "that Kafka decidedly took [his] side" (*Jerusalem*, 79). However, Kafka did not share Scholem's overall dismissive attitude toward the Zionists in the People's Home. He always encouraged Felice and gave moral and practical support by providing her with appropriate reading material for herself as well as for the children. Toward the end of October 1916, he began sending her several song books, including a Zionist Blau-Weiß songbook for the children (LF 528 [BF 733]). In November he sent her F. W. Foerster's *Jugendlehre* (Youth Education) (LF 504 [BF 702]) and even read it himself (DII 165 [T 804]) so that he could discuss it with her (LF 503, 507–8 [BF 701, 706–8]). For the children he tried to find whatever Jewish books were available and suitable. Thus, he notified her, "The Jüdische Verlag is supposed to be bringing out a Hanukkah book" (LF 533 [BF 740]), a volume which he also acquired for himself.[23] He wrote that Sholom Aleichem was "too sarcastic and complicated" (LF 510–11 [BF 711]), and he feared that *Stories from the Bible* by Sholem Asch[24] (1914)—a retelling of Genesis—might be a little "too childish" (LF 512 [BF 713]), since Felice had told him that the girls were reading classical drama already; so he sent Peretz's *Popular Tales* (LF 512 [BF 713]).[25]

In order to help Felice build a library for the children, he also sent her "Schaffstein's little blue books" for her group of girls, because these were devoted to fiction, and he promised to send their counterpart for boys, Schaffstein's nationalistic, colonialist little green books (LF 531–2 [BF 738]).[26] Given the children's traumatic experience during the war and the colonial orientation of the People's Home—preparation for migration to Palestine—it is not surprising that Kafka would choose nationalistic books for the boys that were about war experiences, struggles, and the successful conquering of foreign lands. At the same time, he sent Chamisso's *Peter Schlemihl* (1814), Dickens's *Little Dorrit,* and other books from "Jewish booksellers" (LF 538 [BF 746]) to the children. Such practical community work reconciled Kafka with overtly ideological and political forms of Zionism. Increasingly he came to regard the Zionist movement in very practical terms as a necessary means to a more important goal.

Max Brod believes that the reasons for Kafka's support of Felice's activities in the People's Home were primarily ethical and illustrates this by quoting a saying Kafka was fond of, one "by the wise Rabbi Tarfon from the book *Pirké awot,* that is, *Sayings of the Fathers:* 'It is not up to you to complete the work—nonetheless, you should not stand passively on the side'" (PK 115).[27] Echoing Bergmann (or Berdyczewski), Kafka certainly reminds Felice at all times that the important part of her work is relating to people: the "main thing is the human element, only the human element" and Zionism "is not something that separates well-meaning people" (LF 498, 501 [BF 694, 697–98]). He does so to make her less apprehensive about the politics behind the Zionist enterprise: "Through the Jewish Home other forces, much nearer to my heart, are set in motion and take effect. Zionism, accessible to most Jews of today, at least in its outer fringes, is but an entrance to something far more important" (LF 482 [BF 675]). By this time Kafka had come to consider Zionism a necessary step toward a much more important result. His friend Felix Weltsch, though, a committed Zionist himself, observed that Kafka "at all times saw [Zionism] only in terms of preparing the way and never as a drive and inspiration itself."²⁸ However, Kafka, did see Zionism as more than this, as "positively the only path, or threshold to it, that can lead to spiritual liberation," especially because of its "youthful vigorous method, youthful vigor generally," and he believed "where other means might fail it kindles national aspirations by invoking the ancient prodigious past" (LF 500–501 [BF 696–97]; translation modified).

Kafka's letters to Felice end between December 1916 and early January 1917 because their relationship was in a state of crisis. There are no further letters until September 1917, when Kafka informs her of his tuberculosis, which leads to their official breakup. This explains why we hear no more about the Jewish People's Home. But in 1917 there was a general renewed interest in Jewish education in Prague, and an increasing number of voices requested the establishment of "The Jewish People's Home in Prague" (S 18 Jan. 1918:3–4). Though this project was never realized, Brod and others spent the following years planning the establishment of a Jewish elementary school. The first parents' meeting in connection with it was held on 6 November 1917, and the Zionist Oskar Epstein gave a lecture called "The Education of Our Children and Our Life" (BKB 483n.71). Brod discussed the evening with Kafka, but neither of them was present (BKB 191).

SOCIALIST ZIONISM/ZIONIST FEMINISM:
LILY BRAUN'S *Memoirs of a Female Socialist*

Zionism, nationalism, socialism, and feminism were all emerging political forces in the early twentieth century. Different as these movements were in their political goals, they all critiqued existing social structures and values. Frequently, intellectuals of this period were drawn to socialist-zionist, zionist-feminist, or socialist-feminist alliances. Gustav Landauer, for instance, who gave his support to the Jewish People's Home in Berlin, was a socialist with an interest in Zionism. Kafka and Brod themselves were leaning toward a form of socialist Zionism. Moreover, in his admiration for the writer and feminist Lily Braun (1865–1916),²⁹ Kafka made it clear that he saw a connection between the socialist-Zionist activities and Lily Braun's socialist-feminist struggle. There are many correspondences between Kafka's and Braun's views, experiences, and social engagements.

In May 1915 Kafka had sent Braun's autobiography, *Memoirs of a Female Socialist* (1909–11), to Felice because "this life really is worth sharing. How it longs to sacrifice itself, and does! A veritable suicide and a resurrection while still alive.... I am glad you are reading it" (LF 454 [BF 638]). Kafka's enthusiastic response reveals sympathy for Braun's socialist-feminist engagement, but he is even more impressed by her personal courage, dedication, and self-sacrifice. To be sure, Kafka was no feminist; nor did he have an inordinate concern with the feminist movement. But he was always critical about cultural practices that excluded women and in 1911 commented, "the fact that women are excluded from the study of the Talmud is really destructive of Jewish family life; when the man wants to discuss learned Talmudic matters—the very core of his life—with guests, the women withdraw to the next room or rather must withdraw" (DI 196 [T 317]; translation modified). Kafka also cared about and consciously furthered an interest in Zionism in the young women around him, be it Felice, Ottla, his second fiancée Julie Woryzeck, or Minze Eisner, a young woman he befriended in 1920.

In 1916, after Felice decided to become involved with the Jewish People's Home, Kafka suggested that she read the *Memoirs of a Female Socialist* again (LF 486 [BF 679]), "for the kind of work to be done there at first, even a faint breath of the spirit pervading the *Memoirs* ... would be sufficient" (LF 498 [BF 694]). From this point on, the book's significance for Kafka lies in relation to his and his friends' Zionist activities: "By the way, I recently gave Max a copy of the *Memoirs,* and I am about to give one to Ottla; I am giving them away right and left. They are more appropriate for this day and age and more to the point than anything else I know, as well as being the liveliest encouragement" (LF 499 [BF 695]; LOF 46 [BO 83]). In commentaries such as these we see that Kafka considered the feminist movement a close historical parallel to the Zionist movement.

The histories of Zionism and feminism share an experience of oppression, a feeling of "Otherness" and discrimination. Sander Gilman writes: "given any historical tradition of perceiving the Other, whether as Jew, black, homosexual, or woman, there are variations in emphasis and structure in the code of Otherness. The projections concerning the Jew are different because they occur in different contexts, but they consist of the same raw material as do all other codes of Otherness."[30] Lily Braun herself compares the black liberation movement in the United States with socialist-feminist activities (626) and admires "a well-known Austrian writer, whose courageous books screamed out the entire suffering of the Jewish people who had been persecuted and suppressed for centuries" (288). The forms of discrimination addressed by Kafka and Braun are, for the most part, the result of racism and sexism, but they also involve fixed notions of social hierarchy that determine an individual's place in society. Kafka saw Braun's struggle largely in terms of class: "She suffered a great deal from the morality of her class, but she struggled through it like a conquering angel" (LFF 244 [Br 282]; 1920; translation modified). The Prussian values of her class are permeated with sexism, racism, and elitism, and they affect not only her as a woman but determine as well the treatment of individuals who are lower on the social hierarchy or belong to what is now called a "minority group." This is how Lily Braun's "feminist" struggle could become paradigmatic for Kafka.

Braun's upbringing was clearly determined by the sexism in her environment. She evidently had literary talent and wanted to write but could do so only at night because her mother insisted that she spend the entire day on chores. When Braun complained that she would not have to do this if she were a man, her mother replied: "Certainly not! . . . but since you are a woman you have to learn early that we never belong to ourselves" (161). Similarly, her aunt tore up her writing with the words, "I cannot stand having ink-splattering females around me. . . . A woman should in any event never live for herself, only for others" (107). The women of the previous generation had fully internalized the power relations imposed on their sex and did not believe that a woman had a right to her own identity, to develop her own individuality. The popular literature of the day, written by women of her mother's generation, preached in ever-new variations that "the man is the goal and purpose of your life" (47) and thus reinforced the passive female role model. By the time Braun reached the age of eighteen, she had come to detest not only German literature written by women but also her own sex: "A new reason for my antipathy towards women. I only ask myself: are we so small, so empty, so unfeminine—or is this what they have made of us?" (148)

Anti-Semitism was just as pronounced as sexism, both in Braun's class and in German society as a whole, and she inadvertently supports Kafka's skepticism about the promise held out by the Enlightenment when she describes how baptism and assimilation had not erased the ethnic identity of one of her uncles: "Even as late as the fourth generation, the holy water of baptism had not managed to wash away the memory of the family history" (39).

Moreover, her attempt to break with the Prussian values of the previous generation and search for a "female identity" in her own right is not very different from the Zionists' struggle for a Jewish identity. Both went against the "German" values of the German and Jewish middle and upper-middle classes and understood that assimilation into the dominant, male, Prussian (or Austro-Hungarian) culture was no solution to sexism or anti-Semitism. Just as women had internalized the dominant male values of German society, so had the Jews in their desire to assimilate. Both lost their identities in the process, and what remained in abundance, for the Jews as well as the women—as Sander Gilman's study *Jewish Self-Hatred* has shown—were the psychological effects of discrimination and assimilation: loss of identity, Jewish self-hatred, and Jewish anti-Semitism. Braun, too, was beginning to show the typical markers of the oppressed: a hatred of her own kind and a form of self-hatred. She describes these psychological consequences of oppression, her pent-up frustration, in terms that recall the animal discourse of the Zionists: "In cruel self-mutilation I wrote in one of my little blue books: 'Some uncanny, wild animal lives in my innermost being. It tears apart the firmest iron chains. Since my childhood it has driven me from passion to passion'" (158).

Ironically, it was Braun's mother who in the end acknowledged the detrimental self-destructive effect of the submissive female role model when she regained her freedom after her husband died: "You will come to experience it yourself, how the duty to live for others can drive us women almost to self-annihilation" (587). As a young woman Braun found fulfillment only in her reading. Friedrich Nietzsche's writings had a tremendous impact on her, and she also read Henrik Ibsen's works, "I didn't read them—I drank them like a thirsty person in the desert drinks fresh water. . . . And I saw Tradition and Convention without their colorful garb as naked lies, and at one glance I understood the doll house existence of women. Did I, too, not live by performing tricks for others?!" (208) We will see later how the ape in Kafka's "A Report to an Academy" performs similar "tricks." Growing up with Nietzsche and Ibsen, Braun rebelled and came to reject the values of her class. When she accompanies her husband to vote, for instance, she is told: "Out with the women! . . . Involuntarily I made a fist and with proudly raised head walked past the protester into the hall" (370). She also rejected the traditional forms of address, when people used her husband's title with her, which made her no more than an extension of her husband: "please—do not address me as 'Mrs Professor,' I abhor women's titles unless they are earned by the women themselves" (369).

As for Kafka, he rejected the values of the assimilated Jewish middle class, which his father had internalized: "here too you were conforming with the general method of treating sons in the Jewish middle class, which was the measure of things for you, or at least with the values of that class" (DF 177 [Z 44]).[31] Unlike Kafka's father, who showed disdain for the lower-class Yiddish actors, Kafka and Braun identified with the underprivileged—the working classes or the lower-class Eastern European Jew. They believed that there were individuals in these groups who still had an identity, who represented the "authentic," uncontaminated working-class person or the "authentic" unassimilated Jew.[32]

Further parallels lie in the types of activities that Braun and Kafka participated in. For one, there was Hugo Bergmann's *völkische Kleinarbeit* (practical community work), such as attending "Jewish parent evenings," establishing Jewish kindergartens and schools, supporting the Jewish refugee school during World War I or the Berlin Jewish People's Home. This type of *Kleinarbeit* (small community work), albeit in a socialist-feminist context, is also what Braun cared about. It was a great revelation for Braun when she participated in the "opening of a workers' restaurant" (Braun 629) in France together with Anatole France and Jean Jaurès, the French socialist leader. This restaurant ensured that families could have a cheap meal even if the mothers were working, which gave Braun the idea to create "household cooperative associations":

> In the working class quarters of the big cities every block of tenements should be equipped with a central kitchen, which provides the tenants with their meals ... Daycare and kindergartens should be added, where those children can stay who are without their mothers during the day. ... One of the most important aspects of the woman's question is to find a solution for women to free them from the double work load of domestic work and work outside of the home. And what is true for the working class woman is equally true of the intellectually active woman. (Braun 630)

Ironically, she encountered much opposition from the Social Democratic Party, which considered this type of community work "distractions from the main goal, i.e. the realization of socialism, and from the political struggle which alone is important" (Braun 647).

Like Kafka, Braun was also involved in educational projects: she helped found an "educational club for working class women" (590), participated in a "school project," and listened to talks about the "vocational school of the future, which would replace the cramming school of the present" (741), based on Pestalozzi's educational philosophy. She and her husband finally discovered a school for their son that was not imbued with Prussian values, one "where young people can develop into free and happy individuals, by exercising their body and mind, alternating between play and work, a school whose principal is brave enough to block out the restrictive and cold-hearted Prussian mind-set" (568–69).

Yet, true acceptance for the emancipated and politically engaged woman seemed to be an unreachable goal. Braun realized that except for a few men who respected her, ultimately she was not taken seriously; she felt "the German scholar's lack of regard for women who are entering his circle" (297). There are various examples of chauvinism in many of the Social Democratic leaders who agreed only in theory that women should be treated as equals.[33] But while many Zionists were also chauvinistic in their personal relations with women, at the same time, within the Prague Zionist circle, women were invited to participate and some came to hold important positions.[34] Moreover, these men not only included the women in their political activities, but they also engaged in making women more literate. Kafka himself participated in such activities and he also showed real insight into the importance of an education for women. The question of feminism arose between him and Felice, because at one point he replied, "You probably wanted to frighten me with your remark about the equality of women?" (LF 497 [BF 692]; translation modified). When it came to educating the children in the People's Home, he was the one who pointed out to her the chauvinism in the educational text by Foerster that the teachers were using: "Incidentally, have you noticed that Foerster, to begin with at least, pays no particular attention to the education of girls? This gives you the opportunity to supplement according to your own experience" (LF 509 [BF 709]). Kafka encouraged his fiancée to do her part in redefining stereotypical gender models.

Unlike these Jewish men, the German men described in Braun's memoir found it difficult to identify with the women's plight. Even men of a working-class background considered themselves liberated and superior and the women as substandard and caught up in psychological warfare. Major Social Democratic leaders highlighted the psychological symptoms of oppression in women in order to dismiss the feminist movement. Thus, Ignaz Auer comments, "[Women] have all the bad qualities of the suppressed in the most concentrated form" (Braun 598). And Social Democratic leader August Bebel (who wrote the 1879 book *Woman and Socialism,* arguing for women's emancipation) remarks: "With women you have to expect that they will be seized with horror. In the Middle Ages they would have burned you at the stake, today you will be railed at by 100 mouths foaming with rage and speared on 100 quills" (Braun, 499). Interestingly enough, Braun finally identified the impossibility of being treated as an equal in German society as something that was culture specific. On a visit to England she realized: "Strange: we were taken seriously: I waited in vain for the patronizing benevolent smile on the men's faces, with which my own countrymen tend to regard the political woman" (417). Braun never explicitly made the connection between the treatment of Jews and women. Kafka, however, by seeing her struggle as paradigmatic, raises fundamental questions that are significant for understanding the relationship between race and gender in regards to the hegemonic patriarchal power structures of the time.

The Curse of Assimilation: "A Report to an Academy"

"A Report to an Academy" was published in the November 1917 issue of Martin Buber's journal *Der Jude*. Max Brod immediately identified it as "the most original satire of assimilation which has ever been written! Read it again in the last issue of the 'Jew.' The assimilationist who does not want freedom, not eternity, only a way out!"[35] The ape Rotpeter can be seen as a caricature of the Jewish assimilationist, the successful social climber who despises his origins and who is overly sensitive about drawing attention to his "true" identity. Kafka here exposes the previous generations' optimism, their faith in equality, tolerance, and emancipation, as a mistake, the "wrong way out." In addition, the ape's report may well represent a reply to the enthusiastic "First Report" published by the Berlin Jewish People's Home, disclosing the tortured psyche of one of their educational experiments.

The ape Rotpeter was caught on the Gold Coast in Africa and brought to a zoo in Hamburg, Germany. Many Jewish refugees from the East left Europe from Hamburg on their way to America. Unlike them, the ape cannot leave and ends up in a zoo. The link between the Gold Coast and Eastern European Jewish culture presents itself when we remember that Kafka compared the Hasidic Jews he visited with Brod and Langer in 1915 to "a tribe of African savages" (FK 153). Moreover, the fact that Kafka chose to use the Gold Coast as the home of the ape is significant as well, because there is an inside joke here in the word combination "Gold Coast," which links it with Jewish culture: proper names with "gold" in them are very common Jewish names. Furthermore, Kafka's use of the word *stamme* (originating from) instead of *komme* (coming from) (E 323 ["I belong to the Gold Coast," CS 251]) clearly echoes the nouns *Abstammung* (extraction) or even *Abstammungslehre* (theory of evolution). The ape Rotpeter, then, is hinting at his origins in a roundabout, ironic way, referring to Eastern Europe via Africa and alluding to Darwin's theory of evolution in order to present Eastern European Jewish culture as a backwater, pre-evolutionary and uncivilized.

Rotpeter claims that his evolution into a "human" was never based on a free decision. Caught in the cage, he says, "I had no way out but I had to devise one, for without it I could not live.... Only a way out; right or left, or in any direction" (CS 253–4 [E 326]). He decided not to be "stubborn" (CS 250 [E 322]) and hold onto his previous ape existence but rather to assimilate into the dominant culture. This way Rotpeter gets out of the Hamburg zoo and becomes a performer, making a living as a freak on "all the great variety stages of the civilized world" (CS 251 [E 323]). Over the years he becomes so "human" that he is accepted in educated circles and has reached the height of recognition when he is invited to report to the learned Academy. However, the price the ape has had to pay for his "successful" assimilation is high. Rotpeter achieves success, as Leo Weinstein argues quite rightly, by doing "his best to meet this strange universe on *its* terms rather than on his own."[36] Yet, herein lies precisely his problem: not only is Rotpeter aping or copying his environment (compare the German *nachäffen*), but he pushes himself to internalize the values of the dominant society, which makes him increasingly masochistic: "Ah, one learns when one has to; one learns when one needs a way out; one learns at all costs. One stands over oneself with a whip; one flays oneself at the slightest opposition" (CS 258 [E 331]). Kafka shows little sympathy for the ape and satirizes the path of his evolution, which Rotpeter, in hindsight, calls his "forced career" (CS 250 [E 322]).

For one, Kafka caricatures the myth of the German Enlightenment that the previous generation of Jews so blindly believed in. The average humans who help the ape along, those who work for the hunting expedition Firma Hagenbeck, are anything but civilized and enlightened. They are represented as uncultivated, lower-class boors. The first thing the ape learns from them is to shake hands (CS 251 [E 323]); otherwise they are loud, rough, and vulgar with each other (CS 254 [E 327]); sadistic with those who are inferior, such as the ape (CS 257 [E 330]); and they smoke and indulge in red wine and Schnapps (CS 251, 256 [E 323, E 329–30]). Physically big and heavy, they slap themselves on their knees when they get excited, and they are in fact so slow that if they want to rub their eyes, they are said to lift their hands as if they were weights (CS 254 [E 327]). The ape's representation of the upper social levels of "German" society is equally ironic. Rotpeter's progress is so rapid that he uses up "many teachers, indeed, several teachers at once" (CS 258 [E 332]). Here Kafka satirizes the anti-Semitic stereotype of the ruthless Jewish social climber when Rotpeter's "success" becomes such a trial for the "slow" Germans that one of them even has to be admitted to the hospital and, to top it off, Rotpeter is soon in a position to employ his teachers (CS 258 [E 332]). If anything, his teaching experience has made Rotpeter disdainful of the humans around him and openly sarcastic about the achievements of the Age of Reason and Humanity: "That progress of mine! How the rays of knowledge penetrated from all sides into my awakening brain!" (CS 258 [E 332]).

Regarding the ape's "career," Spector reminds us specifically of the "training" of the Galician schoolchildren in the Prague refugee school and at the Berlin Jewish People's Home, which was "presided over primarily by well-meaning assimilated Jews" (193). Despite his enthusiastic response, Kafka had found the "First Report" of the Jewish People's Home flawed, because "above all, and continuously, there is some arrogance in the Report" (LF 522 [BF 725]). The ape, therefore, may well be the "successful" product of such educational efforts to "enlighten" him. Rotpeter is not thankful but openly resentful and ridicules the "gentlemen" at the Academy by reminding them of their "life as apes" (250).

Kafka also knew the metaphor of the "trained animal" for the assimilated Jew from Mendele's novel *The Mare*.[37] A satire of assimilation and the Enlightenment, this novel is equally sarcastic about the promises held out by the ideals of the Enlightenment. Here, the protagonist Izzy belongs to the "Society for the Prevention of Cruelty to Animals" and believes in Enlightenment values. But the old mare, who represents the Jewish people in exile, sneers at him: "It's pure theater! By God! Modern times really deserve the name: The Age of Moaning, Talking, and Blabbering!" (Pinès, *Histoire*, 189; Neugroschel 617). She does not believe that a "modern" education will help her and she proves to be right. Izzy has written a "report" to the Society, and they reply that before they can do anything for her, the mare has to give up her present way of life and adapt to their customs; they demand total assimilation:

> First of all, the mare ought to have her elflocks removed. Let her become more presentable. In order to avoid a great measure of conflict on this issue

and to improve her condition in the future, it is, in our opinion, necessary to do something about her dreadful ignorance. She has to be led onto the right path, she has to be trained and educated, taught how to walk properly, etc, etc. Then, when she has learned all the tricks required of a trained horse, she will be worthy of our commiseration, and our society will stand by her and not permit any maltreatment of her. (Pinès, *Histoire,* 189; Neugroschel 610)

The mare responds by asserting her own identity, as miserable as it may be, and challenges the Society's position: "'What right do you have to prevent someone from eating, from breathing freely, until he masters some trick or other?'" (Pinès, *Histoire,* 192; Neugroschel 618–19). She resents this kind of "education" and calls it "monkey business," which means being taught "some trick or other": "'What's the use of lovely harnesses, expensive decorations . . .—all these rewards for clever performance?' And she sneers, 'Dance, little animals, dance!'" (Neugroschel 618–19, 606)

Unlike the Mare, Kafka's ape pursues the path of assimilation, but his fate illustrates that the mare's skepticism is justified. Kafka satirizes the consequences of the ape's decision to assimilate when he highlights his schizophrenic existence in German society. Renouncing his own nature ever more and replacing it with the values of the dominant culture, Rotpeter quickly internalizes the stereotypes society projects on his kind. That this cannot remain without an effect on his sense of identity is self-evident. He is self-deprecating toward himself ("free ape as I was" [CS 250; E 322]) and also projects these stereotypes onto other members of his group. We see this when he shows scorn for the other "performing ape Peter" and arrogantly stresses that he is proud of the distance between his new identity and his earlier existence (CS 251 [E 324]). Kafka here mocks the assimilated Jew's oversensitivity about revealing his origins.

Moreover, parodying the Haskalah motto, "Be a man in the street and a Jew at home,"[38] which Rotpeter quickly absorbs, Kafka satirizes his strict separation of home and social life: when he comes home from "social gatherings" he finds his "half-trained chimpanzee wife" waiting for him and "takes comfort from her as apes do" (E 333 [CS 259]). In fact, he is paranoid about being with his chimpanzee wife in broad daylight, "for she has the insane look of the bewildered half-broken animal in her eye; no one else sees it, but I do, and I cannot bear it" (CS 259 [E 333]). If he is indeed the only one who can see the "trained animal" in her, there should be no problem being seen with her in public. The ape's behavior accords with Gilman's observation of "how Jews see the dominant society seeing them and how they project their anxiety about this manner of being seen onto other Jews as a means of externalizing their own status anxiety" (*Self-Hatred*, 11). Rotpeter is pathetic in his constant attempts to downplay his "Otherness," as, for instance, when he is so eager to show how much he is really appreciated and accepted by humans (CS 251 [E 323]). Always careful not to offend, he is downright masochistic when he excuses one of his tormentors who holds a burning pipe to his fur (CS 257 [E 330]). Rubinstein rightly perceives Rotpeter's "craven reluctance to accuse the members of the audience of having persecuted him. He can hardly avoid doing this if he remembers his past in any detail: when he does mention some of these torments, he is careful to excuse his tormentors."[39]

Richard Lichtheim's *Das Programm des Zionismus* (The Zionist Agenda), a book that Kafka owned, represents this phenomenon as follows: "The systematic aping of foreign manners, anxious glances in the direction of the 'others,' the artificial covering up of anything that might stick out as Jewish, this becomes the Law of Life. Already we have a Jewish anti-semitism which is both disgusting and comical at the same time, which tries to justify antisemitism and to demonstrate Jewish inferiority. Zionism wants to lead us out of this spiritual wasteland" (26). This description fits Rotpeter well.

Another Zionist text that was in Kafka's possession, a 1901 pamphlet by Max Mandelstamm (1839–1912), a close friend of Theodor Herzl's, also illustrates that Kafka's satire was understood and shared by many of his contemporaries. Mandelstamm, too, draws an analogy between the assimilated Jew and an ape:

> With his long "caftan" and side-locks, the Jew lightheartedly throws his Jewish consciousness over board and adopts all the indecent behaviour of his environment and sacrifices all his respectable customs that have made his people weatherproof for centuries. . . . one doesn't know what one should be more surprised at: the false legend of the Jews' critical faculties or *their capacity for "mimicry" which surpasses the achievement of the most advanced ape*, or at their masochism which stamps them as repugnant buffoons and makes them despicable in the very circles they want to push their way into).[40]

Like Max Brod, any contemporary Zionist reader would have understood Kafka's caricature of the assimilated Jew. Jewish self-hatred, Jewish anti-Semitism, and status anxiety, as we observe it through Rotpeter, were frequent topics of discussion among Kafka's friends, as well as in many

Zionist publications. Moreover, if the ape's report is also a counter-report to the optimistic "First Report" published by the Berlin Jewish People's Home, then the Western Zionists are part of the satire and their educational fantasies about "humanizing" the Eastern European refugees are exposed as an error.

There is, to be sure, a certain playfulness when Kafka deflects German/Jewish stereotypes humorously. However, what Richard Lichtheim in 1913 could still see as "disgusting and comical at the same time" is almost unanimously perceived as deeply offensive now. The problematic is obvious when one thinks of the consequences of "changing a few words, namely, 'äffisch' to 'jüdisch,' 'Affentum' to 'Judentum,' and 'Affe' to 'Jude'" (Kauf 362). Kafka's attitude to Judaism seems disparaging, and critics have easily attached labels of self-hatred and Jewish anti-Semitism. For Kafka and many contemporary Zionists, though, these were the very "diseases" they were trying to combat. They firmly believed that assimilation had made the Jewish mind sick. Max Brod even talked about "structural afflictions of the Jewish soul"[41] and humorously suggested the Jewish people needed "at least 200 years of holidays and fresh air."[42] For Kafka and his friends, Zionism represented a first step toward regeneration.

Many Zionist writers did not hesitate to incorporate anti-Semitic elements into their literary and political texts, and they did not shrink from ridiculing assimilationists. Much of this writing was borderline in the sense that anti-Semitic discourses and Zionist discourses were often indistinguishable; the same metaphors and literary devices were used by Zionists and anti-Semites alike and, quite consciously, too, for ideological purposes. As Anita Shapira states: "The Jewish national movement derived most of its diverse concepts and paradigms from the conceptual arsenal of the European national and social movements. Yet this same fruitful reservoir was also tapped at the same time by the anti-Semitic movements."[43]

But anti-Semites generally do not distinguish between assimilated Jews and Zionists, Czech or German Jews, reform or orthodox or Hasidic or business Jews; nor do they care much about these groups' identity problems. For them, Jews are Jews. And even if many formal elements of Zionist and anti-Semitic discourses overlap, one has to look at the writer's intention and the function of those formal elements in the respective texts. If these texts were intended to harm, degrade, debase, or eliminate a whole group of people—that is to say, if they have that kind of malicious intent—then they are anti-Semitic. If, however, they were understood as self-criticism or self-irony or even self-help by and within the group itself, then they are not.

As with Max Mandelstamm and other Zionists, Kafka's *intention* was not anti- but pro-Semitic. Either writer would have been very surprised to be called anti-Semitic in the post-Holocaust sense of the word. In a letter to his lover Milena in 1920, Kafka uses the term in a positive sense, calling one of her articles "excellent, sharp and mean, anti-Semitic and magnificent" (LM 153 [BM 206–7; translation modified]). Kafka was therefore not only aware of the offensive elements in his satires; he approved of them. Thus, he urged Elsa Brod (who read "A Report" at a public gathering) not to leave anything out: "And should the text contain something dirty, don't leave it out. If one wished to clean it up really, there would be no end to it" (LFF 168 [Br 197]; translation modified). The Zionists believed, in a Freudian fashion, that by exposing the "disease," they were making a step toward healing.

"A Report" contains much that is "dirty," such as the ironic play on the anti-Semitic discourse on circumcision when the ape remarks he loves pulling down his pants in front of visitors and insists: "I can take my trousers down before anyone if I like" (CS 252 [E 324]). Does the ape's willingness to expose "the mark of the Jew"[44] not suggest an ironic counterdiscourse, especially since Rotpeter ridicules the journalist who criticizes him for revealing himself in public? If the journalist pulled his own pants down, he counters, "that would be quite another story, and I will let it stand to his credit that he does not do it" (CS 252 [E 324]). Moreover, Rotpeter inverts the stereotypes that were imposed on him and directs them back at his audience. He is very aware of being put on display and can hardly hold back his resentment because he knows that he is invited by the Academy in order to be rewarded for his "tricks," his "monkey business," his "clever performance." Polite and ingratiating on the surface, he is mocking his audience at the same time. Kafka has given the ape a voice to express his feelings, and his words are "*aimed at* the all-knowing academy" (Gilman, *Self-Hatred*, 282; my emphasis). There is a nasty twist to Rotpeter's humor in relation to those who have allowed or rather pressured him to assimilate. He needs to feel superior and despises society for making assimilation so easy for him and for its lack of sophistication, "always the same faces, the same movements, often it seemed to me there was only the same man. So this man or these men walked about unimpeded. . . . It was so easy to imitate these people" (CS 255 [E 328–9]). Rotpeter's report therefore functions both as a means of self-assertion and as a form of revenge on society.

It should not be forgotten that Jonathan Swift and Gustave Flaubert were among Kafka's favorite writers, both great ironists and Flaubert, in particular, like Kafka, was a highly self-conscious artist, perfectionist in formal inscription, dissector of human consciousness. Kafka's last companion, Dora Diamant, perceptively describes Kafka's "method" as one of dissection: "cold, practical, gifted with a sure hand."[45] In his satires of Jewish life in the Diaspora, Kafka is something of a Jewish Flaubert. Rotpeter's fundamental unhappiness reveals that no matter how much respect he may have won from the Academy and other individuals who crossed his path, he will never gain universal acceptance. The rest of humanity will never be able to tell the difference between him and any other "ape." The stigma of his "racial" identity will always be with him; it is imprinted on him, like the scar below his hip, or in his very language, which critics have easily identified as "Mauscheln."[46] Zionists like Mandelstamm scorned the assimilationists' inability to acknowledge this and to draw their conclusions from it. Like them, Kafka exposes it all: "Everything is open; . . . there is nothing to conceal" (CS 252 [E 324]). For this story, too, the printing process of the torture machine in "The Penal Colony" is an appropriate metaphor for Kafka's writing, relentlessly exposing the ongoing act of discovery through inscription.

❧ 6 ❦

Anti-Semitism and Self-Hatred

(1916–1924)

ANTI-SEMITISM AND ASSIMILATION

Zweig, Grünberg, Brod

Rotpeter's profound self-hatred is matched by no other figure in Kafka's writing—not even by Gregor Samsa, who would have ample reason to hate himself. But self-hatred and anti-Semitism were frequent themes in many contemporary writings, such as Arnold Zweig's play *Ritual Murder in Hungary* (1914),[1] for which Zweig (along with his other work) received the Kleist Prize in 1915. Kafka was awarded the Fontane Prize at about the same time, and both awards were announced together in *Selbstwehr* (S 10 Dec. 1915:7). Arnold Zweig (1887–1968), like Kafka, had Zionist sympathies and later, in 1923, began to work for the Zionist newspaper *Jüdische Rundschau*.

Kafka was deeply touched when he read Zweig's play (in October 1916), which is based on the blood libel trial at Tisza Eszlar in Hungary in 1882–83. A young boy, Móric Scharf, is accused of ritual murder and made to testify against his family and fellow Jews. In real life he was pardoned after a long trial; however, in Zweig's version, Scharf feels so ashamed and guilty for having betrayed his people that he takes his own life. Kafka was critical of the drama, but it moved him emotionally: "its supernatural scenes are as contrived and feeble as I would have expected from what I know of Zweig's work. The terrestrial scenes on the other hand are intensely alive, taken no doubt largely from the excellent records of the case.... I no longer see him [it][2] the way I used to. At one point I had to stop reading, sit down on the sofa, and weep. It's years since I wept" (LF

530 [BF 735–36]). Kafka was affected by Zweig's changes to the original event, by his shift to Western Zionist concerns, such as self-hatred.

A specifically Eastern perspective is provided by Kafka's friend Abraham Grünberg, who had come to Prague with the refugees in 1914. In November 1916 he presented Kafka with a copy of his 1916 book *Ein jüdisch-polnisch-russisches Jubiläum* (A Jewish-Polish-Russian Jubilee), dedicated to him with the following inscription: "Not being a Zionist means only wanting to think back two or three generations [*Nicht Nationaljude sein, heißt nur zwei oder drei Generationen zurückdenken wollen*]" (KB 137, 139).[3] Grünberg's book is an eyewitness account of a pogrom in his home town of Siedlce in 1906 and largely autobiographical: the author had been involved with the "Bund," the Jewish socialist organization, and describes the Bund's participation in the Russian revolution and their fight for freedom. However, after initial hopes for political equality through the October Manifesto (1905), there was quick disillusionment only a few days later "when the first news came in of the pogroms in Kiev, Odessa, as well as in other cities, which lasted several days" (9). These pogroms took place in about seven hundred cities in Russia, Poland, and Ukraine:

> In the weeks following the granting of fundamental civil rights and political liberties, pogroms directed mainly at Jews but also affecting students, intellectuals, and other national minorities broke out in hundreds of cities, towns, and villages, resulting in deaths and injuries to thousands of people. In the port city of Odessa alone, the police reported that at least 400 Jews and 100 non-Jews were killed and approximately 300 people, mostly Jews, were injured, with slightly over 1,600 Jewish houses, apartments, and stores incurring damage. These official figures undoubtedly underestimate the true extent of the damage, as other informed sources indicate substantially higher numbers of persons killed and injured. . . . Indeed, no other city in the Russian Empire in 1905 experienced a pogrom comparable in its destruction and violence to the one unleashed against the Jews of Odessa.[4]

Grünberg also mentions the Beilis affair in connection with eugenics, the scientific evidence that was cited against Beilis at his trial in order to demonstrate the threat of the biological and physiological superiority of the Jews (11). Given the continual presence of anti-Semitism over the centuries, these are no isolated incidents that affect only "two or three generations." Grünberg's dedication to Kafka is a reminder that connections must be made among past, present, and future historical realities.

Max Brod, like Zweig, was preoccupied with self-hatred in his play *Eine Königin Esther*[5] (Queen Esther), which Kafka read in December 1917 (LFF 180–82 [Br 212–15]). *Queen Esther* is a retelling of the traditional Purim story in which Esther, who is the wife of the Persian King Ahasuerus, saves the Jews from a pogrom that has been planned by the King's evil minister, Haman. Kafka admired "a large part of the prelude, almost everything that pertained to Haman" (LFF 180 [Br 213]) and especially "the second act, which moved me greatly, and the whole section on the Jews" (LFF 181 [Br 213]). Here we have a condensed "history of the millennia" (LFF 182 [Br 214]). Compared to the historical Purim story, the most significant change in Brod's version is that Haman is no gentile minister but turns out to be a self-hating Jew who wants to destroy his own people (*Esther*, 107). Haman is not a villain but a complex character: disillusioned and cynical, a "good human being" but psychologically sick (77). In the end, when he reveals to Esther that he is Jewish as well and this is why he loves her so much, she replies, "I only understand why you hate the Jews so much" (106). Haman outlines Esther's function throughout the centuries as having had to wrestle with him. The message of the drama is thus that the "enemy" is not *outside* but rather *within* the Jewish community. The meek gentile king in the story is no threat; he does not understand what is happening. But Esther has had to protect the Jews from themselves for centuries—the curse is self-hatred. Esther loves Haman, but while making love to him she must kill him in order to preserve her people (110). Kafka was so taken by the play that he read it out in its entirety to his sister Ottla (LFF 180 [Br 213, BKB 211]).

Anti-Semitism at Home and Abroad

Rising anti-Semitism throughout 1920 culminated in the Prague riots of November. But even before this event, Kafka addressed different forms of anti-Semitism in his letters from the sanatoriums where he was convalescing and especially in his correspondence with his non-Jewish lover Milena Jesenská. Generally he was sensitive and ironic about it, but in his letters to Milena he frequently resorted to expressions of self-hatred. Early on in their relationship he had already described a nearly pathological desire "to stuff them all, simply as Jews (me included) into, say, the drawer of the laundry chest. Next I'd wait, open the drawer a little to see if they've all suffocated, and if not, shut the drawer again and keep doing this to the end" (LM 46 [BM 61]). Similarly, Kafka remarked to Brod and Weltsch from Meran (April 1920), "what horrid Jewish energies live on close to bursting inside a baptized Jew, only to be modulated in the Christian children of a Christian mother" (LFF 232 [Br 269]).

Kafka also recounted how he became the subject of curiosity among the non-Jewish guests in his hotel. About one of them—a general, who was trying to make out his accent—Kafka says with great irony: "So now explain to those true German military eyes what you really are" (LFF 233 [Br 270]). When he revealed only that he was from Prague, this was not good enough, and after they had eaten, the man "once more began to wonder about the sound of my German." Kafka thought he was perhaps more irritated by his looks than by his German, and noted that as soon as he revealed he was Jewish everyone at his table got up and left (LFF 233 [Br 271]). This may have been a coincidence, he acknowledged, and a sign of his own paranoia. We can see that this type of situation bothered him also, because a few months later he related to Milena how an acquaintance of hers had remembered his sister as "a Jewish curiosity" (LM 162 [BM 219]). A further scene at the dinner table revealed how anti-Semitism "displays itself in all its typical innocence": "The colonel, talking to me in private, charges the general . . . with 'stupid anti-Semitism.' When they talk about Jewish rascality, brazenness, cowardice, they laugh with a certain admiration and, to boot, apologize to me. . . . It is only Jewish Socialists and Communists who are not forgiven; these are drowned in the soup and cut up small with the roast" (LFF 237 [Br 275]).

Furthermore, still in Meran, Kafka came across an "editorial on Zionism" in a Catholic newspaper, which made available passages from *The Protocols of the Elders of Zion,* one of the most notorious anti-Semitic texts of the end of the nineteenth century, which argued that a secret Jewish conspiracy, the Elders of Zion, wanted to take over the entire world. *The Protocols* had been written before the First Zionist Congress in 1897 (where these Elders of Zion supposedly convened to conspire against the world) but were not published until 1905, by the mystic priest Sergius Nilus. The text had from the beginning been exposed as a forgery, but it was very popular and kept being reprinted and used to incite the Russian population to pogroms. After the Russian Revolution in 1917, Russian emigrants brought *The Protocols* to Western Europe, and the first translations came out in 1920.

Initially, Kafka found the excerpts "too tedious" (LFF 235 [Br 273]), but then he did recount the newspaper's argument to Felix Weltsch:

> According to [the author], Zionism was created by Freemasonry—a creation already partially absorbed by Bolshevism—for the destruction of all

existent institutions and the establishment of Jewish domination of the world. All this was decided at the first Basel Congress, which ostensibly was negotiating about various trifling matters in order to gain outward approval for the organization, but privately was concerned only with the methods for achieving that domination of the world. . . . There were some quoted passages from these protocols of "The Elders of Zion," as the participants in the Congress called themselves. The quotations were at once stupid and frightening, just like the editorial. (LFF 235–36 [Br 273])

In the middle of November 1920, Kafka told Milena about the anti-Semitic Czech paper *"Venkov,* which is now printing very much against the Jews" (LM 215 [BM 291]). *Venkov,* the official newspaper of the Czech Agrarian Party, had begun to run anti-Semitic articles in late September and launched an active hate campaign. Finally, the newly founded Jewish National Council, of which Brod was vice chairman, wrote an official letter of complaint "about the pogrom hysteria" (S 1 Oct. 1920:2). *Venkov* printed the letter from the Council and used it for further anti-Semitic propaganda. This was in turn published by *Selbstwehr*:

> It is strange how sensitive the Jews are wherever and whenever someone touches one of their kind. Immediately there are protests, lamentations, denunciations. . . . We personally had the pleasure to get to know them in our editorial offices when they acted—in their Magyarian ways—with the incredible insolence that they usually show to the poor Slovak people whom they consider so inferior. . . . For the greatest and most perfidious desecrators of the Czech people were and are again "accidentally" the Viennese and Prague Jewish journalists and our greatest enemy in the whole world until now was and has been the Jewish journalist. . . . But in relation to the pogroms, let us give the following explanation: we have only stated facts, that pogroms have broken out immediately wherever Bolsheviks were driven out of office. We have therefore warned the Jews not to place themselves at the head of bolshevism. Whether they follow our advice or not is their business. We only repeat: the Jewish National Council should take note that our people will not tolerate Bolshevik activities as calmly as the Russian people did! (S 8 Oct. 1920:4–5)

The situation became increasingly heated. The two national Jewish newspapers in Prague, *Selbstwehr* and *Zidovske prahy,* together responded with an "Open letter to the Editorial Board of 'Venkov'" (S 8 Oct. 1920:1).

Kafka was present when the events culminated in anti-Semitic riots, and "editorial offices of German newspapers were ransacked, German speaking passersby were beaten up, the German National Theater was confiscated, the archive of the Jewish City Hall was plundered, and Hebrew manuscripts were burnt on the street in front of the Old New Synagogue" (KH 57). He wrote to Milena that he had "been spending every afternoon outside on the streets, wallowing in anti-Semitic hate" (LM 212–13 [BM 288]), and "in the end he runs into an angry mob on the Eisengasse, hot in pursuit of Jews" (LM 218 [BM 295]). When the police were called in to protect the Jewish population, he felt "the unsavory shame of living under constant protection" (LM 213 [BM 288]). All of Kafka's friends were affected by these events: they found expression in Felix Weltsch's article "World Antisemitism and World Salvation" and in Max Brod's "Paths to Jewish Self-Recognition," both of which were printed on the front page of *Selbstwehr* (S 22 Oct. 1920:1–2). As for Kafka, on October 24 he wrote "A Little Fable," in which a mouse comments that she finds the world is getting smaller every day. She has been running and running but finally she has reached the last room. If she keeps running now she will run straight into the trap in the corner. "You only have to change your direction," said the cat, and then it ate her.

Two months after the November riots, an old lady in a sanatorium in Matliary, Hungary, attached herself to Kafka because he spoke Czech. He was not too pleased and happy when he discovered that his Jewishness might actually protect him this time, for he had overheard her saying "that her favorite paper was *Venkov*, especially because of its editorials. Delighted, I have been thinking of that all evening" (LFF 256 [Br 298]). He insisted to Brod that he was not suffering from "a persecution complex [*Verfolgungswahn*]," but he had learned "by experience that no place remains unoccupied and if *I* do not sit high on my horse, the persecutor will be sitting there" (LFF 257 [Br 298]; translation modified).

However, in a letter to Ottla he later admitted he had been mistaken in his first impressions of the old Czech lady: he learned more about her life and realized that she was "a poor, friendly creature, very unhappy (the disease has raged in her family), but still cheerful" (LOF 61 [BO 107]). When he revealed his Jewishness, she "did not 'exterminate' me ... but was just a little more friendly to me, as for that matter I was to her" (LOF 61 [BO 107]). Kafka knew to distinguish between different levels of anti-Semitism. There was the ignorant anti-Semitism that showed its, as he put it ironically, "typical innocence" and was part of daily life; there was the "evil innocence" lurking in the social environment, as in Oskar Baum's novel of 1913; and there were politically motivated forms of anti-Semitism, which he took quite seriously and whose consequences frightened him.

Assimilation: Jakob Wassermann and Karl Kraus

The growing racial tensions increased Kafka's skepticism about the value of assimilation, which he had long shared with many Zionists.[6] His advice to his sister Ottla in 1919, regarding her impending marriage to a non-Jew, makes the difficulty abundantly clear:

> You know that you are doing something extraordinary, and that it is good to do the extraordinary, but also extraordinarily difficult. But if you never forget the responsibility of such a difficult action, if you are aware that you are stepping out of line as confidently as, say, David out of the army, and if in spite of this awareness you keep believing that you have the strength to carry the thing to a good end, then you will have done more than if—to end with a poor joke—if you had married ten Jews. (LOF 37 [BO 69])

Kafka was less concerned than Max Brod about her loss of Judaism (LOF 38 [BO 70]); rather, he was worried because mixed marriages were difficult to maintain in this political climate. The Jews in Czechoslovakia especially were caught in a double bind: they were seen as Germans by the Czechs and as Jews by the Germans. In this respect Kafka remarked in 1921 about his superior, the director of the insurance company, that he was a very good man who had been very kind to him in particular, "though political motives have played a part, for then he could say to the Germans that he had treated one of theirs with exceptional kindness, even though the man was only a Jew" (LFF 265–66 [Br 308]).

When Jakob Wassermann's autobiography *My Life as German and Jew* appeared in 1921, it was debated and reviewed in many places in terms of Wassermann's precarious position as a "German writer." Wassermann (1873–1934) was a very popular German-Jewish novelist in the 1920s and 1930s and is probably best known today for his novel *Caspar Hauser* (1908), about a foundling who is ostracized by his community and comes to an untimely death. Wassermann had always been hesitant about Zionism. For instance, in 1910 Brod and Oskar Baum had attended a Bar Kochba evening (KH 375), where the guest speaker, Wassermann, suddenly declined to talk about the position of the Jewish artist in German literature (as had been announced) because he believed that someone who is "himself involved in the struggle cannot lecture about the struggle." Instead, he began to read from his novel *Die Juden von Zirndorf* (The Jews of Zirndorf, 1897), which still "expresses everything he has to say about Jewish men and women even today" (S 2 Jan. 1910:4). *The Jews of Zirndorf* has as its subject matter the coexistence of Jews and Gentiles in the Nuremberg area. Anti-Semitism is pervasive, but a dialogue between Jews and gentiles for the most part solves the problems, leads to a greater insight into racial prejudice, and eventually dissolves ethnic boundaries. Even though a fin-de-siècle mood prevails in the novel, the end holds out the possibility of a more hopeful future for Jews in Germany. Wassermann clearly belonged to an earlier generation.

In January 1922 Felix Weltsch added his voice to the public debate and published a long article in *Selbstwehr* on "Wassermann's Life as a German and Jew"; he wanted to make one further distinction that he did not think other reviewers had made. Everyone knows, he argued, that Wasserman's goal has always been "to be a German through and through without denying his Jewishness." With the publication of his latest book, though, readers had generally latched onto the last chapter with its refrain "It is in vain" and argued that he had failed in his efforts at assimilation. Herein lies the misrepresentation: "Wassermann does not argue that his complete assimilation into German culture was unsuccessful . . .—but rather: that he did not succeed in conveying his conviction to the German people. . . . And thus Wassermann exhausts himself in bitter complaints against the German people, whom he loves, whom he regards as his people, and who never fail to regard him as an Outsider" (S 13 Jan. 1922:2–3).[7]

In 1921, as well as in 1922, Kafka analyzed the tortured existence of the Jewish writer and believed it had to do with "young Jews and their Jewishness, with the frightful inner predicament of these generations" (LFF 288 [Br 337]). He made these observations in response to the most famous assimilated literary Jew, Karl Kraus, after reading the latter's polemic against Kafka's friend, the Jewish poet, playwright, and novelist Franz Werfel (LFF 287, 477 [Br 336, 513]). Karl Kraus was the well-known Austrian journalist, satirist, and playwright. Not only was he an acculturated Viennese Jew, but he had left the Jewish community in 1899 and converted to Catholicism in 1911. Kraus was famous for his attacks on nationalism, hypocrisy, and corruption in his magazine *Die Fackel* (The Torch) as well as for his diatribes against many (Jewish) writers and intellectuals.

Kafka's following remarks concern young Western Jewish writers, whom Kraus represented par excellence, and he also draws on the paradigmatic case of Wassermann.

> Most young Jews who began to write German wanted to leave Jewishness behind them. . . . But with their posterior legs they were still glued to their father's Jewishness and with their waving anterior legs they found no new ground. The ensuing despair became their inspiration (LFF 289 [Br 337], June 1921). And even if Wassermann should rise at four in the morning day after day and his whole life long plow up the Nuremberg region from end to end, the land would still not respond to him and he would have to take pretty whisperings in the air for its response. (LFF 347 [Br 400], July 1922)

These two evaluations of the contemporary Jewish predicament complement each other and reveal Kafka's consistent pessimism: he saw no hope for the future. The last citation is in response to Friedrich von der Leyen's anti-Semitic literary history, *German Art in Modern Times*,[8] which Kafka compares to Hans Blüher's anti-Semitic work *Secessio Judaica*: "It seems accompanying music to the *Secessio Judaica* and it is astonishing how within a minute a reader . . . can organize things. . . . : German property not to be annexed by any Jews" (LFF 346–47 [Br 400]). Von der Leyen makes it very clear that Jewish writers do not belong and that Wassermann does not deserve his place next to Thomas Mann, where he is often placed.

Wassermann's art has "something cold, brooding, demoralizing, a cruelty which evokes fear rather than love" that characterizes "the art of this race" (310). There is nothing natural, everything is technique and artifice: we see in him "cold calculation," "cruel logical consistency," "the entire art is derivative" (313). More than anything, Wassermann does not have a "specifically German psychology," and the same is true of Werfel, Schnitzler, and Sternheim; "we shiver in the coldness of these hearts" (314). Neither is Brod spared. The section "Unser Land" (Our Country), which Kafka singles out, includes a short paragraph that compares "the Wherwolf by [Hermann] Löns with the attempts of Max Brod—how incredibly these dialectical analyses, these artificially organized ideas contrast with the overflowing life in the work of Löns, and how cold and artificial seems their presence" (von der Leyen 345). Kafka also points out that Brod's novel "*Tycho* was found, in all due respect, suspiciously dialectic" (LFF 347 [Br 400]). Von der Leyen makes clear that there is no place for Jewish writers in German culture, because "first of all we need the German man, purified and hardened in the fire of his history" (391). It is astonishing that his literary history represents a "moderate German position" for Kafka (LFF 346 [Br 399]).

Within the context of the Wassermann debate—about whether a Jewish artist can be a "German writer"—we also have to situate one of Kafka's most famous statements from June 1921, which insists that "Jewish literature" cannot be "German literature": "*First of all, the product of their despair could not be German literature, though outwardly it seemed to be so. They existed among three impossibilities. . . . The impossibility of not writing, the impossibility of writing German, the impossibility of writing differently. One might also add a fourth impossibility, the impossibility of writing*" (LFF 289 [Br 337–38]; my emphasis). For Kafka, German-Jewish writers are in exile within the very German language they are using—their only means of communication. These remarks are still part of Kafka's critique of Karl Kraus (June 1921), but here as elsewhere during this period Kafka's usually critical, astute analysis merges with expressions of self-hatred and anti-Semitic rhetoric. Thus he continues "that in German only the dialects are really alive, and except for them, only the most individual High German" and then finishes off his sentence with the anti-Semitic comment that "all the rest, the linguistic middle ground, is nothing but embers which can only be brought to a semblance of life when excessively lively Jewish hands rummage through them" (LFF 288 [Br 337]). He goes as far as considering the presence of "mauscheln" within the German language as an "appropriation of someone else's property" and Jewish literature "a gypsy literature which had stolen the German child out of its cradle" (LFF 288, 289 [Br 336, 338]).

After this detour, Kafka swings back to his critique of Karl Kraus, arguing that while *mauscheln* characterizes the language of nearly all Jewish writers, "no one can *mauscheln* like Kraus, although in this German-Jewish world hardly anyone can do anything else" (LFF 288 [Br 336]). Kafka often greatly enjoyed Kraus's witty, cynical writings and was unhappy when he missed an issue of *Die Fackel*. But Kraus's unforgiving tirade against many Jewish writers and his arrogant, self-confident, and disrespectful comments about Judaism (not to mention Zionism) did not escape Kafka's criticism: "In the hell of German-Jewish writing . . . Karl Kraus is the great guard and disciplinarian and that is his merit. Only, when he acts like this, he forgets that he himself also belongs in this hell with those who are to be punished" (FK1, 275).

OF DEVILS AND DEMONS AND ABSENT TALMUDISTS:
HANS BLÜHER'S *Secessio Judaica*

Hans Blüher (1888–1955) was "one of the most fascinating figures of the intellectual scene" (Gilman, *Patient,* 158) during this period. He was involved with the German Youth Movement (*Wandervogelbewegung*) from its very beginning (1896) and quickly became one of their leaders; he was also well-known for "his two-volume study of the homoeroticism of the youth movement." This study, as well as "his development of the concept of bisexuality were heavily indebted to Sigmund Freud's early work" (Gilman, *Patient,* 158). Blüher had a liberating effect on many contemporaries. Kafka read his psychoanalytic work *The Role of the Erotic in Male Society* (1917) and welcomed his critique of bourgeois heterosexual society (Baioni, *Judentum,* 194–96; Gilman, *Patient,* 158–60). Blüher also had a tremendous influence on the Zionist hiking clubs. The Zionist youth movement Blau-Weiß (Blue-White), for instance, during World War I, advocated male bonding "not without an erotic dimension (drawn from Blüher's theories), [and was] sympathetic to the cult of the *Führer* and totalitarianism."[9]

Blüher's anti-Semitic work *Secessio Judaica: Philosophical Foundation for the Historical Situation of Judaism and the Anti-Semitic Movement*[10] (1922) aims at creating a scholarly and philosophical foundation for German nationalism. *Secessio Judaica* refers to a specific historical moment when this foundation could be established: the time when Jews involved in the Zionist movement started to break away from German culture. In contrast to Kafka's earlier reaction to the "tedious" *Protocols of the Elders of Zion,* reading Blüher was a different matter and created a sense of urgency for a response to him (LFF 330 [Br 380]). Blüher was a more challenging anti-Semite because he believed that German nationalism had much to learn from Jewish history, particularly from the Zionist movement. Kafka here encountered a mixture of mythical, pseudo-scientific anti-Semitism that tried to legitimize its racial bias ironically by using arguments that Kafka and his Zionist friends employed themselves. Kafka attempted to refute Blüher in his diary (DII 224–25, 230–31 [T 912, 923–24]) but eventually could not continue because he shared many of Blüher's ideas about the place of Jews in German society.

Kafka was not surprised by Blüher's sweeping generalizations; his initial response even contains an element of admiration: "Objections to be made against the book: he has popularized it, and with a will, moreover—and with magic. How he escapes the dangers" (DII 224–25 [T 912]). One difficulty he has is that he fears almost anything he has to say will sound profoundly ironic, yet "there is nothing further from [my] mind, in face of this book, than irony" (DII 231 [T 923]). Kafka immediately recognized the personal nature of Blüher's anti-Semitism: "He calls himself an anti-Semite without hatred . . . and he really is that; yet he easily awakens the suspicion, almost with his every remark, that he is an enemy of the Jews, whether out of happy hatred or unhappy love" (DII 231 [T 923]). Given the homoerotic framework of Blüher's life and work, the last phrase does "ask", "is Blüher in love with the Jews or does he hate the Jews because they make him love them?" (Gilman, *Patient,* 163). Kafka insisted that "attention must be called" to these logical "errors" in Blüher's argument so that one is not "at the very outset . . . rendered incapable of going on" (DII 231 [T 923–24]).

Yet, soon Kafka was unable to continue and instead encouraged his friend Robert Klopstock: "Somewhere in my ancestry I too must have a Talmudist, I should hope, but he does not embolden me enough to go ahead, so I set you to it. It does not have to be a refutation, only an answer to the appeal. That ought to be very tempting. And there is indeed a temptation to let one's flock graze on this German and yet not entirely alien pasture, after the fashion of the Jews" (LFF 330 [Br 380]). Gilman rightly points out that Kafka here "stresses his own Jewishness against Blüher's hypocritical 'Germanness'" (*Patient,* 162), but he and Binder also see self-deprecatory elements. Binder interprets the phrase "after the fashion of the Jews" as derogatory (KH 572), whereas Gilman sees Kafka's comment about his virtually absent Talmudist ancestor as self-deprecatory, "Kafka sees his own psyche as *deformed* by his Jewish ancestry" (*Patient,* 163; my emphasis). But these readings ignore that Kafka is after all "hoping" to have a Talmudist in his ancestry and finds it "tempting" to reply to Blüher "in the fashion of the Jews." The very repetition of the phrase "and there is indeed a temptation" testifies rather to a feeling of defiance than of self-deprecation.

What is very suggestive, though, is Gilman's linking the phrase "after the fashion of the Jews" with Freud (*Patient,* 162). In 1920 Kafka drew a comparison between the method of psychoanalysis and the Talmud: "There is no pleasure in spending any time on psychoanalysis, and I keep as aloof from it as I possibly can. . . . Jewry has always produced its sufferings and joys almost simultaneously with the appropriate Rashi commentary, and thus it is in this case too" (W 272, H 202, NII 529–30). By appealing to Klopstock to respond to Blüher, Kafka is asking another Jew to beat Blüher at his Freudian/Talmudic game.

For Kafka, the "temptation" lies not so much in rejecting Blüher out of hand. After all, "[i]t does not have to be a refutation," and "[Blüher's] perception, insofar as it concerns the Jews and not the other peoples, is profound and true" (DII 231 [T 924]). Like his contemporaries, Kafka had internalized many of the racial and biological discourses of his time, particularly those that circulated in "a broad grey area where ideas and images derived from Jew-hatred can continue to exist, reconstituted into Jewish national conceptions" (Shapira 220). Blüher's main argument in the "grey area" is that anti-Semitism and Zionism have much in common: they even agree on the most essential element by asserting the racial distinctiveness of the Jew. Blüher was familiar with the Zionist position because he participated in the "constant dialogue since the end of the 19th century between the anti-Semitic movement and the Jewish national movement" (Shapira 220). In fact, he is included in a collection of essays, *Der Jud ist schuld* (The Jew is Guilty),[11] which also features articles by Brod, Salten, Theilhaber, and Holitscher.

Blüher (like Kafka) considers the Jew's appropriation of German culture inappropriate (*Secessio,* 53). The Jew, therefore, has no foundation, no "essence," and has out of necessity shown himself to be very skilled at metamorphosis into virtually any culture. Kafka's "Report to an Academy" deals with this problem, but where Kafka highlights the psychological tragedy of the ape protagonist (his anger, resentment, how he harms himself more than others), Blüher sees the assimilated Jew as a threat. For Blüher the Jews have appropriated Germanness too well, and this very success—their invisibility—makes them dangerous. What needs to be done is to make the Jew visible, only then can he be removed from German culture: "Abandon Mimicry [ape-like imitation], separate from the German substance and retreat: *secessio judaica*" (*Secessio,* 39). Here Zionist ideology nicely merges with Blüher's racial agenda. Blüher even expresses admiration for Zionists because they make the Jew visible: "They do the worst which can happen to a Jew today: they loudly call out the name 'Jew!' and say 'I am.' They are the most annoying trouble-makers that Judaism has ever had to deal with" (*Secessio,* 21).

But then again he twists the argument and gives it a biological-racial dimension, welcoming Zionism because it will reveal to the German the "physiognomic distinctiveness" (*Secessio,* 55) of the Jew: "Our sensory organs will grow more alert and one will immediately sense . . . the movement of the Jew, his gait, his gesture, the way his fingers grow out of his hand, his hairline, his eyes and the tongue of the Jew. . . . We will be so sure that no error is possible and the latent ghetto in which the Jew lives today will manifest itself" (*Secessio*, 55). Here the self-proclaimed "anti-Semite without hatred" has found a way of distorting Zionist ideology by combining it with the "old" vulgar anti-Semitism, which draws on all the usual physiognomic associations with the Jewish body. More importantly, Blüher's wish that the Jew be made visible was more than one man's strange obsession: during the Nazi period the yellow star became the symbolic marker of the need to construct artificial difference.

Shortly after reading Blüher, Kafka externalizes the anti-Semitic picture of the Jew through literary creation. Gilman has rightly observed that Kafka's response to the racial discourses is often "mediated by texts," for this gives him the "control which the culture around him denies him" (*Patient*, 158). We can see such control mechanisms or distancing devices in Eduard Raban from "Wedding Preparations in the Country" (1907–8), who splits into two selves, sending one into the world while the other stays safely at home—in bed! Similarly, in "The Truth about Sancho Panza" (1917), Sancho liberates himself from his "devil" Don Quixote, sends him out into the world and follows at a safe distance (CS 430 ["demon"]; E 350 ["Teufel"]). Moreover, in direct relation to Blüher, we encounter another split personality in a 1923 letter to Kafka's former lover Milena Jesenská.

Responding to Milena's article "The Devil at the Hearth," which is about unhappiness in marital relationships, Kafka argues that this article is about a Christian-Jewish marriage (Milena and her husband Ernst Pollak), and its offspring is her essay. For Kafka, Milena's article is like a child who sees what the parents themselves have never seen, the "devil at the hearth" who is tearing this child of mixed parentage apart. The metaphor of the "devil," a common anti-Semitic stereotype, is an externalization of the "devilish" psychological disposition of assimilated German-speaking Jews and thus symbolizes a failed German-Jewish symbiosis. Kafka is drawing here on Blüher's discussion in *Secessio Judaica* about the psychological struggle in offspring who are half-Jewish and half-German:

> Whoever marries a Jewess, places in his children two great ancient destinies that cannot tolerate each other, and splits apart their nature at the core. . . . These Jew bastards are unhappy and cause destruction. They are always longing to be connected to the German component of their inheritance— which brings forth a peculiar voice in this part of their personality. There is no doubt that it is often possible to bring about the victory of the German

side and thus salvation. If this is not successful, then throughout one's whole life one will be torn between two antagonistic fates: *secessio judaica* in one's very biological make-up. (38)

What is so interesting is that Kafka in his letter to Milena has created just such a child torn in this fashion, a creature, he says, that never existed before:

> And now the child of this marriage is standing here looking all around and the first thing he sees is the devil at the hearth, a terrible apparition which didn't even exist before the child was born. At any rate it was unknown to the child's parents. In general, the Jews who had reached their—I almost wrote: happy—end did not know this particular devil; they could no longer differentiate among various infernal things, they considered the whole world a devil and the devil's work.... But on the other hand, the child sees the devil standing over his hearth very exactly. And now the struggle of the parents begins in the child, the struggle of their convictions trying to escape the devil. Again and again the angel hauls the Jews on high, to where they should defend themselves, and again and again they fall back down and the angel has to return with them if he doesn't want them to be swallowed up completely. (LM 229 [BM 310])

Kafka was not against his sister Ottla's marriage to a gentile, and he loved Milena more than any of his previous Jewish lovers. But Milena also happened to be married to a Jew who did not treat her well and had affairs with many other women (FK 223–24), whom Kafka here types as one of those "Jews who ... could no longer differentiate among various infernal things, they considered the whole world a devil and the devil's work." By association, Kafka blames all Jews, himself included, for the suffering Milena experienced in this relationship.[12]

More than that, Kafka takes individual phrases out of Milena's article and develops a Jewish-Christian (devil-angel) dialogue in which Milena's (the angel's) "true" love is juxtaposed with her Jewish lover's cynicism, atheism, and materialism. This is again reminiscent of Blüher, who stresses that the Jew can never express true love, because underneath everything there is only deceit and "pure materialism" (*Secessio*, 24). Blüher also, at the end of *Secessio Judaica,* formulates the irreconcilable antinomies between Jew and anti-Semite in the form of a dialogue (63–64). In his own fictionalization, Kafka can be said to project his personal anxieties into this dialogue when he applauds Milena for liberating herself in the end from the Jew/devil (her husband/ Kafka himself): "At this point at last, at last, good heavens, the angel pushes the Jews back down and frees himself" (LM 231 [BM 312]). This letter is a good example of Kafka's masochism and personal-political nihilism: liberation here is clearly not meant for the Jews, and the sequence of events fits the pattern of many of Kafka's texts, where liberation is usually for others and not for the protagonist.

Kafka's reading of Blüher and von der Leyen, an "accompanying music to the *Secessio Judaica*" (LFF 346 [Br 400]), reinforced his belief that there was no future for Jews in German culture. The child's sighting of the "devil" exemplifies this nihilistic vision. Like Walter Benjamin's "angel of history" (Paul Klee's painting *Angelus Novus*), the child sees nothing but debris, and there is no promise of salvation as the storm from Paradise propels this young generation into the future.[13] No doubt contemporary political events contributed to Kafka's pessimistic outlook that there is "plenty of hope—for God—no end of hope—only not for us" (FK 75).

In March 1921 Kafka alluded to the assassination of the revolutionary leader Gustav Landauer (1919) after the *Freikorps* putsch of the Munich Communist government: "And Bavaria? . . . they receive foreigners very reluctantly there, and they receive Jews only to kill them" (LOF 67 [BO 116]). He was also not surprised to hear about the murder of the Jewish politician Walter Rathenau: "It's incomprehensible that they let him live as long as they did," he said, and "so consistent with the linked destinies of Jews and Germans" (LFF 328 [Br 378]). In July 1922 Kafka was still preoccupied with the Rathenau murder and expressed fear of going to Germany (LFF 338 [Br 390]).

Furthermore, after the anti-Semitic November riots in 1920, Kafka voiced feelings of revolt and self-hatred: "The other day I heard someone call the Jews a 'mangy race.' Isn't it natural to leave a place where one is so hated? (Zionism or national feeling isn't needed for this at all). The heroism of staying on is nonetheless merely the heroism of cockroaches which cannot be exterminated, even from the bathroom" (LM 213 [BM 288]). Kafka knew that going away was the only "way out" when he agreed with the anti-Semitic Czech newspaper: "The *Venkov* is very correct. Emigrate, Milena, emigrate!" (LM 216 [BM 292]). This is why Kafka, who never fully embraced Zionist ideology, in the last years of his life increasingly supported Zionist activities and for a while seriously considered starting a new life in Palestine. His illness, however, prevented him from realizing this goal.

Life as a Farce: Which Way Out?

"Jackals and Arabs": Diaspora as Dead End

"Jackals and Arabs" was published in the October issue of *Der Jude* in 1917. For centuries these jackals have been waiting for someone to redeem them, and many critics have therefore discussed this text as a satire of Diaspora existence,[14] seen from the point of view of a Northern traveler, who could be identified as an acculturated "German-speaking Prague Jew" (Spector 192). Kafka may even have intended a specific allusion to Max Nordau here, for it was common knowledge that after his "conversion" from assimilated Jew to "enlightened" Zionist, Nordau had "changed his name from Südfeld (southern field) to Nordau (northern meadow)" in order to symbolize his "break with the past."[15] The third figure in the constellation is the Arabs, to whom the jackals are subservient. However, since the place of the action is not specifically identified, critics regard the Arab-Jewish relationship as symptomatic of the age-old strife between the Jews and any other host culture. From this perspective, the story can be discussed as a Zionist satire of life in the Diaspora.

The meeting between the traveler from the "enlightened North" and the jackals can be seen as an East-West encounter. The jackals immediately latch onto the Northerner, convinced they have at last found their true acculturated master: "we have been waiting endless years for you; my mother waited for you, and her mother, and all our foremothers right back to the first mother of all the jackals. It is true, believe me!" (CS 408 [E 280]). But the Northern traveler cannot take them seriously. They live according to the Law in order to be worthy of a "Messiah" figure who could come at any time. They are hoping against all odds, because their "Messiah" has never appeared and the Northerner is told by the Arab that he is not the first whom they have taken to be their true redeemer (CS 410 [E 283]). The Eastern Jews' hopeless wait for the coming of the Messiah is a topos in Zionist discourse, which advocated action rather than passivity.

Moreover, the jackals' entire history seems to be one great incomprehensible obsession with ritual and blood. References to ritual slaughter here merge with Jewish dietary restrictions and "modern" contemporary allusions, especially anti-Semitic stereotypes and ritual murder. On the one hand, the Northerner hears from the Arab that it is the jackals' "profession"[16] to drain blood out of animals and witnesses himself how obsessed they are with keeping ancient laws that have to do with ritual purity ("cleanliness, nothing but cleanliness is what we want" [CS 409; E 282]). Their religious observance is well characterized as a Jewish "profession" since it dictates every minute of their lives; yet this "profession" of bloodletting echoes the anti-Semitic ritual murder and ritual slaughter fantasies associated with Jews. The jackals resent the fact that the Arabs kill animals without draining their blood before they eat them; to them this is barbaric and against their ritual laws. Therefore they tear apart every carcass that is thrown their way so that all the blood gushes out: "the camel's blood was already lying in pools, reeking to heaven, the carcass was torn wide open in many places" (CS 411 [E 284]). This description recalls a passage in Arnold Zweig's *Ritual Murder in Hungary,* which states that "the book of Deuteronomy" forbids eating "any blood, because blood contains the soul; therefore . . . you shall pour it on the ground like water" (*Ritualmord,* 79). The jackals keep repeating this ritual again and again, but the irony is that they are performing it on a dead body, which empties not only the ritual but their whole existence of all meaning. However, the fact that they are using only dead animals is highly significant in a different way, for it shows that they are not "ritual murderers or slaughterers" since they do not kill. Kafka must have been aware of the contemporary critique of ritual slaughter, or *shehitah,* which involved charges that draining the blood of animals while they were still alive was brutal and inhumane. Gilman convincingly argues that Kafka is here "parodically rewrit[ing] the debate about *shehitah*" (*Patient,* 151).

The most obvious association with ritual slaughter is ritual murder. Gilman highlights the complexity of the jackal metaphor further when he points out that the jackals are also "ritual murderers in this ironic replay of the anti-Semitic stereotypes of the day" (151). Indeed, their "performance" for the Northern traveler turns into a mock ritual murder scene, which the Arab finds quite entertaining, commenting, with a happy laugh, that the jackals' whole existence has become a spectacle, performed for every traveler who comes their way (CS 135 [E 283]).[17] The farce begins after the jackals have acquainted the traveler with their rituals and state their need for a sacrifice, which "agrees with our old tradition" (CS 409 [E 281]).

Understandably, the "enlightened" traveler becomes rather anxious when he learns that they want to sacrifice an Arab, especially when they hasten to explain that they are "not proposing to kill them" (CS 409 [E 281]) and turn to the Northerner instead (to do it for them). Gilman rightly perceives that their "noble" sentiment testifies less to human decency or their strict adherence to the Law but rather reveals that they are "too cowardly and weak to draw this blood themselves" (*Patient*, 151). This is part of Kafka's satire, for now the jackals turn to the traveler to perform the ritual and plead, in mock religious discourse: "Therefore, oh Lord, therefore dear Lord, with the help of your all-powerful hands, cut their throats through with these scissors."[18] The scene ends with the ludicrous picture of a jackal bringing a small pair of rusty sewing scissors (a parody of yet another stereotypical Jewish profession) "dangling from an eye tooth" (CS 410 [E 283]). The scene is comical and turns their plight into a travesty: the Jewish tailor's "rusty" equipment is ritually unclean and ludicrously inappropriate for ritual slaughter or murder.

The jackals' life in exile and their longing for redemption is perceived as a farce by the Western world around them. "Jackals and Arabs," therefore, fits the often scathing critiques of Jewish life in the Diaspora in Zionist publications such as *Der Jude* or *Selbstwehr*. For all the Zionist critique of the Western assimilated Jew, the Western Zionists still thought of the West as more civilized than the East. Diaspora Jews were frequently depicted as wild animals in Zionist literature, as we saw, for instance, in Hans Bloch's "The Legend of Theodor Herzl," where the Jews were "ravenous beasts with glaring eyes and foaming jowls" ("Legende," 57) and remained in this state until their redeemer appeared in the form of the Western, acculturated Jew Theodor Herzl. It is not far from these "savages" to the wild blood sucking animals of anti-Semitic fantasies. Zionist and anti-Semitic metaphors merge in Kafka's text, for the jackals are saturated with the common stereotypes: they have a peculiar smell, they whine, and at the end of the story their natural instincts burst forth as soon as they see the carcass of the dead camel. They forget everything else (the Arabs, their hatred) in their obstinate insistence on blood letting, which is identified not with custom but with instinct. In the end the jackals "represent the Western fantasy of the Jews as always haunting the edges of 'culture,' unable to truly alter their instincts" (Gilman, *Patient*, 150). Here Kafka sees Diaspora existence through a Zionist and anti-Semitic lens.

At the Second Zionist Congress, 1898, Max Nordau called for the "muscle Jew," urging Jews to "become men of muscle instead of remaining slaves to their nerves. Strengthening of muscle must go hand in hand with the building of character—that is manliness, dignity and self-respect" (Mosse xxvii); the jackals obviously show none of these qualities, they are "slaves to their nerves." And not only Nordau but also Kafka and many of his Zionist friends believed this was a sign of degeneracy—a disease for which they had to find a cure. The jackals have managed to survive in the face of oppression, but they have paid a very high price. Their present form of existence is a dead-end, because they find themselves in a dilemma for which there seems to be no solution: on the one hand, observance of the Law is their only way of keeping their cultural identity; on the other hand, it has made them hopelessly out of touch with the modern world. Moreover, their desperate attempts to preserve their cultural identity make the jackals adhere to a perverted myth of "the Chosen People," which is no more tolerant of the dominant culture than are the views of the dominant culture regarding them.

In the end, Kafka's psychological subtlety distinguishes his satire from the overtly ideological Zionist literature of his day. Just as there was no way out for the ape in "Report to an Academy," the jackals (who choose the opposite path by resisting assimilation) are equally caught. Kafka's euphoric reaction to reading "Jackals and Arabs" in *Der Jude* passionately conveys this feeling of being caged in: "The orgy while reading the story in *Der Jude*. Like a squirrel in its cage. Bliss of movement, despair over constriction, craziness of endurance, feeling of misery confronted with the repose of what is external. All this both simultaneously and alternately, yet still in the filth of the end a sun-ray of bliss" (W 71 [H 52, 324; NII 30]; translation modified).

The frantic, caged-in wild squirrel appropriately characterizes the no-win situation the jackals find themselves in. The story's many echoes to contemporary discourses are well captured in the phrase "both simultaneously and alternately," with its many levels of signification going in several directions at the same time. Kafka's satire highlights the contemporary anti-Semitic/Zionist stereotypes about the Eastern Jew, ritual murder fantasies, the critique of ritual slaughter and also externalizes an internal metamorphosis that is the result of the jackals' life in exile. Gilman pointed out Kafka's "ironic replay of the anti-Semitic stereotypes of the day" (*Patient*, 151), but unfortunately he did not develop this notion, for ironic distance points to the existence of "linguistic weapons" and by extension to an existing counterdiscourse. Unwilling to compromise their beliefs, building their life on hope and faith, backward rather than forward looking, waiting for help and redemption to come to them from the outside, the jackals seek a solution to their plight. "Jackals and Arabs" exposes the price for survival in the form of a tragicomic satire and calls out for a solution without resorting to the heavy pathos of much contemporary Zionist writing.

"A Fratricide"

Ritual murder is also the main theme in "A Fratricide," written in July or August 1917. Critics have generally seen this story as a rewriting of the biblical Cain and Abel story, but this leaves out many other allusions, such as the significance of Shakespeare's Julia (Juliet), the name the murderer gives to the victim's wife, who is seen waiting for her husband by the window because tonight he is a little late. Upon committing the murder, Schmar cries out: "Wese! In vain will Julia wait for you!" (CS 403 [E 262]; translation modified). This contemporary Jewish tragedy incorporates not only the romantic love story from Shakespeare's *Romeo and Juliet* but also includes allusions to Greek mythology through Pallas, the voyeur and sole witness to the murder.

The preparations for the "ritual murder" are staged like a scene in a play. The murder weapon is "half a bayonet and half a kitchen knife" (CS 402 [E 261]), and Kafka emphasizes the ritualistic motion of the knife going "right into the throat and left into the throat and a third time deep into the belly" (CS 403 [E 262]). This is quite likely "a ritual reenactment of *shehitah*" (Gilman, *Patient,* 154), and one should also not miss the graceful, ritualistic gestures that precede the murder. In his preparation for the killing, murderer Schmar elegantly swings the cutting edge of his knife and, like a Jewish fiddler, draws "it like a violin bow across his boot sole while he bent forward, standing on one leg" (CS 402 [E 261]). This links the ritual murderer to a Jew: his name, Schmar, may also give him away, since it echoes the Jewish prayer "Shmah Israel,"[19] but *Schmarrn* in German also means an unreal tale, a joke, or plain nonsense.

The sound the murdered Wese makes when he is slit open—"Water rats, slit open, give out such a sound as Wese" (CS 403 [E 262])—characterizes Wese in an interesting way. Binder notes that Kafka, in 1913, compared "juicy Jewish sausages" to "water rats": "those juicy Jewish sausages (at least here in Prague that's what they are like, plump as water rats) can be cut up by every relative all over the place (the sound of the taut sausage skin being cut has rung in my ears since childhood)" (LF 163 [BF 259–60; KK 216]). Sausages and beer were a favorite diet in the Kafka household, especially at social gatherings. To Kafka, who would not touch this kind of food (as a vegetarian and someone who preferred healthy drinks like milk), all these revolting sounds created "a feeling of happiness. Meat can be steaming around me, mugs of beer drained in huge drafts" (LF 163 [BF 259]). The victim Wese is therefore a nondescript Everyman, a "friend" and "alehouse crony" (CS 403 [262]) who works all day long in his office, has a daily routine, and goes home in the evening to his wife. His name also carries different associations that characterize his fate: "Wesen" identifies him as a human being; *gewesen,* the past participle of "to be," hints already at his demise, while *verwesen* refers to the decomposition of his dead body.

Ironically, there is no moral condemnation of the crime or the murderer. On the contrary, after the deed Schmar experiences a feeling of liberation and exclaims in expressionistic fashion: "The bliss of murder! The relief, the soaring ecstasy from the shedding of another's blood!" (CS 403 [E 262]). Is the murder only a power game or perhaps an act of rebellion? Schmar alludes to Goethe's poem "Prometheus" when he tells his dead victim sarcastically that all is over now, though "not all the trees that blossomed have borne fruit" (CS 403 [E 262]; KK 216). Prometheus's scorn of Zeus and the gods, as well as his rebellion against their authority in Goethe's poem, find a parallel here in Schmar's outrageous interference with human life. Unlike Prometheus, who is creating man in his own image, Schmar has decided to end someone's life. Schmar is playing God. In addition, the narrative is highly ironic, because heaven just does not care. When Wese leaves the office and steps out into the street, the sound of the doorbell is so loud that it extends "right over the town and up to heaven" (CS 403 [E 262]). But heaven will not help Wese. The night sky even lures the victim into the dark, small side street where the murderer is waiting. Moreover, when he looks up into the sky the narrator says: "Nothing up there draws together in a pattern to interpret the very immediate future for him; everything stays in its senseless, inscrutable place" (CS 403 [E 262]; translation modified). And Wese walks straight into the murder weapon.

During this whole time, the private citizen Pallas has been watching the murder preparations intently from his window, "his dressing gown girt around his portly body" (CS 402 [E 261]), a well-fed, well-off, satisfied citizen. In Greek mythology Pallas is a brave giant, the friend of Athena, whom she kills by accident and whose name she then places in front of her own to remember him by. However, there is no fighting spirit in this modern, comfortable citizen with his big, round belly. The narrator asks why he did not interfere and gets no answer: "Why did Pallas, the private citizen who was watching it all from his window nearby . . . permit it to happen? Unriddle the mysteries of human nature!" (CS 402 [E 261]).

This modern Pallas does not deserve to be remembered for any heroic deeds, for he deliberately arrives on the scene when it is too late. Like Kafka's Odysseus, he is another decadent Greek. When Pallas testifies as an outraged witness, he and murderer Schmar examine each other: "The result of the scrutiny satisfies, Schmar comes to no conclusion" (CS 404 [E 263]; translation modified). Faced with Pallas, Schmar feels as nauseated as when the sensational crowd approaches the scene of the crime soon after, where Wese's wife has now thrown herself over her husband's dead body in a theatrical gesture of despair. Their Romeo and Juliet romance, if they ever had one, is over. Her passion is theatrical and fake. Schmar turns away in final disgust, "fighting down with difficulty the last of his nausea" (CS 404 [E 263].

Murder victim Wese could have been saved if Pallas had intervened or called others to the rescue. As a matter of fact, murderer Schmar never attempted to hide his elaborate preparations. He even held the knife into the light of the moon and made unnecessary noise: "the blade glittered; not enough for Schmar; he struck it against the bricks of the pavement till the sparks flew" (CS 402 [E 261]). Schmar wanted to draw attention to himself, and while he did draw Pallas's attention, the witness, instead of helping the victim, chose to enjoy the pleasure of being a voyeur to the deed. Ironically, after the crime this same man steps up as a "righteous witness" (gentile). *Evil Innocence* had been the title of Oskar Baum's "small-town novel," which exposed the arbitrary psychology of scapegoating and suggested that the social environment was at least as guilty as the "criminals" themselves. The murderer's nausea in "A Fratricide" is the result of the hypocrisy all around.

The fact that Schmar is likened to a Jewish fiddler and the murder weapon to the bow of a violin superimposes and at the same time deflates contemporary anti-Semitic stereotypes by conjuring up this Chagallian surreal figure from Jewish folklore, who is playing in limbo, from a roof top or suspended in the air. In a modern world that is the reverse of German classicism and romanticism, the Jewish fiddler introduces a note of sadness and vulnerability; Schmar's Promethean rebellion is botched, Goethe's dreams of flowering trees are over, and the Shakespearean romantic tragedy (where young love is extinguished by two clashing "families") is emptied of all meaning.

From the earliest biblical times of Cain and Abel—where a "brother" was willing to kill a "brother"—well into modernity, Schmar's murder represents another "history of the millennia" (LFF 182 [Br 214]), which is characterized by hatred of the "Other." In this modern version of an old tale, given the overt and noisy murder preparations, murderer Schmar appears to be testing to see if he can actually get away with committing a real ritual murder. It is astonishing and nauseating to see how easy murdering was and is. Given this state of affairs, the missing sign from heaven suggests that as far as the future is concerned, it does not look promising.

Creatures in Limbo: "A Crossbreed," "The Cares of a Family Man," and "The Animal in the Synagogue"

In 1911 Kafka had argued that Western European Judaism found itself "in a transition whose end is clearly unpredictable and about which those most closely affected are not concerned, but, like all people truly in transition, bear what is imposed upon them" (DI 190–91 [T 311–12]). Many animals in Kafka's texts are "transitional creatures" whose prospects for survival look bleak. These animals are mostly in limbo and alone. One of them, the creature in "A Crossbreed" (March 1917), is a kind of *Mischling*, half-cat, half-lamb. As big as a lamb, it has the head and claws of a cat, and the rest of the body from both animals equally. The crossbreed is torn between its two contradictory personalities and defeated by them because each side cancels the other out: the cat in it wants it to attack the lamb, but the lamb in it is afraid of the cat and unable to attack. Though it has the cat's "fang-like teeth" (CS 426 [E 320]) and claws, the crossbreed cannot attack anything or anyone; it has never been able to kill one of the chickens whom it stalks for hours on end and "has never yet seized an opportunity for murder" (CS 426 [E 320]). It cannot even call for help because it has no voice to make itself heard. With its split identity, the animal is paralyzed and "like all people truly in transition [bears] what is imposed upon [it]." Like the ape or the jackals, the crossbreed stands out as a curiosity and is "a great source of entertainment" (CS 426 [E320]). But unlike the former two animals the crossbreed has a good life as a pet: during visiting hours all the children in the neighborhood come and play with it. In turn, it is loyal to the "family" who raised it, though it is also essentially alone, belonging neither here nor there: "though it has countless step-relations in the world, [it] has perhaps not a single blood relation" (CS 427 [E 321]). Also, it is the last of its kind and will eventually die out.

Given the crossbreed's harmonious existence, it comes as a surprise when we hear that the owner wonders if it were not best to end its torn existence through the slaughterer's knife. But he cannot grant the animal deliverance from his predicament because he inherited it and "as a legacy [*Erbstück*] I must deny it that" (CS 427 [E 321]). The owner of the crossbreed is no rebellious Zionist, because he accepts his inheritance, and the two are still so intertwined that when the crossbreed cries the owner does not know whose tears these are, the animal's or his (CS 427). However, he feels it should not survive, because there is no place for it in the present except in his family's home, and even there it has already—over time—become a symbol increasingly divested of its signification (the animal still "thinks" that the family understands it, but the reader learns that the "father" sometimes only pretends that communication is possible [CS 427]).[20]

Another existence in limbo is Odradek, in "The Cares of a Family Man" (April 1917), who has no fixed home. Odradek is an inanimate object, neither human nor animal and yet alive. The survival of Odradek is almost painful for the family man to think about. This story was published not only in the *Country Doctor* collection (1919) but also in the Chanukah issue of *Selbstwehr* (S 19 Dec. 1919:5–6). Here it has its place among other Chanukah stories and is immediately followed by a little story on the *Trenderl*, the German term for *dreydl*, a spinning top, a toy for children. Odradek himself is as elusive as his name: he is and is not a *dreydl*. He represents what Theodor W. Adorno, in his insistence on the importance of literalness in Kafka, called an "association joke"[21]—that is, when Kafka takes objects, words, idiomatic expressions or common phrases literally and makes them appear as personifications in his texts. Odradek is also described as a "star," but this Star of David lives alone, has no purpose, and certainly has no religious or cultural significance. What bothers the family man who narrates the story is that an existence such as Odradek's, without meaning, empty, and hollow as his laughter, seems set to survive everyone.

A further theme of survival is played out in Kafka's only story with a specifically Jewish subject matter and one that deals explicitly with persecution, "The Animal in the Synagogue" (1920–22).[22] Here, a martenlike creature has for centuries called a synagogue its home. Its favorite spot is high up, close to the women's section, towering above the men. Many small synagogues in Eastern Europe had animal pictures on the walls. Though there is no evidence that there were any drawings in the synagogues in Prague, Kafka would not have had to travel far to see them in the country. It is quite plausible that he created this story from such a motif on the wall and made the animal come alive. The text says the animal's color "does resemble that of the paint inside the synagogue, only it is a little brighter" (P 49 [E 405]).

Considering the Second Commandment against graven images, it is not surprising that the animal has continually been threatened with expulsion: "There is evidence, however, that at that time the question whether the presence of such an animal might be tolerated in the house of God was investigated from the point of view of the Law and the Commandments. Opinions were sought from various celebrated rabbis, views were divided, the majority were for the expulsion of the animal and a reconsecration of the house of God" (P 57 [E 408–9]). The rabbis considered such animal pictures a distraction to prayer. However, despite many attempts to remove them, animal wall paintings survived as part of the folk tradition and remained a popular art form in synagogue decorations.[23]

In Kafka's story the "graven" image is freed from its fixed, "graven," position; it takes on a life of its own and escapes when in danger. Kafka also enables the animal to survive by eliminating narrative situations that pose a threat to its existence, employing his mock-Midrash as a tool. The animal lives in constant fear of being expelled, even though it has survived the rabbinic decision until now. On the one hand, this might mean that the rabbis' decree to remove it was never carried out and the danger is over. On the other hand, if it has not been carried out yet, then the expulsion might still occur. However, the narrator immediately eliminates this danger, interjecting that even if they still wanted to carry out the decision, a practical question needs to be solved first: the animal has to be caught. As with Odradek (who is "extraordinarily nimble and can never be laid hold of" [CS 428 (E 344)]), this is hardly possible: "in reality it was simply impossible to catch the animal, and hence it was also impossible to drive it out for good" (P 57 [E 409]). The lack of closure on the thematic level is echoed on the narrative level. The movement of the narrative goes in spirals and is potentially endless as possible interjections allow for continual narrative expansion. Thus, we hear that even though no one has ever succeeded in driving the animal out, this does not necessarily mean that no attempts have been made in the past. At this point there is room for a longer story, the recounting of a legend that the narrator says exists in the folklore of his people. But as soon as the legend begins, the narrative breaks off.

There can be no closure on the narrative level, because the persecution of the animal will be repeated in another fashion in the future. Standing at the Ark of the Covenant—the only time when it feels protected and is not afraid—"it seems to be gazing at the congregation with its bright, unwinking, and perhaps lidless eyes" as if it had something to tell them "but it is certainly not looking at anybody, it is only facing the dangers lying ahead by which it feels itself threatened" (P 55 [E 408]; translation modified). The narrator, who repeatedly comments on the animal's safety, seems perplexed: "What danger has it to fear, anyway? Who intends it any harm?" (P 55 [E 408])

But the animal, whose lidless eyes are always open, stands for much more than a zodiac on the wall in the synagogue. Like the crossbreed, it represents the memory of the past; but unlike the crossbreed, it carries its knowledge into the future. Though misunderstood by present and past generations, it has always been a symbol of the future: "Is it the memory of times long past or the premonition of times to come? Does this old animal perhaps know more than the three generations of those who are gathered together in the synagogue?" (P 57 [E 408]). In this regard, Kafka's friend Abraham Grünberg's dedication—"Not being a Zionist means only wanting to think back two or three generations"—can be seen as a warning. The blindness of past and present generations does not bode well for the future. The animal knows so much more than the three generations assembled in the synagogue that its fear becomes prophetic: the congregation may be unable to connect the past and the present with the future, but the danger that lies ahead is real.

4. One of many animal paintings on the ceiling of the Junction Shul, Knesset Israel. Built in 1911, this is the oldest synagogue in Toronto, Canada, that is still used today.

7

The Dream of Palestine

(1917–1924)

MORE *Völkische Kleinarbeit*

Hebrew Studies: Moses Rath

Around May 1917 Kafka began to teach himself Hebrew, working through Moses Rath's *Textbook of the Hebrew Language for School and Self-Instruction: The Language of Our People.*[1] *Selbstwehr* calls it "the best textbook for learning Hebrew for primarily practical purposes" (S 25 Feb. 1916:7), but Alfred Bodenheimer maintains it was "nothing of the sort... and provided secular Hebrew students with mainly classical (biblical) vocabulary and material."[2] The vocabulary is vocalized throughout, which facilitates reading, but otherwise the book is not easy; the grammar gets complicated immediately and is often not explained clearly.

When Max Brod found out about Kafka's studies several months later, he was taken aback: "His revelation that he had been learning Hebrew, forty-five lessons in Rath's handbook; never said anything to me about it. So he was trying me out when he asked me some time ago, with every appearance of innocence, how do you count in Hebrew. This making a big secret of everything" (FK 163 [10 Sept. 1917]). Forty-five lessons is quite a bit, considering, too, that Kafka was preoccupied with his extensive literary production at the beginning of the year, the elaborate wedding preparations with Felice in the summer, and his first hemorrhages in August. It is about a third of the whole Hebrew book (there are 150 lessons), plus there is a long, comprehensive introduction to plow through before one starts with the individual lessons. However, it is not impossible, because the initial lessons are very short.

Kafka continued working on Hebrew when he was convalescing on a farm in Zürau, a little village outside of Prague, with his sister Ottla from September 1917 through April 1918 (Binder, "Hebräischstudien," 134). Max Brod likely participated in some way during the summer, because in September he wrote a letter to Kafka in Hebrew. Kafka replied (from Turnau, where he was this time) that Brod's Hebrew was "not bad; there are a few mistakes at the beginning, but once you get into it, you make no errors" (LFF 205 [Br 243]). They repeatedly wrote letters to each other in Hebrew in 1923 as well (Binder, "Hebräischstudien," 134, 146). Kafka further continued his Hebrew studies when he was recovering in Schelesen (November–December 1918),[3] this time from the Spanish flu, a disastrous epidemic that killed more than twenty million people. From there he suggested sending Brod "a list of questions on Hebrew matters ... and we will have a correspondence in Hebrew [einen hebräischen Verkehr]" (LFF 209 [Br 246–47]). His next letter includes two pages with questions about Hebrew grammar, much of it in Hebrew script (LFF 209 [Br 247]).

In January 1919, Kafka left Prague again for three months in Schelesen, where he studied Hebrew with another patient using Moses Rath's textbook.[4] At the same time, his engagement with Felice having earlier been broken, he became romantically involved with Julie Wohryzek, who would become his second fiancée. After his return to Prague at the end of March, he must have begun his Hebrew lessons with his friend Friedrich Thieberger.[5] Thieberger, the son of a rabbi, was initially hesitant because he knew ancient Hebrew better than modern Hebrew, but Kafka would hear of no excuses ("Erinnerungen," 52). Apparently, Kafka had already studied "the first lessons from the textbook by Moses Rath" on his own,[6] and they got together "for many weeks ... at fixed times at [Kafka's] place, most of the time in a little room overlooking the courtyard behind the kitchen. He was very serious about his vocabulary book and written exercises and very annoyed when there were inaccuracies in the structure of the book." Thieberger especially noticed "the storyteller" in Kafka, "the joy of spinning yarns about little details and drawing from them as much warmth as possible" ("Erinnerungen," 52).

Lesson 63 in Moses Rath begins with a little story called "In the Forest." The scene is typically European. Here, two children, their parents, and a maid are going into the forest for a picnic. The sun is shining, and they sing a Hebrew song as they walk along. One sentence is of particular interest here: "On a branch sat a small squirrel, licking its paws." This is the only reference to the squirrel in the story, and one of the questions that follows the text is "What did the squirrel do?" Kafka's answer is to respond with a story. In his notebooks we find the following passage: "Climbing. *Snait*. It was a squirrel, it was a squirrel, a wild female nutcracker, a jumper, a climber, and her bushy tail was famous in all the forests. This squirrel, this squirrel was always traveling, always searching, it couldn't talk about this, not because it lacked the power of speech but because it had absolutely no time" (W 236 [H 176, NII 546]; translation modified). Kafka wrote the word *Snait* (squirrel) in Hebrew letters; curiously, there are no squirrels in Israel. This lesson, as well as many others, reveals Moses Rath's "Western" frame of reference.[7] The squirrel piece possibly falls into the period of the Thieberger lessons;[8] by 1919 Kafka may well have progressed as far as Lesson 63.

That summer back in Prague, he and Julie were looking for an apartment and planning their wedding. During this time, Kafka may have taken further Hebrew classes with his friends Irma Singer, Felix Weltsch, and possibly Brod. Irma remembers that she, Kafka, and Weltsch decided to leave their Hebrew class in order to take private lessons with Langer. These classes ended before Irma Singer emigrated to Palestine in 1920.[9] In the fall of 1919, Kafka returned once more to Schelesen (4–20 November), where he wrote his famous "Letter to His Father" (who opposed the marriage to Julie) before returning to Prague to resume his work at the insurance company. Kafka must have kept up his Hebrew during this period as well, because in the spring of 1920, while convalescing in Meran (3 April–28 June 1920), he was proud that he could use a little Hebrew with one of the guests, a "Turkish-Jewish rug dealer, with whom I exchanged my scanty words of Hebrew" (LFF 232 [Br 269–70]). In 1921 Kafka sent Klopstock a copy of Moses Rath's Hebrew book (LFF 311, 314 [KF 31, Br 364, 365]), along with Hugo Bergmann's collection of articles on cultural Zionism, *Jawne und Jerusalem*. Though neither text was part of his personal library, Kafka does not seem to have sent him his own Hebrew book, since the critical edition maintains he was working on Lesson 105 in Moses Rath in the fall and spring of 1923–24 in Berlin (NIIA 135–36).

Planting for Palestine

Gardening had been one of Kafka's hobbies as early as 1913, when he worked in vegetable gardens as well as at the Pomological Institute for Viniculture and Gardening in Troya, close to Prague. At the farmhouse in Zürau in 1917–18 he fed the animals (Ottla had bought a horse, a pig, goats, and geese) and worked in the garden and fields. Upon returning to

Prague, he again spent all summer at the Pomological Institute, and when he was vacationing in Turnau (September 1918) he did gardening "in the largest nursery in Bohemia (Maschek, Turnau)" (LFF 261 [Br 301; C 155; Bokhove, "Zionism," 48]). Obviously there was more to this than gardening for relaxation. Kafka was seriously interested in Zionist educational projects that established agricultural schools to prepare individuals for life in Palestine and attempted to get many of his friends involved in such Zionist related activities.

Ottla gained her first practical agricultural experience in Zürau, and after that she began "an apprenticeship in an agricultural winter school in Friedland [in the Iser mountains]" (C 156; Wagnerová, *Familie Kafka*, 164, 167). For the paper she had to present to her class, Kafka recommended she make use of a "renowned study on land reform: Adolf Damaschke's *Die Bodenreform*" (1902), which was "declared the basis of the policy of the future state" at the Zionist Congress in 1903 (Bokhove, "Zionism," 49). Furthermore, Kafka pushed to get her into the Hachschara, an agricultural school near Cologne (LFF 228, 467n.9 [Br 264, 511n.2]). He even promised to donate a thousand crowns to the Jewish National Fund if Ottla were to be successful, but the place was full (LFF 227–28 [Br 264–65]). Several of her friends from the Club of Jewish Women and Girls actually emigrated to Palestine in 1920, but Ottla married Josef David, a non-Jew, in July 1920 (Wagnerová 167).

Kafka also urged Minze Eisner, a young woman he had befriended, to join a Jewish agricultural school and recommended the Israelitische Gartenbauschule (Israelite Agricultural School) in Ahlem; yet all the places she applied for were full as well (LFF 226–27 [Br 263–65]). Kafka knew through Ottla that the school near Cologne, too, would admit new students no sooner than the following April, and even that was uncertain. When Minze was eventually accepted at Ahlem, it did not work out. She complained, for instance, about the literature they were reading; "Gogol, Hafiz, Li-Po: a somewhat random choice," Kafka admitted, but then he stressed not to expect too much since it was "an affair of West European Jewry, where all such things may be on the verge of breakdown. Perhaps you yourself will someday carry a beam from Ahlem to Palestine." Once again he recommended reading Lily Braun's *Memoirs of a Female Socialist* (LFF 244 [Br 282]). Minze left Ahlem in 1921 (LFF 260 [Br 300]).

From 1917 on Kafka's involvement in Zionist cultural activities increased. When Buber chose "A Report to an Academy" and "Jackals and Arab" for publication in *Der Jude*, he replied: "So I shall be published in

Der Jude after all, and always thought that impossible" (LFF 132 [Buber, *Briefwechsel* 1:494]). He also recommended poems by Rudolf Fuchs and Ernst Feigl to Buber, as well as Löwy's article about the Yiddish theater. His attachment to *Selbstwehr* became even stronger after Nelly Thieberger edited the paper from 1917 to 1919 and Felix Weltsch took over in 1919. Binder points out

> that in the last years of his life Kafka asked to have the Zionist weekly *Selbstwehr* sent to him outside of Prague, that he eagerly awaited the appearance of each issue, complained about postal irregularities, . . . borrowed issues (Br 273 and 332), encouraged friends to contribute to it . . . and even solicited subscriptions (Br 332 and 336). His solidarity with the goals of the paper is also apparent when—on three occasions in the last years of his life—he made texts available for publication in special issues for Jewish holidays: "An Imperial Message" (September 24, 1919), "The Cares of a Family Man" (December 19, 1919) and "An Old Manuscript" (September 30, 1921). (KH 572).

The importance of *Selbstwehr* for Kafka is quite obvious when he remarks in 1923 that he has been reading "no books, no newspapers, no magazines, or rather, yes, *Selbstwehr*" (LFF 394 [Br 459]).

Social events were still important, but often Kafka could not participate for health reasons. Thus, he could not attend the Twelfth or Thirteenth Zionist Congresses in Karlsbad in 1921 and 1923 (LFF 377, 378–79 [Br 440, 442, 443]; KH 575). Instead, he encouraged friends to pursue Zionist-related activities. In February 1919 he asked Max Brod to send him his essay "The Third Phase of Zionism"—which dealt with "Jewish-national social and cultural projects and activities initiated in the diaspora"[10]—for Julie Wohryzek (LFF 213 [Br 252]). When Kafka discussed Brod's essay with Julie, he was very pleased to discover that her previous "fiancé, who was killed in the war, was a Zionist, her sister goes to Jewish lectures, her best friend is a member of the Blue-White and 'never misses a lecture by Max Brod'" (LFF 214 [Br 253]). Moreover, in January 1921 he found it "odd" that Brod "hesitat[ed] to throw all [his] professional energies . . . into Zionism" (LFF 257 [Br 299]).

Kafka certainly did what he could to make a Zionist of Klopstock, "a Budapest Jew. . . . anti-Zionist, his guides are Jesus und Dostoevski" (LFF 259 [Br 302]). In November he sent him the copy of Moses Rath's text, and when Klopstock became more receptive to Zionist ideas, Kafka highlighted the importance of his medical studies, for doctors are actually needed in "Palestine, which is now happily beginning to enter your frame of reference" (LFF 313 [Br 364]). Kafka was well informed about the many practical considerations that complicated emigration and relates the example of an acquaintance who gave up his law studies, retrained as an apprentice mechanic, and "in the spring he will leave for Palestine" (LFF 313–14 [Br 365)]. He also invited Klopstock to contribute to the Jewish monthly *Ha-Auhel* (The Tent) (LFF 382 [Br 446]) and *Selbstwehr*—"the magazine is wide open to you" (LFF 395 [Br 459])—and he informed him that "this year [1923] an overwhelming abundance of Hebrew affairs is being planned in Prague" (LFF 392 [Br 460]). In his insistence that others participate in Zionist activities, one almost forgets that Kafka was very ill already, and yet he still contributed his share of *völkische Kleinarbeit*.

Finally, there had been talk of either Felix Weltsch or Kafka replacing Martin Buber as editor of *Der Jude* in 1922. Kafka makes clear that Weltsch should take on the position and calls it a "joke" to even consider him, or an idea that occurred to someone "in a semicomatose moment": "How could I think of such a thing, with my boundless ignorance of affairs, my complete lack of connection with people, the absence of any firm Jewish ground under my feet? No, no" (LFF 349 [Br 403–4]). But Kafka's modesty here cannot be taken at face value—the very fact that his name should have come up as a possible successor suggests that his friends, too, thought of him as seriously committed to Zionist affairs and capable of taking on this position.

"Dates" in Palestine: "Die besitzlose Arbeiterschaft"

What has frequently been overlooked in Kafka studies is Kafka's interest in socialist-Zionist projects and in contemporary life in Palestine. Kafka was influenced here by the cultural Zionism of the Second Aliya (1904–14). Secular and socialist in outlook, they stressed the Hebrew language, "adopted Spartan ideals and high standards of personal behaviour and rejected all emblems of comfort such as smart clothes, strong drink, tobacco and the ownership of personal possessions. They survived on a diet of lentils and bean soup and lived in mud huts."[11] Max Brod was the first to draw attention to Kafka's "socialist plan, 'Workers Without Possessions,' which later without his knowledge became a reality in many respects in the collective settlements in Palestine" (FK1, 298). Critics are in agreement that it was meant for Palestine: "Most frugal existence. Eat only what is absolutely necessary, for instance as a minimum subsistence wage which is in a certain sense also a maximum wage, bread, water, dates. The food of the poorest of the poor, the shelter of the poorest of the poor" ("Workers without Possessions" [W 119 (NII 106)]; translation modified).[12] The "dates" give the location away and identify the working plan laid out here as Kafka's vision of life in an early kibbutz. Davis Trietsch points out that the date fruit was called "the bread of the desert" because "it served the natives as main nourishment, raw, dried or cooked, [and] for people who lived around oases it constituted the only nourishment for three quarters of the year."[13] One could make honey from the fruit as well as a wine-like juice; the leaves could be eaten as palm cabbage, and the dried dates provided food for months.

Kafka's plan outlines the workers' "duties" and "rights" in an environment that has no need for money or material possessions. One should only own a simple gown as well as some books and food. Everything else should go to the poor. Everyone should earn his or her living through work alone, and a supervisor might delegate work to the workers. Other duties include the workers' relationship to the employer. Kafka is adamant that he wants no lawyers there: no legal courts should ever be involved, and one should only have personal relationships based on trust. Later he will stress to Klopstock that "the average set of lawyers . . . must first be ground to dust before they may reach Palestine. Palestine needs earth but it does not need lawyers" (LFF 313 [Br 365]). As for workers' "rights," Kafka lists a maximum labor of six hours and in the case of heavy physical labor four to five hours of work a day. There will also be hospitals and old-age homes to provide for the sick and old.

Many Zionists who were involved in creating new social structures in Palestine drew up such plans. For instance, Max Brod's study, *Socialism in Zionism*[14] (1920), which Kafka owned, contains a much more elaborately worked out project for the social organization of a future state in Palestine. Brod takes issue with various ideological groups, such as the Zionist Ha-Poel haTzair (The Young Worker), founded in 1905 by members of the Second Aliya, as well as the socialist Bund. Ha-Poel haTzair "devoted considerable efforts to practical ways of assisting workers, such as by creating cooperative workshops, kitchens and stores, sick funds, labor exchanges and workers' libraries" (Bregman, *History*, 12). Here we have the labor Zionists' form of socialism: more *völkische Kleinarbeit* in Palestine.

In March or April 1920 Kafka attended a meeting of the socialist Zionist party Zeire Zion (Zionist Youth) and Ha-Poel haTzair, where he was introduced to Aharon D. Gordon (1856–1922), one of the leaders of the

Zionist labor movement, and spoke with Palestinian Jews. Hugo Bergmann was present as well; apparently this event took place a month before Bergmann's immigration to Palestine (Bokhove, "Zionism," 47; KH 506). Gordon had migrated to Palestine in 1904 and begun life as an agricultural laborer in the first small settlement in the country, Petah Tikvah (Gateway of Hope), founded in the 1870s. He then moved on to the second settlement, Rishon Le-Zion (First of Zion), founded in the 1880s; and when Kafka met him in 1919 he had just moved to the kibbutz Deganya (cornflower), founded in 1910, which represented the beginning of the kibbutz movement in Palestine. Gordon's speech was published in *Selbstwehr* (S 2 and 23 Apr. 1920:5, 4 [Bokhove, "Zionism," 47]). In July 1920 Kafka attended yet another evening event where he talked to a Palestinian Jew, "a small, almost tiny, weak, bearded man with one eye. But thinking about him cost me half the night" (LM 121 [BM 162]).

Kafka also showed interest in the political situation in Palestine. Since he could not attend the Twelfth Zionist Congress in Karlsbad in 1921, he read the *Kongreßzeitung* (Congress newspaper), which was published by *Selbstwehr* "with news and extracts from the speeches" (LFF 303, 478n.94; Br 354, 363); however, Kafka liked only one issue, which dealt with "proposals for intensive agriculture," and found the rest "not worth reading— dry extracts from speeches" (LFF 310 [Br 363]). But he was very interested in the daily political reality of Palestine. Before the Balfour Declaration on November 1917, when Britain gave political support for a Jewish homeland in Palestine, Kafka remarked to Brod, "What things are going on in Palestine!" (LFF 142 [Br 167]), referring to Field Marshall Allenby's "campaign against the Turks in Palestine which was to end Turkish rule in that region in November 1918" (LFF 453nn.35, 120). When the Balfour Declaration was passed, this caused many racial and political problems. In 1919 Brod writes to Kafka about a "dream in which I was tormented by Jewish and Zionist catastrophes. The situation in Palestine was critical at the time" (Br 510n.3).

Kafka was equally preoccupied with the racial conflicts there when he complained to Felix Weltsch in 1920 that he had not received *Selbstwehr*: "And just at this moment, when Palestine, according to a newspaper story, has been overrun by Bedouins and perhaps the little bookbinder's workbench in the corner has been smashed" (LFF 239 [Br 277]). Here Kafka is toying with the idea of becoming a "bookbinder in Palestine" (Br 512n.14). The racial turbulence continued: in 1921 in Jaffa, for instance, forty-seven Jews were killed during an Arab attack.[15] All the newspapers Kafka read

The Dream of Palestine (1917–1924)   173

and/or subscribed to, such as *Selbstwehr, Der Jude, Das jüdische Echo,* or *Die Welt,* provided readers with continual reports about the situation in Palestine: harvesting disasters, racial tensions and clashes, what diseases occurred where and when, the present state of the hospitals, job prospects, and so forth. Kafka and Brod shared this information.

Moreover, in 1921 Kafka went to see *Schiwath Zion*[16] (Return to Zion) (DII 197 [T 870; K 205]), a silent film by Ya'akov Ben Dov that depicts the lives of the *chaluzim* (pioneers) after coming to Palestine. The film shows pioneers engaged in the hard physical labor that was required for building roads and settlements. There are pictures of individuals hammering away at blocks of rock in the heat for days on end. Famous Zionist leaders are shown on their visit to Palestine, as well as politicians involved in the Balfour Declaration. The film witnesses the arrival of First British High Commissioner Sir Herbert Samuel in June 1920 and shows the revisionist leader Vladimir Jabotinsky as he is released from prison, walking away with his mother by his side. Jabotinsky had been arrested by the British during the Arab riots in April 1920 as leader of the military *Haganah* (self-defense) unit. A few months later, he and others were pardoned by Sir Herbert Samuel and released from prison.

Finally, Kafka read literature about daily life in Palestine: he owned a volume of short stories, *Jewish Peasants* (1919),[17] by the Hebrew writer and Zionist Shlomo Zemach (1886–1974). These short stories are written in very realistic prose and depict the lives of villagers, the hardships of daily survival in Israel, and conflicts and racial tensions with the Arabs. Many stories deal with Arab attacks and the hatred that builds on the Jewish side. In one such story, "Brachfeld" (Barren Field), we are told about a Jewish man who is badly injured after an Arab attack: in his "frozen look there was irreconcilable hatred" (15), and he is overwhelmed by his desire for revenge, "the spilled blood ... cried out from the depth for retaliation and the cut off finger lying in the mud called out: Revenge, Revenge!" (17).

The Jewish Elementary School of Prague

In the meantime, on the home front in Prague, the Zionists were still working on establishing the Jewish elementary school. Brod and others fought for six years in order to realize this project. It was the Czech Jewish assimilationists who opposed the school most vehemently, and they occupied the administrative positions that needed to be consulted in this matter. To get around their objections, the Zionists decided to adopt Czech as the language of instruction, and this is why, in the end, the school became a

Jewish private school with Czech as the language of instruction and with particular consideration for German. When the elementary school finally opened on 6 September 1920,[18] Max Brod made the opening speech, which Kafka and Brod had supposedly written together (FK1 271–72). The school started out with only seventeen students (Brod, "Jüdische Schule," 345). For the first ten years the president was Viktor Kohn (1885–1957), a schoolmate of Brod's who was also related to the father's side of Kafka's family. Like Kafka and Brod, Kohn had also been involved with the Jewish refugees during World War I; he was the "founder of a centre for the absorption, accommodation and treatment of Jewish refugees from Eastern Europe upon the cessation of World War I."[19]

For the first year (1920–21) there exists only one class record book.[20] The basic subjects (languages, zoology, biology, arithmetic, geography) were taught, and the teaching was innovative because it was visually oriented, much of it done using pictures of animals, birds, plants, and other subjects or objects. In the second year, Kafka persuaded his sister Valli (1890–1942) to send her daughter Lotte (1914–31) to the school. At this time there were already two classes. Lotte was taught by a young teacher named Arnstein, whom Kafka highly respected.[21] Lotte's older sister, Marianne Steiner (1913–2001), recollected: "Erwin Arnstein was a marvellous teacher and all children, myself included, adored him. His method, for Prague of that time, was revolutionary indeed. The children were asked to call him Erwin (not "Herr Lehrer" as was the custom then); he introduced plasticine and encouraged the children to use their imagination and create models of everyday life: a wedding, a funeral etc. When he left Prague with his fiancée Klara, we children were heartbroken."[22]

In 1922 Lotte's mother, Valli, became involved in the school as well, in the sense that she "would help out on outings to the countryside, supervising the children" (Steiner, personal correspondence). Kafka himself participated in parent evenings, and if he was unable to attend he generally kept informed about school activities. On one particular occasion he read his friend Felix Weltsch's review article (in *Selbstwehr*) on the parents' evening he missed (LFF 337 [Br 389]). He was especially interested this time because Valli had spoken, and he asked Brod for further details: "How did the Parents' Evening go (on the personal plane)? How did my sister speak? Have they pupils for next year?" (LFF 341 [Br 393]) In the fall of 1921, Kafka encouraged his sister Elli (1889–1941) to send her son Felix (1911–40) away from the assimilationist home environment to the innovative non-Jewish school in Hellerau,[23] which furthered the children's creativity and free expression. However, Kafka's niece Marianne Steiner does not remember "Felix having been sent to Hellerau, but Franz tried to persuade Elli to send her daughter Gerty (1912–1972) there, but she was sent to Switzerland, I think to Lausanne" (Steiner, personal correspondence). For Kafka it was absolutely detrimental to Felix that he had spent all of his ten years in Prague, "where prosperous Jews are affected by a particular spirit from which children cannot be shielded . . . To be able to save one's own child from that, what good fortune!" (LFF 290–91 [Br 339–40]).

The popular teacher Erwin Arnstein left the school in February 1923, when he and his fiancée emigrated to Palestine. In May 1923 *Selbstwehr* printed an article by Arnstein from Tel Aviv on the front page.[24] Arnstein returned to Prague after a year or two to obtain his doctorate and stayed for about twelve months; then he went back to Palestine. Kafka never saw him again, but Marianne Steiner, who visited Arnstein in Jerusalem in 1950, recalls that he showed her "Kafka's slim book 'Der Heizer,' a gift from the author with the inscription: 'For Erwin Arnstein, with many thanks for the happiness which radiated from him'" (Steiner, personal correspondence). Until shortly before his death, Kafka kept informed about school affairs through family and friends as well as through his reading of *Selbstwehr* (LFF 396 [Br 463]).

After Kafka's death, the Jewish elementary school kept growing. Valli remained a teacher or helper until the Nazi invasion. In the 1930s Dr. Richard Feder, a rabbi in Prague, was involved, and with increasingly less Jewish content on the curriculum, his "Hebrew textbook" was used "on the side from grades one to five."[25] A Czech book by Feder on Jewish culture was part of Kafka's personal library.[26] In 1936 there was hardly any Jewish content,[27] except for a few handouts, which were typed up, on "Ijar, Dr. Jonas Jeiteles, Scholem Aleichem, Theodor Herzl and Nathan Birnbaum." It was in these years that the school became increasingly important, especially after September 1940 when Jewish children were expelled from all other schools.

Moreover, in the archives of the Jewish Museum of Prague there are hundreds of job applications for the year 1940 with teachers from all German-speaking countries desperately applying for an opening at the school. Those that were hired had excellent qualifications; the teaching was evidently superb. But there were at least sixty children in each class, and with every new transport to the camps, literally from one day to the next, the teachers and students would constantly be replaced by others. It is possible that Kafka's sister Valli was teaching at this time. Since so many students were in need of teachers, much of the teaching did not even take place on the school's premises; there were many little schools in various locations and in private homes in Prague. Valli stayed until October 1941, when she was deported to Lodz.[28]

The school remained open until 1942, when the last children and teachers were sent to the concentration camp Terezin (Theresienstadt). Here, some teaching continued under the guidance of Drs. Richard Feder (1875–1970)[29] and Leo Baeck (1873–1956), both of whom survived the war. Feder, the lesser known of the two, was the only one of his family to survive. After the war he became the rabbi of Prague. The school itself was forgotten; only very few remembered its existence.[30] The building in which it was located became the Jewish Central Museum under the Nazi occupation

5. A 1923 advertisement in *Selbstwehr* asking Jewish parents to send their children to the Jewish elementary school of Prague.

and was apparently intended as "Museum einer ausgestorbenen Rasse" (a museum of a race that has died out). They certainly used it to store many stolen artifacts, not only from Prague but from all over Germany as well. Czech authorities after the war retained the Jewish Museum in the same location where the Nazis had misused it. This is the same building that had at one time also been the home of the Jewish elementary school of Prague.[31]

THE DREAM OF PALESTINE

Jiří Langer and Puah Ben Tovim

Kafka certainly dreamed about going to Palestine. Max Brod remembers that he often talked "about his intention to emigrate to Erez-Israel. He wanted to live there as a simple craftsman. He thought like a Chaluz, a pioneer."[32] But in March 1921 Kafka called these plans "the stuff of dreams" (LO 63 [BO 111]), and instead he learned more Hebrew and Hasidic lore from Jiří Langer and later took further Hebrew lessons from a native speaker, Puah Ben Tovim, who had come from Palestine to study in Europe.

Not much is known about the lessons with Langer. In February 1921 Brod must have consulted Langer about Jewish mysticism, because Kafka asks from the sanatorium in Matliary, "would you bring along one of the kabbalistic texts? I assume it is in Hebrew?" (DFF 260 [Br 303]). After he returned to Prague at the end of August, Kafka (and Brod) may have taken up Hebrew lessons with Langer again (DII 196 [T 868]). Binder believes it is likely "that the hours of instruction were also an introduction to 'hasidism' and 'Kabbalah'" ("Hebräischstudien," 136), and Brod supports this claim when he testifies to Langer's "thorough and unfathomable knowledge: I owe Georg Langer an endless amount of information specifically in the Kabbalistic sciences. Without him I could not have written my 'Rëubeni'" ("Zwanziger Jahre," 54).

Langer was a writer and a scholar as well. His first book, *Die Erotik der Kabbala* (Eroticism of the Kabbala),[33] is a scholarly study of erotic sexuality that permeates Kabbalistic mythology and rabbinic fantasies. It also contains sections on Hasidic life, and one of these, "On the Life of the Hasidim," was printed in *Selbstwehr* just before the book appeared (S 16 Mar. 1923:1–3). Brod edited Langer's book, sent it off for publication, and reviewed it in *Selbstwehr* ("Die Zwanziger Jahre," 54; Oppenheimer, 300n.2). It is unlikely that Kafka knew nothing of these activities. After

Kafka's death, Langer also wrote other studies on religious topics: "On the Function of the Jewish Mezuzah" (1928) and "Jewish Tefillin" (1931) (*Encyclopaedia Judaica*, 10:1420).

When *Eroticism of the Kabbala* appeared, Langer's "piety and reputation for learning led to his being appointed as a teacher at the Jewish College in Prague" (*Nine Gates*, xxi). His family was delighted that he had finally found real employment, but Langer never lasted long in any establishment. His brother recalls: "With his pupils, I am told, he was a great favorite since he was easy-going and always full of humor. He was less liked, however, by the School's Board of Governors since he was very off-hand and unpunctual. His lessons never started on time, and if his attention was taken up with something that he was working on privately, he might even fail to put in an appearance for several days on end" (*Nine Gates*, xxii). Langer's trouble with the authorities and the parents of his students may also have had to do with his sexual orientation; according to Oppenheimer, in later life he pursued his homosexuality "with an extremism comparable with his former devotion to Hasidism" (300). He lost several jobs, and "on one of his enforced holidays he made a journey to Palestine. He went more as a historian than a pilgrim or would-be settler" (*Nine Gates*, xxii).

In the late 1930s Langer was still in Prague, teaching religion classes wherever he could. Jiří Kraus was one of his students in a regular public school, where Langer taught him for two hours a week over a period of two years (1937–38): Kraus was not aware that Langer was gay and only remembers him as a very flamboyant character. Langer took the children out for skating and ice cream, and they learned no religion whatsoever.[34] During this period, Langer was still very productive. In 1937, on the eve of the Nazi destruction of Eastern European Jewry, he recreated the folklore of the Hasidim in his *Nine Gates to the Chassidic Mysteries,* which is well described as a "Chassidic *Thousand and One Nights*" (*Nine Gates*, xxvi). Langer further published "Poems and Songs of Friendship," "the first book of Hebrew verses to be printed at the Jewish printing-works in Old Prague for a whole century" (*Nine Gates*, xxii). In these desperate times he also wrote a "popular book about the Talmud and its origins. He selected and translated into Czech a hundred examples of old Jewish wisdom from the Talmud, the humanism of whose commandments was so directly opposed to the brutalities of Nazi racialism" (*Nine Gates*, xxvi). Plus he composed another book of poems, "Songs of the Rejected," published in 1937 and republished in 1939.

The Dream of Palestine (1917–1924)

Langer eventually left for Slovakia in the fall of 1939, joining others on a route along the Danube to Istanbul. It is in keeping with his character that he filled his suitcases with his favorite books (two hundred of them!) and no warm clothing. Eventually he reached Palestine, but he had become very ill on the journey. Though he received medical treatment, he never truly recovered. Before he died, he translated his Hasidic legends into Hebrew, published a few Hebrew verses in magazines, and dreamed of going back to Prague (*Nine Gates,* xxix). He died in Tel Aviv in March 1943.

As Kafka's health began to fail, his dreams about going to Palestine grew stronger and his Hebrew studies intensified. At the end of January 1923, he began to take lessons with Puah Ben Tovim, a nineteen-year-old native speaker who had come to Prague to study: "Born and raised in Jerusalem, the daughter of the Hebrew writer Salman Ben-Tovim, she was among the first of the new generation to grow up with Hebrew as her native tongue" (Pawel, "Kafka's Hebrew Teacher," 21). She was bilingual in German and Hebrew, and Hugo Bergmann had sent her to study in Prague to further her education.³⁵ Puah met with Kafka for his Hebrew lessons on a daily basis over a period of five months, after which she left for Berlin to continue her studies (NIIA 131).

According to Binder, "the Palestine project was the driving force behind [Kafka's] study of the language" ("Hebräischstudien," 151). Kafka was enthusiastic about Palestine and kept asking Puah about Jerusalem and forging plans to accompany her when she returned home (Menczel-Ben-Tovim, "Hebräischlehrerin," 166). In April 1923 he told Klopstock about Bergmann's return from Palestine and how "exciting and tempting [it was] to be with him" (LFF 370 [Br 433]). The Prague Zionists organized a series of lectures for Bergmann at the Zionist club Keren Hayesod, where Bergmann spoke about "The Situation in Palestine." After one of these lectures Kafka came up to him and said, "You gave this talk only for me" (Bergmann, "Erinnerungen," 746).³⁶

Kafka's Hebrew notebooks from this time contain Zionist agricultural vocabulary such as "pitchfork," "pumpkin," "cattle breeding," "weather," apart from a mass of practical, everyday expressions. Many of the words he wrote down are early Zionist vocabulary no longer used in modern Hebrew. Some of the sections are marked "Pua"; then again he writes "at Bergmann's place." Kafka obviously used these occasions when they got together as an opportunity to improve his Hebrew. He wrote down the words for "bookbinder" and "waiter" (his imaginary professions in Palestine [PK 116]) or "fairy tale" on several sheets and vocabulary such as "horse," "saddle," "galloping," "spores." Much of the vocabulary seems to come from little stories, fairy tales, and even from a "newspaper," which he mentions in the margin.[37]

During these gatherings with Bergmann, there may also have been talk about Jewish education because Kafka marked down the name "Kugel" on his Hebrew sheets: Chaim Kugel was involved in Jewish education, especially with Hebrew schools.[38] When Puah left Prague in June 1923, Kafka had to rely on books again and acquired *Halashon,* a Hebrew book that was listed in *Selbstwehr* as one of the "newest publications" (S 15 June 1923:2), and attempted to work through it on his own.[39]

During the Third Aliya (1919–23), 26,900 Jews emigrated to Palestine (Bregman 19), and after Hugo Bergmann's visit, Kafka seriously contemplated going there as well. While vacationing in Müritz in July 1923, he received his first letter in Hebrew from Bergmann. Kafka replied that his holiday was to test his fitness for travel to Palestine. A letter to Bergmann's wife, Else, also reveals that Kafka planned to go (LFF 373 [Br 436]). Else Bergmann was in Prague at the time and must have encouraged Kafka to accompany her on her return to Jerusalem. But the decision was made for him when she informed him by the middle of July that "'all the berths are already taken'" (LFF 374 [Br 438]). Though he must have been disappointed, Kafka immediately presented his wish as almost presumptuous (LFF 374 [Br 437–38]). Else still tried to make the journey possible, but Hugo Bergmann repeatedly argued against Kafka's visit, urging her to consider that they had no room, that Kafka was very sick and needed too much care, and if he came they would not be able to spend enough time with their children. Bergmann was adamant, suggesting that "perhaps it would be better if Franz waited in Europe until after your departure," and once she was back she would see herself if she could manage the household under those circumstances.[40]

Luckily, other interests of a more personal nature were now holding Kafka back as well, because this was the time when his last companion, Dora Diamant, came into his life. From his holiday in Müritz, Kafka wrote to Klopstock that he was "learning far less Hebrew than in Prague"; however, there was something else that more than made up for this, "a camp affiliated with the Berlin Jewish People's Home . . . with many Hebrew-speaking, healthy, and cheerful children" (LFF 372 [Br 435]). This is where he met Dora. She was twenty-four or twenty-five years old, had lived in Berlin for three years, was originally from Bedzin, Poland, and came from an Orthodox family; her father was a follower of the Hasidic Gerer Rebbe.

Dora rebelled against her upbringing, joined a theater group, and later, at the beginning of World War I, the Zionist Hebraica Association, where she "studied Hebrew with a passion" (Diamant, *Last Love,* 2–5, 9, 21, 25). She, too, wanted to go to Palestine. During the war years she was influenced by Theodor Herzl, and when she was in Berlin one of her role models was "Clara Zetkin, a passionate socialist and feminist, a founder of the women's international suffrage movement, a leading political figure and member of the German Reichstag" (Diamant 21, 4). Dora later married a German Jewish Communist, was actively involved in the underground, and even spoke at a "left-wing Socialist rally" (Diamant 24). She survived World War II first in Russia and then escaped to England with her daughter in 1939 and remained in England. In 1949 she visited Israel to see family members who had survived, and at this time she also met Max Brod and Felix Weltsch again (Diamant 271–72). She died in London in 1952.

When Kafka met Dora, she was working as a volunteer for the "Berlin Jewish People's holiday camp for refugee children" (Diamant 3). His involvement with the young people in the Jewish People's Home and his delight in them are documented in his letters to Brod and Else Bergmann, in which he expresses joy at being able to celebrate the Sabbath with the children, "for the first time in my life, I think" (LFF 373 [Br 437]), and even considered going to the "Jewish Harvest Festival" (Sukkoth) with Dora (LFF 383 [Br 448]). Yet, ultimately he was looking for something more permanent, since he was only "a guest here" (LFF 377 [Br 441]). In July 1923 he already contemplated moving to Berlin to live with Dora. His letters to Klopstock foreshadow Kafka's own plans when he recommends that his friend should perhaps "go to the dirty Jewish streets of Berlin" (LFF 374 [Br 438]) and asks, "Would you feel like moving to Berlin? Closer, very close to the Jews?" (LFF 378 [Br 442]).

"Berliner Möglichkeiten"

By September 1923, Palestine had clearly been replaced by other hopes: "In any case Palestine would have been beyond me; in view of the possibilities in Berlin [*Berliner Möglichkeiten*] it would not even be urgent" (LFF 380 [Br 445]). At the end of September, Kafka moved to Berlin. Initially, he planned to attend the "famous gardening school at Dahlem," but when he heard more about it from a Palestinian friend of Dora's, he felt mentally and physically incapable of doing so (LFF 389 [Br 455]; Diamant 57). He continued with his Hebrew, and after a month he had read "thirty-two pages of a novel by Brenner, a page every day. The book is entitled *Shekhol ve-Kishalon* [Barrenness and Failure]" (LFF 390 [Br 456]; see LFF 395 [Br 459]). Josef Chajim Brenner (1861–1921) emigrated to Palestine in 1909, was active in the socialist-Zionist movement, and was murdered during the Arab riots in May 1921. Kafka states that he read "only Hebrew" (LFF 394 [Br 459]), but even though his Hebrew was respectable enough for communication in oral and written form, he emphasizes repeatedly how much he was struggling with the Brenner text.[41] Kafka also attempted to read biblical Hebrew with Dora. When he came to Berlin, Dora was already enrolled at the reformed Rabbinic Institute in Berlin, the "Hochschule für die Wissenschaft des Judentums" (Academy for Jewish Studies) (Diamant 14). Soon both Kafka and Dora began attending classes there together.

The Academy for Jewish Studies

The Berlin Rabbinic Institute was founded in 1872. Attendance was free of charge, and one of the leitmotifs of this new institution was "to stay independent of the authorities of the state, the community, and the synagogues."[42] Even though the Academy did consider it a priority to educate those who wanted to be rabbis, preachers, or religion teachers, "the private Jewish individual should be offered the opportunity to inform himself in a scientific way about the 'treasures and fate of the Jewish spirit'" (*Festschrift*, 12). Anyone who was interested (women and non-Jews as well) was invited to come and study biblical, Talmudic, and rabbinic texts in the original (*Festschrift*, 20).

Moreover, the name "Hochschule" (academy) indicates that the level of instruction was comparable to that of a university. The professors teaching at the institution were very distinguished scholars: David Cassel and Abraham Geiger (Kafka had books by both of them in his library [KH 149, 113]) as well as Israel Lewy and Hajim Steintal.[43] Max Brod mentions that Kafka "attended all the lectures by Professor Torczyner and Professor Guttmann."[44] These professors were there already in 1920, together with Leo Baeck: Baeck was teaching Midrash; Julius Guttmann, author of *The Philosophy of Judaism,* was lecturing on Jewish history; and Harry Torczyner taught his controversial commentary on the Book of Job.[45] But they were the really big names. It seems highly unlikely that Kafka attended all of Guttmann's and Torczyner's lectures, though it is of course possible that he heard a few, because students in the *Präparandie*, preparatory classes, where Kafka was, were allowed to sit in on some occasions (*Festschrift*, 79).

Kafka mentions the Academy frequently in his letters (LFF 399, 401, 402–3 [Br 466, 468, 470]; LO 85 [BO 141]). He told Felix Weltsch that he attended courses twice a week (LF 399 [Br 466]) and also stressed that he was taking preparatory courses: "Of course I am not a proper student, am only in the preparatory school, and have only one teacher there, moreover go seldom" (LF 403 [Br 470]). These preparatory courses had become a necessity because many people did not bring the required knowledge of Hebrew and the Scriptures (*Festschrift*, 61). In fact, since 1884, the Academy offered "private sessions for beginners," and a "coach" was needed as well in order to prepare them for the lectures on the Talmud: "In the *Präparandie* courses were offered by the scholars Dr. Barol, Dr. Grünthal and Dr. Rosenthal on the Bible and the Commentaries, Hebrew Grammar, Mishna, Talmud and on the prayer book" (*Neununddreissigster Bericht* [1921], 11).

Niels Bokhove recently discovered that Kafka's teacher was Rabbi Dr. Julius Grünthal (1875–1943). Grünthal's son, the Israeli composer Josef Tal, remembers his father talking about Kafka and even recalls Kafka and Dora visiting their family's home. He describes his father as a very absentminded, unworldly scholar and recounts that "his father's lost commentaries on the Talmud were unreplaceable intellectual treasures. Such things must have been discussed in his talks with Kafka. I cannot imagine what other things they could have had in common."[46] Bokhove links the representation of the peaceful stillness of the "Castle Keep" in "The Burrow" to the Academy, and the description of a teacher in a fragment from this period fits Grünthal.[47]

Kafka and Dora apparently studied sections of the Talmud in the preparatory classes, and Kafka recommended Talmud lessons to Klopstock (LFF 402 [Br 470]). According to Dora, she attended the halakha section of the course, while Kafka went to the aggadah part: she recalls that Kafka treated the aggadic legends like Grimm fairy tales.[48] The following texts were taught at the Academy: "apart from the Babylonian they also drew in great detail on the Jerusalem Talmud, and examined halakhic as well as aggadic Midrashim and the Baraita texts. Individual lectures were also given separately on these topics over the years" (*Festschrift*, 34). In particular, Kafka worked with the "*Traktat Berachot* . . . in the bilingual edition by E. M. Pinner (Berlin 1842)" (KH 574),[49] which is "among the easiest of the tractates... and because of its wealth of Aggada it is perhaps the most suitable with which to commence the study of the Talmud."[50]

Kafka's studies at the Academy, then, facilitated his reading of the Scriptures. Yet, a distanced irony is still present in Kafka's personal observations when he describes the Academy as "a refuge of peace in the wild and woolly Berlin and in the wild and woolly regions of the mind" and also finds it "rather odd to the point of grotesquerie and beyond that to the point of intangible delicacy (namely the liberal-reformist tone and scholarly aspects of the whole thing)" (LFF 402–3 [Br 470]). Kafka was under no illusion about his Talmud studies when he told Klopstock, "You won't completely understand it, but what does that matter? You will hear it from far away; what else is it but news from afar" (LFF 402 [Br 470]). In addition, he admits to Brod in January 1924 that he has "not really become used to reading [*Lernen*] the Talmud, aside from the fact that this is not at all real 'reading' [*Lernen*], only a formal kind of pleasure without a base" (Br 472; my translation).[51] *Lernen* (lejnen) in Yiddish refers to reading/reciting the Talmud. In the end, Kafka was too sick to attend further classes or lectures. Neither he nor Dora mentions any problems, but Nahum Glatzer claims that "the masters of the academy disliked the presence of the unmarried couple in their sacred precincts and delegated a younger colleague to convey the message to the strange student. It can be presumed that Kafka, anyway ill, ceased his visits."[52]

Though Kafka's health of course made it impossible to even contemplate such a move, Palestine remained a dream for both of them: they would open a restaurant in Tel Aviv with Dora as cook and Kafka as waiter. Dora remembers that they "constantly played with the idea of leaving Berlin and immigrating to Palestine to begin a new life.... He loved to play with great seriousness and care the role of the waiter for me.... He had an entire room to serve and the game lasted sometimes fifteen minutes while the meal got cold" (Diamant 49). Kafka also liked to have a little part of the religious life: "After four months, [Dora recounts] Franz knew the 'Got fun Avrum' by heart, as a child knows the fairy tales which have been told to him countless times.... Every Saturday night he never failed to ask [her], and [she] recited [the prayer] for him" (Diamant 77). "Got fun Avrum" (God of Abraham) is a traditional Hasidic prayer recited at the end of the Sabbath, composed in Yiddish by Rabbi Levi Yitzchok of Berditchev (1740–1810). Dora is careful to highlight that these prayers were like "fairy tales" for him. However, when Kafka wrote to Dora's father, seeking permission to marry her "although he was not a practicing Jew," he insisted he was not just pretending to be "a repentant one, seeking to return" (Diamant 109). The answer he received was "No."

DREAMS AND REALITIES

"The Jews Are Our Dogs": "Jackals and Arabs"

Since the jackals reside not only in the European Diaspora but also in Palestine, "Jackals and Arabs" can also be placed within the context of contemporary Zionist history. Written in January 1917, the story was published in *Der Jude* a month before the incisive Balfour Declaration was issued. During World War I, many negotiations between Zionist and world leaders had taken place concerning the realization of Herzl's political dream, and Britain had increasingly supported the Zionist aspirations to establish a national homeland for the Jewish people in Palestine. The British decision became known as the Balfour Declaration, since it was presented in the form of a short letter by Arthur James Lord Balfour to Lord Rothschild. This letter symbolizes the first political recognition of Zionist political goals by a major world power. When "Jackals and Arabs" was published, these negotiations were in full swing. The Balfour letter was discussed by the British cabinet on 3 September and 5 October 1917 (Bregman 17). Martin Buber published Kafka's story in mid-October 1917.

If we interpret "Jackals" only as a satire directed against those Diaspora Jews who are passively waiting for the coming of the Messiah, this reading does not take into account the presence of the Arabs and the fact that the jackals' Messiah is very "human." These jackals turn to any European for help and rather indiscriminately: "every European is just the man that Fate has chosen for them. They have the most lunatic hopes, these beasts; they're just fools, utter fools. That's why we like them; they are our dogs; finer dogs than any of yours" (CS 410 [E 283]). The jackals are caricatured for their overhasty judgment in trying to find support for their cause. The Northern traveler, a European Nordau figure whom they have chosen this time, finds it hard to take their obstinacy seriously. John Milfull comments: "That this bitter satire on Zionist Messianism should have been published in Martin Buber's periodical *Der Jude* is in many ways the high point of Kafka's irony."[53] One could argue that in "Jackals" Kafka is drawing on the history of the First (1882–1903) and Second (1904—14) Aliya.

The first Jews to immigrate in the nineteenth century were the religious (Orthodox) Jews, who arrived even before 1882 and certainly before the

First Zionist Congress in Basel in 1897. They came from Russia, escaping from persecution and pogroms after the reign of Czar Alexander II, and were not political and not interested in founding a new state. However, many Jews of the Second Aliya (1904–14), who started to come at the time when Kafka's traveler from the North is visiting, were Westerners and secular, enlightened socialists and labor Zionists (Bregman, 11–12). Visiting Palestine before or during WWI was a shock for many a Western, Northern visitor investigating the new "homeland." There were swamps to drain, diseases like malaria was rampant, and the living conditions were very hard. A tiny Jewish minority was living amidst many Arabs, and these religious Jews were living in the past, adhering to old traditions. During the period of the First Zionist Congress in Basle (1897), "some 400,000 Arabs and a Jewish minority of 50, 000 or so lived on this land." At the time of the Balfour Declaration (1917), the population in Palestine was "around 87 percent Arab," or about "55, 000 [Jews] compared with some 560, 000 Arabs" (Bregman 7, 17, 19).

Ironically, when the Northern traveler arrives, Herzl's Old-New Land does not seem to point to a new beginning. The jackals are filled with superstition, waiting for a Messiah to redeem them and clinging to their old traditions. The traveler does not know what to think of them. The political reality seems like a continuation of the old in a new disguise, especially in the way power constellations are playing themselves out, since the jackals are constantly whipped by the Arabs. As a result, they are filled with scorn and hate, and it seems as if the Jews are caught in a "continual exile," no matter what country they live in. The Arab's last comment is "Marvellous creatures, aren't they? And how they hate us!" (CS 411 [E 284]).

Moreover, as in the Diaspora, it is not only the dominant group—here the Arabs—that is responsible for the clash of cultures and the lack of understanding. The jackals make a point of informing the traveler of their scorn for the Arabs: "You are indeed a stranger here . . . or you would know that never in the history of the world has any jackal been afraid of an Arab. Why should we fear them? Is it not misfortune enough for us to be exiled among such creatures?" (CS 408 [E 281]). The jackals adopt a self-satisfied and self-righteous stance and flatly deny the Arabs' views any legitimacy, projecting a presumptuous and calculating nature onto them that has no place for "reason": "Not a spark of intelligence, let me tell you, can be struck from their cold arrogance" (CS 408 [E 281]). Not only did the religious Jews of the First Aliya think of themselves as superior to the Arabs, but many Western Zionists as well believed not only in the superiority of the "civilized" Western over the Eastern Jews but were just as derogatory in their description of the Arabs as uneducated and uncivilized. Arthur Holitscher, for instance, calls the Arab "a primitive monster, separated from Western man by an abyss a thousand years wide" (79).

The jackals' arrogant rejection of the Arabs in Kafka's story is absolutely closed-minded: they refuse to talk to the Arabs, insisting that communication is impossible, and instead "turn tail and flee into cleaner air, into the desert" (CS 409 [E 281]). The jackals are no less tolerant of Arab culture than the Arabs are of them. However, it is to be noted that the Arab in Kafka's text appears more civilized than the jackals, and Kafka's Western traveler, unlike many Zionists, is not condescending toward the Arabs—he is traveling with them and is shown around the country. He does not take sides and remains an observer.[54]

In 1921, after the Arab riots of 1920, Holitscher argues that Arab racism toward the Jews was a result of World War I and the pending Balfour Declaration. There were no major clashes before 1914 and no acute racism (Holitscher 83). During the war, however, and especially after the Balfour Declaration, racist sentiments grew. For instance, there was a common militant Arab slogan that could be heard among the Arabs in the towns: "Palestine is our land, and the Jews our dogs."[55] The Arab in "Jackals and Arabs" repeats this very slogan: "they are our dogs; finer dogs than any of yours" (CS 410 [E 283]). Kafka's story thus incorporates contemporary concerns and political realities in Palestine during World War I. While Herzl's novel *Alt-Neuland* (Old-New Land, 1902) had envisioned a peaceful coexistence of Arabs, Jews, men, and women in Palestine, Kafka was less optimistic. Holitscher, too, warns in 1922 that Westerners are naive when they believe they have found solutions to the racial clash: "At the Zionist Congress in Karlsbad [1921] a respectable professor from Berlin went so far as to claim that the University of Jerusalem should create a chair for Arabic Literature—this would immediately bring the races closer to each other and reconcile them" (80). Holitscher concludes: "Those who have never been in Palestine, who have never seen the Falachas [Ethiopian Jews] and Bedouins [nomads], should not participate in discussions concerning the Arab question and the Palestinian Arab" (80).

In "Jackals and Arabs" contemporary Jewish-Arab conflicts in Palestine have become the subject matter of Kafka's fiction. The story is more than a Zionist critique of Diaspora Jewry: "delving deeper" and "drawing one deeper into it" (LF 421 [BF 596]); it appears to be caricaturing Zionist messianism from the perspective of an outsider who, like many Zionist emissaries, is a "modern" Western visitor to an Arab country—another Northerner (or Nordau figure). Yet it is also much more than a critique of Zionist messianism, since the focus is just as much on the continuing racial conflicts in Herzl's "promised land." "Jackals and Arabs" represents a satiric "West meets Old-New Land" encounter in Palestine at the time of the Balfour Declaration.

"Investigations of a Dog"

In the light of contemporary Zionism, "Investigations of a Dog" (1922) satirizes the "dog's life" many Jews led in the Diaspora, which has reached a dead end and is characterized as "an endless [aberration] [*Irren*]" (CS 300 [E 436]). *Irren* in the sense of *umherirren,* wandering around confused, brings to mind the myth of the Wandering Jew, as well as the phrase *sich irren,* to make an error. The dogs' wandering is presented as the result of an erroneous decision, and from then on "error" seems to mark their whole existence (echoing Berdyczewski's argument in Bergmann's article "Jawne and Jerusalem"). Yet in their very midst a young dog is embarking on an educational experiment, trying to teach himself about the culture of his people. Now an old dog, he recounts the struggles of his youth. Significantly, also looking back (in January 1922, before writing "Investigations"), Kafka felt that his involvement with Zionism had been detrimental to his writing: "All such writing is an assault on the frontiers; if Zionism had not intervened, it might easily have developed into a new secret doctrine, a Kabbalah" (DII 202–3 [T 878]). In "Investigations," Zionism not only informs the young dog's rebellion against his community but also interferes with his attempts to find spiritual sustenance in the traditions of the past.

Like many Zionists, the dog narrator believes it cannot be right that the dogs are "holding firmly to laws that are not those of the dog world, but are actually directed against it" (CS 280 [E 413]). He is bothered by this, and his Zionist sympathies are obvious in his desire to escape the "dog's life" and to question and speak up where the others are silent (CS 297 [E 432]). No encouragement can be expected from the dog community, because these dogs are resigned to their fate, filled with apathy, and old before their time. There is also no school for the young "scholarly dog" (Robertson, *Judaism,* 83) who is so curious and eager to learn. The problem is that he is pretty much on his own (CS 293 [E 427]), and his lonely research illustrates how frustrating and self-defeating contemporary attempts at Jewish self-education could be.

The dog's rebellion begins in his youth when he starts investigating and questioning the dog community's obsession with *Nahrungswissenschaft*, the science of nurture (CS 315 [E 454]), which has "occupied us since the dawn of time, it is the chief object of all our meditation" (CS 286 [E 421]). Kafka's humorous compound word *Nahrungswissenschaft* (which recalls Kafka's studies at the *Hochschule für die Wissenschaft des Judentums* [Academy of Jewish Studies]) can be taken to refer to Jewish dietary restrictions and by extension to the Talmud, where a plethora of commentaries discusses the suitability of different kinds of food from the point of view of religious ritual. Truly, the rabbinic commentaries surpass the understanding of most "dogs" (CS 286–87 [E 421]), and the narrator therefore questions the need for this "science" (CS 299 [435]). Thus, it is not only the laws of the dominant society but the dogs' own laws, the Scriptures themselves, which are seen as furthering a defeatist attitude within the community, and the narrator imputes this desire for defeat to the dogs. These charges are typical of Zionist discourse. Ahad Ha'am wrote "that the Jews are no longer the people of Scripture but the slaves of Scripture" (Böhm, *Bewegung*, 5), and Hugo Bergmann (via Berdyczewski) insisted that "The Jews want the *Galuth* [Exile]" (*Jawne*, 36).

However, the Zionists themselves are equally concerned with *Nahrungswissenschaft* as they are particularly obsessed with "preparation of the ground [*Bodenbearbeitung*]" (CS 303 [E 439, 440]). Many of the Zionist publications that Kafka read dealt with practical matters such as the preparation of the land in Palestine. The innumerable volumes of Zionist publications seem just as inexhaustible as the many volumes of the Talmud. The charge here is that the Zionists' rebellion against tradition has led to an excessive intellectualism, which interferes just as much with the pursuit of a spiritual regeneration of the Jewish people as traditional dogma had done before.

Throughout "Investigations," the dog attempts to free himself but is continually blocked either by dietary and ritual laws or by discussions about the cultivation of the land, debated by the traditionalist and Zionist quarters alike. What made him rebel initially, as a very young dog, was his discovery that a spiritual dimension indeed existed when he encountered the seven music dogs who sang without producing a sound. Here we have an allusion to Jewish mysticism. In Peretz's story "Cabalists," the highest moment of revelation is accompanied by music that has "no sound at all, pure spirit" (*Treasury*, 222). In Kafka's story, too, the essential quality of the dogs' music is its spirituality: "They did not speak, they did not sing, they remained generally silent. . . . Everything was music, the lifting and setting down of their feet, certain turns of the head, their running and their standing still" (CS 281 [E 414]).

In his ongoing research he keeps searching for just this emotional, spiritual sustenance and argues that the Law has at all times included a spiritual dimension. He refers to tradition itself, to the "auxiliary perfecting processes of incantation, dance, and song" (CS 303 [E 440]). This spiritual dimension is less concerned with "the ground food in the narrower sense, and serve[s] principally to attract the food from above" (CS 303–4 [E 440]). The description of traditional ceremonies where dogs "gaze upwards," jump in the air, and send magical "incantations [*Zaubersprüche*]" (CS 304 [E 441]) instead of prayers heavenwards is very playful. The dog performs many experiments to prove the validity of a spiritual dimension—some humorous, others disastrous and nearly tragic.

"Investigations" is no linear narrative; it is highly associative and contains many narrative breaks that are filled in by humorous anecdotal commentary that resembles anecdotes in rabbinic texts. Apart from the "music dogs," there are the famous "air dogs [*Lufthunde*]," a play on the Yiddish term *Luftmensch*, air people, a metaphor that is applied to those who have no income and must rely on the community for support. They were frequently criticized in Zionist discourse (CS 295 [E 429]); however, the narrator dog takes their side since he has never seen a single one who exhibited such negative characteristics and continues to believe in them (CS 294 [E 429]). He annuls the criticism directed against them by rendering it humorous, once again by taking the metaphor literally. The depiction of the dogs soaring in the air is a comic device, and Kafka uses it in order to transform the air dogs' supposedly senseless existence into a meaningful one. As with the music dogs before them—whom he admired for their "courage" and "power to endure" (CS 282 [E 416])—the strength of these dogs, too, lies in their survival: their stubbornness shows that "in spite of obstacles which appear insurmountable to our understanding, no dog species, however curious, ever dies out, once it exists, or, at least, not without a tough struggle, not without being capable of putting up a successful defense for a long time" (CS 296 [E 431–32]).

Such narrative reversals illustrate the challenge Kafka's writing represents for tradition, convention, or political dogma. As Benjamin said in 1938, Kafka's texts "do not modestly lie at the feet of doctrine, as aggadah [legends, anecdotes] lies at the feet of halakha [Law]. When they have crouched down, they unexpectedly raise a mighty paw against it" (Scholem,

Correspondence, 225 [B 87]). Seven years earlier Scholem had called Benjamin's secular interpretation a "presumptuous supposition," comparing it to the blasphemous nature of an attempt to paraphrase in words the quest for a divine judgment (B 64–65). But such an attempt is indeed depicted in "Investigations" when the little dog succeeds in showing that food is actually attracted to someone who is hungry. Again, the Midrashic technique is to take the metaphor "spiritual food" literally: the dog imagines what it would be like if "the food were to come of itself from above, and without going near the ground were to knock at my teeth for admittance" (CS 306 [E 443–44]). Here we have a parody of a biblical motif (manna in the wilderness descending on man) and of a mystical motif (the doorkeeper). The narrator's fertile imagination has produced a kind of *Luftnahrung* (air food) that pursues the little dog from above and ridicules any kind of religious quest (CS 305 [E 442]).

A subsequent anecdote further supports Benjamin's argument. Having been told that his experiments are not convincing, the little dog turns to traditional practices where the way to redemption is through self-negation and fasting. Again the narrator exploits this anecdote for creative storytelling. Before he started on his fasting experiment, the little dog had actually made sure that his point of departure was according to the Law. He knew that in a famous disputation a sage at one time wanted to prohibit fasting. But another sage intervened and answered, significantly with a question, in good Talmudic fashion: "But who would ever think of fasting?" (CS 310 [E 447]), implying that it would never occur to anyone in his right mind to do such a thing. The first sage found this answer so convincing that he no longer saw any need to prohibit fasting. But, the narrator intervenes, this does not solve the problem; since no law had been formulated, the question still needs to be asked: "Is not fasting really forbidden after all?" (CS 310 [E 447–48]).

The function of this parody of Talmudic reasoning is to satirize the seriousness and naiveté of the young dog: desperately in search of a straightforward "law" that he can apply to his present circumstances, he eagerly reassures himself that fasting is not forbidden and goes ahead with his experiment. Naturally, the results are catastrophic. He is starving, has spells of delirium, and suddenly comes to realize that the commentators' views had been downright wrong. Kafka's secular perspective is clear: the dog himself admits that he "was laboring to undermine the laws of the science of nutrition" (CS 308 [E 445]; translation modified). His experiments show that he has reduced the Law to a mere functional, literal level.

This becomes increasingly obvious in the little dog's final "assault on the frontiers," when he stubbornly persists in his fasting and pushes the situation to its very limit. At the climax he experiences what Scholem described to Benjamin as "the nothingness of Revelation." Though Scholem defines this phrase as "a state in which revelation *appears to be* without meaning" (*Correspondence,* 142; my emphasis [B 82]), in Kafka's text there literally is no meaning: "here and now was the hour of deadly earnest, here my inquiries should have shown their value, but where was the Science now? Here was only a dog snapping helplessly at the empty air" (CS 311 [E 449]; translation modified). This is the "presumptuous supposition!!" Scholem perceived and objected to in Benjamin's reading of Kafka. But Benjamin is proven right in that Kafka's dog here is raising a mighty paw against halakha.

Moreover, observance of the Law is ridiculed in the immediately following episode with the hunting dog who insists that the little dog *must* get out of his way. The little dog challenges this new halakha, "nothing but musts. Can you explain to me why we must?" and receives the reply, "No . . . but there's nothing that needs to be explained, these are natural, self-evident things" (CS 313 [E 452]). The humor of the situation lies in the pun on the German *müssen,* which in formal speech means "to have to" in the sense of "must" and, more prosaically "to urinate." This is what leads to the misunderstanding.

The anecdotal encounter with the hunting dog has the function of providing final liberation. The dog's singing frees the little dog from himself, and "pursued by the melody, I flew from the spot in the most grandiose leaps" (CS 314 [E 453]; translation modified). The singing again evokes the kabbalistic music from Jewish mysticism. Just as the little dog notices that "in the depth of his chest the hound was preparing to upraise a song" (CS 313 [E 452], in Peretz's "Cabalists," too, a fasting scholar who is about to be admitted as a singer to the heavenly host, hears that "'something within me hummed, like the beginning of a melody. . . . Then I heard the melody sing within me'" (*Treasury,* 222). Similarly, Kafka's dog suddenly understands "something such as no dog before me had ever seen . . . I thought I saw that the hound was already singing without knowing it" (CS 314 [E452]).

More than that, Kafka's hunting dog has stepped right out of the world of contemporary fairy tales. He is what we might call a sort of "Bambi Kabbala dog." *Bambi* was written by Felix Salten (who, incidentally, was an avid hunter in real life). Salten's deer world, an allegory of Jewish history with a Zionist message,[56] finds an equivalent in Kafka's dog universe. Though there is no ironclad proof that Kafka knew this text before it was published,[57] the similarities are far too striking not to attract our attention. The sudden appearance of Bambi's father, when Bambi is lying on the ground in a pool of blood, incapable of going on, is strikingly similar to the scene in "Investigations." The narrator dog, also lying in his blood, is comparable to Bambi, and the hunting dog to Bambi's father.

The description of Kafka's hunting dog suggests a deer as much as a dog: "He was lean, long-legged, brown with a patch of white here and there, and had a fine, strong, piercing glance. 'What are you doing here?' he asked. 'You must leave this place'" (CS 312 [E 450]). In Salten's novel the eyes of Bambi's father are also described as remarkable: they are dark, deep, penetrating, kind, and proud. In addition, Bambi's father uses very similar words when he commands his son to get up and come with him. Moreover, in both texts the protagonists begin searching for answers to their many questions, isolate themselves from their community, and set out alone to find their way. And finally, both protagonists are rescued by a "father" figure.

However, Kafka's hunting dog and Salten's King of the Forest have rather different functions. In Zionist discourses, the idolized leader Theodor Herzl was often referred to as "the King" or "the Prince."[58] Salten greatly admired Herzl, who died young in 1904, and offers a fairy-tale solution, promising the continuity of the line as Bambi replaces his father and becomes the King of the Forest himself. Herzl's famous slogan, "Wenn du nur willst, ist es kein Märchen" (If you really wish for it, it will be no fairy tale), comes to mind. *Bambi* ends with the hope that there will be new leaders and a strong independent community in the future. In contrast, Kafka's hunting dog is no idealized Herzl figure or political leader. Not only does he need to urinate in the very place where the little dog is lying in his blood, but the eroticism that manifests itself in Bambi's love and admiration for his father is transformed in Kafka's story into the hunting dog's (incipiently erotic) advances and the little dog just wanting him to go away (CS 313 [E451]).

The dog more likely alludes to Kafka's lover Milena Jesenská, whose eyes were equally remarkable, "strong, blue [and] penetrating" (Binder, *Erzählungen*, 261, 293–94). All of a sudden, despite the little dog's misgivings, a miracle happens: the hunting dog begins to sing, and the little dog is literally carried away by the melody, which seems to exist independently of the hunting dog, soaring in the air and coming toward him, existing for him alone. This melody gives the little dog the necessary strength to "fly away" (in the original German) as in a fairy tale.

Salten makes sure that Bambi stands his ground against all adversity and passes on a different political message, but Kafka offers his own creative "fairy-tale" solution when he describes the little dog's miraculous rescue. There seems to be no irony: in hindsight, the narrator comments that even if this experience was "an error it had nonetheless a sort of grandeur, and it remains the sole, even if delusive, reality that I have rescued from my period of fasting and carried over with me into this world" (CS 314 [E 453]; translation modified). The memory of this experience (which alludes to his great love for Milena) helps the little dog return to his humble existence and live out his life at peace with the other dogs. These anecdotes, and especially the scene with the Bambi Kabbala dog, are not just "beginnings" for a new kind of writing, the new type of folkloristic Kabbala, which Kafka said existed already in his earlier work. Rather, Kafka has created his own imaginary world out of the contemporary discourses (traditional, Zionist, mystic, children's literature) available to him. This world is not only a clear interdiscursive construction but a counterdiscourse to Zionism and tradition.

Within the folkloristic cultural framework, a new literary voice has emerged that has momentarily liberated the narrator from his dog life and removed him not to a Zionist world but to an imaginary one that resembles the associative fantasies in a Chagall painting. Does not Kafka's entire representation of the Jewish world in "Investigations of a Dog" evolve out of a humorous play on the Yiddish term *Luftmensch* (air person)? Here, *Luftmenschen* are transformed into dogs of various strange breeds: Zionists with their *Lufthunger* (air hunger), the spiritualists with their *Luftnahrung* (air nourishment), the incredible *Lufthunde* (air dogs) themselves, the ecstatic *Musikhunde* (music dogs)—not forgetting Milena, the Bambi Kabbala dog. These imaginary creatures pursue many strange "professions" (CS 279 [vocations]; E 413 [Berufe]): mostly *Nahrungswissenschaft* (the science of nutrition) and *Bodenbearbeitung* (the cultivation of the land), but those of a more spiritual orientation go as far as practicing the art of *Musikwissenschaft* (the science of music).

In this Dog Universe characterized by metamorphosis and error, a little dog undertakes his "assault on the frontiers" in a manner not unlike Josef K.'s struggle (and perhaps even the travails of the ape Rotpeter). Along the way he encounters halakhas of various kinds, challenges them, and exposes them as errors. Real miracles occur when "meaningless existences" like "air dogs," or the little dog himself, are transformed into something "wonderful."

But let us not be taken in by fantasies and miracles. Josef K. may think he has an important position at the bank, yet his world—and this, too, is like a Chagall painting—comes tumbling down, and soon he himself is no more than a *Luftmensch*. The reality of *The Trial* is that the accused are degraded and treated like dogs: merchant Block is Huld's "dog," and Josef K. is killed "like a dog." These human characters share the fate of Kafka's animals because they all live out their lives alone, amongst the garbage, on staircases, in the desert, in a variety show, or—as in Kafka's last story—like the mice in "Josephine the Singer," "always on their last legs."

"Josephine the Singer, or the Mouse Folk"

The old dog-narrator concluded that he learned very little in his youth and found it aggravating that even later he "never seriously tackled the science of music" (CS 315 [E 454]). In "Josephine the Singer" (1924) the study of *Musikwissenschaft* becomes central. Just as in "Investigations," where Kafka employed the nutrition metaphor *Nahrungswissenschaft* and drew on the various connotations of *Bodenbearbeitung* for his satire of traditional Judaism as well as of Zionism, in "Josephine" we see him employ various connotations of "the science of music." The main question is whether Josephine's singing is an art form or not.

Josephine is another rebellious child, and her insistence that her singing is "art" is all the more surprising since she has had no formal training. The mice people, too, have no school at all, and thus there is no opportunity for developing any child's creative side or artistic talent. The mouse narrator deplores the absence of a national education for the mice children: "Other races [*Völker*] may foster their children carefully, schools may be erected for their little ones, out of these schools the children may come pouring daily, the future of the race [*die Zukunft des Volkes*]. . . . We have no schools" (CS 368 [E 528]). This passage echoes contemporary Zionist discourses, as does the repetition of "Volk" [people] throughout the entire story.[59] Kafka avoids the word "race," *Rasse,* and thereby makes a clear distinction between non-Jewish racist and *völkish* Zionist discourses, which the English translation does not make. The argument in "Josephine" is that the mice are a "people" like other peoples and have the same needs. In fact, schools are said to exist for everyone else—only not for them. And the mice children are just as much in need of an education, especially since they seem to have great potential: they are sprightly and enthusiastic, "merrily lisping or chirping so long as they cannot yet pipe" (CS 369 [E 528–29]).

We hear that frequent attempts have been made by the community to improve this state of affairs, to offer greater individual freedom, space for creativity, room to play and to develop self-confidence (CS 368 [E 528]). These plans recall Kafka's interest in creative, innovative, liberating forms of education. The need for some kind of action is agreed upon by most, yet all attempts to create a more appropriate educational environment have so far gone nowhere: "one approves these demands, one makes attempts to meet them, but soon all the old ways are back again" (CS 368 [E 528]). This situation has serious consequences for the formation of an identity amongst the mice children. Without any schooling appropriate to their needs, they develop no pride in their own culture. They are quickly robbed of their childhood, their youth, and spend their lives "pfeifen auf dem letzten Loch [always on their last legs]." Josephine makes an art of this *pfeifen*, piping, indulging in every nuance.

One could argue that much of the story develops out of this idiomatic expression, "pfeifen auf dem letzten Loch," to be on one's last legs or to gasp, and that Kafka is playing with its literal and metaphorical meanings.[60] How indeed can Josephine claim she is an artist who deserves special treatment and understanding if her piping sounds like everyone else's piping? (CS 361 [E 519]) There are different opinions about the musical talent of the mice people. For one, there are those who flatly deny the mice *any* musical talent since "we are not in general a music-loving race [*sic.:* *"Geschlecht,"* lineage, family]" (CS 360 [E 518]). Considering that the mice metaphor is drawn from anti-Semitic discourses, this charge finds its strongest expression in Richard Wagner's *Das Judentum in der Musik* (Judaism in Music, 1850).[61] Kafka is conveying the stereotype here, but it is unlikely that he internalized these anti-Semitic stereotypes so much that he simply reproduced them without critical distance. How would one then explain that he has Josephine singing until her last breath? Kafka knew Yiddish songs, Hasidic music and dances, as well as "temple melodies" from the synagogue. When the Eastern European Jewish refugees came to Prague in 1914, Brod's great enjoyment came from the Hasidic music sung during the services that he, as well as Kafka, attended.[62]

At the same time, the narrator is acknowledging that the music the mice are producing now in the form of Josephine's "singing" might not be art. He admits he is "half in sympathy" with the opposition that does not grant her singing the status of art (CS 362 [E 521]). There are those, he explains, who argue that Josephine's "piping" is part of their tradition, their cultural heritage: "Although we are unmusical we have a tradition of singing; in the old days our people did sing; this is mentioned in legends and some songs have actually survived, which, it is true, no one can now sing" (CS 361 [E 519]). In this case, Josephine's "art" represents a tradition in decline, since what used to be "singing" has now, at the end of a long history of cultural repression, become *pfeifen*, piping, whistling, squeaking.

Marek Nekula has equated the piping with Yiddish and Josephine's "singing" with the Hebrew lessons of the young Puah Ben Tovim (42). Though "piping" may not refer to Yiddish alone but to *Mauscheln*, the "language" of the Diaspora Jews in general, Nekula's insight that her singing might be an allusion to "Hebrew classes" does not seem so farfetched. One could elaborate here that what used to be real "singing" in the past might indeed refer to old Hebrew prayers that no one can sing anymore. Moreover, *Musikwissenschaft*, the science of music, also recalls the Academy of Jewish Studies, the *Hochschule für die Wissenschaft des Judentums*. Kafka explicitly referred to reciting the Talmud there, and during religious services the Torah is always chanted and there are "signs" indicating melodies in the text. Significantly, Josephine is described like a female cantor.

The narrator does not admire her "piping," and temple melodies were the one kind of Jewish music Kafka was not enthusiastic about. At one time he described them as annoying, and another time he remarked that the lament is senseless.[63] However, the narrator does acknowledge that everyone who sits in front of Josephine understands her: "And when you take a seat before her, you understand her; opposition is possible only at a distance, when you sit before her, you know: this piping of hers is no piping" (CS 362 [E 521). The phrase "when you sit before her," which is repeated twice here, identifies Josephine as some kind of *Vorbeter*, someone who leads others in prayer (piping).

As a matter of fact, Jewish music was just beginning to establish itself as an art form in the synagogues in Western Jewish culture. Generally it did suffer from the fact that cantors or other performers had very little musical training, and congregations "had been annoyed by singing habits perpetuated by inertia alone or by barren experimentation" (*Encyclopaedia Judaica*, 12:650). A sign of greater "art" was the introduction of organ and choir to the synagogue. These were relatively new additions that Kafka was familiar with because his friend Oskar Baum played the organ in the synagogue (Rybar 205). But Kafka and Brod in any event preferred the more "authentic" services with the Eastern European refugees (without organ or choir) to the innovations of the assimilated Western congregations.

There is no accompaniment to Josephine's song—neither by a musical instrument nor by a choir. Josephine's art, if one can call it that, is still without artifice and completely natural, and its peculiar strength lies in creating a feeling of togetherness, which imparts momentary peace. Though Bokhove related the peaceful stillness of the "Castle Keep" in "The Burrow" to the Academy for Jewish Studies ("Friedensort," 48), there is another echo in "Josephine" here, for when she stops singing, the audience feels peaceful. Kafka had called the Academy "a refuge of peace" (LFF 402 [Br 470]) and described the teaching there as "rather odd to the point of grotesquerie and beyond that to the point of intangible delicacy [namely the liberal-reformist tone and scholarly aspects of the whole thing]" (LFF 403 [Br 470]). Similarly, Josephine's singing distinguishes itself from the other *pfeifen* only through its vulnerability, "at most . . . through being delicate or weak" (CS 361[E 520]).

But even if Josephine's piping is no longer art or "singing," its effect is the same as in the traditions of the past, because her music brings about peace and harmony. Her singing, "when you sit before her," is a struggle during which everyone is silent. But then she stops: "Here in the brief intervals between their struggles our people dream, it is as if the limbs of each were loosened, as if the harried individual once in a while could relax and stretch himself at ease in the great, warm bed of the community" (CS 370 [E 530]). This feeling of harmony evokes an understanding of the mice people's shared history similar to the intended effect of Theodor Herzl's famous refrain, "Wir sind ein Volk, Ein Volk," "We are a people, One people, united," which echoes through *The Jewish State* (1896).

But this is the Zionist dream. In real life, Josephine's music is an art form that "pfeift auf dem letzten Loch"—is on its last legs. She represents a late phase of a once-heroic musical past, and her fate is clear: she will disappear like all the other heroes before her (CS 376 [E 538]). However, in this last story, as in his very last diary entry, Kafka expresses his firm belief (which is "more than consolation") that Josephine will lose herself "happily" in her people, "[who] as a whole . . . surrender unconditionally to no one" (CS 376, 371 [E 538, 532)]). The narrator knows that her stubbornness and determination will live on in them and continue beyond her death.

It was the memory of a simple "folk" tradition that lent Josephine the strength to carry on and cling to her art until her last breath. She was deluded when she thought her people did not understand her and in her arrogance challenged them with "Ich pfeife auf eueren Schutz [I don't give a damn for your protection]." The narrator, for one, responded ironically, because he understood her pun and also spoke for the community: "Ja, ja, du pfeifst," denken wir [Yes, yes, you are piping, we think]" (CS 366 [E 525]; my translation). In fact, the community took care of her all along: "So the people [*das Volk*] look after Josephine much as a father takes into his care a child whose little hand . . . is stretched out to him" (CS 365 [E 524–25]).[64] The idiomatic expression "ich pfeif dir was," "I'll pipe you something" or "I'll do what I want, I don't care if you like it," expresses the superior, childish attitude that Josephine—literally and figuratively— held on to all her life. This "little woman" is certainly one of Kafka's most defiant protagonists, but she too–the only female heroine–"will happily lose herself in the numberless throng of the heroes of our people, and soon, since we are no historians, will rise to the heights of redemption and be forgotten like all her brothers" (CS 376 [E 538]).

Conclusion

Like Josephine, millions of Jews disappeared without a trace twenty years later. Kafka did not live to see the Holocaust, but his personal as well as his fictional writings reproduce, echo, and ironically refract many of the discourses that led up to the *Shoah* and helped bring it about. To be sure, Walter Benjamin rightly argued that Kafka had no prophetic vision; however, Kafka listened intently not only to tradition but also to the discourses that surrounded him. His representation of the jackals and the ape, for instance, was so obviously anti-Semitic that the animals can be seen as personifications of verbal expressions that make "visible" the contemporary Zionist and anti-Semitic discourses by literally representing Jews as what they were said to be: jackal-like pariahs and ape-like imitators and imposters. Yet, how representative of the period would Kafka's stories be if they did not contain present-day concerns, fears, and prejudice?

In his personal life, Kafka was preoccupied with contemporary counterdiscourses to the anti-Semitic political reality. These are the many Jewish discourses (the rich folklore tradition and Zionism) that he identified with and which make up his cultural Zionism. His participation in small community work (*völkische Kleinarbeit*) and his furthering of a Jewish education stand out here in particular. However, Kafka seems to be far more sympathetic to contemporary Zionism in the letters to his friends than in his literary works. Here Zionism is not only represented critically, he even singles it out for interfering with his literary creativity and consciously draws on other Jewish discourses (biblical, Talmudic, mystic, folkloric, etc.). Kafka's extensive readings demonstrate his broad interest in Jewish culture and reveal his keen desire to learn about Judaism, though he was well aware that "it would require genius of an unimaginable kind to strike root again in the old centuries, or create the old centuries anew" (DII 203 [T 878; 1922]).

Despite his great interest in Jewish culture, Kafka was never a religious believer. In 1921, in the sanatorium in Matliary, he was annoyed with "a young half-pious Hungarian Jew" directly under his balcony who, "in his reclining chair, comfortably outstretched with one hand over his head, the other thrust deep into his fly, ... all day long cheerfully keeps on humming temple melodies (What a people!)" (LFF 283 [Br 330]). And in 1922 Kafka described himself as "alienated from the faith, so that a father cannot even expect him to say the prayers for the rest of his soul" (LFF 347 [Br 401]). At the same time, Kafka was curious about religious life. Thus, he enjoyed his visit with Langer and the Hasidim in 1916, and we hear that he was "intrigued with Jewish prayer rituals" in 1924 and told Max Brod that he wanted *tefillin*, "the philacteries used by Orthodox Jews" (Diamant 26). But Kafka's friend Friedrich Thieberger was surely right when he stressed that Kafka was never very familiar with religious Judaism: in January 1923 he missed the bar mitzvah of Oskar Baum's son because he did not know "that the ceremony can only take place on a Saturday" (LFF 368 [Br 428]). In September 1923, the very possibility that he might be "attending the Jewish Harvest Festival" with Dora immediately elicited the cautious rejoinder, "a risky venture for her as for me. I probably won't do it" (LFF 383 [Br 448]).

Ultimately, it was not religious faith or ritual that Kafka wanted. He cared about people and being part of a community. Already in 1912, when he criticized the Yiddish plays, it was the individual actors who counted most (DI 215 [T 349]). The same is true in 1916 when he remarked to Felice that "the main thing is the human element, only the human element" (LF 498 [BF 694]) and that "Zionism is not something that separates well-meaning people" (LF 501 [BF 697–98]. Moreover, a sentence from Schimon bar Jochai, which Kafka read out to Brod from a tattered Talmud anthology, further underlines the humanist quality of Kafka's cultural Zionism: "'A miracle happened to me; therefore I will set up an institution which will be of benefit to all'" (FK1, 233). Finally, in 1924, when Brod suggested someone he knew who was versed in the Scriptures, Kafka felt that "having a man in the vicinity who knows something about these things would be a certain encouragement to me" but he would "probably be more interested in the man than in the things" (LFF 405 [Br 472]). Kafka's personal Zionism was influenced by Hugo Bergmann's practical or spiritual form of cultural Zionism, which was indebted especially to Micha Josef Berdyczewski, bin Gorion, who is largely forgotten today. For Berdyczewski, Judaism was identical with humanity ("We are Jews only because we are human beings that are part of the Jewish people and our humanity is our Judaism").

A similar emphasis on the "human" element is evident in Kafka's fiction. For instance, "A Report to an Academy" is perhaps his most obvious Zionist text with its critique of the Enlightenment and assimilation. Yet at the same time the story's psychological realism highlights the tragedy of the ape's tortured existence—a dimension that is entirely missing in the monological contemporary Zionist critiques of assimilation. Or we may think of the impact of Josephine's singing on the mice community as conjuring up Theodor Herzl's magic words, "we are a people, one people united," yet nonetheless Josephine is far too individualistic (and arrogant) to listen to anyone but herself. She is "human" (with many flaws) and not a spokesperson for a political ideology. Gregor Samsa as well is "human" inside his vermin body; the crossbreed is not killed by the butcher's knife but treated humanely; the dog in "Investigations" no longer rebels but becomes reconciled with the other sad Diaspora dogs; and the narrator in "Josephine" is not upset about her disappearance but accepts it as part of life. Though Zionist concerns are visible in many of Kafka's texts, there is no political Zionist message, nor are there activist Zionist heroes—only human beings with at best more weaknesses than strengths. One could even argue that Kafka is deliberately countering the demands of the more political Zionists for an identifiable Jewish discourse by creating stubborn antiheroes who struggle valiantly but never reach any goals.

Kafka's last statement about Judaism occurs shortly before his death and sums up an attitude I have attempted to present here. In a letter to his friend and doctor Robert Klopstock, Kafka discusses "The Memoirs of Arthur Holitscher," which were published under the title *The Life-Story of a Rebel*.[1] Here again we see Kafka's critical distance from assimilated Jews who identified only with German culture (LFF 410 [Br 478]). More than that, Kafka's criticism becomes even stronger when he addresses Holitscher's attitude toward his own Jewish heritage: "The way he complains about Jewishness is embarrassing both for him and for the reader. As if someone at a party were to go on for hours expounding on the features of a certain ailment and furthermore showing it to be incurable, amid general agreement, and after all this is over someone in the corner begins to wail about this particular ailment. And yet there is something fine about it; it is sincere to the point of grotesque wretchedness. Nevertheless, one feels: it might go even further" (LFF 410 [Br 479]).

Ironically, Holitscher's biography testifies to the fact that he had a very eventful life in the company of many of the literary figures of his time, such as Knut Hamsun, Wedekind, Wassermann, the Bohemians in Paris around Oscar Wilde and Lord Alfred Douglas, and Thomas Mann, all of whom he knew personally. To Kafka, Holitscher's resorting to sentimental self-pity at the end of his life seems uncalled for: "For so many years what an aura of Paris and of literature surrounded Holitscher and the titles of his novels—and now here is this aging man crying over the hardships of that whole period. He was unhappy then, but one cannot help thinking: If only I had been unhappy that way just once; I would have still liked to try this way of life just once" (LFF 410 [Br 479]; translation modified). Kafka's scorn for sentimental self-pity is in keeping with his nonillusory attitude toward himself and has characterized his relationship to his own Jewish heritage all along. In his critical and frequently ironic distance to Judaism, Zionism, himself, and others, he remained constant during his life.

Already in 1912 he disliked the Yiddish plays when they became "too monotonous and degenerate[d] into a wailing" (DI 215 [T 349]). In his notebooks, too, we find the same rejection of self-pity in a comment of 1922–23 on a service in the synagogue: "The lament is senseless [to whom does he complain?], the jubilation is ridiculous [the kaleidoscope in the window]. Obviously all he wants is to lead the others in prayer, but then it is indecent to use the Jewish language, then it is quite sufficient for the lament if he spends his life repeating: 'Dog-that-I-am, dog-that-I-am,' and so forth, and we shall all understand him, but for happiness silence is not only sufficient, it is indeed the only thing possible" (W 326 [H 240, NII 333–334]). Lament is rejected in favor of silence. Holitscher's reaction at the end of his life stands in stark contrast to Kafka's, who was very sick when he made these remarks and dead within three months.

In conclusion, Kafka's attitude to Judaism, and Zionism in particular, has frequently been called ambiguous; however, he is actually quite consistent. While he identified with "Zionist longing" on a general level, and in this respect always sympathized with the Zionist movement, he disliked its dogmatism. He also rejected the reassurances that accompany all essentialist beliefs and could never identify with contemporary Zionism when it took the form of a substitute religion. Kafka's Zionism was the humanist Zionism of bin Gurion, Hugo Bergmann, and Max Brod. And though critics may believe that Kafka's wish to migrate to Palestine cannot be taken very seriously (because he must have known that he was too ill for the journey), Kafka did want to go and at one point tried to buy a ticket. One could equally argue that had his illness not prevented him from doing so, Kafka would have migrated to Palestine at a time when his best friends Max Brod and Felix Weltsch did not even consider such a move.

Furthermore, Kafka's literature does not mask or repress contemporary realities. Since he disliked the ideological racial discourses (both Zionist and anti-Semitic) of his period, it should come as no surprise that he refused to allow them to dominate his fiction. This does not mean that his literature is devoid of social reality: in his first major work, "The Judgment," the Beilis ritual murder trial surfaces. Nowhere during this period does Kafka mention the ritual murder trials in his personal correspondence or diary, but the allusion appears here, in his "literature." Moreover, besides anti-Semitic and Zionist rhetoric, a great many other Jewish discourses permeate his writings. In fact, a closer look at some of his literary texts reveals that these other Jewish discourses (of the Yiddish theater, Hasidic tales, Zionism, Jewish anti-Semitism or self-hatred) are actually more prominent in Kafka's fiction than is non-Jewish anti-Semitism. However, after the Holocaust, the loud racial discourses have drowned out the existence of these other Jewish discourses, which Kafka frequently represented in his fiction with humor and ironic distance.

Developing his own private counterdiscourse, Kafka made a political statement. A writer who rejects racial ideologies is not about to reproduce them uncritically in his work, and Kafka clearly avoids any racial labeling in his literary texts. Thus especially his avoidance of the word "Jew" in his fiction is not necessarily, as so many critics have readily concluded, a sign of self-hatred and a repression of his Jewish identity, but rather a conscious choice on Kafka's part: since he rejected stereotyping of any kind (in Zionist or anti-Semitic rhetoric), he had good reason not to give his protagonists a clearly identifiable ethnic identity. Significantly, there is no "Jewish Patient" in "A Country Doctor"; Gregor Samsa is not Jewish, nor is Karl Rossmann or Joseph K. Eric Homberger adds a further dimension to this discussion when he stresses "the need for space . . . a space, within which the writer lays claim to objectivity, independence, and critical distance—distance from Jewishness, perhaps—upon which secular intellectual integrity depends."[2] Kafka needed—insisted on—this space. In "Investigations" the narrator-dog comes to the conclusion that more than anything, he needs freedom to protect his personal space and integrity: "It was this instinct that made me . . . prize freedom higher than everything else. Freedom! Certainly such freedom as is possible today is a wretched business. But nevertheless freedom, nevertheless a possession" (CS 316 [E 455]). The narrator's "possession" is his chronicle, created within "the marvellous *field for play* [der herrliche *Spielraum*]" which Benjamin perceived long ago (Scholem, *Correspondence,* 224 [B 86]). Kafka's literature originates in a "burrow of art," a personal, creative space located in an intellectual battlefield and yet removed from it—a space from which he could creatively engage with the world around him. The animal in "The Burrow" rightly insists that building and protecting this private space is no sign of cowardice: "But you do not know me if you think I am afraid, or that I built my burrow simply out of fear [*Feigheit*: cowardice]" (CS 325 [E 465]).

Kafka's literature is an unlimited counterfiction that dissects, probes, tests, and challenges new and preestablished modes of thinking. His texts are unlimited because they cannot be reduced to allegory, ideology, or the author's own subjectivity. There is also no closure, only further and further unraveling of layers of meaning. "Jackals and Arabs" is a case in point. Many contemporaries would have understood this story as a Zionist satire of Diaspora existence because it employs the typical anti-Semitic metaphors for the religious Eastern European Jews that we find in many polemical Zionist narratives. At the same time, within the context of the Second Aliya, the story also appears to be a satire of contemporary Western Zionism (caricaturing not only the religious jackals but also the Northern visitor who is quite out of touch with the reality of life in Palestine). Furthermore, those readers who were following the immediate historical events with a sense of hope (i.e., the negotiations leading to the Balfour Declaration) would not have missed Kafka's rather bleak prognosis for the future that promises no new beginning in Herzl's Old-New Land, only the continuation of old conflicts in a new disguise.

What is equally fascinating is that this overlap of multiple discourses, in their apparent disjunction, comes across as decidedly postmodern to many readers who are not familiar with the historical-cultural context. Kafka's unfulfilled dream of Palestine exemplifies par excellence a Derridean kind of continual deferment that aptly characterizes the postmodern condition.

On the discursive level, too, we discussed similarities between rabbinic interpretation, Kafka's modernist, ironic mock-Midrash, and deconstructive criticism, which are apparent in the process of unraveling and dismantling discourse, the circular and decidedly nonlinear structure, the continual deferral of meaning from one sign to the next. Critics agree that these discursive features are typically Kafkaesque. Whether we want to see Kafka as a radical modernist, a precursor of a postmodern consciousness or a forerunner of modern deconstruction, the variety and richness of his literary production alone is a challenge to the polemical, monological writing of the period and signals Kafka's independence as a writer. Indeed, by creating a rebellious counterdiscourse with humor and ironic playfulness, Kafka affirms the last words in his diary, "You too have weapons" (DII 232–33 [T 926]). Even now, the fundamental ambiguity of his texts remains his most powerful rhetorical weapon.

6. *Selbstwehr* pays tribute to Franz Kafka (*In Memoriam Franz Kafka*, S 6 June 1924:5).

Notes

INTRODUCTION

1. Max Brod, "Die dritte Phase des Zionismus," *Die Zukunft* 16 (20 Jan. 1917): 1–13.
2. Marthe Robert, *As Lonely as Franz Kafka,* trans. Ralph Mannheim (1979; reprint, New York: Schocken, 1986), 27.
3. According to Jiri Kudela, the census of 1900 reveals that 19,204 Jews lived in Prague districts I–VIII. The whole population of Prague, including the suburbs (Smichov, Karlin, Vinohrady, Žižkov), consisted of 394,030 inhabitants. There were 26,342 Jews ("Die Emigration galizischer und osteuropäischer Juden nach Böhmen und Prag zwischen 1914–1916/17," in *Studia Rosenthaliana,* ed. M. P. Beukers and J. J. Cahen [Amsterdam: University Library of Amsterdam, Bibliotheca Rosenthaliana, 1989], 121 n.4). The Jewish population in all of Bohemia was approximately 85,000 in 1913 (Hugo Bergmann, *Jawne und Jerusalem: Gesammelte Aufsätze* [Berlin: Jüdischer Verlag, 1919], 12).
4. Hartmut Binder, *"Vor dem Gesetz": Einführung in Kafkas Welt* (Stuttgart: Metzler, 1993), 5.
5. See Arnold Band, "Kafka and the Beiliss Affair," *Comparative Literature* 32 (1980): 173; Claus-Ekkehard Bärsch, *Max Brod im "Kampf um das Judentum": Zum Leben und Werk eines deutsch-jüdischen Dichters aus Prag* (Vienna: Passagen Verlag, 1992), 155; and especially Ernst Pawel, "Franz Kafkas Judentum," in *Kafka und das Judentum,* ed. Karl Erich Grözinger et al. (Frankfurt: Jüdischer Verlag bei Athenäum, 1987), 258, 253, 257.
6. Meyer Isser Pinès, *L'Histoire de la littérature judéo-allemande* (Paris: Jouve, 1911).
7. Ritchie Robertson, *Kafka: Judaism, Politics and Literature* (Oxford: Clarendon Press, 1985), 19.
8. Claude Mauriac, "Des lettres d'amour signées Kafka," *Preuves* 69 (Nov. 1956): 73–74.
9. Giuliano Baioni, *Kafka: Letteratura ed ebraismo* (Turin: Einaudi, 1984), 53. See also Baioni's "Zionism, Literature, and the Yiddish Theater," in *Reading Kafka: Prague, Politics, and the Fin-de-Siècle,* ed. Mark Anderson (New York: Schocken, 1989), 108.

10. Régine Robin, *Kafka* (Paris: Pierre Belfond, 1989), 52.

11. Sander Gilman, *Franz Kafka, the Jewish Patient* (New York: Routledge, 1995).

12. Marthe Robert hopes "to discover why Kafka felt obliged to censor the name "Jew" in his work" (*As Lonely as Franz Kafka*, 22). Jean Jofen attributes the absence of "Jewish" markers in Kafka's work to self-hatred and believes this shows "how carefully Kafka tried to hide all traces of these sources, in order to identify himself as a German writer" (*The Jewish Mystic in Kafka* [New York: Peter Lang, 1987], xii).

13. Pavel Petr, *Kafkas Spiele: Selbststilisierung und literarische Komik* (Heidelberg: Carl Winter Universitätsverlag, 1992), 71.

14. Jack Murray, *The Landscapes of Alienation: Ideological Subversion in Kafka, Céline, and Onetti* (Stanford: Stanford Univ. Press, 1991), 6.

15. Gershom Scholem, ed., *The Correspondence of Walter Benjamin and Gershom Scholem 1932–1940* (Cambridge, Mass.: Harvard Univ. Press, 1992), 224, translation modified (hereafter cited as *Correspondence*). See also Walter Benjamin, "Some Reflections on Kafka," in *Illuminations: Essays and Reflections,* ed. Hannah Arendt, trans. Harry Zohn (New York: Schocken, 1969), 143. Compare B 86.

16. Mark Gelber, "Introduction: Kafka in Israel—Preliminary Remarks," in *Kafka, Zionism, and Beyond,* ed. Mark Gelber (Tübingen: Niemeyer Verlag, 2004), 2. Baioni's *Kafka: Letteratura ed ebraismo* includes chapters on "Prague and Martin Buber's Cultural Zionism" and "Zionism and Literature"; his book has been translated into German (*Kafka—Literatur und Judentum,* trans. G. and J. Billen [Stuttgart: Metzler, 1994]), but only one chapter (chap. 2 on the Yiddish theater) has been translated into English (see note 9 above). Ritchie Robertson's *Kafka: Judaism, Politics, and Literature* substantially develops the research done by Anne Oppenheimer in "Franz Kafka's Relation to Judaism" (Ph.D. diss., Oxford University, 1977), places Kafka into his social environment, interprets his texts from various perspectives, and reads Kafka's aphorisms and especially *The Castle* (in his final chapter) from the perspective of Jewish mysticism. Scott Spector's *Prague Territories: National Conflict and Cultural Innovation in Franz Kafka's Fin de Siècle* (Berkeley: Univ. of California Press, 2000) uses Deleuze and Guattari's notion of a minor literature as a point of departure and examines different manifestations of deterritorialization in the work of these Prague writers, arguing that they seek but ultimately fail to achieve reterritorialization.

17. Scholem, ed., *Correspondence,* 225. See Benjamin, *Illuminations,* "Some Reflections," 144 for a more accessible edition. Compare B 87.

18. "Context" is to be understood in the "factual" historical sense, while "(con)text" is to suggest the social text of Kafka's time, or the multiple social discourses (traditional-religious, Zionist, mystic, etc.) surrounding Kafka.

19. Frederick Karl, *Franz Kafka, Representative Man: Prague, Germans, Jews and the Crisis of Modernism* (New York: International Publishing, 1993), 756; Nicholas Murray, *Kafka* (New Haven: Yale Univ. Press, 2004), 300.

20. See Kathi Diamant, *Kafka's Last Love: The Mystery of Dora Diamant* (New York: Basic Books, 2003), 317; and Anthony Northey, "Julie Wohryzek, Franz Kafkas zweite Verlobte," *Freibeuter* (Apr. 1994): 15.

21. Richard Terdiman, *Discourse/Counter-Discourse: The Theory and Practice of*

Symbolic Resistance in Nineteenth-Century France (Ithaca, N.Y.: Cornell University Press, 1985), 16. My use of the term "counter-discourse" is loosely based on Terdiman's study.

22. Scholem called it "a work of highly dubious authenticity that nevertheless was swallowed uncritically by a hungry world, a book the author published (or fabricated) . . . only when Kafka became world famous after the Second World War" (*Walter Benjamin: The Story of a Friendship* [Philadelphia: The Jewish Publication Society of America, 1981], x). See Hartmut Binder, ed., *Kafka Handbuch, Bd. 2: Das Werk und seine Wirkung* (Stuttgart: Alfred Kröner Verlag, 1979), 554–62; Gerhard Kurz, *Traum-Schrecken: Kafkas literarische Existenzanalyse* (Stuttgart: Metzler, 1980), x; Robertson, *Judaism, Politics, and Literature*, xii.

1. KAFKA'S JEWISH PRAGUE (1883–1911)

1. Anthony Northey, "Die Kafkas: Juden? Christen? Tschechen? Deutsche?" in *Kafka und Prag*, ed. Kurt Krolop and H.-D. Zimmermann (Berlin: Walter de Gruyter, 1994), 16; Alena Wagnerová, *Die Familie Kafka aus Prag* (Frankfurt: Fischer, 1997), 57; and Marek Nekula, *Franz Kafkas Sprachen* (Tübingen: Max Niemeyer Verlag, 2003), 66.

2. Anthony Northey, *Kafka's Relatives: Their Lives and His Writing* (New Haven: Yale Univ. Press, 1991), 85. On Kafka's family history, see also KH 124–27 and Klaus Wagenbach, *Franz Kafka: Eine Biographie seiner Jugend 1883–1912* (Bern: Francke Verlag, 1958), 21–22.

3. Wagenbach claims that the grandfather barely managed to make a living to support the children (*Biographie* 12, 16); yet Jeremy Adler argues the grandfather was actually well off and that the myth of the family's poverty was created by Kafka's father to "heighten his own image as a self-made man" (*Kafka* [London: Penguin, 2001], 18).

4. Ernst Pawel, *The Nightmare of Reason* (New York: Farrar, Straus & Giroux, 1984), 6; KH 116.

5. Marsha Rozenblit has shown that "in Czech areas of Bohemia," German language and culture were generally predominant: even Jews who spoke Czech in public would speak German at home (*Reconstructing a National Identity: The Jews of Habsburg Austria during World War I* [Oxford: Oxford Univ. Press, 2001], 27). Nekula, too, argues very convincingly that the father grew up with German, knew a little Yiddish, used German in the army, and spoke Czech to his Czech employees but German at home (45–66).

6. The dates that are given are certainly vague and contradictory. Christoph Stölzl places this event right after the father came to Prague (1881) (*Kafkas böses Böhmen: Zur Sozialgeschichte eines Prager Juden.* [Munich: Text & kritik, 1975], 51). According to Wagenbach, "he was a member of the board of the synagogue on Heinrichgasse, the first Prague synagogue, founded around 1890, where the sermon was delivered in Czech" (*Franz Kafka in Selbstzeugnissen und Bilddokumenten* [Reinbeck: Rowohlt, 1976], 16). Yet another source reports that Kafka's father participated in the 1890s (Citibor Rybar, *Jewish Prague* [Prague: TV Spektrum, 1991], 199).

7. Milada Vilimkova, *Die Prager Judenstadt,* trans. Tomanova-Weisova (Prague: Aventinum, 1990), 135.

8. The father's shifting cultural affiliations are not unusual. In 1920 Franz Kafka describes "a Prague Jew, who until the break-up [of the Habsburg monarchy] (this in confidence) was a member of the Deutsche Haus [German Bohemian Society] as well as of Měštanská Beseda [its Czech equivalent], and now, thanks to his high connections, has obtained his release from the Casino ... and promptly had his son transferred to the Czech Realschule, 'now he won't know either German or Czech, so let him bark'" (LFF 232, 468n.18–20 [Br 270]).

9. PK 130; and Zdenko Vaněk, "Erinnerungen eines Mitschülers," in *"Als Kafka mir entgegenkam . . .": Erinnerungen an Franz Kafka,* ed. H. G. Koch (Berlin: Verlag Klaus Wagenbach, 1995), 37.

10. Hugo Bergmann recalls that "Nathan Grün was a renowned writer and librarian of the Jewish community." Grün and Rabbi Bedrich Knöpfelmacher "published textbooks on Jewish history, which were well-known in their time" (*Tagebücher und Briefe,* vol. 2: *1948–1975,* ed. Miriam Sambursky [Königstein: Jüdischer Verlag bei athenäum, 1985], 697, 708n.1). See also KH 216. Grün's son was a Jewish nationalist (CJ 97).

11. Anna Pouzarovà, "Als Erzieherin in der Familie Kafka," in Koch, ed., *"Als Kafka,"* 65.

12. Stölzl, *"Prag,"* in KH 67; see also Binder "Der Mensch" in KH 217; and Kafka's "Letter to His Father" (DF 172 [Z 42]).

13. The English translation is missing the question mark.

14. Ben Korda, personal unpublished memoirs, 15.

15. I received this information from Karol Sidon, the rabbi of Prague during a meeting in 1993. See also Rybar for further information on the Pinkassynagoge: "In the lower part, in the men's department, there were 177, while in the women's part there were 100. On the gallery, intended exclusively for women, there were 143 seats" (265).

16. For a detailed account of the history of these student associations, see Kieval, "Zionism in Prague: Bar Kochba, 1899–1909" (CJ 93–123); and S. Goshen, "Zionist Students' Organizations," in *The Jews of Czechoslovakia,* vol. 2, ed. Society for the History of Czechoslovak Jews (Philadelphia: The Jewish Publication Society of America, 1971), 173–84.

17. Hugo Bergmann, "Erinnerungen an Franz Kafka," *Universitas: Zeitschrift für Wissenschaft, Kunst und Literatur* 27.7 (1972): 743–44; see also Bergmann, "Schulzeit und Studium," in Koch, ed., *"Als Kafka,"* 17. See Kieval on Bergmann's family background as well as on Bergmann's impact on the Bar Kochba (CJ 100–103, 109).

18. These events are not discussed in his early letters from 1902 on, nor when he begins his diary in 1910. For this reason, they will be mentioned again in subsequent chapters in the chronological order in which they appear in Kafka's readings and writings.

19. *Encyclopaedia Judaica* 15 (Jerusalem: Keter Publishing House, 1971).

20. Lovis M. Wambach, *Ahasver und Kafka: Zur Bedeutung der Judenfeindschaft in dessen Leben und Werk* (Heidelberg: Universitätsverlag C. Winter, 1993), 115.

21. Hans Kohn, "Before 1918 in the Historic Lands," in *The Jews of Czechoslovakia*, vol. 1:17. See also *Judaica* 8:496; and Stölzl, *Böhmen*, 67–74.

22. *Encyclopaedia Judaica* 10 (Jerusalem: Keter Publishing House, 1971), 1066. Concerning Kishinev and other pogroms during this period, see Shlomo Lambroza, "The Pogroms of 1903–1906," in *Pogroms: Anti-Jewish Violence in Modern Russian History*, ed. John D. Klier and Shlomo Lambroza (Cambridge: Cambridge Univ. Press, 1992), 195–247.

23. "Total membership of the Lese- und Redehalle in 1908 was between 150 and 200 students; at the time there were approximately 700 Jewish students in Prague" (CJ 228n.103).

24. Cited in CJ 106. The letter was not written in 1901, as Kieval suggests, and it is available in the original German. It was written in 1902–3, before Hugo Bergmann's travels to Galicia (Bergmann, *Tagebücher und Briefe*, 1:9).

25. Spector mentions that Bergmann "accepted Bar Kochba leadership" in 1901 (82), and Kieval states he joined Bar Kochba "in the fall of 1901" but dates his chairmanship 1903–4 (CJ 100). Binder maintains that Bergmann first joined the Lese- und Redehalle and became a member of Bar Kochba during the winter semester 1902–3 (KH 281, 370).

26. S 7 Feb. 1908:8; see CJ 117. For the history of the *Selbstwehr*, see Achim Jaeger, "'Nichts Jüdisches wird uns fremd sein': Zur Geschichte der Prager 'Selbstwehr' (1907–1938)," *Aschkenaz: Zeitschrift für Geschichte und Kultur der Juden* 15.1 (2005): 151–207.

27. In December 1908, as *Selbstwehr* entered its third year, the newspaper summed up the many reasons for its existence on the front page, in particular the anti-Semitic German School Association and the boycott against Jewish businessmen: "Germans and Czechs turn against the Jew, whom the government abandons without any protection. It must necessarily be the sacred duty of all Jews to stand by and help each other in such a time of need. These are some of the reasons why the paper was founded. It will serve the Jewish people, it will speak up for Judaism" (S 25 Dec. 1908:1). Stölzl discusses the barriers imposed on Jewish academics, the companies' and organizations' reluctance to hire too many Jews, the demand for quotas for Jewish students even at the universities (*Böhmen*, 76–81). See also CJ 116–23, as well as Hartmut Binder, "Franz Kafka und die Wochenschrift Selbstwehr," *Deutsche Vierteljahrsschrift für Literaturwissenschaft und Geistesgeschichte* 41 (1967): 283–304.

28. According to Binder, the Zionist Viktor Kellner, who was a friend of Kafka's in 1912 (DI 272 [T 437]), introduced the members of Bar Kochba to Ahad Ha'am's philosophy in the winter semester of 1907–8. In his lecture he stated that "before each outer liberation one must break away from inner servitude and diaspora," and "the study of Hebrew [was] a crucial test of loyalty for every member of the brotherhood" (KH 370).

29. See SL 48–49; KH 375; and Klara Carmely, *Das Identitätsproblem jüdischer Autoren im deutschen Sprachraum von der Jahrhundertwende bis zu Hitler* (Königstein: Scriptor Verlag, 1981), 138.

30. Kafka mentions "Haam" only once in 1921, though not in relation to the famous Zionist, using the Hebrew meaning of the name as a joke in a letter to his

sister Ottla's family. Since *haam* in German is the colloquial pronunciation for *haben* (to have), Kafka jokes: "[Vera] is surely very talented, after all she already speaks Hebrew, as you write. Haam, you see, is Hebrew and means 'people'" (LOF 75 [BO 128]).

31. Arthur Hertzberg, *The Zionist Idea: A Historical Analysis and Reader* (Philadelphia: The Jewish Publication Society, 1997), 251.

32. See Martin Buber, *Der Jude und sein Judentum: Gesammelte Aufsätze und Reden* (Köln: Joseph Melzer Verlag, 1963): "Das Judentum und die Juden" (9–18), "Das Judentum und die Menschheit" (18–27), "Die Erneuerung des Judentums" (28–46). For the English translation, see Martin Buber, *On Judaism*, ed. Nahum Glatzer (New York: Schocken, 1967).

33. Lore Muerdel Dormer comments, "just as most of his books were forgotten, many facets of his biography became so obscure that to this day major encyclopaedias give faulty information, even about the date of his death" ("Felix Salten," in *Major Figures of Turn-of-the-Century Austrian Literature*, ed. Donald Daviau [Riverside, Calif.: Ariadne Press, 1991], 407). See Iris Bruce, "Which Way Out? Schnitzler's and Salten's Conflicting Responses to Cultural Zionism," in *A Companion to the Works of Arthur Schnitzler*, ed. Dagmar Lorenz (Rochester, N.Y.: Camden House, 2003), 103–26.

34. Karl Kraus, *Die Fackel* 87 (26 Nov. 1901): 23.

35. Kafka's letter is missing in the English translation.

36. Adolf Böhm, *Die zionistische Bewegung: Eine kurze Darstellung ihrer Entwicklung*, vols. 1 and 2 (Berlin: Welt-Verlag, 1920–21), 20–21. Kafka owned this book (KB 109). Max Nordau, however, remarks: "Only the raging antisemitism awakened me and made me aware of my duties towards my own people and the initiative of my dear friend Herzl" (S 6 Aug. 1909:3).

37. Max Brod, *Die Jüdinnen* (1911; Leipzig: Kurt Wolff, 1915).

38. The last diary entry is missing in the English translation. There has been much controversy regarding Kafka's own position. Oppenheimer believes that Kafka "seems to give an onlooker's view of the Jewish problem, with the self-consciousness of one who is not fully identified with the Jewish element in the novel" (39). Binder finds it "remarkable ... that Kafka's own position with regard to Brod's novels corresponds in its ideological bias exactly with the reviews in *Selbstwehr*" ("*Selbstwehr*" 288; KH 376). Baioni rightly stresses that Kafka's review reveals his "disagreement with the Zionist position" ("Zionism," 95). Binder ignores the irony in Kafka's review.

39. It is interesting that the courtroom metaphor is so pervasive in Herrmann's review. In Kafka's story "The Judgment," written a year later (Sept. 1912), the protagonist Georg Bendemann is sentenced to death for his hasty and false assumptions. Furthermore, on the same page as Herrmann's review of Brod's *Die Jüdinnen* there was also an article on the Beilis affair, the ritual murder trial in Kiev, Russia—another *Urteil* (judgment, trial). The word *Urteil* obviously had mixed connotations and associations for Kafka.

40. Kafka expressed his "utmost aversion to the word 'type'" (T 982; 14–20 Sept. 1911—this passage is not included in the English translation of the diaries), a term used frequently in contemporary racial discourses. An article in *Selbstwehr*, for instance, ridicules "the feeling of being ashamed of one's own type" ("The Flight

from the Type," S 30 Apr. 1909:1; see also Gilman, *Patient,* 15) and demands a proud acknowledgment of racial distinctions.

2. THE YIDDISH THEATER (1910–1913)

1. Walter Sokel, "Language and Truth in the Two Worlds of Franz Kafka," *German Quarterly* 52 (1979): 369.
2. Max Brod, *Arnold Beer: Das Schicksal eines Juden* (Berlin: Axel Juncker Verlag, 1912).
3. In Kafka's diary we find the following note: "Card to Max in joy over *Arnold Beer*" (DI 261 [T 420]). For the postcard see LFF 77 [Br 94, 501]; 7 May 1912; (translation modified).
4. See Guido Massino, *Fuoco Inestinguibile: Franz Kafka, Jizchak Löwy e il teatro yiddish polacco* (Rome: Bulzoni Editore, 2002), 16n.7.
5. Max Brod, "Humanistischer Zionismus," in *Auf gespaltenem Pfad. Zum 90. Geburtstag von Margarete Susman,* ed. Manfred Schlosser (Darmstadt: Erato-Pr., 1964), 280.
6. Massino, *Fuoco,* 31n.13. Many thanks to Guido Massino for providing me with the dates for the actors (e-mail correspondence, 8 Nov. 2006). The dates for Urich and Pipes are unknown.
7. See Massino, *Fuoco,* 31nn.14, 15. I thank Nikla Gargano-Luciano for helping me with the Italian original. As Kafka knew, Löwy had been in many major cities, including Paris (DI 114, 115 [T 198, 199–200]). He arrived in Paris around 1904 (Massino, *Fuoco,* 56). He and Urich are listed with a theater company in Berlin, the Bleichmann troupe, from 1907 on. See Peter Sprengel, *Scheunenviertel-Theater: Jüdische Schauspieltruppen und Jiddische Dramatik in Berlin (1900–1918)* (Berlin: Fannei & Walz Verlag, 1995), 91. They performed in Zurich, Basilea, and Vienna and in 1911 went to perform in Karlsbad, where Löwy met the famous New York actor Jacob P. Adler (DI 110 [T 100–101]); see also Sprengel 90–91. He then went to Prague where he and Urich performed with the Tschissiks, Klugs, and Pipes. Urich, for instance, performed in *Sulamith* when Kafka saw it on 13 October 1911. His wife and daughter were actors as well (Sprengel 129n.142).
8. Scripts of *Shulamith* and *Bar Kochba* (Goldfaden); *Die Sedarnacht* (Lateiner); *Der vilder mensh, Got, mensh un tayvel,* and *Herschole Dubrowner* (Gordin) are available in Sprengel, *Scheunenviertel,* 135–256. These are texts that were submitted to the censorship board in Berlin. Note that the dates for these plays indicated in various source materials vary considerably.
9. Hartmut Binder, "Café Savoy," in *Wo Kafka und seine Freunde zu Gast waren: Prager Kaffeehäuser und Vergnügungsstätten in historischen Bilddokumenten* (Prague: Vitalis, 2000), 146.
10. Kafka wrongly identifies the playwright's name as Lateiner (DI 80 [T 58]). As Hans-Gerd Koch points out, the playwrights' names were initially confused by the *Prager Tagblatt* in their advertisements (K 29, 30, 37, 52). Even though Evelyn Torton Beck was unable to identify Lateiner as the author of this play, scholars have assumed

he was the author. See Evelyn Torton Beck, *Kafka and the Yiddish Theater: Its Impact on His Work* (Madison: Univ. of Wisconsin Press, 1971), 23n.35; Robertson, *Judaism*, 16; and Karl, *Kafka*, 285. Sharkansky has now been identified as the author in the commentary to the critical edition of Kafka's diaries [K 29]). See also Sprengel, *Scheunenviertel*, 25, as well as Guido Massino, "Franz Kafka, *Der Meshumed* by Abraham Sharkansky and *Elisha ben Avuyah* by Jakob Gordin," *Journal of the Kafka Society of America* 1.2 (June–Dec. 1996): 30–41.

11. Kafka wrongly identifies the author as "Feimann" (K 30); Evelyn Torton Beck refers to him as Faynman but was unable to find this text (24n.38).

12. The translation wrongly gives this song the name of the Jewish prayer, "Hear, O Israel." Kafka identifies the song as "bore Isroel" (Creator of Israel) (T 352).

13. This section was not included in the English translation.

14. In *Selbstwehr* the title is given as "Elischa ben Abuja" ("Jakob Gordin," S 2 July 1909:3); other renderings are "Elisha ben Avuyah" (Massino, "*Meschumed*," 34) and "Elishe ben Avuya" (Evelyn Beck 23–24n.36). Massino claims that Kafka must have known more than the first act because the Talmudic anecdote in Kafka's diary appears in "an episode from the second act" (DI 122 [T 209]; *Fuoco*, 41n.39). See also the Talmudic anecdote about Elischa ben Abuja, "Der unfromme Gelehrte" (The Infidel Scholar) in Jakob Fromer, introduction, "Der Organismus des Judentums," in *Der babylonische Talmud zur Herstellung einer Realkonkordanz vokalisiert* (Charlottenburg: Selbstverlag des Verfassers, 1909), 61–64 (KB 204); Massino, *Fuoco*, 41n.39.

15. See also Abraham Shulman: "The history of the Yiddish theater was a continuous fight against *shund*, . . . [Gordin] was the first to get rid of stock characters, the first to write dramas about real people. He took upon himself the task of reeducating the actors, teaching them respect for the text and respect for the audience. He taught them to stop reciting and start talking, even whispering. He induced the audience, which had become used to canned spectacles, to sit and watch a real human drama. He even brought the Jewish intelligentsia . . . into the theater" (*New Country: Jewish Immigrants in America* [New York: Scribner's, 1976], 49).

16. See Max Brod, "Eine Jargonbühne in Prag" (Yiddish Theater in Prague), *Prager Tagblatt*, 27 Oct. 1911, 3.

17. The Zionist club "Bar Kochba may have derived its name from the 1897 play *Bar Kochba*, written by the Czech poet and playwright Jaroslav Vrchlický" (CJ 97).

18. Reiner Stach, *Kafka: Die Jahre der Entscheidungen* (Frankfurt: Fischer, 2002), 59. See also Massino, *Fuoco*, 133.

19. Binder believes that this letter was for a "guest performance by Löwy and his troupe" (KH 393). It is possible that Löwy went to Pilsen with the other actors and that they all returned to Prague together; but it is more likely that Löwy wanted to strike out on his own, stayed in Prague, and gave performances in the area.

20. See Hartmut Binder, "The evening of recitals which Kafka organized was a regular event of the club 'Bar Kochba'" (*Selbstwehr*, 289–90).

21. The English translation renders Kafka's phrase "vertrauliche Verkehrssprache der Juden" as "familiar colloquial language of German Jews" (DF 385 [BK 152]). But *Verkehr* can also refer to "traffic" and business transactions. Until today, colloquial

German is infiltrated with Yiddish and Hebrew vocabulary that originally entered the German language through the language of trade. This is still the case in big centers like Berlin but also in the area around Münster, where the trade language, *Masematte*, had a significant Hebrew and Yiddish component. See Margaret Strunge and Karl Kassenbrock, *Masematte: Das Leben und die Sprache der Menschen in Münsters vergessenen Vierteln* (Münster: im Selbstverlag, 1980).

22. Stach incorrectly assumes that Kafka was ridiculing the actors. He claims that Löwy "made himself look ridiculous with his poster on which Mania Tschissik was presented as a 'Primadonna' and he himself as a 'Dramatist.' One can imagine the comments of Berliners passing by," and he further ridicules "the exotic sentimentality of this singing, jumping motley crew, jabbering in Yiddish" (*Entscheidungen*, 53). Not only is Stach presumptuous to assume that Felice would have shared his negative opinion of the actors, but the ironic response he imagines to come from "Berliners passing by" is unfounded because Kafka is talking about "a poster of the company's guest appearance in Leipzig," which just happens to have been printed in Berlin (LF 25 [BF 72]).

23. Kafka assumes the review will be published soon in the *Berliner Tageblatt*. However, "Kurt Pinthus: Jüdisches Theater" appeared in the *Leipziger Tageblatt* (Sprengel 23n.3). It is reprinted in Sprengel, *Scheunenviertel*, 303–7, as well as in Andreas Herzog, ed., *Ost und West: Jüdische Publizistik 1901–1928* (Leipzig: Reclam, 1996), 182–86.

24. After Kafka visited Felice in Berlin, he continued on to Leipzig where he and his friends Franz Werfel, Frantisek Khol (librarian at the National Museum in Prague), and Otto Pick also met up with Löwy (LF 228 [BF 346]; Stach, *Entscheidungen*, 301–2).

25. The evening was advertised and reviewed in *Selbstwehr* (S 30 May 1913: 7, 13 June 1913: 5). A longer article announcing the performance also appeared in the *Prager Tagblatt* on 1 June 1913 (BF 763); this article was commissioned by Kafka but written by his friend Pick (LF 264; BF 392). See also K 140–41.

26. Many thanks to Anthony Northey for sending me the program of their performance on 6 Jan. 1917, which he discovered in the National Archives in Prague. He also came across an earlier performance on 20 Nov. 1916 (*Prager Tagblatt*, no. 322 [20 Nov.1916], AA2). E-mail message, 12 and 14 Nov. 2006.

27. See Martin Buber, *The Letters of Martin Buber: A Life of Dialogue*, ed. Nahum N. Glatzer and Paul Mendes-Flohr, trans. Richard Winston, Clara Winston, and Harry Zohn (New York: Schocken, 1991), 220.

28. In October 1911 Kafka learned that Löwy had syphilis (T 93); in 1912 he remarked, "Löwy, with his severe headaches that probably indicate a serious head ailment" (DI 215 [T 348]). In 1917 Kafka told Brod that Löwy had to remain in a sanatorium for three months (Br 173; KH 490).

29. Isaac Bashevis Singer, "A Friend of Kafka," in *The Collected Stories of Isaac Bashevis Singer* (New York: Farrar, Straus & Giroux, 1982), 277–86.

30. These newspaper articles are collected in the second part of Massino, *Fuoco*, 95–141.

31. Kafka is referring to the first volume of the three-volume edition *Volkstümliche Geschichte der Juden* (Berlin-Wien: R. Löwit Verlag). The year of publication cannot be verified. Kafka owned volumes 2 (1918) and 3 (1923) (KB 136–37). The very first edition of *Volkstümliche Geschichte* was published from 1888 to 1891.

32. This information appears in Brod's foreword to a Yiddish translation of Kafka's *Der Prozes,* trans. Melech Ravitsh (London: Der Kval, 1966).

33. See Willy Stein, "Heinrich Graetz. Zu seinem 20. Todestag" (S 15 Sept. 1911:3).

34. Fromer, *Der babylonische Talmud;* and Salomon Maimon, *Salomon Maimons Lebensgeschichte* (1792), ed. Jakob Fromer (Munich: Georg Müller, 1911).

35. Ritchie Robertson, "Antizionismus, Zionismus: Kafka's Responses to Jewish Nationalism," in *Paths and Labyrinths: Nine Papers Read at the Kafka Symposium Held at the Institute of Germanic Studies on 20 and 21 October 1983* (London: University of London, 1985), 42n.34.

36. One of these critics is Israel Zinberg, a scholar in the field of Yiddish literature, who, in the 1930s, wrote on the same writers as Pinès in his study *The Flowering of Haskalah Literature in Russia.* The other scholar is Ber Borochov, a socialist Zionist leader and theoretician. Both are said to have "stamped the work as dilettantish, a judgment held also by later scholars" (*Encyclopaedia Judaica*, 13:533–34).

37. Milton Hindus, introduction to Isaac Joel Linetski, *The Polish Lad,* trans. Moshe Spiegel (Philadelphia: The Jewish Publication Society of America, 1975), 7.

38. The Yeshivah student in "Cabalists" who has been fasting for days does not find ultimate redemption. When he dies he is admitted as a singer in the heavenly host, but "the master of the yeshivah was not satisfied. 'Only a few fasts more,' he said, sighing, 'and he would have died with the Divine Kiss!'" (Peretz, "Cabalists," in *A Treasury of Yiddish Stories,* ed. Irving Howe and Eliezer Greenberg [New York: Schocken, 1973], 223). Jean Jofen also establishes the connection to "The Hunger Artist" (94).

39. The novel is not mentioned in the English edition of the *Diaries.* The notes Kafka took down from Pinès are incomplete in the English edition.

3. ANTI-SEMITISM AND ZIONIST ACTIVITIES (1911–1915)

1. Michael Berkowitz, *Western Jewry and the Zionist Project 1914–1933* (Cambridge: Cambridge University Press, 1997), 85.

2. *Selbstwehr* carried an article by the journalist Brasul-Bruschkowsky in which he recounts his ordeal to bring out the truth (S 21 June 1912:2–3; see also S 24 May 1912:2).

3. CS 83 [E 55]; see also Robertson, *Judaism,* 12, and Band, "Beiliss Affair," 179.

4. Oskar Baum, *Die böse Unschuld: Ein jüdischer Kleinstadtroman* (Frankfurt: Rütten & Loening, 1913); DII 15 [T 629].

5. The entire article is reprinted in Band, "Beiliss Affair," 176–77.

6. The significance of the Dreyfus affair has also been pointed out by Klaus Wagenbach, *Franz Kafka: In der Strafkolonie: Eine Geschichte aus dem Jahr 1914* (Berlin:

Verlag Klaus Wagenbach, 1975), 67; and Walter Müller-Seidel, *Die Deportation des Menschen: Kafkas Erzählung "In der Strafkolonie" im europäischen Kontext* (Frankfurt: Fischer, 1986), 141–45.

7. See Evelyn Beck, *Yiddish Theater*, 148; Malcolm Pasley, "In the Penal Colony," in *The Kafka Debate*, ed. A. Flores (New York: Gordian Press, 1977), 302.

8. Jochanan Ginat, "Kurt Blumenfeld und der deutsche Zionismus," in Kurt Blumenfeld, *Im Kampf um den Zionismus: Briefe aus fünf Jahrzehnten*, ed. Miriam Sambursky and Jochanan Ginat (Stuttgart: Deutsche Verlags-Anstalt, 1976), 9, 10.

9. Jehuda Reinharz, "Martin Buber's Impact on German Zionism before World War I," *Studies in Zionism* 6 (Autumn 1982): 181–83.

10. Blumenfeld, *Im Kampf um den Zionismus*, 203.

11. See *Palästina-Heft der "Welt"* 14.41/42 (17 Oct. 1910): 1023–27. It was published weekly under the auspices of *Die Welt* (1897–1914), the central organ of the Zionist movement, founded by Theodor Herzl. See also Adolf Böhm's *Zionistische Palästinaarbeit, Heft 1* (Wien: Publikationen des Zionistischen Zentralbureaus Wien IX, 1909): 12–15, 18–20, 28–29, 34–36; and *Palästina: Monatsschrift für die Erschließung Palästinas* (monthly journal for the preparation of the land in Palestine) (Vienna) 9.7/8 (1 Aug. 1912): 191, 192–93.

12. See Niels Bokhove, "'The Entrance to the More Important': Kafka's Personal Zionism," in *Kafka, Zionism, and Beyond*, ed. Mark Gelber (Tübingen: Max Niemeyer Verlag, 2004), 29.

13. Karl Kraus, "Eine Krone für Zion" (1899), in *Frühe Schriften: 1892–1900*, vol. 2 (1897–1900), ed. Johannes J. Braakenburg (München: Kösel-Verlag, 1979), 301–2.

14. "The price up until the mid-1920s was apparently prohibitive for many middle-class and lower-middle-class Jews" (Berkowitz, *Western Jewry*, 131).

15. Martin Buber, "Der Mythos der Juden," in *Vom Judentum: Ein Sammelbuch*, ed. Verein jüdischer Hochschüler Bar Kochba in Prague (Leipzig: K. Wolff, 1913), 21–31; KH 131.

16. Micha Josef bin Gorion, *Die Sagen der Juden: Von der Urzeit: Jüdische Sagen und Mythen*, trans. Rahel Ramberg (1913; Frankfurt: Rütten & Loening, 1919). The 1913 edition of the first volume was part of Kafka's personal library (KB 84).

17. In 1915 Buber asked Kafka to collaborate on *Der Jude*, but Kafka declined (Buber, *Letters*, 182). In 1916, Buber rejected Kafka's "A Dream" (LF 506, 517, 531 [BF 704–5,719, 737]), which was, however, later published in *Das jüdische Prag* (1917) on Buber's recommendation.

18. Richard Lichtheim, *Das Programm des Zionismus* (1911, Berlin: Zionistische Vereinigung für Deutschland, 1913). Brod dedicated the second edition of this book (1913) to Kafka and Felice (KB 116–17).

19. Kafka here combined business with pleasure. He was "the only staff member" to accompany his insurance company's director to the "II. International Congress for Rescue Work and Accident Prevention" in Vienna, 9–13 September (Pawel, *Nightmare*, 188; see KH 450–51).

20. Concerning the photograph, see Reuben Klingsberg, ed., *Exhibition Franz Kafka*

1883–1924: Catalogue: Ta'rukhath Franz Kafka 1883–1924: Katalog (Jerusalem: The Jewish National and Univ. Library, 1969), 25; see also KH 450.

21. *Stenographisches Protokoll der Verhandlungen des XI: Zionisten-Kongresses in Wien vom 2. bis 9. September 1913,* ed. Zionistisches Aktionskomitee (Berlin: Jüdischer Verlag, 1914), 3, 4, 5.

22. *Selbstwehr* advertised that two prominent Zionist leaders would be giving lectures that morning: Menahem Ussischkin on "Jewish Cultural Work in Palestine" and Chaim Weizmann on "The Question Concerning the Foundation of the Jewish University" (S 29 Aug. 1913:1). However, in the end these two speeches did not take place until the evening session (*Stenographisches Protokoll,* 294–300 [Ussischkin's speech], 300–309 [Weizmann's speech]).

23. Bokhove claims Kafka attended both the afternoon and evening sessions ("Zionism," 36), whereas Stach asserts he was tired of the "Buber-Sound" at the congress and in any event had to be at the opening ceremony of the Insurance Congress in the evening (409–10). There is no evidence that Kafka returned for the afternoon sessions, and no doubt he attended the reception for the insurance company congress. But Stach needlessly ridicules the congress and its participants in order to suggest that Kafka skipped the elaborate afternoon program (which included slides from Palestine and Jewish sport) and instead "strolled around in the Schönbrunn park" (409). The timing is incorrect, since Kafka refers to his walk in the park as having taken place "on a rather cool but very sunny *morning*" (LF 348 [BF 502]; my emphasis).

24. Kafka himself calls it "Beamtenverein" [Civil Servant Club] (T 613). The English translation is merely "officials' club" (DI 322). The critical edition identifies it as "Ostensibly a meeting of the 'German Civil Servant Club of the Workers' Accident Insurance Company'" (K 150).

25. Karlheinz Fingerhut, "Ein Beispiel produktiver Lektüreverarbeitung (Max Brods *Arnold Beer* und *Das Urteil*)," in Binder, ed., *Kafka Handbuch,* Bd. 2, 281; see also discussion in Robertson, *Judaism,* 29–32.

26. "Throughout World War I, [Kafka] was draft-deferred as essential at the [Workers' Accident Insurance] institute's request.... Chief Inspector Eugen Pfohl, his immediate superior until 1917, insisted that 'without Kafka, the whole department would collapse'" (Pawel, *Nightmare,* 188). At the end of the war, Kafka was not only a "Senior Secretary," he was "de facto the Institute's most influential administrator after [Director] Marschner" (Anthony DiRenzo, "Golems, Scribes and Tzaddiks: Franz Kafka's Parabolic Paperwork," in *Kafka Kaleidoscope,* ed. M. Wasserman [Delhi, N.Y.: Birch Brook Press, 1999], 21).

27. Claus-Ekkehard Bärsch, *Max Brod im "Kampf um das Judentum,"* 56.

28. Stach claims: "The militant Zionist organization, which he had joined, had left imposing scars on his face" (431). See also Peter-André Alt (*Franz Kafka: Der ewige Sohn: Eine Biographie* [Munich: C. H. Beck, 2005], 300). Kafka does ask Bloch's sister Grete, "And where did he get his scars?" (LF 332 [BF 480]).

29. Hans Bloch, "Die Legende von Theodor Herzl," in *Der Zionitische Student,* ed. K.Z.V. (Kartell Zionistischer Verbindungen) (Berlin: Jüdischer Verlag, n.d. [prob.

1912]), 51–62. In *Letters to Felice*, this story is wrongly identified as a "play" (LF 420), and the German edition of these letters states that the legend was never published (BF 594). The text was published in *Der zionistische Student* (The Zionist Student), which was in Kafka's library (KB 132). The date of publication is not clear: 1920 according to Klaus Wagenbach, "supposedly 1912" according to Jürgen Born. See LF 419–20, 421 (BF 594, 595–96); and Bruce, "'Zionistische Sehnsucht': Franz Kafka und Hans Blochs 'Legende von Theodor Herzl,'" *Neue Zürcher Zeitung* (Switzerland) 101 (2–3 May 1992): 69.

30. According to I. A. White and J. J. White, previous interpretations by Emrich and others stressed "the enigma of the balls which has to be confronted both interpretively and evaluatively" and that they "have no meaning, only a function" ("Blumfeld, an Elderly Bachelor," in *The Kafka Debate*, ed. Angel Flores [New York: Gordian Press, 1977]: 364, 363).

31. Blumenfeld apparently did not grow up Jewish. He came from "a second generation 'Jewish family of German culture,' which mixed in principally Christian circles" and had none of "the spirit of *yiddishkeit* that animated the Eastern Zionist rank and file and which Blumenfeld himself came to admire" (Alan Levenson, "German Zionism and Radical Assimilation before 1914," *Studies in Zionism* 13.1 (1992): 24. See also Ginat, "Blumenfeld," 8.

32. See Clayton Koelb's perceptive discussion of paranomasia: "The imaginary dog is described by its *Bellen*, a trait that is almost instantly transformed by paronomasia into the *Bälle* Blumfeld finds in his room" (*Kafka's Rhetoric: The Passion of Reading* [Ithaca, N.Y.: Cornell Univ. Press, 1989], 35). Koelb rightly argues that Kafka's thinking is not linear but associative, because he finds it "familiar and natural to read hyperbolic language in a way different from the rest of us" (37).

4. FORMS OF CULTURAL RENEWAL (1912–1917)

1. František Langer, "Foreword. My Brother Jiří," in Georg (Jiří) Langer, *Nine Gates to the Chassidic Mysteries*, trans. Stephen Jolly (1961; New York: Behrman House, 1976), xii–xiii.

2. See Max Brod, "Die Zwanziger Jahre in Prag: Kultur aus drei Kulturen," *Magnum* 25 (1961): 54; Langer, *Nine Gates*, xv–xviii; and Pawel, *Nightmare*, 336–37.

3. Binder believes that "the Western Jew who has become assimilated to the Hasidim" (DII 119 [T 733]) refers to Langer (*Gesetz*, 134). The critical edition identifies a certain H. Getzler (K 181n.733).

4. Jofen, *Mystic*, 198–200; Robertson, *Judaism*, 178, and "Western Observers and Eastern Jews," *The Modern Language Review* 83.1 (Jan. 1988): 102.

5. Chajim Bloch, "Aus der Welt der Chassidim" (From the World of the Hasidim), *Das jüdische Echo* (Munich) 38 (1917): 421. Max Brod remembered how "Kafka loved a particular type of joke. They had to be childishly simple, without being indecent" (SL 185). Apparently he especially loved the following joke: "A beggar came to a millionaire and complained that he had not eaten for three days. The millionaire replied in a very friendly way: 'You have to force yourself'" (SL 186).

6. Karl Erich Grözinger, *Kafka and Kabbala*, trans. Susan Hecker Ray (New York: Continuum, 1994), 27.

7. Sander Gilman, *Franz Kafka* (London: Reaktion Books, 2005), 32.

8. Apart from Fromer and Pinès, Kafka owned Ignaz Ziegler's *Die Geistesreligion und das jüdische Religionsgesetz: Ein Beitrag zur Erneuerung des Judentums* (Berlin: Georg Reimer, 1912); see pp. 37–92 KB 132. David Stern cites Ziegler as an authority on Midrash (*Parables in Midrash: Narrative and Exegesis in Rabbinic Literature* [Cambridge, Mass.: Harvard Univ. Press, 1991], 19). Moreover, Malcolm Pasley dates Kafka's reading of *Salomon Maimons Lebensgeschichte* as "preced[ing] his writing of *Der Prozess*" ("Two Literary Sources of Kafka's 'Der Prozess,'" *Forum for Modern Language Studies* 3.2 [Apr. 1967]: 144). See Maimon, *Salomon Maimons Lebensgeschichte*. Maimon highlights the arbitrary nature of Talmudic narrative, discusses kabbalistic exegesis in the *Zohar* with great ironic distance, "summarizes the teachings of Maimonides" (LFF 173 [Br 203]), and explains his major work, *Guide for the Perplexed*. There are also excerpts from the *Babylonian Talmud* ("Traktat Berachot"), the *Jerusalem Talmud*, and from the *Zohar* in *Vom Judentum: Ein Sammelbuch*.

9. A. M. Klein, "Hemlock and Marijuana: Review of *In the Penal Colony: Stories and Short Pieces by Franz Kafka*" (17 Dec. 1948), in *Literary Essays and Reviews*, ed. Usher Caplan and M. W. Steinberg (Toronto: Univ. of Toronto Press, 1987), 276.

10. Jean Starobinski, "Kafka's Judaism," *European Judaism* 8.2 (1974): 28.

11. Chajim Bloch, *Der Prager Golem: Von seiner "Geburt" bis zu seinem "Tod"* (Berlin: Verlag Benjamin Harz, 1920); and Yudl Rosenberg, "The Golem, or The Miraculous Deeds of Rabbi Liva" (1809), in *Great Tales of Jewish Fantasy and the Occult*, ed. and trans. Joachim Neugroschel (1976; reprint, Woodstock, N.Y.: Overlook Press, 1987), 162–225. Bloch himself saw nothing wrong with his plagiarizing, since he encouraged other artists to do likewise: they should use the golem myth creatively in the future, since these legends had great potential and could be further improved "if one of our artists wanted to try his hand at it!" (*Golem*, 14).

12. Arnold L. Goldsmith, *The Golem Remembered, 1909–1980: Variations of a Jewish Legend* (Detroit: Wayne State Univ. Press, 1981), 71.

13. Chajim Bloch, "Aus der Welt der Chassidim," nos. 17, 19, 23, 26, 27, 35, 38.

14. Alexander Eliasberg, ed. and trans., *Sagen polnischer Juden* (Munich: Georg Müller, 1916), 22; KB 81.

15. Howard Schwartz, ed., *Gates to the New City: A Treasury of Modern Jewish Tales* (New York: Avon, 1983), 32.

16. Martin Buber, *Briefwechsel aus sieben Jahrzehnten*, vol. 1: 1897–1918, ed. Grete Schaeder (Heidelberg: Lambert Schneider, 1972), 429.

17. Martin Buber, *Der grosse Maggid und seine Nachfolge* (Frankfurt: Literarische Anstalt Rütten & Loening, 1921), 429.

18. Bin Gorion, foreword to the 1913 edition, *Die Sagen der Juden* (Frankfurt: Insel Verlag, 1962), 10.

19. Bin Gorion, foreword to the 1916 edition, *Der Born Judas: Legenden, Märchen, Erzählungen* (Frankfurt: Jüdischer Verlag im Suhrkamp Verlag, 1993), 7, 9.

20. See Bluma Goldstein, "Franz Kafka's *Ein Landarzt:* A Study in Failure,"

Deutsche Vierteljahresschrift für Literaturwissenschaft und Geistesgeschichte 42 (1968): 745–59; and Jill Robbins, "Kafka's Parables," in *Midrash and Literature,* ed. G. Hartman and S. Budick (New Haven: Yale Univ. Press, 1986), 272–80.

21. See Michel Dentan, *Humour et création littéraire dans l'oeuvre de Kafka* (Geneva: Droz and Minard, 1961), 11–16; J. Malcolm S. Pasley, "Semi-Private Games," in *The Kafka Debate,* ed. Angel Flores (New York: Gordian Press, 1977), 189; F. D. Luke, "Kafka's *Die Verwandlung,*" *Modern Language Review* 46 (1951): 232–45.

22. George Steiner, "K.," in *Language and Silence* (New York: Atheneum, 1970), 121.

23. A. B. Gotlober, "The Gilgul, or The Transmigration," in Neugroschel, ed., *Great Tales,* 394.

24. Stanley Corngold, trans. and ed., *The Metamorphosis by Franz Kafka* (1972; New York: Bantam Books, 1986), xxi.

25. See Evelyn Beck, *Yiddish Theater,* 141; and Meno Spann, *Franz Kafka* (Boston: Twayne, 1976), 73.

26. Evelyn Beck relates only *The Castle* to *Shulamith* (198–200).

27. Marvin Caplan, "'Raisins and Almonds'—Goldfaden's Glory," *Judaism* 42.2 (Spring 1993): 195.

28. Caplan, "'Raisins and Almonds,'" 194. Abraham Goldfaden, "Shulamith," in Sprengel, *Scheuenviertel,* 139; this text of *Shulamith* is a censored version from this period, found in the Berlin police archives.

29. Gershom Scholem, *Major Trends in Jewish Mysticism* (New York: Schocken, 1954), 281.

30. Mendele Mokher Sforim, *The Mare,* in Neugroschel, ed., *Great Tales,* 557.

31. Arthur Green, "Teachings of the Hasidic Masters," in *Back to the Sources: Reading the Classic Jewish Texts,* ed. B. Holtz (New York: Summit Books, 1984), 392.

32. Scholem, *Correspondence,* 135 (translation modified); see B 78.

33. Kurt Weinberg, *Kafkas Dichtungen: Die Travestien eines Mythos* (Bern: Francke Verlag, 1963), 241.

34. David Biale, *Gershom Scholem: Kabbalah and Counter-History* (Cambridge, Mass.: Harvard Univ. Press, 1982), 31.

35. Franz Kafka, *Der Prozes,* 194. See Iris Bruce, "*Der Proceß* in Yiddish, or 'The Importance of Being Humorous,'" *TTR* 7.2 (Fall 1994): 35–62.

36. Michael Greenstein, "Breaking the Mosaic Code: Jewish Literature vs. The Law," *Mosaic* 27.3 (Sept. 1994): 91.

37. Franz Kafka, *The Trial,* trans. Breon Mitchell (New York: Schocken, 1998), 13–14; Kafka, *Der Proceß,* Roman in der Fassung der Handschrift (Frankfurt: Fischer, 1994), 19–20.

38. David Stern, "Midrash," in *Contemporary Jewish Religious Thought,* ed. Arthur A. Cohen and Paul Mendes-Flohr (New York: Charles Scribner's, 1987), 615. In 1939 already Walter Benjamin argued that "the key to Kafka's work is likely to fall into the hands of the person who *is able to extract the comic aspects of Jewish theology*" (Scholem, *Correspondence,* 243; see B 91).

39. A note in the English translation states that the "wheel of life" is "a toy through the aperture of which one perceived the successive positions of a figure affixed to a revolving wheel. It thus created the illusion of motion" (DI 329n.35).

40. Stanley Corngold, *Franz Kafka: The Necessity of Form* (Ithaca, N.Y.: Cornell Univ. Press, 1988), 222.
41. Barry W. Holtz, "Midrash," in Holtz, ed., *Back to the Sources*, 178.
42. Robert Goldenberg, "Talmud," in Holtz, ed., *Back to the Sources*, 156.
43. Several critics have identified the man from the country as an *am ha aretz*, someone who is ignorant of the Law. See Heinz Politzer, *Kafka: Parable and Paradox* (1962; Ithaca, N.Y.: Cornell Univ. Press, 1966), 175; Robertson, *Judaism*, 126; Robert, *Lonely*, 119.
44. Scholem, *Correspondence*, 137; B 79. Robert, too, pointed out that the parable is "accompanied by a commentary in the form of a *midrash*" (*Lonely*, 163).
45. Herford, R. Travers, ed. and trans., *Pirke Aboth: The Ethics of the Talmud; Sayings of the Fathers* (Schocken: New York, 1962), 145.
46. See, for example, Strother B. Purdy, "A Talmudic Analogy to Kafka's Parable Vor dem Gesetz," *Papers on Language and Literature* 4/4 (1968): 420–27; Ulf Abraham, "Mose 'Vor dem Gesetz': Eine bekannte Vorlage zu Kafkas 'Türhüterlegende,'" *Deutsche Vierteljahreszeitschrift für Literaturwissenschaft und Geistesgeschichte* 57.4 (Dec. 1983): 636–50; Karl Erich Grözinger, "Himmlische Gerichte, Wiedergänger und Zwischenweltliche in der ostjüdischen Erzählung," in *Kafka und das Judentum*, ed. Grözinger et al. (Frankfurt: Jüdischer Verlag bei athenäum, 1987); and Gerhard Kurz, "Meinungen zur Schrift. Zur Exegese der Legende 'Vor dem Gesetz' im Roman 'Der Proceß'" in Grözinger et al, eds., *Kafka und das Judentum*, 93–112, 216. Hartmut Binder takes issue with all interpretations of the parable in his study *"Vor dem Gesetz."*
47. Joseph Heinemann, "The Nature of the Aggadah," in Hartman and Budick, eds., *Midrash and Literature*, 42, 43.
48. Henry Sussman, *Franz Kafka: Geometrician of Metaphor* (Madison, Wis.: Coda Press, 1979), 110.
49. Franz Kafka, *Tagebücher 1910–1923*, ed. Max Brod (1948–49; Frankfurt: Fischer, 1976), 310.
50. Franz Kafka, *Parables and Paradoxes*, bilingual edition, Nahum Glatzer, ed. (New York: Schocken, 1961) (hereafter cited as P).
51. Max Brod, "Postscript to the German Edition" (1936), in *Description of a Struggle and the Great Wall of China*, ed. Edwin Muir, trans. W. Muir, E. Muir, T. Stern, and J. Stern (London: Secker & Warburg, 1960), 336–37. See also Franz Kafka, *Shorter Works*, vol. 1, trans. and ed. Malcolm Pasley (London: Secker & Warburg, 1973), xii.
52. Clement Greenberg, "At the Building of the Great Wall of China," in *Franz Kafka Today*, ed. A. Flores and H. Swander (Madison: Univ. of Wisconsin Press, 1964), 77. Weiyan Meng has examined Kafka's transformation of motifs from Chinese tales but agrees with Clement Greenberg that China is a symbol for Diaspora Jewry (*Kafka und China* [Munich: Iudicium Verlag, 1986], 68–90).
53. Stéphane Mosès, "Franz Kafka: 'The Silence of the Sirens,'" *University of Denver Quarterly* 2.2 (Summer 1976): 67.
54. See Clayton Koelb's discussion of their "appearance" in "Kafka and the Sirens," in *The Comparative Perspective on Literature: Approaches to Theory and Practice*, ed. Clayton Koelb and S. Noakes (Ithaca, N.Y.: Cornell Univ. Press, 1988), 310–11.

55. Maurice Blanchot, "The Sirens' Song," in *Selected Essays*, trans. Sasha Rabinovitch (Bloomington: Indiana Univ. Press, 1982): 60. Many thanks to Ramona Uritescu for pointing this article out to me.

56. Stanley Corngold, "Kafka's Double Helix," in *The Necessity of Form*, 105.

57. Shimon Sandbank has called Kafka's oeuvre "a glaring case of Aggadah without Halakha" (*After Kafka: The Influence of Kafka's Fiction* [Athens: University of Georgia Press, 1989], 5). Robert Alter regards Kafka's work as "a body of Aggadah in search of a Halakhah, lore in quest of Law" ("On Walter Benjamin," *Commentary* 48.3 [1969]: 91). See Benjamin's description of Kafka's narratives as "a Haggadah, which continually pauses, lingers in elaborate descriptions, always with the hope and fear at once that it could suddenly encounter the halakhic order and formula, the Law, on the way" and Scholem's critique (BK 42, 89). See Robert Alter on Kafka, Benjamin, and Scholem in *Necessary Angels: Tradition and Modernity in Kafka, Benjamin and Scholem* (Cambridge, Mass.: Harvard Univ. Press, 1991); and David Stern, "Midrash and Indeterminacy," *Critical Inquiry* 15 (Autumn 1988): 132–61.

58. Jacques Derrida, *The Ear of the Other: Otobiography, Transference, Translation*, ed. Christie McDonald, trans. Peggy Kamuf (1982; Lincoln: Univ. of Nebraska Press, 1988), 85.

5. Kafka's Cultural Zionism (1914–1917)

1. Ahad Ha'am, "The Jewish State and the Jewish Problem," in Hertzberg, ed., *The Zionist Idea*, 267.

2. For some of Berdyczewski's essays, see Hertzberg, ed., *The Zionist Idea*, 290–302.

3. Nelly Engel, sister of Friedrich Thieberger, participated in Bergmann's Hebrew classes. See her "Franz Kafka als 'boyfriend,'" in Koch, ed., *"Als Kafka,"* 115, as well as *Selbstwehr* for the Hebrew classes (S 15 Oct. 1913:7) and the Hebrew kindergarden (S 31 Oct. 1913:3).

4. Stölzl refers to an "Epilogue on the Last German Jewish School" in *Selbstwehr* (S 7 Feb. 1913). Kieval's research shows that this trend existed already "since the early 1880s" (CJ 49). See also CJ 46–48, 50–58; and Bergmann, "Schulzeit und Studium," in Koch, ed., *"Als Kafka,"* 13–15.

5. Max Brod, "Jüdische Schule," *Der Jude* 5 (1920–21): 347.

6. See S 6 Mar. 1914:4; DII 20 (T 637); K 162.

7. Chaim Nagler was later caught appropriating large funds for himself. He was shamefully removed from his position as head of the relief committee, but the event was hushed up and he went to fight at the front (Kudela 129).

8. See KH 470; DII 142–43 (T 772–73), LFF 151 (Br 177).

9. Max Brod, "Erfahrungen im ostjüdischen Schulwerk," *Der Jude* 1 (1916–17): 33.

10. Frau Kannengießer is listed in the "refugee list of 1915 as number 1237" (Kudela 126n.12).

11. Marsha Rozenblit confirms that "the process employed for clothing and blanket distribution by Prague's Galician *Hilfskomitee* illustrates a distinct lack of sympathy for those in need. The committee sent postcards to refugees, written in German,

not Yiddish, or Polish, which entitled them to receive clothing at the distribution center, but only if they arrived with these cards at the exact time specified and accompanied by all the people whose names were indicated and none others. Refugees who did not arrive on time lost their right to clothing or blankets" (76).

12. KH 119; Engel, "Franz Kafka als 'boyfriend,'" 114.

13. "Since July 2, 1915 we have had a housekeeping school for girls, who are instructed in cooking, canning fruit, vegetable gardening, poultry farming and dairy farming. All costs are covered by the Interior Ministry. New classes for boys on wood working and pasting and a new parallel class (4th grade for girls) were established" (S 30 July 1915:1).

14. The English translation renders "Gottesdienst" as "Church Services" here, though the context clearly refers to activities with the Jewish refugees. *Gottesdienst* is a neutral term for any religious service; it does not have to refer to a church.

15. Gertrud Weil was one of the women who helped found the Jewish People's Home. See Regina Scheer, *AHAWAH: Das vergessene Haus: Spurensuche in der Berliner Auguststrasse* (Berlin: Aufbau Verlag, 1992), 147–49. Lehmann stayed in Berlin until 1928, when he went to Palestine, where he founded the children's village Ben Schemen, a community for orphans outside of Tel Aviv, and afterwards helped bring children from a Jewish orphanage in Berlin to Palestine.

16. *Das jüdische Volksheim Berlin,* Erster Bericht (First Yearly Report) (May/Dec. 1916). Many thanks to Hermann Simon (Berlin) for sending me this document.

17. Hannah Weiner, "Gershom Scholem and the Jung Juda Youth Group in Berlin, 1913–1918," *Studies in Zionism* 5.1 (1984): 33–34. See the description of the *Volksheim* (People's Home) and settlement idea by Siegfried Lehmann, published under his real name Salomon Lehnert: "Jüdische Volksarbeit," *Der Jude* (1916/17): 104–111. Hideo Nakazawa has related Lehnert's article to Kafka's story "Die Chinesische Mauer." See "Über Die Chinesische Mauer," *Chinesisch-japanisches Germanistentreffen Beijing 1990* (International Culture Publishing Corporation, 1994) 77–95. http://deutsch.c.u_tokyo.ac.jp/~nakazawa/Kafka/china.htm, pp. 77–95; accessed 6 Nov. 2006.

18. Mark K. Smith, "Settlements and Social Action Centres," infed (informal education homepage), ed. Mark K. Smith, Michele Erina Doyle, and Tony Jeffs (March 1999 [updated Jan. 2005]): http://www.infed.org/association/b_settl.htm; accessed 6 Nov. 2006.

19. See also LF 500 (BF 696); and LFF 119 (Br 141).

20. At the end of July he impresses on her that "it is a hundred times more important than the theater, than Klabund, Gerson, or whoever else there may be" (LF 481 [BF 673]). See also LF 477, 479, 480, 481 (BF 668, 671, 672, 673). In August he sends her Max Brod's article in the *Jüdische Rundschau,* "Aus der Notschule für galizische Flüchtlinge in Prag" (From the Emergency School for Galician Refugees in Prague) (LF 482 [BF 675]), and offers to pay her expenses (LF 494 [BF 688–89]).

21. Lily Braun, *Memoiren einer Sozialistin* (Berlin: Dietz, 1985).

22. Gershom Scholem, *From Berlin to Jerusalem: Memoirs of My Youth,* trans. Harry Zohn (Schocken,: New York, 1980), 78.

23. *Moaus Zur: Ein Chanukkahbuch,* ed. S. J. Agnon and Hugo Herrmann (Berlin:

Jüdischer Verlag, 1918). It includes historical information about the origin of Chanukah, the wars of the Maccabees, a translation of psalms and of "narratives and teachings of the midraschim." Furthermore there is an old Yiddish text from 1771 in transliterated German, a section on how Chanukah was celebrated, including prayers and excerpts from the Schulchan Aruch, and essays on the significance of the Menorah.

24. Sholem Asch, *Kleine Geschichten aus der Bibel* (Berlin: Jüdischer Verlag, 1914). The book was advertised in *Selbstwehr* (S 22 May 1914:5).

25. Isaac Leib Peretz, *Volkstümliche Erzählungen* (Berlin: Jüdischer Verlag, 1913). The book was advertised in *Selbstwehr* (30 May 1913:1–3), and excerpts also appeared later (S 30 Apr. 1915:3–4).

26. See John Zilcosky on colonial discourses in the little green books (*Kafka's Travels: Exoticism, Colonialism, and the Traffic of Writing* [New York: Palgrave, 2003], 103–51).

27. Brod also remembered Kafka reading "in a Talmud anthology the words of our teacher from the Roman period Schimon bar Jochai.... The following words: 'A miracle happened to me; therefore I will set up an institution which will benefit all'" (PK 113). Brod highlights Kafka's "humanistic Zionism": "In his own native country, he wishes to be employed in a profession useful to the development of his homeland, and thereby be a part of humanity" ("Humanistischer Zionismus," 280).

28. Felix Weltsch, "Franz Kafkas Geschichtsbewußtsein," in *Deutsches Judentum: Aufstieg und Krise*, ed. Robert Weltsch (Stuttgart: Deutsche Verlags-Anstalt, 1963), 278–79.

29. There is evidence to suggest that Kafka actually met Lily Braun in person: both of their names appear in a "Curliste vom 4. August 1903" of a sanatorium near Dresden. See Cor de Back and Niels Bokhove, *Niederländische Autoren über Franz Kafka 1922–1942* (Amsterdam: Rodopi, 1993). Many thanks to Jürgen Born for this information.

30. Sander Gilman, *Jewish Self-Hatred: Anti-Semitism and the Hidden Language of the Jews* (Baltimore: Johns Hopkins Univ. Press, 1986), 11.

31. For an analysis of the relationship between father and son in terms of class see Iris Bruce, "'A Frosty Hall of Mirrors': *Father Knows Best* in Franz Kafka and Nadine Gordimer," in *Evolving Jewish Identities in German Culture*, ed. Linda Feldman and Diana Orendi (Westport, Conn.: Praeger, 2000), 95–116.

32. When Braun returns to Berlin, she sees in the new parts of the city "a good middle class woman who dressed herself up and thereby completely lost the little bit of true culture which she possessed" (636). Similarly, Kafka's overall preference for Eastern European Jewry over his own assimilated Western upbringing always resurfaces (DII 117, 130 [T 730, 753]; LM 190–91 [BM 258]).

33. Karl Liebknecht, for example, does not take the feminist movement seriously, is dismissive of women, and tells Braun to stay away from them: "Do not pay any attention to women, if you want to achieve anything. They are even more backwards than men, can't be anything else. From where would they have any knowledge, after all, the poor women?" (Braun 433, 434) He is very patriarchal with his wife. August Bebel's wife is also submissive: she is "like a part of this room" (437), and in their discussion she is mostly silent and lets her husband speak.

34. In 1912, the Zionist Club of Jewish Women and Girls was founded in Prague. Kafka's sister Ottla was a member; Elsa Bergmann, Liese Weltsch, and Nelly Thieberger were all leaders at some point. Moreover, in the summer of 1917 Nelly Thieberger became editor of *Selbstwehr* and remained in this position until 1919.

35. Brod's review, "Literarischer Abend des Klubs jüdischer Frauen und Mädchen (December 19, 1917)" was published in *Selbstwehr* (1 Apr. 1918:4). See Jürgen Born et al., eds., *Franz Kafka: Kritik und Rezeption zu seinen Lebzeiten 1912–1924* (Frankfurt: Fischer, 1979), 128, 196. See Robert Kauf, "Once Again: Kafka's 'A Report to an Academy,'" *Modern Language Quarterly* 15.4 (Dec. 1954), 364.

36. Leo Weinstein, "Kafka's Ape: Heel or Hero," *Modern Fiction Studies* 8 (1962–63): 78.

37. *The Mare* is also mentioned by Patrick Bridgwater, "Rotpeters Ahnherren, oder: Der gelehrte Affe in der deutschen Dichtung," *Deutsche Vierteljahrsschrift* 56 (1982): 459; and Wagenbach, *Biographie*, 235n.718, 181.

38. Among other factual information about the Haskalah movement, Kafka noted down this motto from his reading of Pinès: "Principle formulated by Gordon: 'Be a man on the street and a Jew at home'" (DI 224 [T 363]; *Histoire*, 83). Similarly, Bergmann discusses this phrase in *Jawne und Jerusalem*, 18.

39. William Rubinstein, "A Report to an Academy," in *Franz Kafka Today*, ed. A. Flores and H. Swander (Madison: Univ. of Wisconsin Press, 1964), 58.

40. Max Mandelstamm, "Eine Ghettostimme über den Zionismus," in *Separatabzug aus 'Ost und West' [Illustrierte Monatszeitschrift für modernes Judentum]*, ed. Berliner Zionistische Vereinigung (Berlin: Verlag S. Calvary & Co., 1901), 6–7 (emphasis mine); KB 116.

41. Max Brod, "Bemerkungen zur Judenfrage," in *Der Jud ist schuld . . . ? Diskussionsbuch über die Judenfrage* (Basel: Zinnen-Verlag, 1932), 364. Brod here elaborates on self-hatred as well (363–64).

42. Max Brod and Felix Weltsch, *Zionismus als Weltanschauung* (Mähr: R. Färber, 1925), 136; cited in Carmely, *Identitätsproblem*, 143.

43. Anita Shapira, "Anti-Semitism and Zionism," *Modern Judaism* 15.3 (Oct. 1995): 219–20.

44. I am echoing Gilman here. See Gilman, *The Jew's Body* (New York: Routledge, 1991), 76, 80, 87, 91, 98, 119, 155, 165.

45. Marthe Robert, "Une figure de Whitechapel: Notes inédites de Dora Dymant sur Kafka," *Evidences* 4.28 (1952): 42.

46. Karlheinz Fingerhut, *Die Funktion der Tierfiguren im Werke Franz Kafkas* (Bonn: H. Bouvier & Co. Verlag, 1969), 144n.317.

6. ANTI-SEMITISM AND SELF-HATRED (1916–1924)

1. Arnold Zweig, *Ritualmord in Ungarn* (Berlin: Hyperionverlag, 1914). *Selbstwehr* later ran excerpts from *Ritualmord in Ungarn* (S 11 Oct. 1916:2–4).

2. The pronoun *ihn* in the German original can refer to the author or the trial.

3. Abraham Grünberg, *Ein jüdisch-polnisch-russisches Jubiläum: Der große Pogrom*

von Siedlce im Jahre 1906 (Prague: Grafia Selbstverlag, 1916). See Binder for more information on Grünberg (*Gesetz,* 132–33).

4. Robert Weinberg, "The Pogrom of 1905 in Odessa: A Case Study," in *Pogroms: Anti-Jewish Violence in Modern Russian History,* ed. John D. Klier and Schlomo Lambroza (Cambridge: Cambridge Univ. Press, 1992), 248.

5. Max Brod, *Eine Königin Esther* (Leipzig: Kurt Wolff Verlag, 1918).

6. See Hans Kohn, "Das kulturelle Problem des modernen Westjuden," *Der Jude* 5 (1920–21): 281–97.

7. See Siegmund Kaznelson for a critique of Wassermann's book along the same lines, "Um jüdisches Volkstum: Zu Jakob Wassermanns Bekenntnisbuch," *Der Jude* 6.1 (1921–22): 49–52.

8. Friedrich von der Leyen, *Deutsche Dichtung in neuer Zeit* (Jena: Eugen Diederichs, 1922); KH 141.

9. Yehuda Eloni, *Zionismus in Deutschland: Von den Anfängen bis 1914* (Gerlingen: Bleicher Verlag, 1987), 458. Many Zionists were very influenced by Blüher. Arthur Holitscher reports from his travels in Palestine that outside of the works of Marx and Freud he "very frequently" found "books and pamphlets by Hans Blüher" and adds: "Many German and Austrian Chaluzim [pioneers], from the Wandervogel, the free German, Blauweiß-movement, asked me about Blüher, his new writings, changes, impulses" (*Reise durch das jüdische Palästina* [Berlin: S. Fischer Verlag, 1922], 39).

10. Hans Blüher, *Secessio Judaica: Philosophische Grundlegung der Historischen Situation des Judentums und der Antisemitischen Bewegung* (Berlin: Der Weisse Ritter Verlag, 1922).

11. Hans Blüher, "Das Judentum und die falsch gestellte Rassenfrage," in *Der Jud ist schuld . . . ? Diskussionsbuch über die Judenfrage* (Basel: Zinnen-Verlag, 1932), 69–82.

12. In an earlier letter to Milena of 1920, Kafka warns her of Jewish lovers. They are discussing a tragic event, that of the husband of a common friend, Jarmila, committing suicide after finding out that his wife had an affair with another friend, Willy Haas, whom she married a year later. Kafka likens Willy Haas, the Jewish lover (and later editor of the letters to Milena), to a Hilsner type, a ritual murderer who throws himself on gentile women: "I don't understand how whole nations of people could ever have thought of ritual murder before these recent events (at most they may have felt general fear and jealousy, but here there is no question, we see 'Hilsner' committing the crime step by step; what difference does it make that the virgin embraces him at the same time?)" (LM 51 [BM 68]). He also describes Jewish males as "predatory animals" (LM 51 [BM 68]). And though he grants that "these are all exaggerations. . . . because people seeking salvation always throw themselves at women, and these women can be either Christian or Jewish" (LM 51 [BM 68]), he nonetheless warns Milena about himself: "When you talk about the future, don't you sometimes forget that I'm Jewish? . . . Even at your feet, Jews and Judaism remain dangerous" (LM 116 [BM 154]). Willy Haas, as first editor of the *Letters to Milena,* ommitted these passages.

13. Walter Benjamin, "Theses on the Philosophy of History," in *Illuminations,* 257–58. See Gerschom Scholem, "Walter Benjamin and His Angel," in *On Walter Benjamin:*

Critical Essays and Recollections, ed. Gary Smith (Cambridge, Mass.: MIT Press, 1988), 51–89.

14. In an article by Kafka's friend Hugo Bergmann, we read: "The Zionist predicament in the Diaspora is not devoid of tragedy. We are often called the people of the desert, and more or less pitied by those who live in Palestine" (*Jawne,* 12). See also Jens Tismar, "Kafka's *Schakale und Araber* im zionistischen Kontext betrachtet," *Jahrbuch der deutschen Schillergesellschaft* 19 (1975): 312; and Robert Kauf, who pointed out long ago that the "similarity of the fate of the jackals to that of the Jews is fairly obvious" ("Once Again," 365).

15. George Mosse, "Max Nordau and His Degeneration," in *Degeneration,* by Max Nordau. (Lincoln: Univ. of Nebraska Press, 1993), xiii. Many thanks to Don Bruce for this reference.

16. The original German "Beruf" (profession) in "wir lassen sie bei ihrem Beruf" (E 284) does not come across in the English "we'll leave them to their business" (CS 411).

17. The German "Schauspiel" (E 283), which I have rendered as "spectacle" here and which also connotes comedy, theater, farce, is not adequately described by the English "entertainment" (CS 410).

18. "O Herr" also means "Oh, Lord," but the religious connotations do not come across in the Muir translation "dear sir" (CS 410 [E 283]).

19. I owe this insight to Stanley Corngold.

20. All of these sentences are left out of the latest German edition of short stories, which is based on the German critical edition. Compare CS 427 and E 321.

21. The original German is "Assoziationswitz" (my translation here). See "the literalness is driven to the point of a pun" (Theodor W. Adorno, "Notes on Kafka," in *Prisms,* trans. S. Weber and S. Weber [London: Neville Spearman, 1967], 248).

22. Until recently, Nahum Glatzer's German-English bilingual edition, *Parables and Paradoxes* (P), was the only edition that included "The Animal in the Synagogue." The story was written after the end of March 1920 and before 23 June 1922 (E 572, NII 405–11).

23. "Despite harsh rabbinical views based on strict interpretation of the early sources, communities continued to decorate their synagogues as they found fit and appropriate" (Shalom Sabar, 'Synagogue Interior Decoration and the Halakhah,' in *Synagogues without Jews,* ed. Rivka Dorfman and Ben-Zion Dorfman [Philadelphia: Jewish Publication Society, 2000], 316). Many thanks to Rivka and Ben-Zion Dorfman for sharing their information with me. Special thanks to Michael Greenstein who discovered the animal in Toronto.

7. THE DREAM OF PALESTINE (1917–1924)

1. Moses Rath, *Lehrbuch der Hebräischen Sprache für Schul- und Selbstunterricht* (Vienna: Selbstverlag des Verfassers, 1918). Kafka owned the second revised edition that was advertised in *Selbstwehr.* On Kafka's Hebrew studies, see Binder, "Kafkas Hebräischstudien. Ein biographisch interpretatorischer Versuch," in *Zu Franz Kafka,*

ed. G. Heintz (Stuttgart: Klett, 1979), 133–58; Clive Sinclair, "Kafka's Hebrew Teacher," *Encounter* 64.3 (1985): 46–9; Ernst Pawel, "Kafka's Hebrew Teacher," *The American Zionist* 74.1 (Oct./Nov. 1985): 21–22.

2. Alfred Bodenheimer, "A Sign of Sickness and a Symbol of Health: Kafka's Hebrew Notebooks," in Gelber, ed., *Kafka, Zionism, and Beyond*, 263, 265.

3. Pavel Eisner identifies this place as "Zelizy, which he, like the Sudeten Germans, called Schelesen; it is a place in the valley of the Elbe near what was then the linguistic frontier between Czech and Germans where a typically German Jewish vacation colony of Prague residents had been established (Pavel Eisner, *Franz Kafka and Prague*, trans. Lowry Nelson and René Wellek [New York: Arts, 1950], 66).

4. See Hermine Beck, "'Warum lassen Sie die arme Fliege nicht in Ruh,'" in Koch, ed., *"Als Kafka,"* 147.

5. Friedrich Thieberger remembers: "It was shortly after WWI when he asked me if I was willing to teach him Hebrew" ("Erinnerungen an Franz Kafka," *Eckhart* 23 [Oct. 1953]: 52). *Franz Kafka Eine Chronik* (1999) dates the beginning of the Hebrew lessons for the fall of 1918, after Kafka's return from Turnau on 29 September (C 156). However, he became ill with the Spanish flu on 14 October and stayed sick for several months and then left for Schelesen to recover (30 November–22 December 22). Binder's date of spring 1919 is more likely correct (KH 539).

6. See also Friedrich Thieberger, "Kafka und die Thiebergers," in Koch, ed., *"Als Kafka,"* 125–26.

7. Lesson 6, for instance, describes an elementary school class where the children have a slate and slate pencil—this was typical for a European school.

8. It is hard to date Kafka's fragments in general, and this one is no exception. The critical edition suggests the date 1923 because Kafka mentions a squirrel in a letter to his sister of this period (NIIA 134). However, Kafka also mentions a squirrel elsewhere (W 359 [H 263–64]), and he had used the squirrel metaphor as early as 1917 upon reading "Jackals and Arabs" in *Der Jude* (W 71 [H 52, 324; NII 30]). A few pages previous to the squirrel entry, the critical edition identifies Hebrew vocabulary relating to Moses Rath's textbook (NIIA 128).

9. Binder believes these lessons took place in the summer of 1918 with Kafka, Brod, Weltsch, and Irma Singer (KH 539). Miriam (Irma) Singer does not mention Brod; see her "Hebräischstunden mit Kafka," in Koch, ed., *"Als Kafka,"* 140. Singer lived on the Kibbutz Deganya. When she returned to Prague in 1922 for a visit, Kafka presented her with one of his books and dedicated it to her with the inscription: "To accompany you to Daganiah [Deganya]" (143).

10. Mark H. Gelber, "The Image of Kafka in Max Brod's *Zauberreich der Liebe* and its Zionist Implications," in Gelber, ed., *Kafka, Zionism, and Beyond*, 279.

11. Ahron Bregman, *A History of Israel* (Houndmills: Palgrave Macmillan, 2002), 11.

12. Kafka composed this plan in March 1918, while living in Zürau (W 119–20 [NII 105–7; NIIA 48; BB 221–22; H 93–4]). See Brod, "Humanistischer Zionismus," 281; Binder, KH 506–7; Stölzl, *Böhmen*, 129.

13. Davis Trietsch, *Palaestina Handbuch* (Berlin: Verlag Benjamin Harz, 1922), 98.

14. Max Brod, *Sozialismus im Zionismus* (Vienna: R. Löwit Verlag, 1920).

15. See Hugo Bergmann, *Tagebücher und Briefe*, 1:103.

16. For pictures from the film, see the slides reproduced in Hanns Zischler, *Kafka geht ins Kino* (Reinbeck: Rowohlt, 1996), 148–53.

17. Shlomo Zemach, *Jüdische Bauern: Geschichten aus dem neuen Palästina* (Vienna: R. Löwit Verlag, 1919).

18. See "Successful Settlement of the Jewish School Affair: A Jewish School in Prague" (S 8 Sept. 1920:2). "Final approval for the creation of Jewish national schools was given on August 28, 1920, and the first nationally oriented Jewish elementary school with Czech as the language of instruction opened in Prague on September 6 of that same year" (A. M. Rabinowicz, "The Jewish Minority," in *The Jews of Czechoslovakia*, 1:215). See also Brod, "Jüdische Schule," 345.

19. Amira Kohn-Trattner, personal correspondence, 1995–96.

20. The documentary material on the school was made available to me through the help of the Jewish Museum in Prague.

21. See LF 396 (Br 463); KH 575; and Binder, "*Selbstwehr*," 295.

22. I am grateful to the late Marianne Steiner for this information (letter to the author, 16 March 1995).

23. Many thanks to Niels Bokhove for his information on this school. The innovative educational methods were decisive for Kafka: "There are schools in Palestine which are more akin to us and perhaps more important. But for proximity and minimal risk there is probably nothing like Hellerau" (LFF 290 [Br 339]). "Hellerau was founded in 1909 as a garden city outside of Dresden. . . . It had . . . Emile Jaques-Dalcroze's School for Eurythmics which Kafka had visited in 1914. In 1921 a progressive school, the Neue Schule, was established; A. S. Neill (1883–1973), later the creator of Summerhill, was a cofounder" (LFF 477n.78).

24. Erwin Arnstein, "Schabath in Tel Aviv" (S 18 May 1923:1).

25. Archival material in the Jewish Museum of Prague; letter by Dr. Gustav Sicher, n.d.

26. Richard Feder, ed., *Zidovské Besídky: Kniha První: Pro zabavu a pouceni dospelesjsi mladeze zidovske* [Jewish Book of Entertainment, V. 1. For the Entertainment and Instruction of the Grown up Jewish Youth] (Roudnice: Nákladem Vlastním, 1912). The book includes humorous anecdotes, Midrashic legends, and Talmudic wisdom (KB 34).

27. The following entries constituted the curriculum: "Inge and the Easter Bunnies," "With Singing and Music Through the Year," "This and That in Earnest and Fun," "Holidays by the Ocean," "Funny Stories," "Rübezahl," "Robinson Crusoe," "Whatever You Want," "A Thousand and One Nights," "Die Schildbürger," "Reineke Fuchs," "Gulliver's Travels."

28. I would like to thank Arno Pařik for this information (personal correspondence, 6 March 1993) and for translating many Czech documents, which allowed me to reconstruct the history of the school. He was instrumental for putting me in touch with earlier students of the Jewish elementary school.

29. Many thanks to Helen Epstein for providing me with Feder's dates.

30. In 1992, when I began searching for the Jewish elementary school in Prague, my inquiries at the Jewish Museum on Jachymova 3 were unsuccessful. I later came across the school's address in *Selbstwehr:* the address was identical with the address of the Jewish Museum. In 2001, the museum moved to a different location.

31. Many thanks to (the late) Marianne Steiner (London), Arno Pařik (Prague), Anna Lorencova (Prague), Rosa and Walter Brössler (Tel Aviv), Amira Kohn-Trattner (New York), Hermann Simon (Berlin), Ben Korda (Edmonton), and Jiři Kraus (Edmonton) for sharing their information with me over the years. Without their help, this narrative would not have been possible.

32. Max Brod, "Franz Kafka und der Zionismus," *Emuna* 10.1–2 (1975): 34. See also FK1:270–71; and PK 116.

33. Jiři Langer, *Die Erotik der Kabbala* (Prague: Dr. Josef Flesch Verlag, 1923).

34. Jiři Kraus, personal memoirs. Max Brod, too, mentions Langer's skating: "Interestingly enough, Langer was much less proud of his thorough and unfathomable knowledge than of his skill in skating" (PK 181). His brother states that "he even wrote an instruction book on figure-skating" (*Nine Gates,* xxiii).

35. Puah Menczel-Ben-Tovim, "Ich war Kafkas Hebräischlehrerin," in Koch, ed., *"Als Kafka,"* 165.

36. Kafka read a very similar response in Lily Braun's autobiography when a friend of hers made a spirited defense of socialism. When Lily thanked him, he replied, "I really only made this little speech for you" (Braun 644).

37. Many thanks to Michael Greenstein for examining the Hebrew sheets with me, as well as to Hans-Gerd Koch (Forschungsstelle für Prager deutsche Literatur) for providing me with this unpublished material. Bodenheimer also confirms that Kafka's notes are "mostly composed" of "everyday words" ("Hebrew Notebooks," 269).

38. If "Kugel" indeed refers to the Zionist Chaim Kugel, he is identical with the later mayor of a suburb of Tel Aviv after World War II (Aryeh Sole, "Subcarpathian Ruthenia: 1918–1938," in *The Jews of Czechoslovakia,* 1:144–45).

39. See Samuel Loeb Gordon, *Halashon* ("The Language"—Hebrew textbook), vol. 3 (Warsaw: Ch. Goldberg, n.d. [probably 1919]). It contains a sheet of Hebrew exercises in Kafka's handwriting (KB 152), but Kafka did not get all that far in it because there is nothing underlined after page 47.

40. See Bergmann, *Tagebücher und Briefe,* 1:182–83.

41. See LFF 388, 390, 395 (Br 453, 456, 459). Robert Alter points out that Kafka's difficulty may also have had to do with Brenner's pessimism (*Necessary Angels,* 40). Brenner is a starkly realistic and psychologically brooding Dostoevskian writer not known for an optimistic philosophy of life. But neither is Kafka.

42. J. Elbogen and J. Höniger, *Lehranstalt für die Wissenschaft des Judentums: Festschrift zur Einweihung des eigenen Heims* (Berlin: N.p., 1907), 14, 1. Many thanks to Renate Kirchner from the Institutum Judaicum (Berlin) for helping me access this material.

43. Cassel taught Jewish history and literature, Semitic linguistics, and biblical exegesis; Geiger history of Judaism and its literature; Steintal comparative history of religion, biblical exegesis, and language studies; and Lewy the Talmudic subjects, as much for their scientific treatment as for the halakhic and practical studies (*Festschrift*, 24, 27, 31, 33).

44. Brod's comment appears in the introduction to a Yiddish translation of Kafka's *Trial*, see Franz Kafka, *Der Prozes*.

45. *Hochschule für die Wissenschaft des Judentums. Neununddreissigster Bericht* (Berlin: Druck H. Itzkowski, 1921), 10.

46. Niels Bokhove, 'Friedensort in den wilden Gegenden des Innern': Kafka en de Berlijnse 'Hochschule für die Wissenschaft des Judentums,'" "*Berlin als Zwischenstation*": *Franz Kafka in Berlin 1923–1924, Kwartaalblad van de Nederlandse Franz Kafka-Kring* 7. 2 and 3 (May 1999): 47, 48. See also Bokhove, "Zionism," 55.

47. See Kafka's description: "He had, for instance, my teacher's beard, this stiff, thin, sticking out, grey-black beard which covered the upper lip and the whole chin" (NII 551). See Bokhove, "Friedensort," 49.

48. Nicolas Baudy, "Entretiens avec Dora Dymant: Compagne de Kafka," *Evidences* 2.8 (1950): 22.

49. Binder's information comes from Hugo Bergmann himself. Pinner's edition of the *Traktat Berakhot* is the first scholarly translation into German and was probably the standard Talmud edition used in rabbinic institutes at the time. There are extensive commentaries and explanations, the Hebrew text is vocalized, and the tractate is prefaced with a long introduction to the Talmud by the Enlightenment philosopher Maimonides.

50. Maurice Simon, introduction to *Berakot: Hebrew-English Edition of the Babylonian Talmud*, ed. Rabbi Dr. I. Epstein (London: The Soncino Press, 1960).

51. The English translation is incorrect: "it isn't that I've taken up studying—aside from the fact that I am not really pursuing these studies but only doing them for pleasure without the necessary groundwork" (LFF 404–5).

52. Nahum Glatzer, *The Loves of Franz Kafka* (New York: Schocken, 1986), 73. No source is given to substantiate this claim.

53. John Milfull, "The Messiah and the Direction of History: Walter Benjamin, Isaac Bashevis Singer and Franz Kafka," in *Festschrift für E. W. Herd*, ed. August Obermayer (Dunedin, New Zealand: Dept. of German, University of Otago, 1980), 185, 184.

54. In a similar vein, as late as 1920 Kafka distances himself from an arrogant Zionist nationalism: "By the way, this Judaism that looks down so haughtily on the Germans is more than I bargained for" (LFF 245 [Br 282]).

55. "This land is our land. The Jews are our dogs!" Arthur Holitscher reports that these "slogans" reverberated throughout Jerusalem during the time of the November pogrom of 1921 (85).

56. See Bruce, "'Which Way Out?'" 112–17.

57. *Bambi* "was serialized in 1922 in the *Neue Freie Presse* [Vienna]" (Dormer, "Felix Salten," 413).

58. Brod's first impression of Herzl was of "a King with an Assyrian full beard" (SL 49). Adolf Böhm describes him as "the picture of the new Jew" who exhibits "pride, strength, power, nobility, grandeur" and is "a true prince," a "royal Jew" with "dark sparkling eyes and imperious gestures" (*Bewegung*, 181–83; KH 109). Kafka also read Herzl's *Diaries* after they appeared in 1922 (KH 573). For the religious mystical aura staged around Herzl, see Michael Berkowitz, *Zionist Culture and West European Jewry before the First World War* (Cambridge: Cambridge Univ. Press, 1993), 27–30, 136.

59. *Volk* (people) derives from contemporary *völkish* discourses, which were shared by all nationalist movements. With the growing nationalism (Czech, Jewish, German, etc.) after WWI, the word *Volk* appears everywhere. Even *Selbstwehr,* which started out as a "Unabhängige jüdische Wochenschrift" (Independent Jewish Weekly) officially became a "Jüdisches Volksblatt" (Paper of the Jewish People) in 1922. Furthermore, a great many articles during this period discuss national education, such as Bergmann's "Ways of Educating the People" (S 13 Jan. 1922:4).

60. Throughout the story, Kafka is playing with the literal meaning of *pfeifen,* to whistle, and its various idiomatic expressions, such as "auf etwas pfeifen" (not to give a damn) in the phrase: "Ich pfeife auf eueren Schutz, sagt sie dann. 'Ja, ja, du pfeifst,' denken wir [I don't give a damn about your protection, she says then. Yes, yes, you are piping, we think]" (E 525). The standard English translation is: "Your protection isn't worth an old song, she says then. Sure, sure, old song, we think" (CS 365–66). The most important pun is the idiomatic phrase "pfeifen auf dem letzten Loch"—literally "to pipe on or out of the last hole, to be on one's last legs, at one's last gasp." In idiomatic German "pfeifen *auf*" as well as "pfeifen *aus* dem letzten Loch" are used interchangeably. "Pfeifen *auf*" keeps the musical connection (as in playing *on* an instrument), but "pfeifen *aus* dem letzten Loch" is equally used.

61. For a discussion of Josephine's singing and Wagner, see Mark M. Anderson, *Kafka's Clothes: Ornament and Aestheticism in the Habsburg Fin de Siècle* (Oxford: Clarendon Press, 1992), 197; see also Gilman, *Patient,* 1–40.

62. "Since the Galician refugees have come to Prague, I have often attended Eastern European Jewish prayer services—the most sublime feeling ever that I have been fortunate enough to experience" (Brod, "Jüdische Volksmelodien," *Der Jude* 1 [1916–17]: 344). DII 128 (T 745, K 184).

63. See LFF 283 (Br 330); and W 326 (H 240, NII 333–334). Sometimes Kafka did not like the Yiddish plays either, "because they degenerate into a wailing" (DII 215 [T 349]).

64. Compare the letter to Minze Eisner in early 1923, where Kafka uses a similar analogy: "One cannot help imagining a child left to play by itself who undertakes some incredible adventure of climbing up on a chair or something of the sort. But the father whom it has wholly forgotten is looking on after all, and prospects are much brighter than they seem. The father might, for example, be the Jewish people" (LFF 369 [Br 428–29]).

CONCLUSION

1. Arthur Holitscher, *Lebensgeschichte eines Rebellen* (Berlin: S. Fischer Verlag, 1924).

2. Eric Homberger, "Some Uses for Jewish Ambivalence: Abraham Cahan and Michael Gold," in *Between "Race" and Culture: Representations of "the Jew" in English and American Literature,* ed. Bryan Cheyette (Stanford, Calif.: Stanford Univ. Press, 1996), 167.

Kafka's Talmud

Works Cited

Abraham, Ulf. "Mose 'Vor dem Gesetz': Eine bekannte Vorlage zu Kafkas 'Türhüterlegende.'" *Deutsche Vierteljahreszeitschrift für Literaturwissenschaft und Geistesgeschichte* 57.4 (December 1983): 636–50.
Adler, Jeremy. *Kafka*. London: Penguin, 2001.
Adorno, Theodor W. "Notes on Kafka." In *Prisms*. Trans. S. Weber and S. Weber. London: Neville Spearman, 1967. 243–71.
Ahad Ha'am [Asher Ginsberg]. "The Jewish State and the Jewish Problem." 1897. In Hertzberg, ed., *The Zionist Idea*. 262–69.
Alt, Peter-André. *Franz Kafka: Der ewige Sohn: Eine Biographie*. Munich: C. H. Beck, 2005.
Alter, Robert. *Necessary Angels: Tradition and Modernity in Kafka, Benjamin, and Scholem*. Cambridge, Mass.: Harvard University Press, 1991.
———. "On Walter Benjamin." *Commentary* 48.3 (1969): 86–93.
Anderson, Mark. *Kafka's Clothes: Ornament and Aestheticism in the Habsburg Fin de Siècle*. Oxford: Clarendon Press, 1992.
Asch, Schalom. *Kleine Geschichten aus der Bibel*. Berlin: Jüdischer Verlag, 1914.
Back, Cor de, and Niels Bokhove. *Niederländische Autoren über Franz Kafka 1922–1942*. Amsterdam: Rodopi, 1993.
Baioni, Giuliano. *Kafka: Letteratura ed ebraismo*. Turin: Einaudi, 1984.
———. *Kafka: Literatur und Judentum*. Trans. G. Billen and J. Billen. Stuttgart: Metzler, 1994.
———. "Zionism, Literature, and the Yiddish Theater." In *Reading Kafka: Prague, Politics, and the Fin-de-Siècle*. Ed. Mark Anderson. New York: Schocken, 1989. 95–115. Translation of part of "Gli Attori di Lemberg" from *Kafka: Letteratura ed ebraismo*.
Band, Arnold. "Kafka and the Beiliss Affair." *Comparative Literature* 32 (1980): 168–83.
Bärsch, Claus-Ekkehard. *Max Brod im "Kampf um das Judentum": Zum Leben und Werk eines deutsch-jüdischen Dichters aus Prag*. Vienna: Passagen Verlag, 1992.

Baudy, Nicolas. "Entretiens avec Dora Dymant: Compagne de Kafka." *Evidences* 2.8 (1950): 21–25.

Baum, Oskar. *Die böse Unschuld: Ein jüdischer Kleinstadtroman.* Frankfurt: Rütten & Loening, 1913.

Beck, Evelyn Torton. *Kafka and the Yiddish Theater: Its Impact on His Work.* Madison: University of Wisconsin Press, 1971.

Beck, Hermine. "'Warum lassen Sie die arme Fliege nicht in Ruh.' . . ." In Koch, ed., *"Als Kafka."* 146–48.

Benjamin, Walter. *Benjamin über Kafka: Texte, Briefzeugnisse, Aufzeichnungen.* Ed. Hermann Schweppenhäuser. Frankfurt: Suhrkamp, 1981. Abbreviated in text as B.

———. "Some Reflections on Kafka." In *Illuminations: Essays and Reflections.* Ed. Hannah Arendt. Trans. Harry Zohn. New York: Schocken, 1968. 141–45.

———. "Theses on the Philosophy of History." In *Illuminations.* Ed. Hannah Arendt. Trans. Harry Zohn. New York: Schocken, 1968. 257–58.

Bergmann, Hugo. "Erinnerungen an Franz Kafka." *Universitas: Zeitschrift für Wissenschaft, Kunst und Literatur* 27.7 (1972): 739–50.

———. *Jawne und Jerusalem: Gesammelte Aufsätze.* Berlin: Jüdischer Verlag, 1919.

———. "Schulzeit und Studium." In Koch, ed., *"Als Kafka."* 13–24.

———. *Tagebücher und Briefe.* Vols. 1: *1901–1948* and 2: *1948–1975.* Ed. Miriam Sambursky. Königstein: Jüdischer Verlag bei Athenäum, 1985.

Berkowitz, Michael. *Western Jewry and the Zionist Project, 1914–1933.* Cambridge: Cambridge University Press, 1997.

———. *Zionist Culture and West European Jewry before the First World War.* Cambridge: Cambridge University Press, 1993.

Biale, David. *Gershom Scholem: Kabbalah and Counter-History.* Cambridge, Mass.: Harvard University Press, 1982.

Binder, Hartmut. "Café Savoy." In *Wo Kafka und seine Freunde zu Gast waren: Prager Kaffeehäuser und Vergnügungsstätten in historischen Bilddokumenten.* Prague: Vitalis, 2000. 146–51.

———. "Franz Kafka und die Wochenschrift *Selbstwehr.*" *Deutsche Vierteljahrsschrift für Literaturwissenschaft und Geistesgeschichte* 41 (1967): 283–304. English version in *Yearbook XII of the Leo Baeck Institute.* Ed. Robert Weltsch. London: East and West Library, 1967. 135–48.

———. *Kafka-Kommentar zu sämtlichen Erzählungen.* 1975. Munich: Winkler Verlag, 1986. Abbreviated in the text as KK.

———. "Kafkas Hebräischstudien." In *Zu Franz Kafka.* Ed. Günter Heintz. Stuttgart: Klett, 1979. 133–58.

———. *"Vor dem Gesetz": Einführung in Kafkas Welt.* Stuttgart: Verlag J. B. Metzler, 1993.

———, ed. *Kafka Handbuch Bd. 1: Der Mensch und seine Zeit.* Stuttgart: Alfred Kröner Verlag, 1979. Abbreviated in text as KH.

———, ed. *Kafka Handbuch Bd. 2: Das Werk und seine Wirkung.* Stuttgart: Alfred Kröner Verlag, 1979.

Blanchot, Maurice. "The Sirens' Song." In *Selected Essays*. Trans. Sasha Rabinovitch. Bloomington: Indiana University Press, 1982. 59–65.

Bloch, Chajim. "Aus der Welt der Chassidim." *Das jüdische Echo* nos. 17, 19, 23, 26, 27, 35, 38 (1917).

———. *Der Prager Golem: Von seiner "Geburt" bis zu seinem "Tod."* Berlin: Verlag Benjamin Harz, 1920.

Bloch, Hans. "Die Legende von Theodor Herzl." In *Der Zionistische Student*. Ed. K.Z.V. (Kartell Zionistischer Verbindungen). Berlin: Jüdischer Verlag, n.d. (probably 1912). 51–62.

Blüher, Hans. "Das Judentum und die falsch gestellte Rassenfrage." In *Der Jud ist schuld . . . ? Diskussionsbuch über die Judenfrage*. Basel: Zinnen-Verlag, 1932. 69–82.

———. *Secessio Judaica: Philosophische Grundlegung der Historischen Situation des Judentums und der Antisemitischen Bewegung*. Berlin: Der Weisse Ritter Verlag, 1922.

Blumenfeld, Kurt. *Im Kampf um den Zionismus: Briefe aus fünf Jahrzehnten*. Ed. Miriam Sambursky and Jochanan Ginat. Stuttgart: Deutsche Verlags-Anstalt, 1976.

Bodenheimer, Alfred. "A Sign of Sickness and a Symbol of Health: Kafka's Hebrew Notebooks." In Gelber, ed., *Kafka, Zionism, and Beyond*. 259–70.

Böhm, Adolf. *Die zionistische Bewegung: Eine kurze Darstellung ihrer Entwicklung*. Vols. 1 and 2. Teil. Berlin: Welt-Verlag, 1920–21.

———. *Zionistische Palästinaarbeit, Heft 1*. Vienna: Publikationen des Zionistischen Zentralbureaus Wien IX, 1909.

Bokhove, Niels. "'The Entrance to the More Important': Kafka's Personal Zionism." In Gelber, ed., *Kafka, Zionism, and Beyond*. 23–58.

———. "'Friedensort in den wilden Gegenden des Innern': Kafka en de Berlijnse 'Hochschule für die Wissenschaft des Judentums.'" *"Berlin als Zwischenstation": Franz Kafka in Berlin 1923–1924. Kwartaalblad van de Nederlandse Franz Kafka-Kring* 7. 2–3 (May 1999): 43–49.

Born, Jürgen. *Kafkas Bibliothek: Ein beschreibendes Verzeichnis*. Frankfurt: Fischer, 1990. Abbreviated in text as KB.

———, et al., eds. *Franz Kafka: Kritik und Rezeption zu seinen Lebzeiten 1912–1924*. Frankfurt: Fischer, 1979.

Braun, Lily. *Memoiren einer Sozialistin*. Berlin: Dietz, 1985.

Bregman Ahron. *A History of Israel*. Houndmills: Palgrave Macmillan, 2002.

Bridgwater, Patrick. "Rotpeters Ahnherren, oder: Der gelehrte Affe in der deutschen Dichtung." *Deutsche Vierteljahrsschrift* 56 (1982): 447–62.

Brod, Max. *Arnold Beer: Das Schicksal eines Juden*. Berlin: Axel Juncker Verlag, 1912.

———. "Bemerkungen zur Judenfrage." In *Der Jud ist schuld . . . ? Diskussionsbuch über die Judenfrage*. Basel: Zinnen-Verlag, 1932. 363–65.

———. "Die dritte Phase des Zionismus." *Die Zukunft* 16 (20 January 1917): 1–13.

———. "Erfahrungen im ostjüdischen Schulwerk." *Der Jude* 1 (1916–17): 32–36.

———. *Franz Kafka. A Biography*. Schocken: New York, 1960. Abbreviated in text as FK.

———. "Franz Kafka und der Zionismus." *Emuna* 10.1/2 (1975): 33–36.

———. "Humanistischer Zionismus im Werk Kafkas." In *Auf gespaltenem Pfad:*

Zum 90. Geburtstag von Margarete Susman. Ed. Manfred Schlosser. Darmstadt: Erato-Pr., 1964. 278–81.

———. "Eine Jargonbühre in Prag" (Yiddish Theater in Prague). *Prager Tagblatt* (27 October 1911): 3.

———. *Die Jüdinnen.* 1911. Leipzig: Kurt Wolff, 1915.

———. "Jüdische Schule." *Der Jude* 5 (1920–21): 345–48.

———. "Jüdische Volksmelodien." *Der Jude* 1 (1916–17): 344–45.

———. *Eine Königin Esther.* Leipzig: Kurt Wolff Verlag, 1918.

———. *Der Prager Kreis.* Frankfurt: Suhrkamp, 1979. Abbreviated in text as PK.

———. *Sozialismus im Zionismus.* Vienna: R. Löwit Verlag, 1920.

———. *Streitbares Leben, 1884–1968.* München: F. A. Herbig, 1969. Abbreviated in text as SL.

———. *Über Franz Kafka.* Frankfurt: Fischer, 1977. Abbreviated in text as FK1.

———. "Die Zwanziger Jahre in Prag: Kultur aus drei Kulturen." *Magnum* 25 (1961): 54.

———, and Felix Weltsch. *Zionismus als Weltanschauung.* Mähr.-Ostrau: R. Färber, 1925.

Bruce, Iris. "'A Frosty Hall of Mirrors': *Father Knows Best* in Franz Kafka and Nadine Gordimer." In *Evolving Jewish Identities in German Culture.* Ed. Linda Feldman and Diana Orendi. Westport, Conn.: Praeger, 2000. 95–116.

———. "*Der Proceß* in Yiddish, or 'The Importance of Being Humorous.'" *TTR* 7.2 (Fall 1994): 35–62.

———. "Which Way Out? Schnitzler's and Salten's Conflicting Responses to Cultural Zionism." In *A Companion to the Works of Arthur Schnitzler.* Ed. Dagmar Lorenz. Rochester, N.Y.: Camden House, 2003. 103–26.

———. "'Zionistische Sehnsucht': Franz Kafka und Hans Blochs 'Legende von Theodor Herzl.'" *Neue Zürcher Zeitung* (Switzerland) 101 (2–3 May 1992): 69.

Buber, Martin. *Briefwechsel aus sieben Jahrzehnten,* Vol. 1: *1897–1918.* Ed. Grete Schaeder. Heidelberg: Lambert Schneider, 1972.

———. *Der grosse Maggid und seine Nachfolge.* Frankfurt: Literarische Anstalt Rütten & Loening, 1921.

———. *Der Jude und sein Judentum: Gesammelte Aufsätze und Reden.* Cologne: Joseph Melzer Verlag, 1963.

———. "Der Mythos der Juden." In *Vom Judentum: Ein Sammelbuch.* Ed. Verein jüdischer Hochschüler Bar Kochba. Leipzig: K. Wolff, 1913. 21–31.

———. *On Judaism.* Ed. Nahum Glatzer. New York: Schocken, 1967.

———. *The Letters of Martin Buber: A Life of Dialogue.* Ed. Nahum N. Glatzer and Paul Mendes-Flohr. Trans. Richard Winston, Clara Winston, and Harry Zohn. New York: Schocken, 1991.

Caplan, Marvin. "'Raisins and Almonds'—Goldfaden's Glory." *Judaism* 42.2 (Spring 1993): 193–200.

Carmely, Klara P. *Das Identitätsproblem jüdischer Autoren im deutschen Sprachraum von der Jahrhundertwende bis zu Hitler.* Königstein: Scriptor Verlag, 1981.

Corngold, Stanley. *Franz Kafka: The Necessity of Form*. Ithaca, N.Y.: Cornell University Press, 1988.

———, trans. and ed. *The Metamorphosis by Franz Kafka*. 1972. New York: Bantam Books, 1986.

Dentan, Michel. *Humour et création littéraire dans l'oeuvre de Kafka*. Geneva: Droz and Minard, 1961.

Derrida, Jacques. *The Ear of the Other: Otobiography, Transference, Translation*. Ed. Christie McDonald. Trans. Peggy Kamuf. Lincoln: University of Nebraska Press, 1988.

Diamant, Kathi. *Kafka's Last Love: The Mystery of Dora Diamant*. New York: Basic Books, 2003.

DiRenzo, Anthony. "Golems, Scribes and Tzaddiks: Franz Kafka's Parabolic Paperwork." In *Kafka Kaleidoscope*. Ed. M. Wasserman. Delhi, N.Y.: Birch Brook Press, 1999. 17–38.

Dormer, Lore Muerdel. "Felix Salten." In *Major Figures of Turn-of-the-Century Austrian Literature*. Ed. Donald Daviau. Riverside, Calif.: Ariadne Press, 1991: 405–40.

Eisner, Pavel. *Franz Kafka and Prague*. Trans. Lowry Nelson and René Wellek. New York: Arts, Inc., 1950.

Elbogen, J., and J. Höniger. *Lehranstalt für die Wissenschaft des Judentums: Festschrift zur Einweihung des eigenen Heims*. Berlin: N.p., 1907.

Eliasberg, Alexander, ed. and trans. *Sagen polnischer Juden*. Munich: Georg Müller, 1916.

Eloni, Yehuda. *Zionismus in Deutschland: Von den Anfängen bis 1914*. Gerlingen: Bleicher Verlag, 1987.

Encyclopaedia Judaica. Jerusalem: Keter Publishing House, 1971.

Engel, Nelly. "Franz Kafka als 'boyfriend.'" In Koch, ed., *"Als Kafka,"* 112–20.

Fingerhut, Karlheinz. "Ein Beispiel produktiver Lektüreverarbeitung (Max Brods *Arnold Beer* und *Das Urteil*)." In Binder, ed., *Kafka Handbuch Bd. 2*. 278–82.

———. *Die Funktion der Tierfiguren im Werke Franz Kafkas*. Bonn: H. Bouvier & Co., 1969.

Flores, Angel. *The Kafka Debate*. New York: Gordian Press, 1977.

———, and H. Swander, eds. *Franz Kafka Today*. Madison: University of Wisconsin Press, 1964.

Fromer, Jakob. Introduction: "Der Organismus des Judentums." In *Der babylonische Talmud zur Herstellung einer Realkonkordanz vokalisiert*. Charlottenburg: Selbstverlag des Verfassers, 1909.

Gelber, Mark H., ed. *Kafka, Zionism, and Beyond*. Tübingen: Max Niemeyer Verlag, 2004.

Gilman, Sander. *Franz Kafka*. London: Reaktion Books, 2005.

———. *Franz Kafka: The Jewish Patient*. New York: Routledge, 1995.

———. *Jewish Self-Hatred: Anti-Semitism and the Hidden Language of the Jews*. Baltimore: Johns Hopkins University Press, 1986.

———. *The Jew's Body*. New York: Routledge, 1991.

Ginat, Jochanan. "Kurt Blumenfeld und der deutsche Zionismus." In *Im Kampf um den Zionismus*. By Kurt Blumenfeld. 7–37.
Glatzer, Nahum N. *The Loves of Franz Kafka*. New York: Schocken, 1986.
Goldenberg, Robert. "Talmud." In Holtz, ed., *Back to the Sources*. 129–75.
Goldfaden, Abraham. "Shulamith," in Sprengel, *Scheuenviertel-Theater: Jüdische Schauspieltruppen und Jiddische Dramatik in Berlin (1900–1918)*. Berlin: Fannei & Walz Verlag, 1995. 135–63.
Goldsmith, Arnold L. *The Golem Remembered, 1909–1980: Variations of a Jewish Legend*. Detroit: Wayne State University Press, 1981.
Goldstein, Bluma. "Franz Kafka's *Ein Landarzt:* A Study in Failure." *Deutsche Vierteljahresschrift für Literaturwissenschaft und Geistesgeschichte* 42 (1968): 745–59.
Gorion, Micha Josef bin. *Der Born Judas: Legenden, Märchen, Erzählungen*. Frankfurt: Jüdischer Verlag im Suhrkamp Verlag, 1993.
———. Foreword to the 1913 edition of *Die Sagen der Juden*. Frankfurt: Insel Verlag, 1962.
———. *Die Sagen der Juden: Von der Urzeit. Jüdische Sagen und Mythen*. Trans. Rahel Ramberg. 1913. Frankfurt: Rütten & Loening, 1919.
Goshen, S. "Zionist Students' Organizations." In *The Jews of Czechoslovakia*. 2:173–84.
Gotlober, A. B. "The Gilgul, or The Transmigration." In Neugroschel, ed., *Great Tales of Jewish Fantasy and the Occult*. 386–434.
Graetz, Heinrich. *Volkstümliche Geschichte der Juden*. Vols. 1–3. Berlin: R. Löwit Verlag, 1923.
Green, Arthur. "Teachings of the Hasidic Masters." In Holtz, ed., *Back to the Sources*. 361–401.
Greenberg, Clement. "At the Building of the Great Wall of China." In Flores and Swander, eds., *Franz Kafka Today*. 77–81.
Greenstein, Michael. "Breaking the Mosaic Code: Jewish Literature vs. the Law." *Mosaic* 27.3 (September 1994): 87–106.
Grözinger, Karl Erich. *Kafka and Kabbala*. Trans. Susan Hecker Ray. New York: Continuum, 1994. Originally published as *Kafka und die Kabbala: Das Jüdische in Werk und Denken von Franz Kafka*. Frankfurt: Eichborn Verlag, 1992.
———, et al., eds. *Kafka und das Judentum*. Frankfurt: Jüdischer Verlag bei Athenäum, 1987.
Grünberg, Abraham. *Ein jüdisch-polnisch-russisches Jubiläum: Der große Pogrom von Siedlce im Jahre 1906*. Prague: Grafia-Selbstverlag, 1916.
Hartman, G., and S. Budick, eds. *Midrash and Literature*. New Haven, Conn.: Yale University Press, 1986.
Heinemann, Joseph. "The Nature of the Aggadah." In Hartman and Budick, eds., *Midrash and Literature*. 41–55.
Herford, R. Travers, ed. and trans. *Pirke Aboth: The Ethics of the Talmud: Sayings of the Fathers*. Schocken: New York, 1962.
Hermes, Roger, Waltraud John, Hans-Gerd Koch, and Anita Widera, eds. *Franz Kafka: Eine Chronik*. Berlin: Verlag Klaus Wagenbach, 1999. Abbreviated in text as C.

Hertzberg, Arthur. *The Zionist Idea: A Historical Analysis and Reader*. Philadelphia: Jewish Publication Society, 1997.

Herzog, Andreas, ed. *Ost und West: Jüdische Publizistik 1901–1928*. Leipzig: Reclam, 1996.

Holitscher, Arthur. *Reise durch das jüdische Palästina*. Berlin: S. Fischer Verlag, 1922.

Holtz, Barry W., ed. *Back to the Sources: Reading the Classic Jewish Texts*. New York: Summit Books, 1984.

Homberger, Eric. "Some Uses for Jewish Ambivalence: Abraham Cahan and Michael Gold." In *Between "Race" and Culture: Representations of "the Jew" in English and American Literature*. Ed. Bryan Cheyette. Stanford: Stanford University Press, 1996.

Jaeger, Achim. "'Nichts Jüdisches wird uns fremd sein': Zur Geschichte der Prager 'Selbstwehr' (1907–1938)." *Aschkenaz: Zeitschrift für Geschichte und Kultur der Juden* 15.1 (2005): 151–207.

The Jews of Czechoslovakia. Ed. Society for the History of Czechoslovak Jews. Vols. 1 and 2. Philadelphia: The Jewish Publication Society of America, 1968–72.

Jofen, Jean. *The Jewish Mystic in Kafka*. New York: Peter Lang, 1987.

Das jüdische Volksheim Berlin. Erster Bericht (May–December 1916).

Kafka, Franz. *Beim Bau der chinesischen Mauer und andere Schriften aus dem Nachlaß in der Fassung der Handschrift*. Ed. Hans-Gerd Koch. Frankfurt: Fischer Taschenbuch Verlag, 1994. Abbreviated in text as BB.

———. *Beschreibung eines Kampfes und andere Schriften aus dem Nachlaß in der assung der Handschrift*. Ed. Hans-Gerd Koch. Frankfurt: Fischer Taschenbuch Verlag, 1994. Abbreviated in text as BK.

———. *Briefe, 1902–1924*. Ed. Max Brod. Frankfurt: Fischer, 1975. Abbreviated in text as Br.

———. *Brief an den Vater*. Frankfurt: Fischer, 1979. Abbreviated in text as BV.

———. *Briefe an Felice*. Ed. E. Heller and J. Born. Frankfurt: Fischer, 1976. Abbreviated in text as BF.

———. *Briefe an Milena*. Ed. Jürgen Born and Michael Müller. Frankfurt: Fischer Taschenbuch Verlag, 1986. Abbreviated in text as BM.

———. *Briefe an Ottla und die Familie*. Ed. H. Binder and K. Wagenbach. Frankfurt: Fischer, 1981. Abbreviated in text as BO.

———. *The Complete Stories*. Ed. Nahum N. Glatzer. New York: Schocken, 1971. Abbreviated in text as CS.

———. *Dearest Father: Stories and Other Writings*. Trans. Ernst Kaiser and Ethel Wilkins. New York: Schocken, 1954. Abbreviated in text as DF.

———. *Description of a Struggle and the Great Wall of China*. Ed. Edwin Muir. Trans. W. Muir, E. Muir, T. Stern, and J. Stern. London: Secker & Warburg, 1960.

———. *The Diaries of Franz Kafka, 1910–1913*. Ed. Max Brod. Trans. Joseph Kresh. New York: Schocken, 1948. Abbreviated in text as DI.

———. *The Diaries of Franz Kafka, 1914–1923*. Ed. Max Brod. Trans. Martin Greenberg, with Hannah Arendt. New York: Schocken, 1949. Abbreviated in text as DII.

——. *Erzählungen und andere ausgewählte Prosa*. Ed. Roger Hermes. Frankfurt: Fischer, 1996. Abbreviated in text as E.
——. *Hochzeitsvorbereitungen auf dem Lande und andere Prosa aus dem Nachlaß*. Ed. Max Brod. Frankfurt: Fischer, 1980. Abbreviated in text as H.
——. *Letters to Felice*. Ed. Erich Heller and Jürgen Born. Trans. James Stern and Elisabeth Duckworth. New York: Schocken, 1973. Abbreviated in text as LF.
——. *Letters to Friends, Family, and Editors*. Trans. Richard and Clara Winston. New York: Schocken, 1977. Abbreviated in text as LFF.
——. *Letters to Milena*. Trans. Philip Boehm. New York: Schocken, 1990. Abbreviated in text as LM.
——. *Letters to Ottla and the Family*. New York: Schocken, 1982. Abbreviated in text as LOF.
——. *Nachgelassene Schriften und Fragmente* II. Ed. Jost Schillemeit. Frankfurt: Fischer, 1992. Abbreviated in text as NII.
——. *Nachgelassene Schriften und Fragmente* II. Apparatband. Ed. Jost Schillemeit. Frankfurt: Fischer, 1992. Abbreviated in text as NIIA.
——. *Parables and Paradoxes*. Ed. Nahum Glatzer. 1935. New York: Schocken, 1983.
——. *Der Prozes*. Trans. Melech Ravitch. Illus. Yossl Bergner. New York: Der Kval, 1966.
——. *Der Proceß*. Roman in der Fassung der Handschrift. Frankfurt: Fischer, 1994.
——. *Shorter Works*. Vol. 1. Trans. and ed. Malcolm Pasley. London: Secker & Warburg, 1973.
——. *Tagebücher, 1910–1923*. Ed. Max Brod. 1948–49. Frankfurt: Fischer, 1976.
——. *Tagebücher in der Fassung der Handschrift*. Eds. Hans-Gerd Koch, Michael Müller and Malcolm Pasley. Frankfurt: Fischer, 1990. Abbreviated in text as T.
——. *Tagebücher in der Fassung der Handschrift: Kommentarband*. Eds. Hans-Gerd Koch, Michael Müller, and Malcolm Pasley. Frankfurt: Fischer, 1990. Abbreviated in text as K.
——. *The Trial*. Trans. Breon Mitchell. New York: Schocken, 1998.
——. *Wedding Preparations in the Country and Other Posthumous Prose Writings*. Trans. E. Kaiser and E. Wilkins. Notes by Max Brod. London: Secker & Warburg, 1954. Abbreviated in text as W.
——. *Zur Frage der Gesetze und andere Schriften aus dem Nachlaß in der Fassung der Handschrift*. Ed. Jost Schillemeit. Frankfurt: Fischer Taschenbuch Verlag, 1994. Abbreviated in text as Z.
Karl, Frederick. *Franz Kafka, Representative Man: Prague, Germans, Jews and the Crisis of Modernism*. New York: International Publishing, 1993.
Kauf, Robert. "Once Again: Kafka's 'A Report to an Academy.'" *Modern Language Quarterly* 15.4 (December 1954): 359–65.
Kaznelson, Siegmund. "Um jüdisches Volkstum: Zu Jakob Wassermanns Bekenntnisbuch." *Der Jude* 6.1 (1921–22): 49–52.
Kieval, Hillel. J. *The Making of Czech Jewry: National Conflict and Jewish Society in Bohemia, 1870–1918*. New York: Oxford Univ. Press, 1988. Abbreviated in text as CJ.

Klein, A. M. "Hemlock and Marijuana. Review of *In the Penal Colony: Stories and Short Pieces by Franz Kafka*" (17 December 1948). In *Literary Essays and Reviews*. Ed. Usher Caplan and M. W. Steinbery. Toronto: University of Toronto Press, 1987. 275–78.
Klier, John D., and Shlomo Lambroza, eds. *Pogroms: Anti-Jewish Violence in Modern Russian History*. Cambridge: Cambridge University Press, 1992.
Klingsberg, Reuben, ed. *Exhibition Franz Kafka, 1883–1924: Catalogue*. Jerusalem: Jewish National and University Library, 1969.
Koch, H. G., ed. *"Als Kafka mir entgegenkam . . .": Erinnerungen an Franz Kafka*. Berlin: Verlag Klaus Wagenbach, 1995.
Koelb, Clayton. "Kafka and the Sirens." In *The Comparative Perspective on Literature: Approaches to Theory and Practice*. Ed. C. Koelb and S. Noakes. Ithaca, N.Y.: Cornell University Press, 1988. 300–314.
———. *Kafka's Rhetoric: The Passion of Reading*. Ithaca, N.Y.: Cornell University Press, 1989.
Kohn, Hans. "Before 1918 in the Historic Lands." In *The Jews of Czechoslovakia*. 1:12–20.
———. "Das kulturelle Problem des modernen Westjuden." *Der Jude* 5 (1920–21): 281–97.
Kraus, Karl. *Die Fackel* 87 (26 Nov. 1901): 12–23.
———. "Eine Krone für Zion" (1899). In *Frühe Schriften. 1892–1900: Zweiter Band. 1897–1900*. Ed. Joh. J. Braakenburg. München: Kösel-Verlag, 1979. 298–314.
Kudela, Jiří. "Die Emigration galizischer und osteuropäischer Juden nach Böhmen und Prag zwischen 1914–1916/17." In *Studia Rosenthaliana*. Ed. M. P. Beukers and J. J. Cahen. Amsterdam: University Library of Amsterdam, Bibliotheca Rosenthaliana, 1989. 119–34.
Kurz, Gerhard. "Meinungen zur Schrift. Zur Exegese der Legende 'Vor dem Gesetz' im Roman 'Der Proceß.'" In Grözinger et al., eds., *Kafka und das Judentum*. 209–23.
———. *Traum-Schrecken: Kafkas literarische Existenzanalyse*. Stuttgart: Metzler, 1980.
Langer, Georg (Jiří). *Die Erotik der Kabbala*. 1923. Munich: Eugen Diederichs Verlag, 1989.
———. *Nine Gates to the Chassidic Mysteries*. Trans. Stephen Jolly. 1961. New York: Behrman House, 1976.
Lehnert, Salomon. "Jüdische Volksarbeit." *Der Jude* (1916–17): 104–11.
Levenson, Alan. "German Zionism and Radical Assimilation before 1914." *Studies in Zionism* 13.1 (1992): 21–41.
Leyen, Friedrich von der. *Deutsche Dichtung in neuer Zeit*. Jena: Eugen Diederichs, 1922.
Lichtheim, Richard. *Das Programm des Zionismus*. 1911. Berlin: Zionistische Vereinigung für Deutschland, 1913.
Linetski, Isaac Joel. *The Polish Lad*. Trans. Moshe Spiegel. Philadelphia: Jewish Publication Society of America, 1975.
Luke, F. D. "Kafka's *Die Verwandlung*." *Modern Language Review* 46 (1951): 232–45.
Maimon, Salomon. *Salomon Maimons Lebensgeschichte* (1792). Ed. Jakob Fromer. Munich: Georg Müller, 1911.

Mandelstamm, Max. "Eine Ghettostimme über den Zionismus." In *Separatabzug aus "Ost und West"* [*Illustrierte Monatszeitschrift für modernes Judentum*]. Ed. Berliner Zionistische Vereinigung. Berlin: Verlag S. Calvary & Co., 1901. 1–14.

Massino, Guido. "Franz Kafka, *Der Meshumed* by Abraham Sharkansky and *Elisha ben Avuyah* by Jakob Gordin." *Journal of the Kafka Society of America* 1.2 (June–December 1996): 30–41.

———. *Fuoco Inestinguibile: Franz Kafka, Jizchak Löwy e il teatro yiddish polacco*. Rome: Bulzoni Editore, 2002.

Mauriac, Claude. "Des lettres d'amour signées Kafka." *Preuves* 69 (November 1956): 72–75.

Max Brod, Franz Kafka: Eine Freundschaft. Bd. 1, Reiseaufzeichnungen. Ed. Malcolm Pasley. Frankfurt: Fischer, 1987. Abbreviated in text as BKR.

Max Brod, Franz Kafka: Eine Freundschaft. Bd. 2, Briefwechsel. Ed. Malcolm Pasley. Frankfurt: Fischer, 1989. Abbreviated in text as BKB.

Meng, Weiyan. *Kafka und China*. Munich: Judicium, 1986.

Milfull, John. "The Messiah and the Direction of History: Walter Benjamin, Isaac Bashevis Singer and Franz Kafka." In *Festschrift für E. W. Herd*. Ed. August Obermayer. Dunedin, New Zealand: Department of German, University of Otago, 1980. 180–87.

Moaus Zur: Ein Chanukkahbuch. Ed. S. J. Agnon and Hugo Herrmann. Berlin: Jüdischer Verlag, 1918.

Mosès, Stéphane. "Franz Kafka: 'The Silence of the Sirens.'" *University of Denver Quarterly* 2.2 (Summer 1976): 62–78.

Mosse, George. "Max Nordau and His Degeneration." In *Degeneration*. By Max Nordau. Lincoln: University of Nebraska Press, 1993. xiii–xxxvi.

Moykher-Sforim, Mendele. *The Mare*. In Neugroschel, ed., *Great Tales of Jewish Fantasy and the Occult*. 545–663.

Müller-Seidel, Walter. *Die Deportation des Menschen: Kafkas Erzählung "In der Strafkolonie" im europäischen Kontext*. Frankfurt: Fischer, 1986.

Murray, Jack. *The Landscapes of Alienation: Ideological Subversion in Kafka, Céline, and Onetti*. Stanford: Stanford University Press, 1991.

Murray, Nicholas. *Kafka*. New Haven, Conn.: Yale University Press, 2004.

Nakazawa, Hideo. "Über Die Chinesische Mauer." Available at http://deutsch.c.u-tokyo.ac.jp/~nakazawa/Kafka/china.pdf. Paper for *Chinesisch-japanisches Germanistentreffen: Dokumentation der Tagungsbeiträge*, Beijing 1990. First published: Beijing: International Culture Publishing, 1994.

Nekula, Marek. *Franz Kafkas Sprachen*. Tübingen: Max Niemeyer Verlag, 2003.

Neugroschel, Joachim, ed. and trans. *Great Tales of Jewish Fantasy and the Occult*. Woodstock, N.Y.: Overlook Press, 1976.

Northey, Anthony. "Julie Wohryzek, Franz Kafkas zweite Verlobte." *Freibeuter* (April 1994): 2–16.

———. "Die Kafkas: Juden? Christen? Tschechen? Deutsche?" In *Kafka und Prag*. Ed. Kurt Krolop and H.-D. Zimmermann. Berlin: Walter de Gruyter, 1994. 11–32.

———. *Kafka's Relatives: Their Lives and His Writing*. New Haven, Conn.: Yale University Press, 1991.
Oppenheimer, Anne. "Franz Kafka's Relation to Judaism." Ph.D. diss. Oxford University, 1977.
Palästina-Heft der "Welt" 14.41–42 (17 October 1910).
Palästina: Monatsschrift für die Erschließung Palästinas (Vienna) 9.7–8 (1 August 1912).
Pasley, J. Malcolm S. "In the Penal Colony." In Flores, ed. *The Kafka Debate*. 298–303.
———. "Semi-Private Games." In Flores, ed., *The Kafka Debate*. 188–205.
———. "Two Literary Sources of Kafka's 'Der Prozess.'" *Forum for Modern Language Studies* 3.2 (April 1967): 142–47.
Pawel, Ernst. "Franz Kafkas Judentum." In Grözinger et al., eds., *Kafka und das Judentum*. 253–58.
———. "Kafka's Hebrew Teacher." *The American Zionist* 74.1 (Oct./Nov. 1985): 21–22.
———. *The Nightmare of Reason*. New York: Farrar, Straus & Giroux, 1984.
Peretz, Isaac Leib. "Cabalists." In *A Treasury of Yiddish Stories*. Ed. Irving Howe and Eliezer Greenberg. New York: Schocken, 1973. 219–23.
———. *Volkstümliche Erzählungen*. Berlin: Jüdischer Verlag, 1913.
Petr, Pavel. *Kafkas Spiele: Selbststilisierung und literarische Komik*. Heidelberg: Carl Winter Universitätsverlag, 1992.
Pinès, Meyer Isser. *L'Histoire de la littérature judéo-allemande*. Paris: Jouve, 1911.
Politzer, Heinz. *Kafka: Parable and Paradox*. 1962. Ithaca, N.Y.: Cornell University Press, 1966.
Purdy, Strother B. "A Talmudic Analogy to Kafka's Parable *Vor dem Gesetz*." *Papers on Language and Literature* 4.4 (1968): 420–27.
Rabinowicz, Aharon Moshe. "The Jewish Minority." In *The Jews of Czechoslovakia*. 1:155–265.
Rath, Moses. *Lehrbuch der Hebräischen Sprache für Schul- und Selbstunterricht: Mit Schlüssel und Wörterverzeichnis*. 3d ed. Vienna: Selbstverlag des Autors, 1918.
Reinharz, Jehuda. "Martin Buber's Impact on German Zionism before World War I." *Studies in Zionism* 6 (Autumn 1982): 171–83.
Robbins, Jill. "Kafka's Parables." In Hartman and Budick, eds., *Midrash and Literature*. 265–84.
Robert, Marthe. *As Lonely as Franz Kafka*. Trans. Ralph Mannheim. 1979. New York: Schocken, 1986.
———. "Une figure de Whitechapel: Notes inédites de Dora Dymant sur Kafka." *Evidences* 4.28 (1952): 38–42.
Robertson, Ritchie. "Antizionismus, Zionismus: Kafka's Responses to Jewish Nationalism." In *Paths and Labyrinths: Nine Papers Read at the Kafka Symposium Held at the Institute of Germanic Studies on 20 and 21 October 1983*. London: University of London, 1985. 25–42.
———. *Kafka: Judaism, Politics and Literature*. Oxford: Clarendon Press, 1985.
———. "Western Observers and Eastern Jews." *The Modern Language Review* 83.1 (January 1988): 87–105.
Robin, Régine. *Kafka*. Paris: Pierre Belfond, 1989.

Rosenberg, Yudl. "The Golem, or The Miraculous Deeds of Rabbi Liva" (1809). In Neugroschel, ed. and trans., *Great Tales of Jewish Fantasy and the Occult*. 162–225.

Rozenblit, Marsha. *Reconstructing a National Identity: The Jews of Habsburg Austria during World War I*. Oxford: Oxford University Press, 2001.

Rubinstein, William C. "A Report to an Academy." In Flores and Swander, eds., *Franz Kafka Today*. 55–60.

Rybar, Citibor. *Jewish Prague*. Prague: TV Spektrum, 1991.

Sabar, Shalom. "Synagogue Interior Decoration and the Halakhah." In *Synagogues Without Jews*. Ed. Rivka Dorfman and Ben-Zion Dorfman. Philadelphia: The Jewish Publication Society, 2000. 308–17.

Sandbank, Shimon. *After Kafka: The Influence of Kafka's Fiction*. Athens: University of Georgia Press, 1989.

Scheer, Regina. *AHAWAH: Das Vergessene Haus: Spurensuche in der Berliner Auguststrasse*. Berlin: Aufbau Verlag, 1992.

Scholem, Gershom G. *From Berlin to Jerusalem: Memoirs of My Youth*. Trans. Harry Zohn. Schocken: New York, 1980.

———. *Major Trends in Jewish Mysticism*. New York: Schocken, 1954.

———. "Walter Benjamin and His Angel." In *On Walter Benjamin: Critical Essays and Recollections*. Ed. Gary Smith. Cambridge, Mass.: MIT Press, 1988. 51–89.

———. *Walter Benjamin: The Story of a Friendship*. Trans. Harry Zohn. 1975. Philadelphia: Jewish Publication Society of America, 1981.

———, ed. *The Correspondence of Walter Benjamin and Gershom Scholem, 1932–1940*. Trans. Gary Smith and Andre Lefevere. Cambridge, Mass.: Harvard University Press, 1992.

Schwartz, Howard, ed. *Gates to the New City: A Treasury of Modern Jewish Tales*. New York: Avon, 1983.

Selbstwehr [Independent Jewish weekly, Prague]. Abbreviated in text as S.

Shapira, Anita. "Anti-Semitism and Zionism." *Modern Judaism* 15.3 (October 1995): 215–32.

Shedletzky, Itta. "Im Spannungsfeld Heine-Kafka: Deutsch-jüdische Belletristik und Literaturdiskussion zwischen Emanzipation, Assimilation und Zionismus." In *Auseinandersetzungen um jiddische Sprache und Literatur: Jüdische Komponenten in der deutschen Literatur—die Assimilationskontroverse*. Ed. Walter Röll and Hans-Peter Bayersdörfer. Tübingen: Max Niemeyer Verlag, 1986. 113–21.

Shulman, Abraham. *New Country: Jewish Immigrants in America*. New York: Scribner, 1967.

Simon, Maurice. Introduction to *Berakot: Hebrew-English Edition of the Babylonian Talmud*. Ed. Rabbi Dr. I. Epstein. London: Soncino Press, 1960.

Sinclair, Clive. "Kafka's Hebrew Teacher." *Encounter* 64.3 (1985): 46–49.

Singer, Isaac Bashevis. "A Friend of Kafka." In *The Collected Stories of Isaac Bashevis Singer*. New York: Farrar, Straus & Giroux, 1982. 277–86.

Singer, Miriam. "Hebräischstunden mit Kafka." In Koch, ed., *"Als Kafka."* 140–43.

Sokel, Walter. "Language and Truth in the Two Worlds of Franz Kafka." *German Quarterly* 52 (1979): 364–84.

Sole, Aryeh. "Subcarpathian Ruthenia: 1918–1938." In *The Jews of Czechoslovakia*. 1:125–54.
Spann, Meno. *Franz Kafka*. Boston: Twayne, 1976.
Spector, Scott. *Prague Territories: National Conflict and Cultural Innovation in Franz Kafka's Fin-de Siècle*. Berkeley: University of California Press, 2000.
Sprengel, Peter. *Scheunenviertel-Theater: Jüdische Schauspieltruppen und Jiddische Dramatik in Berlin (1900–1918)*. Berlin: Fannei & Walz Verlag, 1995.
Stach, Reiner. *Kafka: Die Jahre der Entscheidungen*. Frankfurt: Fischer, 2002.
Starobinski, Jean. "Kafka's Judaism." *European Judaism* 8.2 (1974): 27–29.
Steiner, George. "K." In *Language and Silence*. New York: Atheneum, 1970. 118–26.
Stenographisches Protokoll der Verhandlungen des XI: Zionisten-Kongresses in Wien vom 2. bis 9. September 1913. Ed. Zionistisches Aktionskomitee. Berlin: Jüdischer Verlag, 1914.
Stern, David. "Midrash." In *Contemporary Jewish Religious Thought*. Ed. Arthur A. Cohen and Paul Mendes-Flohr. New York: Scribner, 1987. 613–20.
———. "Midrash and Indeterminacy." *Critical Inquiry* 15 (Autumn 1988): 132–61.
———. *Parables in Midrash: Narrative and Exegesis in Rabbinic Literature*. Cambridge, Mass.: Harvard University Press, 1991.
Stölzl, Christoph. *Kafkas böses Böhmen: Zur Sozialgeschichte eines Prager Juden*. Munich: Text & kritik, 1975.
———. "Prag." In Binder, ed., *Kafka Handbuch*. 40–100.
Strunge, Margaret, and Karl Kassenbrock, eds. *Masematte: Das Leben und die Sprache der Menschen in Münsters vergessenen Vierteln*. Münster: im Selbstverlag, 1980.
Sussman, Henry S. *Franz Kafka: Geometrician of Metaphor*. Madison, Wis.: Coda Press, 1979.
Terdiman, Richard. *Discourse/Counter-Discourse: The Theory and Practice of Symbolic Resistance in Nineteenth-Century France*. Ithaca, N.Y.: Cornell University Press, 1985.
Thieberger, Friedrich. "Erinnerungen an Franz Kafka." *Eckhart* 23 (October 1953): 49–53.
———. "Kafka und die Thiebergers." In Koch, ed., *"Als Kafka."* 121–27.
Tismar, Jens. "Kafka's *Schakale und Araber* im zionistischen Kontext betrachtet." *Jahrbuch der deutschen Schillergesellschaft* 19 (1975): 306–23.
A Treasury of Yiddish Stories. Ed. Irving Howe and Eliezer Greenberg. New York: Schocken, 1973.
Trietsch, Davis. *Palaestina Handbuch*. Berlin: Verlag Benjamin Harz, 1922.
Vaněk, Zdenko. "Erinnerungen eines Mitschülers." In Koch, ed., *"Als Kafka."* 37–38.
Verein jüdischer Hochschüler Bar Kochba in Prag, ed. *Vom Judentum: Ein Sammelbuch*. Leipzig: K. Wolff, 1913.
Vilimkova, Milada. *Die Prager Judenstadt*. Trans. Tomanova-Weisova. Prague: Aventinum, 1990.
Wagenbach, Klaus. *Franz Kafka: Eine Biographie seiner Jugend, 1883–1912*. Bern: Francke Verlag, 1958.
———. *Franz Kafka: In der Strafkolonie: Eine Geschichte aus dem Jahr 1914*. Berlin: Verlag Klaus Wagenbach, 1975.

———. *Franz Kafka in Selbstzeugnissen und Bilddokumenten.* 1964. Reinbeck: Rowohlt, 1976.

Wagnerová, Alena. *Die Familie Kafka aus Prag.* Frankfurt: Fischer, 1997.

Wambach, Lovis M. *Ahasver und Kafka: Zur Bedeutung der Judenfeindschaft in dessen Leben und Werk.* Heidelberg: Universitätsverlag C. Winter, 1993.

Weinberg, Kurt. *Kafkas Dichtungen: Die Travestien eines Mythos.* Bern: Francke Verlag, 1963.

Weinberg, Robert. "The Pogrom of 1905 in Odessa: A Case Study." In Klier and Lambroza, eds., *Pogroms.* 248–89.

Weiner, Hannah. "Gershom Scholem and the Jung Juda Youth Group in Berlin, 1913–1918." *Studies in Zionism* 5.1 (1984): 29–42.

Weinstein, Leo. "Kafka's Ape: Heel or Hero." *Modern Fiction Studies* 8 (1962–63): 75–79.

Weltsch, Felix. "Franz Kafkas Geschichtsbewußtsein." In *Deutsches Judentum: Aufstieg und Krise.* Ed. Robert Weltsch. Stuttgart: Deutsche Verlags-Anstalt, 1963. 271–88.

Wetscherek, Hugo, ed. *Kafkas letzter Freund: Der Nachlaß Robert Klopstock, 1899–1972.* Vienna: Inlibris, 2003. Abbreviated in text as KF.

White, I. A., and J. J. White. "Blumfeld, an Elderly Bachelor." In Flores, ed., *The Kafka Debate.* 354–66.

Zemach, Shlomo. *Jüdische Bauern: Geschichten aus dem neuen Palästina.* Vienna: R. Löwit Verlag, 1919.

Ziegler, Ignaz. *Die Geistesreligion und das jüdische Religionsgesetz: Ein Beitrag zur Erneuerung des Judentums.* Berlin: Georg Reimer, 1912.

Zilcosky, John. *Kafka's Travels: Exoticism, Colonialism, and the Traffic of Writing.* New York: Palgrave, 2003.

Zischler, Hanns. *Kafka geht ins Kino.* Reinbeck: Rowohlt, 1996.

Zweig, Arnold. *Ritualmord in Ungarn.* Berlin: Hyperionverlag, 1914.

Index

Abramovitsh, Shalom Yakov (S.Y.). *See* Sforim, Mendele Mokher
Adorno, Theodor W., 162, 230n.21
aggadah, 9, 93, 103, 107, 110, 183, 184, 190, 225n.57
Agnon, S. Y., vii
agricultural schools, 168, 181–82
Ahad Ha'am (Asher Ginsberg), 4, 21, 189; and Bialik, 58; and cultural Zionism, 22, 23, 24, 28, 65, 69–70, 113–14
Aleichem, Sholom (Sholem Rabinovitsh), 40, 44, 52, 53, 123, 175; *The Bloody Hoax*, 60
Allenby, Field Marshal Edmund, 172
am ha aretz, 99, 102, 104, 224n.43
Anders, Günter, 7
anti-Semitism, 16–20, 57–64, 126, 138–64, 200; and Jewish nationalism, 135; and "Rozhinkes mit Mandlen," 97; stereotypes, 32, 132, 154, 155, 157, 160, 196; and Zionism 29, 76, 214n.36
Arabs, 154–56, 185–88; racism, 187; riots, 173, 182, 187; Western Zionist perception of, 187
Arnstein, Erwin, 174, 175
Asch, Sholem, 123, 227n.24

assimilation, 63, 133, 197, 202; and Lily Braun, 126, 127; Czech, 173; *Die Jüdinnen*, 30; and Kafka's family, 15, 35; and Kraus, 145–47; in "Die Legende von Theodor Herzl," 80; and Nordau, 154; in "A Report to an Academy," 127, 130–37; as threat, 150; and Wassermann, 144–45, 146, 147; Zionist critique of, 29–31, 73, 133, 135, 156

Baal Shem Tov, 86
Baeck, Leo, 176, 182
Baioni, Giuliano, 7, 8, 45, 148, 210n.16
Balfour Declaration, 75, 172, 173, 185, 186, 187, 188
Band, Arnold, 57
Barissia (militant Zionist student organization in Prague), 22, 23, 71
Bar Kochba (Zionist student organization in Prague), 17, 20, 21, 22, 23–24, 26, 70, 71, 72, 73, 77, 144, 216n.17; and Yiddish theater, 34, 41, 44, 49
Barol, Moses, 183
Bauer, Felice, vii, 3, 5, 24, 25, 49, 74, 125, 217n.24; and Berlin Jewish People's Home, 119–24; engagement

Bauer, Felice (*continued*)
to Kafka, 73, 166; and Palestine, 69, 72; and Rosh Hashanah, 91; and Yiddish actors, 48
Baum, Oskar, 11, 44, 144, 197, 201; *Evil Innocence,* 60–61, 160
Beck, Evelyn Torton, 49, 215n.10, 216n.11
Beilis, Menahem Mendel, ritual murder trial of, 57–60, 61, 63, 139, 204
Belzer, rabbi of, 85, 86, 87, 89–90
Ben Bag Bag, 102, 104
Ben Dov, Ya'kov, *Schiwath Zion* (film), 173
Benjamin, Walter, 5, 8, 9, 98, 110, 190–92, 200, 205; "angel of history," 153
Ben Tovim, Puah, 177, 179, 180, 197
Ben Tovim, Salman, 179
Berdyczewski, Micha Josef (bin Gorion): and cultural Zionism, 4, 24, 113–14, 120, 123, 188, 189, 202, 203; *The Legends of the Jews,* 72, 93, 107, 108; *The Well of Juda,* 94
Bergmann, Else, 22, 73, 78, 180, 181
Bergmann, Hugo, 11, 17, 20, 41, 71, 76, 79, 91, 201–2, 203; and cultural Zionism, 4, 21–22, 23–24, 123, 128; emigration to Palestine, 70, 71, 172, 179, 180; "Jawne and Jerusalem," 113–15, 188, 189; *Jawne und Jerusalem,* 167; "Moses and the Present," 77
Bialik, Chaim Nachman, 44; and Ahad Ha'am, 58; "In the City of Slaughter," 40, 58
Binder, Hartmut, 12, 14, 15, 16, 19, 20, 21, 23, 25, 29, 30, 44, 49, 73, 77, 78, 79, 82, 143, 144, 149, 158, 166, 169, 172, 177, 179, 182, 184, 193, 221n.3
Birnbaum, Nathan (Mathias Acher), 4, 21, 175; and Ahad Ha'am, 22; and diaspora nationalism, 65; and evening of Jewish Folksongs, 43–44, 65–66; idealizations of Yiddish culture, 36, 66; and Kadimah, 65

Blau-Weiss (Blue-White, Jewish Youth Organization), 81, 117; 169; and homoeroticism, 148; song book, 122
Bloch, Chajim, Hasidic tales by, 90–91, 92–93, 222n.11
Bloch, Grete, 80
Bloch, Hans, 80, 220n.28; "The Legend of Theodor Herzl," 80–81, 82, 104, 156, 220n.29
Blumenfeld, Kurt, 67–68, 81, 221n.31
Blüher, Hans, 148–49, 229n.9; *The Role of the Erotic in Male Society,* 148; *Secessio Judaica,* 146, 148–53
Bodenheimer, Alfred, 165, 233n.37
Bokhove, Niels, 75, 168, 172, 183, 198
Böhm, Adolf, 29, 69–70, 189, 214n.36
Braun, Lily, 124–30; animal imagery, 127; *Memoirs of a Female Socialist,* 121, 124–25, 168; sexism, 125–26, 127, 129–30, 227n.33
Bregman, Ahron, 171, 180, 185, 186
Brenner, Josef Chajim, 182, 233n.41; *Barrenness and Failure,* 182
Brod, Elsa, 78, 136
Brod, Max, vii, 4, 5, 9, 11, 13, 19, 22, 36, 59, 85, 91, 92, 94, 113, 124, 138, 143, 144, 150, 181, 201; and Ahad Ha'am and Herzl, 24; *Arnold Beer,* 35, 36, 78, 79, 80; and Bar Kochba, 23, 24–25, 29; and Buber, 28, 93; *Die Jüdinnen,* 30–33, 35, 57, 78; *Eine Königin Esther,* 140; estrangement with Kafka, 77; and ethical Zionism, 123, 203; evening with Felice Bauer, 48, 69; and Hasidism, 119; Hebrew lessons with Kafka, 165, 166, 167; on humor in *The Trial,* 100; and Jewish elementary school, 173, 174; and Jewish refugees, 117, 197; and Jewish refugee school, 115, 118, 119; on Kafka and jokes, 221n.5; on Kafka's "Report to an Academy," 130, 134; and Lese- und Redehalle, 17, 20, 21; Lichtheim's *The Zionist Agenda,* 73; Lily Braun's *Memoirs of a*

Index   255

Female Socialist, 125; and Löwy, 49, 50; "Religion and Nation" (lecture), 86, 118; religious fanaticism of, 89; religious upbringing of, 14, 15, 135; *Rëubeni,* 177; selection criteria for Kafka's stories, 106–7; *Socialism in Zionism,* 171; on situation in Palestine, 172; "The Third Phase of Zionism," 3, 169; *Tycho Brahe,* 146; on "Workers without Possessions," 170; and Yiddish theater, 34, 41; reaction to Zionist critique of *Die Jüdinnen,* 30–33, 57

Buber, Martin, 4, 21, 22, 30, 33, 35, 36, 56, 65, 66, 71, 80, 88, 92, 185; *Der Jude* (The Jew), 23, 49, 130, 168, 169, 170; "Drei Reden über das Judentum" (Three Lectures on Judaism), 23, 24, 25, 28, 29, 214n.32; *The Great Maggid and His Successors,* 93; Hasidic tales by, 72–73, 92, 93, 99, 122; on "Jewish Myth" (lecture), 72–73; and Jewish People's Home, 119; at Third Zionist Congress (1899), 24

Caplan, Marvin, 96, 97
Cassel, David, 182
Central Association for the Preservation of Jewish Affairs, 19, 59, 117–18
Chagall, Marc, 160, 194, 195
Chamisso, Adalbert, 123
Chaplin, Charlie, 95
colonialism, 63, 68, 123, 227n.26
Corngold, Stanley, 95, 101, 110–11
circumcision, 35, 43, 136
Czech anti-Semitism, 60, 142–44
Czech National Theater, 39; contrasted with German theater, 43

Damaschke, Adolf, *Die Bodenreform* (Land Reform), 168
Darwin, Charles, 131
Deganya, 172, 231n.9
Derrida, Jacques, 111, 205
Diamant, Dora, 5, 10, 137, 180, 181, 182, 183, 184; Hebrew studies, 181; influence of Clara Zetkin and Theodor Herzl, 181
Diamant, Kathi, 181, 182, 184
Diaspora, 4, 21, 24, 28, 65, 80, 81, 107, 197, 202, 224n.52, 230n.14; and cultural Zionism, 113–15; Zionist satire of, 137, 154, 156, 185–88; Zionist satire of, in "Jackals and Arabs," 205. See also *Galuth*
Dick, Aisik Meier, 52
Dickens, Charles, 123
Dienesohn, Jacob, 52
discourses, 194; anti-Semitic, 32, 136, 196, 200, 204, 205; borderline (Zionist and anti-Semitic), 135, 148, 150; counterdiscourse, 11, 157, 194, 200, 204, 205, 206, 210n.21; Expressionist, 80; Jewish, 200, 202, 204; Kafkaesque, 61; Mauscheln, 137, 147, 197; racial, 8, 80, 195; Talmudic, 9, 91, 92, 94, 149, 222n.8 (*see also* Midrash); Talmudic, in "Investigations of a Dog," 191; Talmudic, in *The Trial,* 99–105; *völkisch,* 195, 235n.59; Yiddishisms, 87, 93; Zionist, 30–33, 58, 80, 82, 195
Don Quixote, 102, 107, 151
Dreyfus Affair, 18, 19, 20, 61, 63

Eastern European Judaism, 6, 7, 16, 33, 42, 88–90, 118–19, 128, 130, 131, 157, 162; and Africa, 130; "authentic" Judaism, 34, 128; prayer service, 89, 118–19, 226n.14; prejudice against, 45, 187, 205; realistic depiction of, in *Arnold Beer,* 36, 42, 54–56, 88; refugees, 49, 116–24, 130, 174, 181, 197, 225n.11; romanticized, 9, 65, 66; West needs East, 120–22; West needs East, in contrast to refugees, 118–19, 197, 227n.32
Ehrenfels, Christian von, 66–67
Ehrenstein, Albert, 73

Ehrentreu, Chanoch Heinrich, 44
Einstein, Albert, 68
Eisner, Minze, 125, 168, 235n.64
Eliasberg, Alexander, *Tales of Polish Jews,* 93
Engel, Alfred, 118
Enlightenment, 6, 26, 28, 44, 45, 47, 80, 126, 132, 202; anti-Enlightenment, 73; caricature of German Enlightenment in "A Report to an Academy," 130–32; Kafka and Lily Braun, 126; and Nordau, 154. *See also* Haskalah
Eysoldt, Gertrud, 72, 93

Fackel, Die, 26, 145, 147
Feder, Richard, 175, 176, 232n.26
Feigl, Ernst, 169
Feinmann, Sigmund: *Der Vitse-kenig* (play), 37; *Vicekönig* (Viceroy, play), 43
Feiwel, Berthold, 21, 22
feminism: and Academy of Jewish Studies, 182; and Kafka, 129; role of women in Judaism, 116, 125; and Zionism, 124–30
Fingerhut, Karlheinz, 79
Flaubert, Gustave, 33, 136, 137
Foerster, F. W., 122
fraternities and student organizations. *See* Bar Kochba; Barissia; Germania; Lese- und Redehalle der deutschen Studenten in Prag (Reading and Lecture Group of German Students in Prague); Lese- und Redehalle der jüdischen Hochschüler in Prag (Reading and Lecture Group of Jewish Students in Prague)
Freud, Sigmund, 29, 87, 136, 148, 149
Frischmann, David, 44, 46
Fromer, Jakob: "The Organism of Judaism," 50, 102, 216n.14; *Salomon Maimon's Life History,* 51
Frug, Samuel, 44, 46, 52
Fuchs, Rudolf, 169

Galuth (exile), 114–15, 189. *See also* Diaspora
Gegenwartsarbeit (work in the present), 21–22
Geiger, Abraham, 182
Germania (nationalist German student organization), 16, 20, 21
Gilman, Sander, 7–8, 136, 151; anti-Semitic discourse, 32, 107; on Blüher, 148, 149; on Christian von Ehrenfels, 66–67; Dreyfus affair, 18, 61; on "A Fratricide," 158; on "Jackals and Arabs," 155, 157; Otherness, 125, 133–34
Ginat, Jochanan, 68
Glatzer, Nahum, 106–8, 184
Goethe, Johann Wolfgang von, 40, 53, 159, 160
Goldfaden, Abraham, 37, 40, 52, 53, 96; *Bar Kochba* (play), 37, 41, 96; *Shulamith* (play), 37, 39, 43, 48, 96
Golem, legend of the, 13, 92, 94, 105–6
Gordin, Jakob, 52, 53, 216n.15; *Elisha ben Abuyah* (play), 37, 40, 54, 216n.14; *Got, mensh un tayvel* (play), 37, 40, 48, 54; *Di Shkhite* (play), 37, 42, 54; *Der vilder mensh* (play), 37, 40, 215n.8
Gordon, Aharon D., 133, 171–72, 228n.38
Gorion, Micha Josef bin. *See* Berdyczewski, Micha Josef
Gotlober, A. B., 95
Graetz, Heinrich, 50
Greek mythology: Homer, 33, 108–12, 118; Pallas, 158; Prometheus, 159
Greenberg, Clement, 107
Greenstein, Michael, 100
Grodek, rabbi of, 86, 89, 119
Grözinger, 16, 91
Grün, Nathan, 14, 212n.10
Grünberg, Abraham, 117, 138, 164; *A Jewish-Polish-Russian Jubilee,* 139
Grünthal, Julius, 183
Guttmann, Julius, 182, 183

Haas, Willy, 6, 229n.12
Ha-Auel (The Tent, Jewish monthly), 170
halakha, 9, 101, 110, 183, 190, 192, 194, 225n.57
Hamsun, Knut, 203
Ha-Poel haTzair (The Young Worker, political party), 171
Hasidism, 54–55, 85, 86, 88–89, 98, 122, 130, 177, 178, 201; Hasidic songs, 44, 196
Haskalah (Jewish Enlightenment), 7, 44, 52, 54, 97; anti-Haskalah, 51; Haskalah motto, 133 (see also Gordon, Aharon D.)
Hebrew language, 14, 77, 78, 115, 116, 122, 170, 180, 183, 203; and Felice Bauer, 69; Hebrew literature, 46, 85, 179; Hebrew script in "In the Penal Colony," 63; at Zionist Congress, 75, 76
Hebrew University of Jerusalem, 76
Heine, Heinrich, 46, 53
Hermann, Elli (née Kafka), 174
Hermann, Felix (Kafka's nephew), 35, 43, 119, 174, 175
Hermann, Gerty (Kafka's niece), 175
Herrmann, Hugo, 23, 30, 31, 32, 35, 42, 57, 78
Herrmann, Leo, 22, 23, 25, 30; as editor of Selbstwehr (1910–13), 24
Herzl, Theodor, 4, 22, 23, 24, 26, 65, 70, 71, 74, 75, 80, 134, 156, 175, 181, 185, 186, 193, 202, 205, 235n.58; The Jewish State, 78, 198; Old-New Land, 69, 187
Herzliya Gymnasium, 70–71, 74, 76
Hilsner, Leopold, ritual murder trial of, 18, 19, 20, 229n.12
Hindus, Milton, 55
Hochschule für die Wissenschaft des Judentums (Academy of Jewish Studies), 182–84, 189, 197, 198, 234n.43
Holitscher, Arthur, 150, 187, 202–3, 229n.9

Holtz, Barry, 101
Homberger, Eric, 204
homoeroticism: Blüher, 148, 149; Kafka and Löwy, 39; Langer, 87, 178

Ibsen, Henrik, 127
Israelitische Kultusgemeinde [IKG] (Jewish Central Community), 117

Jabotinsky, Vladimir, 58, 173
Janouch, Gustav, 11, 211n.22
Jeiteles, Jonas, 175
Jerusalem, 175, 179, 180
Jesenskà, Milena, 140, 152, 193, 194; "The Devil at the Hearth," 6, 151–53
Jew is Guilty, The, 150
Jewish anti-Semitism, 29, 134, 135
Jewish Civil Servants' Club, 77
Jewish education, 76, 115–24, 128, 135, 188, 195; Prague Jewish elementary school, 173–77, 232n.18, 232n.26, 232n.27; Prague refugee school, 118, 119, 132, 226n.13; stereotypical gender roles in Jewish People's Home, 120, 129
Jewish music: Eastern European prayer services, 235n.62; in "Josephine the Singer," 196–97; "Rozhinkes mit Mandlen" (Yiddish song), 96–97; Yiddish songs, 34, 36, 37, 39, 43, 65, 66, 196
Jewish mysticism, 98, 103, 177, 189, 192
Jewish National Fund, 74; and Kafka, 168
Jewish novel, 30–33, 78–79
Jewish People's Home in Berlin, 119–24, 130, 132, 135, 180–81
Jewish People's Home in Prague, 124
Jewish self-hatred, 127; in Brod, 140–41; by Kafka, 140–41, 147, 149, 152–53, 210n.12; in "Report to an Academy," 131, 133–35; in Zweig, 138–39
Jofen, Jean, 7

Jude, Der (journal), 11; and Kafka, 156, 170, 173; Kafka published in, 82, 130, 154, 168–69, 185
Jüdische Echo, Das, 92, 93, 173
jüdische Prag, Das (The Jewish Prague), 79
Jüdische Rundschau, 138
Jüdischer Volksverein (Jewish People's Club), 86

Kabbala, 87, 99, 103, 177, 192; Kabbalistic literature, 85, 86, 94, 177; and Kafka, 188, 194
Kafka, Franz: agriculture, interest in, 167–68, 179, 181–82, 189; at Academy of Jewish Studies, 182–84, 197; celebrates Sabbath with children and Dora, 181, 184; as *chaluz* [pioneer]), 177; loves Chajim Bloch's Hasidic tales, 90–91, 92-93; dates in Palestine, 5; dreams of emigrating to Palestine, 153, 177, 184, 204; dislikes Buber's Hasidic tales, 73, 93; encourages friends to emigrate to Palestine, 49, 168, 170; and "eighteen-minute matzos," 89; and *eruv*, 88; and *Halashon* (Hebrew textbook), 180; Hebrew notebooks, 179–80; Hebrew lessons with Langer, 177; Hebrew lessons with Puah Ben Tovim, 177, 179–80; Hebrew lessons with Thieberger, 165-67; Hebrew studies, 4, 122, 165–66, 180, 183-84, 197; and humanist Zionism, 113–114, 120, 123, 167, 202, 203, 227n.27; loves Yiddish play "Mensch muß man sein" (To Be a Human Being), 36; loves Yiddish songs, 34, 36; meets A. D. Gordon, 171–72; on Palestine travelers, 70–71, 82; plans trips to Palestine, 69, 72, 179–180; reads Brenner, *Barrenness and Failure*, 182; rejection of racial discourses, 30–33, 80; and Sabbath angels, 89; sees film *Schiwath Zion* (Ben Dov, Ya'akov), 173; Sukkoth with Dora, 181, 201; takes nephew to Chanukah play, 119; vision of early kibbutz, 170–73
Kafka, works of: "Abraham" (fragment), 94; *Amerika* (*Der Verschollene*), 48, 204; "The Animal in the Synagogue," 161, 162–64; "Before the Law," 81, 82, 99; "Blumfeld, an Elderly Bachelor," 81–84; "The Burrow," 183, 205; "The Cares of a Family Man," 161, 162, 163, 169; "A Country Doctor," 204; "A Crossbreed," 161–62, 164; "A Fratricide," 158–61; "Golem" (fragment), 105–6, 107; "A Hunger Artist," 94; "An Imperial Message," 107, 169; "In the Penal Colony," 57, 61–65, 103, 137; "Introductory Talk on the Yiddish Language," 6–7, 44–47, 66, 67; "Investigations of a Dog," 188–95, 202; "Jackals and Arabs," 80–81, 154–57, 161, 167, 185–88, 200, 205; "Josephine the Singer, or the Mouse Folk," 195–99, 200, 235n.60; "The Judgment," 48, 57, 59, 78–79, 97, 204, 214n.39; "Leopards in the Temple," 110; "Letter to His Father," 20, 102, 167; "Literature of Small Nations," 42; "A Little Fable," 143; *The Metamorphosis*, 3, 48, 59, 94–99, 138, 202, 204; "An Old Manuscript," 169; *Parables and Paradoxes*, 106–8; "A Report to an Academy," 81, 127, 130–37, 138, 150, 157, 161, 168, 202; "The Silence of the Sirens," 108–12; "The Stoker," 175; *The Trial*, 57, 61, 63, 195, 204; "The Truth about Sancho Panza," 102, 151; *Wedding Preparations in the Country*, 151; "Workers Without Possessions, 5, 170–71
Kafka, Elli and Valli (sisters). *See* Hermann, Elli; Pollàk, Valli

Kafka, Hermann (father), 12–14, 44, 45, 117
Kafka, Jakob (grandfather), 13
Kafka, Julie (née Löwy, mother), 12, 13, 45
Kafka, Ottla (sister), 77, 116, 125, 143, 144, 152, 166; and Jewish education, 116; marriage to Josef David, 144, 152, 168; and *Queen Esther*, 140; (Zionist) agricultural education, 167, 168
Katznelson, Sigmund (Albrecht Hellmann, editor of *Selbstwehr* [1913–18]), 79
Kellner, Viktor, 70, 71, 73, 213n.28
Keren Hayesod (Palestinian Foundation Fund, Prague Zionist club), 179
Kieval, Hillel, 6, 16, 17, 19, 20, 21, 22, 23, 25, 43, 65, 68, 71, 116, 212nn.16–17, 213nn.23–25
Kishinev pogrom (1903), 18, 20, 40, 58
Klein, A. M., 92
Klopstock, Robert, 149, 167, 169–70, 171, 181, 202
Klug, Flora (Yiddish actress), 34, 37, 38, 40, 43, 49
Koelb, Clayton, 82
Kohn, Hans, 213n.21
Kohn, Viktor, 174
Kraus, Karl, 71, 75–76, 83, 144, 145, 147; *Die Fackel* (The Torch), 145
Kraus, Jiří, 178
Kudela, Jiří, 116, 117, 118

Landauer, Gustav, 119, 124, 153
Langer, FrantiJišiek, 85, 86
Langer, Jiří, 85–87, 88, 89, 90, 118, 119, 130, 177, 178, 201, 221n.3, 233n.34; *Eroticism of the Kabbala*, 177, 178; "Jewish Tefillin," 178; *Nine Gates to the Chassidic Mysteries*, 86, 178; "On the Function of the Jewish Mezuzah," 178; popularization of the Talmud, 178

Lateiner, Joseph, 40, 52, 53; *Blimele, di perle fun Varshe* (play), 37, 42; *Di Seydernacht* (play), 37, 38, 39, 43, 48; *Dovid's Fidele* (play), 37, 42
Lehmann, Siegfried (S. Lehnert), 119, 120; argument with Scholem, 121–22
Lese- und Redehalle der deutschen Studenten in Prag (Reading and Lecture Group of German Students in Prague), 16–17, 20–21
Lese- und Redehalle der jüdischen Hochschüler in Prag (Reading and Lecture Group of Jewish Students in Prague), 21
Lewy, Israel, 182
Leyen, Friedrich von der, *German Art in Modern Times*, 146–47, 153
Lichtheim, Richard, *The Zionist Agenda*, 73, 134, 135
Liebgold, Bashia and Salmen (Yiddish actors), 37, 42, 50
Linetski, Joel, 52, 56; *The Polish Lad*, 54–55
Lombroso, Cesare, 67
Löns, Hermann, 146
Löw, Hugo, 70, 71
Löwy, Itzhak, 36, 39, 40, 41, 44, 48, 49, 50, 66, 169, 216n.19; anecdotes, 88–89; at Kafka's nephew's circumcision, 35, 43; reads from *Di Shkhite* (Gordin), 42; reads from *Got, mensh un tayvel* and *Elisha ben Abuyah* (Gordin), 40; reads "In Shkhite-Stot" (Bialik), 40, 58; Yiddish evening performance, 46–47, 67
Löwy, Joseph and Alfred (Kafka's uncles), 12; and Dreyfus affair, 18, 19
Lukács, Georg, 7

Maccabäa (Jewish nationalist organization), 16
Maimonides, 51, 92
Mandelstamm, Max, 134, 136, 137
Mann, Thomas, 146, 203
Masaryk, Tomàš, 19

Massino, Guido, 37, 48, 50, 88
Mauriac, Claude, 6
Mauscheln, das, 137, 147, 197
Mendele. *See* Sforim, Mendele Mokher
Midrash: at Academy of Jewish Studies, 183; and Kafka's "Creation of the Golem," 105–7; Kafka's mock-Midrash and deconstruction, 163, 205–6; in Kafka's "Silence of the Sirens," 108–12; and narrative transformation, 92, 93–94, 222n.8; in *The Trial,* 100–105. *See also* discourses (Talmudic)
Milfull, John, 185
Mirbeau, Octave, *The Garden of Torturers,* as source for "In the Penal Colony," 61
Mishnah, 51, 92, 183
Mosès, Stéphane, 108, 111
Mosse, George, 156

nationalism: Czech, 14, 19, 115; German, 16, 30, 146, 148; Jewish, 16, 30, 42, 65; Jewish nationalism and humanism, 120; similarities between German and Jewish nationalism, 146, 150; and Yiddish plays, 96
Nekula, Marek, 13, 14, 197
Neugroschel, 132–33
Nietzsche, Friedrich, 28, 113, 127
Nordau, Max, 54, 65, 67, 154, 185, 188, 214n.36; "muscle Jew," 156
Northey, Anthony, 18–19; on Yiddish actors, 41, 217n.26

Oppenheimer, Anne, 7, 86, 87, 177, 178, 210n.16

Palästina (Viennese Zionist journal), 11, 24, 69, 70
Palestine, 4, 5, 10, 46, 69, 77, 82, 86, 189; and anti-Semitism, 153; Bedouins in, 172, 187; and Bergmann, 115, 172; and Buber, 28; colonization of, 68; cultural center in, 113; emigration to, 167, 170, 172, 175, 179, 180, 181, 182, 184, 185, 204; and Kraus, 83; and Langer, 178, 179; and Löwy, 49; Maccabees in first Hebrew school, 71; practical Zionism at Eleventh Zionist Congress, 70–75; situation in, 77, 173, 179, 187–88, 205
Passover, 15, 91; "eighteen-minute matzos," 89; ritual murder charges during Passover/Easter, 18, 19, 38, 57, 58
Pawel, Ernst, 20, 29, 54, 179
Peretz, Isaac Leib, 52, 53, 54, 78; "Cabalists," 189, 192, 218n.38; *Popular Tales,* 123
Pestalozzi, Johann H., 128
Petah Tikvah, 172
Pick, Otto, 73,
Pinès, Meyer Isser, 96, 97; *Histoire,* 5, 6, 46, 50, 51–56, 132–33; at Zionist Congresses, 54, 73
Pinthus, Kurt, 48
Pirke Avot (Sayings of the Fathers), 123
Pollàk, Lotte (Kafka's niece), 174
Pollàk, Marianne (Kafka's niece). *See* Steiner, Marianne
Pollàk, Valli (née Kafka, sister), 174, 175, 176
Pouzarovà, Anna, 15
Prager Tagblatt (German liberal daily newspaper), 41, 70
Protocols of the Elders of Zion, 141, 148

Rabbi Loew, 13, 92, 106
Rashi, 51; and psychoanalysis, 149
Rath, Moses, *Textbook of the Hebrew Language for School and Self-Instruction,* 165, 166–67, 169
Rathenau, Walter, murder of, 153
Ravitsh, Melech, 99
Richter, Moses: *Moishe Khayit als Gemaynderat* (play), 37, 42; *Reb Herzele Miyuches* (play), 37, 43, 44
Rishon Le-Zion (Palestinian settlement), 172

ritual murder: Beilis trial, 57–60; Beilis, *The Trial,* and "In the Penal Colony," 61–64; in "A Fratricide," 158–61; in "Jackals and Arabs," 154–57; in "The Judgment," 59–60; Tisza Eszlar and *Ritual Murder in Hungary,* 138–39 *(see also* Zweig); trials and accusations (Dreyfus, Hilsner, Kishinev, Tisza Eszlar), 18–20
ritual slaughter (shehitah), 62, 63, 154, 155, 157
Robert, Marthe, 4
Robertson, Ritchie, 7, 8, 49, 51, 85, 88, 188, 210n.16
Robin, Régine, 7, 44, 51
Rosenfeld, Morris, 40, 44, 45, 46
Rozenblit, Marsha, 117, 118
Rubinstein, William C., 134
Ruppin, Arthur, 70, 75
Rybar, 13, 197, 212n.15

Salten, Felix, 24, 25–26, 150, 214n.33; *Bambi,* 25, 192–94; on "Jewish Modernity," 77–78; on "The Lapse from Judaism," 26–27
Scholem, Gershom, 5, 8, 98, 99, 110, 190–91, 205; and Berlin Jewish People's Home, 121–22
Schopenhauer, Arthur, 21
Selbstwehr ("Self-Defense," Independent Jewish weekly), 11, 24, 40, 41, 170, 175; and anti-Semitism, 22, 57–60, 61, 62–64, 142, 143, 213n.27; Brod attacked in, 29; 31, 33; Buber in, 27, 28, 72; editorial meetings with Kafka, 79; on Hebrew textbook by Moses Rath, 165; on Hebrew textbook *Halashon,* 180; and Herzl, 23; 169; and Jewish education, 71, 116, 118, 124, 174, 176; Kafka's "Before the Law" in, 81, 82, 99; Kafka's "The Cares of a Family Man" in, 162, 169; Kafka's circular for Yiddish actors in, 43; Kafka's Fontane Prize announced in, 138; Kafka's "An Imperial Message" in, 107, Kafka's "An Old Manuscript" in, 169; Langer in, 177; as publisher of *Kongreßzeitung* (covering Zionist congresses), 172; review of Kafka's Yiddish evening in, 47; Salten in, 25, 26–27, 77; on "small nations," 42
Shakespeare, William, 33, 40, 53, 158, 160
Shapira, Anita, 135, 150
Sharkansky, Abraham, 53; *Kol-Nidre* (play), 37, 38, 40; *Der Meshumed* (play), 37, 38
Singer, Irma, 167, 231n.9
Singer, Isaac Bashevis, 49–50
Sforim, Mendele Mokher (Abramovitsh), 52, 54, 55, 56; *The Mare,* 52, 97–98, 132–33
Sokel, Walter, 35
Sokolov, Nahum, 69, 75
Spector, Scott, 8, 132, 154, 210n.16
Sprengel, Peter, 39, 40, 41, 48, 215n.7
Stach, Reiner, 73, 217n.22
Starobinski, Jean, 92
Stein, Hugo, 116
Steiner, George, 94
Steiner, Marianne (née Pollàk, Kafka's niece), 174, 175
Steinthal, Hajim, 182
Stern, David, 104
Stern, Siegbert, 119
Sternheim, Carl, 82, 146
Stölzl, Christoph, 14, 17, 19, 115
Swift, Jonathan, 136

Talmud: Kafka and, 38, 42, 51, 53, 88, 92, 94, 101, 125, 149, 182–84, 197, 201, 227n.27; Langer and, 178. *See also* discourses (Talmudic)
Tel Aviv, 69, 175, 179, 184
Theilhaber, Felix, 66–67, 150
Thieberger, Friedrich, 201; as Kafka's Hebrew teacher, 27, 166, 167, 231n.5
Thieberger, Nelly, 78; as editor of *Selbstwehr* (1917–19), 169

Tisza Eszlar, ritual murder trial of, 18, 59, 138
Torah, 15, 53, 86, 87, 96, 104, 197
Torczyner, Harry, 182, 183
Trietsch, Davis, 68, 171
Tschissik, Mania (Yiddish actress), 34, 36, 38, 42, 43, 50

Ussischkin, Menahem, 75, 76

Venkov (anti-Semitic Czech newspaper), 142, 143, 153
Vom Judentum (On Judaism), 23

Wagenbach, Klaus, 14, 17
Wagner, Richard, 30, 196
Wagnerovà, Alena, 13, 168
Wambach, Lovis M., 18
Wandervogel (German youth group), 148
Warburg, Otto, 74
Wassermann, Jakob, 144, 146, 147, 203; *Caspar Hauser*, 144; *The Jews of Zirndorf*, 145; *My Life as German and Jew*, 144
Weinberg, Kurt, 99
Weinberg, Salcia (Yiddish actress), 36
Weinstein, Leo, 131
Weizmann, Chaim, 74, 76
Welt, Die (Zionist journal), 173
Weltsch, Felix, 4, 11, 19, 43, 59, 73, 90, 123, 140, 141, 170, 181, 183; as editor of *Selbstwehr* (1919–early 1940s), 169; Hebrew lessons with Kafka, 167
Weltsch, Lise, 73, 74, 78, 79
Weltsch, Robert, 73
Werfel, Franz, 19, 59, 121, 145, 146
Western European Judaism, 35, 146, 156, 161, 168; West meets East, 90–91
Wilde, Oscar, 203

Wohryzek, Julie, 3, 10, 125, 166, 167, 169
Wolffsohn, David, 74

Yiddish theater, 34–56, 169, 201, 203, 215n.7, 215n.8; contrasted with German theater, 34; disdain for actors, 44, 45, 128, 217n.22. *See also* Feinmann, Sigmund; Goldfaden, Abraham; Gordin, Jakob; Lateiner, Joseph; Richter, Moses; Sharkansky, Abraham
Yom Kippur, 15, 16, 38, 91, 102; *kapora* ritual in *The Trial*, 104; Kol Nidre, 16, 119

Zeire Zion (Zionist Youth, socialist Zionist party), 171
Zemach, Shlomo, *Jewish Peasants*, 173
Zidovske prahy (Zionist newspaper in Prague), 142
Zionism: Arab opposition to, 182, 187; cultural vs. political, 4, 22, 65, 68, 69–70, 71; socialist, 46, 170–72, 182, 186; World Zionist Organization (WZO), 67; WZO's Palestine office, 70, 74
Zionist Congresses, World: First (Basel, 1897), 17, 65, 71, 76, 141, 186; Second (Basel, 1898), 156; Third (Basel, 1899), 24; Fifth (Basel, 1901), 54; Tenth (Basel, 1911), 74; Eleventh (Vienna, 1913), 54, 73–77, 83; Twelfth (Karlsbad, 1921), 74, 169, 172, 187; Thirteenth (Karlsbad, 1923), 169
Zionist Women's Organizations, 78, 115, 119, 168, 228nn.34–35
Zola, Émile, 19
Zweig, Arnold, *Ritual Murder in Hungary*, 138–39, 155

STUDIES IN GERMAN JEWISH CULTURAL
HISTORY AND LITERATURE

Kafka and Cultural Zionism: Dates in Palestine
IRIS BRUCE

Spinoza's Modernity: Mendelssohn, Lessing, and Heine
WILLI GOETSCHEL

*Jewish Scholarship and Culture in Nineteenth-Century Germany:
Between History and Faith*
NILS ROEMER